St. Francis of Assisi

St. Francis of Assisi

First and Second Life of St. Francis with
selections from
The Treatise on the Miracles of Blessed Francis

by

Thomas of Celano

Translated from the Latin
with introduction and footnotes
by
Placid Hermann, O.F.M.

Franciscan Press
Quincy University
1800 College Avenue
Quincy, Illinois 62301-2699
Telephone: 217-228-5670 • FAX: 217-228-5672

Library of Congress Cataloging-in-Publication Data:

Thomas of Celano, fl. 1257.
  [Selections. English. 1988]

   St. Francis of Assisi: first and second life of St. Francis with selections from the Treatise on the miracles of blessed Francis/by Thomas of Celano; translated from the Latin with introduction and footnotes by Placid Hermann.

     p. cm.
  Bibliography: p.
  Includes index.
  ISBN 0-8199-0554-2
  1. Francis of Assisi, Saint, 1182-1226. 2. Christian saints–Italy–Assisi–Biography. 3. Assisi (Italy)–Biography. I. Title
BX4700.F6P452 1988
271'.3'024–dc19
  [B]   88-21470
                                              CIP

FOREWORD

A saint who has attracted the admiration and love of people of all faiths for over seven hundred years is a saint who must indeed have a message for all ages. Such a saint is Francis of Assisi.

St. Francis came upon a world that was fast turning away from God and devoting itself to purely worldly interests; a world that was intent upon material wealth rather than upon spiritual health; a world that was torn by strife between classes and by wars between cities and states. But Francis towered above the people of his time like the golden cross of Brother Sylvester's vision that proceeded from the mouth of the saint to reach to the heavens and to extend its arms to embrace the whole world; and Francis drew the world after him by living the Gospel life, a life of complete detachment from the things of this world, a life of justice and charity toward all, a life of love of God above all things.

The world today is even more sorely afflicted than was the world of St. Francis' day. True, the world has made much progress. Men have dug deep to discover the secrets of the atom; they have put on wings to soar into the far reaches of space. But, by and large, they have turned their newly found knowledge of the atom to harness its potency for destructive purposes, and they have used their knowledge of space to prepare missiles that can be hurled to the farthest corners of the earth to bring searing destruction upon their enemies. As a result, the whole world is at odds with itself, one half of it threatening to destroy as much as is necessary to fasten its materialistic way of life upon every country of the world; the other half ready to defend itself against this immoral and rashly brazen enemy.

Strangely enough, however, this other half of the world, our half, is committed, to a very large extent, to the same basic philosophy of life as the other half. Our scientists, succeeding as they have never succeeded before in probing the secrets of nature, have not, however, come nearer to the God of nature; as a matter of fact, many of them seem to think that since science can uncover the mysteries of nature, science itself is an all-sufficient god. Many other people, too, pursuing the pleasures of the day, are unaware of either God or of their neighbor or of any obligation to serve God or care about their neighbor. Moral responsibility does not exist for them and sin is equated merely with illness.

How sadly deluded the world is! How much in need it is of St. Francis of Assisi! Francis understood nature too; in a way, even better than do the scientists; but Francis turned from the creature to embrace the Creator. Francis understood himself too; and renouncing the world and all his possessions, he clung to Christ, the Redeemer, with a love that in the end marked his own body with the wounds of the body of Christ. And Francis understood the hearts of his fellowmen; and he mapped out a way of life for them that would assuredly bring them to God and to perfection, and to peace and happiness even in this world.

There are many ways of coming to know Francis and his message to the world. But surely, the best way to come to know him is to see him through the eyes of those who knew him when he trod the roads and fields of his native Assisi. That is why it seems opportune at this time to give to the world a new translation of a biography of the saint by one who walked with him; one who was familiar with those who first followed the way he set out for them; one, therefore, who knew St. Francis and his ideals as only a contemporary and a friend could know them.

In preparing this translation of Thomas of Celano's two lives of St. Francis and of some selections from the *Treatise on the Miracles of Blessed Francis,* we have made use of the work of countless Franciscans of both the present and the past, and of others too who were not Franciscans. How does one go about expressing thanks to so many who have done so much work ahead of one? To do so to each individually would take a volume much larger even than this present volume. To do so only in general is but a faint recognition of such immense and such important labors. But, lacking any other way of doing it, we say simply that without their work this work would have been totally impossible. All of us, however, will be well rewarded if this work contributes in some small way toward bringing people closer to St. Francis, and through him, to Christ, our King.

PLACID HERMANN O.F.M.

CONTENTS

PART I
The First Life of St. Francis

PART II
The Second Life of St. Francis

How, while Francis was praying, the devil showed him

PART III
Treatise on the Miracles of Blessed
Francis, Selections

INTRODUCTION

1
THE AUTHOR

Brother Thomas, the first biographer of St. Francis of Assisi, was born in the little town of Celano in central Italy.[1] Accordingly, he is always known as Brother Thomas of Celano. The year of his birth, however, is not known with any degree of certainty. A recent writer in *Ecclesia* (1960), a monthly publication from the Vatican, expressed the opinion that Brother Thomas was born in 1185. Though this cannot as yet be regarded as certain, it may at least be close to the actual date, for we know from the other facts of his life that he was born some time during the closing years of the twelfth century. The name of his family is likewise unknown.

It is very probable that Brother Thomas entered the Franciscan Order between the years 1213 and 1216, and quite likely in the year 1215. This conclusion seems to follow from what he himself says in his *First Life of St. Francis,* numbers 56-57. There, after telling of Francis' unsuccessful attempt to go to Morocco as a missionary, he implies that Almighty God had his own personal welfare in view in thus frustrating Francis' desire to carry the word of God to that country and his desire for martyrdom. Brother Thomas writes: "But the good God, whom it pleased in his kindness to be mindful of me and of many others, *withstood him to his face* (Gal. 2, 11) when he had traveled as far as Spain; and, that he might not go any farther, he recalled him from the journey he had begun by a prolonged illness."[2] Brother Thomas then goes on to tell how very shortly after Francis' return to the Portiuncula, "some educated and noble men"[3] were received into the order. Most authors think that Brother Thomas was among these men. Accordingly, since Francis' unsuccessful journey to Morocco took place most probably during the winter of 1213-1214,[4] and since he was turned back while he was in Spain, he must have returned to the Portiuncula late in 1214 or early in 1215. Not long thereafter[5] Thomas was received into the order along with the other educated and noble men of whom he speaks. Some think that he had already been ordained a priest before his entry into the order.

Nothing is known of the life of Brother Thomas during the first years he was a member of the Franciscan Order. The first information we get concerning him comes to us from the *Chronicle of Brother Jordan of Giano.*[6] Brother Jordan tells us that among the brothers chosen to undertake the founding of the order in Germany in 1221 was "Thomas of Celano, who later wrote both a first and a second *Legenda* of St. Francis."[7] These brothers were chosen at the general chapter of 1221, held at Assisi,[8] and they left for Germany about three months later, in September 1221. On October 16 they arrived at Augsburg under the leadership of Brother Caesar of Speyer, who had been appointed at that same chapter the first minister provincial of Germany. The following year, 1222, Brother Caesar held a provincial chapter at Worms, and in this chapter Brother Thomas of Celano was appointed custos of Mainz, Worms, Cologne, and Speyer.[9] In 1223 Brother Caesar appointed Brother Thomas to serve as vicar provincial in Germany while he himself attended the general chapter of the order at Assisi.[10] This general chapter relieved Brother Caesar of his office and appointed Brother Albert of Pisa to succeed him as minister provincial of Germany.

Brother Thomas was still in Germany on September 8, 1223, because, on the authority of Brother

Jordan,[11] he was present at the provincial chapter held at Speyer on that day. Apparently he was relieved of his office of custos at this time. The German province was divided in this chapter into four custodies, according to Brother Jordan, who gives the names of the four who were appointed custodes and of the four custodies over which they were to preside. Brother Thomas is not named among them.[12] It is quite generally assumed that Brother Thomas left Germany about this time, or shortly thereafter, and returned to Italy. He is not mentioned anymore in connection with the German province,[13] but he is known to have been in Italy a little later.

Apparently Brother Thomas did not have any really close contact with St. Francis during the last years of the saint's life. True, he does give a rather complete account of these last years, especially 1224-1226; but his account is based only in part upon what he himself experienced, and otherwise, as he himself says, upon what he could learn from others.[14] However, his description of the ceremonies of Francis' canonization gives the impression that he was present for that solemn ceremony on July 16, 1228. It was on this occasion too, or perhaps somewhat earlier, that Pope Gregory IX commissioned Brother Thomas to write his *First Life of St. Francis.*

In 1230 Brother Thomas was living in Assisi. It was there that Brother Jordan of Giano visited him after he had completed his business with the minister general[15] on behalf of the minister provincial of the Rhine.[16] Brother Thomas gave some relics of St. Francis to Brother Jordan to take back to Germany.[17] No doubt, Brother Thomas was present that year at the translation ceremonies, when St. Francis' body was taken from the church of St. George in Assisi, where he was first buried, to the new basilica of St. Francis.[18]

Brother Thomas is not heard of in the early sources of Franciscan history for the next fourteen years. Then, at the general chapter of the order held at Genoa in 1244, the newly elected minister general, Crescentius of Jesi,[19] asked Brother Thomas to write a second life of St. Francis, and he issued an order that whatever material could be gathered together by the brothers concerning the life and miracles of St. Francis should be sent to the minister general.[20] The response to this order was generous, and Brother Thomas used this material for the writing of his second life of St. Francis.

Several years later, probably shortly before 1250, Brother Thomas was again asked to write about St. Francis, this time by the new minister general, John of Parma.[21] The new work, the *Treatise on the Miracles of Blessed Francis,* was written between the years 1250-1253. Most likely Brother Thomas was living at Assisi during the writing of this treatise as well as during the writing of the earlier *Second Life.* And it is quite likely that he was still living in that city when he wrote his last work, the *Legenda Sanctae Clarae,* during the years 1255-1256. This life of St. Clare was written at the order of Pope Alexander IV.[22]

It seems that Brother Thomas spent the last years of his life, with the exception of the years spent at Assisi writing the life of St. Clare, in Tagliacozzo, in the custody of the Marches. Apparently he had charge of the Poor Clare nuns of the monastery of St. John of Varro. He died in 1260 or not long thereafter and was buried in the Poor Clare monastery. However, the Poor Clares gave up this monastery in 1476; and in 1506, by order of Pope Julian II, it became the property of the Friars Minor Conventual. In 1516 Brother Thomas' body was laid to rest behind the high altar of their church, and at the beginning of the eighteenth century it was clothed in the habit of the Friars Minor Conventual and laid to rest under the high altar at Tagliacozzo. The tomb is marked with this inscription:

> B. THOMAS DE CELANO S.F.D.
> SCRIPTOR CRONICAR ET SEQUENTIAE
> MORTUOR[23]

2

THE WORKS OF THOMAS OF CELANO

The *First Life of St. Francis*

On April 29, 1228, Pope Gregory IX issued a Bull authorizing the building of a church to honor St. Francis of Assisi.[24] This was done in anticipation of the canonization of the saint, three months later, July 16, 1228. It is likely that already at this time Pope Gregory commissioned Thomas of Celano to write the first biography of the new saint. In any case he did so at some time during the months that followed, or at least on the day of the canonization itself. Celano himself tells us that he wrote the *First Life of St. Francis* "at the command of our lord, the gloriously reigning Pope Gregory."[25]

Brother Thomas must have set to work immediately on this first life of the founder of the order, for, if we can trust a note in one manuscript of the work, the completed biography was presented to the pope and received his approbation seven months later, on February 25, 1229. This, the Paris manuscript, dating back to at least the fourteenth century, says: *Apud Perusium felix dominus papa Gregorius nonus secundo gloriosi pontificatus sui anno quinto Kal. martii legendam hanc recepit, confirmavit, et censuit fore tenendum.*[26] At any rate, whether this statement of the Paris manuscript is correct or not, the biography must certainly have been completed before May 25, 1230, for it does not make mention of the very important event that took place on that day, namely, the translation of the remains of St. Francis from the church of St. George in Assisi to the new basilica that was being erected to honor the saint.

Just why Pope Gregory IX chose Brother Thomas of Celano for this task is not known. However, he was admirably suited for the task. He was a learned man, probably one of those "educated and noble men" who were admitted into the order shortly after Francis' return from Spain. The work itself shows that the author was both a skilled literary craftsman and a painstaking artist.[27] Whether or not he had become known by reason of some other literary work and for that reason drew the attention of the holy father is not known. There is a possibility, in no way proven however, that he might have been the author of the *Sacrum Commercium S. Francisci cum Domina Paupertate*,[28] a little allegorical work that is dated 1227. If this were so, there would then be at hand an excellent reason why Pope Gregory should have chosen him from among many others for this task, for the *Sacrum Commercium* is a literary gem.

The *First Life* is prefaced by a Prologue in which Brother Thomas tells briefly of the command of Pope Gregory IX to write the life and how he intends to proceed. The life itself is divided into three *opuscula* or books. The first book, which "follows the historical order,"[29] tells of the years of Francis' early youth, his conversion, the founding of the order, his holy life and teaching; and it concludes with an account of Francis' celebration of Christmas at Greccio in 1223. The historical order, however, is followed only in a general way, not with precision. The second book gives an account of the last two years of Francis' life on earth and covers above all the stigmatization,

xxvi

the death, and the burial of the saint. The third book consists of two parts. The first part tells of the canonization of St. Francis on July 16, 1228, and the second part recounts the miracles that were accepted and read as a part of that colorful ceremony of canonization. The life closes with a short Epilogue in which the author asks to be remembered before God by the reader.

Brother Thomas used as his sources for this *First Life* his own personal experience and the testimony of reliable witnesses.[30] He himself, however, could not have spent too much time in the company of St. Francis, as is evident from the brief chronology of his life given above. Hence he had to rely to a great extent on the testimony of others. These others, no doubt, included many of Francis' early companions who were still living, men like Brother Leo, Brother Rufino, Brother Angelo, and many others, as the occasion arose. He could also consult Brother Elias, who had been Francis' vicar from 1221 until the election of John Parenti as minister general in 1227. He could also consult Pope Gregory IX, who already as Cardinal Hugolino had been a close friend of the saint. Bishop Guido, too, of Assisi, and St. Clare, Francis' first daughter, and her companions were likewise available.

Furthermore, Brother Thomas had access to Francis' own writings, which he seems to have had at hand, since he quotes from or alludes to them quite frequently, such things as the Rule of 1221, the Rule of 1223, the *Testament, The Canticle of our Brother the Sun,* the admonitions of St. Francis, and other writings. He used also Brother Elias' letter announcing the death of St. Francis to the brothers around the world and the Bull of Canonization. Whether or not he was able to make use of the official *Acta* of the process of canonization, we do not know; these official *Acta* are no longer extant. However, the fact that he did make use of such *Acta* in writing his life of St. Clare leads us to believe that he did surely make use of them for his life of St. Francis, at least if they were at all available to him. There were, of course, no other *legendae* in existence at this time concerning St. Francis' life, since Celano's was the first biography of the saint.[31]

This *First Life*, no doubt, is the most important document concerning St. Francis and things Franciscan that we have, written as it was so soon after the saint's death and presented as the official biography of the saint, commissioned by Pope Gregory IX, for the general edification of the faithful.

The *Second Life of St. Francis*

In the general chapter of the order held at Genoa in 1244 the minister general, Crescentius of Jesi, "commanded all the friars to send to him in writing whatever they could know with certainty about the life, signs, and wonders of Blessed Francis."[32] The response to this appeal was generous. Brother Leo, Brother Rufino, and Brother Angelo, in particular, gathered together what they could from their own experience and from the experience of others of the early companions of St. Francis and transmitted this material to the minister general along with a covering letter explaining what they had done.

This letter is addressed to the minister general, "our reverend father and brother in Christ, by the grace of God minister general," by "Brother Leo, Brother Rufino, and Brother Angelo, onetime companions, though unworthy, of the most blessed Francis." These companions refer to the command issued at the general chapter of Genoa and then go on to describe their procedure:

it seemed good to us who lived with him for a long time, though we were unworthy, to present to your holiness a few things we are sure of from among the many things he did, things which we ourselves saw or which we could learn from other holy brothers, and especially from Brother Philip, the visitator of the Poor Ladies, Brother Illuminato of Rieti, Brother Masseo of Marignano, and Brother John, the companion of the venerable Brother Giles, who had learned many things from that same Brother Giles and from Brother Bernard of blessed memory, the first companion of the blessed Francis.

The three companions then go on to say that they are not writing these things "after the fashion of a legend, since legends have already been written about his life and the miracles the Lord performed through him." On the contrary, they say they are presenting these things as so many "flowers gathered from a delightful meadow," flowers they regard as more beautiful than the rest. "We are not offering, therefore," they go on to say, "a continuous story, for we have omitted many things that have already been written in the legends mentioned before in so truthful and brilliant a style."[33] Apparently the three companions were not looking forward to an entirely new life of St. Francis, for they added: "these few things which we have written you can insert in the legends already mentioned, if your discretion sees fit to do so." They closed their letter with this thought: "We believe that if these things had been known to the venerable men who wrote the legends mentioned before, they would certainly not have passed them by, but would have embellished them with their own style and handed them down for a remembrance to those who would come after them."

The letter is dated: Greccio, August 11, 1246.[34]

Some time after the command of the minister general in this matter had been issued, Crescentius also asked Brother Thomas of Celano to undertake the writing of a second life of St. Francis. This may have been at that same general chapter of 1244 or at some time during the following two years. The chronicler Brother Salimbene, writing between 1282 and 1288, says: "He [Crescentius] ordered Brother Thomas of Celano, who had written the first legend of Blessed Francis, to write another book, inasmuch as many things had been uncovered about the blessed Francis that had not been written down."[35] Moreover, Brother Thomas himself refers to this command in the Prologue of the *Second Life*: "It has pleased the entire holy assembly of the past general chapter and you, Most Reverend Father, not without the disposition of divine wisdom, to enjoin upon our littleness that we set down in writing ... the deeds and also the words of our glorious father Francis, inasmuch as they were better known to us than to the rest because of our close association with him and our mutual intimacy. We hasten to obey with humble devotion the holy injunctions which we cannot pass over."[36]

The companions of St. Francis forwarded this material to the minister general, as was indicated, on August 11, 1246. This material was then given to Brother Thomas to be used in the composition of a new life of St. Francis. It need not be supposed, however, that Brother Thomas relied solely on this material. It would have been only natural for him to have gathered material himself ever since he had completed the *First Life,* for he must have realized that much could be added to the things he had been able to learn at that time. Furthermore, the command of the minister general had been issued to all the brothers, not merely to those who had been close companions of St. Francis. It may well be, therefore, that Brother Thomas received other material too, in addition to what he received from the three companions, either by word of mouth or in writing.

In any case, Brother Thomas set to work on a new life of St. Francis. It is evident especially from the Prologue of the *Life* and from the prayer that concludes it that Brother Thomas regarded himself as being rather the spokesman of the brothers who had supplied most of the material than as writing simply in his own name. In the Prologue quoted above he is speaking in the first person plural and in the name of those who were close associates and intimates of St. Francis. Furthermore, in the so-called *Prayer of Francis' Companions to Him*,[37] the first person plural is used consistently, as though the several companions and Brother Thomas were speaking as one.

Nevertheless, there can be no doubt at all about Celano being really the sole author of the whole. Already in the Prologue he refers to himself as the author when he says that the present work contains certain things that were not included in the earlier work because "they had not come to the notice of the author."[38] Again, throughout the work, when the first person is used, it is always, with few exceptions,[39] the first person singular.[40] Finally, it is evident from the third section of the concluding prayer that Thomas alone is the author, for though this prayer is put upon the lips of the several companions in a rather elaborate apostrophe, it has a very personal reference to the one author: "We beseech you also with all the affection of our hearts, most kind Father, for this your son who now and earlier has devotedly written your praises. He, together with us, offers and dedicates this little work." Beyond a doubt, therefore, Thomas of Celano is the sole author of the

Second Life, even though, in a sense, he regards himself as the spokesman for those who supplied the material for the new life.

The *Second Life* is often call the *Memoriale in Desiderio Animae* from the opening words of Book One. The whole work begins with the aforementioned Prologue, which tells how the life came to be written and closes with a dedication to the minister general. The dedication consists of a play on the name *Crescentius*: "so that the things that are approved as well said by your learned judgment may indeed grow together with your name *Crescentius* and be multiplied in Christ. Amen." The life itself is divided into two books. The first book is comparatively short and covers much the same period that was covered in the first book of the *First Life*: the naming of Francis at baptism, the conversion of Francis, the founding of the order, the appointment of Cardinal Hugolino as protector of the order. However, it is evident that Brother Thomas is writing this section only as a supplement to what had already been said in the *First Life*, for it repeats little, but only adds details. The second book treats a variety of subjects in a rather systematic and logical arrangement of the material. As Brother Thomas says, it is his intention to bring out "what was the good and acceptable will of Francis both for himself and for his followers in every practice of heavenly discipline and in zeal for the highest perfection which he ever had toward God in his sacred affections and toward men in his examples."[41] Certain miracles are inserted, "as occasion for inserting them presents itself."[42] The latter part of this second book returns again to the chronological order and treats of Francis' illnesses, his stigmatization, death, canonization, and translation. However, the latter part of this section is missing and nothing actually is said concerning the translation of his remains from the church of St. George to the lower church of the new basilica. But one can easily return to the *First Life* to supply the conclusion of the canonization ceremonies and to the *Legenda ad usum chori* for at least a brief note concerning the translation.[43]

As was said, Brother Thomas dedicated the *Second Life* to the minister general who had asked him to write it, Crescentius of Jesi. No doubt, when Brother Thomas had completed the life, he forwarded it to the minister general. However, Crescentius did not go personally to the next general chapter, July 13, 1247, and he was released from his office "because of his insufficiencies."[44] Still, he did forward to the chapter Brother Thomas' work; and John of Parma, who was elected minister general at this chapter, confirmed the *Second Life* either at the chapter itself or not long thereafter.[45] Obviously, therefore, the *Second Life* was written for the most part between August 11, 1246, the date on which the three companions sent their material to the minister general, and July 13, 1247, the date of the general chapter held at Lyons.

During the past seventy-five years or so there has been much discussion over the relationship between the material submitted to the minister general by the three companions and the several works that are in one way or another dependent upon that material, especially the *Second Life* of Celano, the so-called *Legenda Trium Sociorum* (or *The Legend of the Three Companions*), and the *Speculum Perfectionis* (or *Mirror of Perfection*). The letter of the three companions, spoken of above, is generally found as a preface to the *Legenda Trium Sociorum*. Obviously it does not belong there, for the eighteen or so chapters of this legend are written after the fashion of a legend and not merely as a collection of "flowers gathered from a delightful meadow," contrary to what the three companions say in their letter.

Up to 1894, however, the *Legenda Trium Sociorum* was quite generally accepted as the authentic work of Brothers Leo, Rufino, and Angelo. Even so, some doubt arose when Stanislaus Melchiorri published in 1856 an Italian text of the work that dated back to the sixteenth century,[46] which in its turn was a copy of a still older text. This text contained much additional material over what was contained in the traditional Latin text.[47] But the editor explained this material as additions made by the copyist from Thomas of Celano, St. Bonaventure, Bartholomew of Pisa, and the *Speculum Vitae*.

When Paul Sabatier published his life of St. Francis in 1894,[48] he proposed the theory that the *Legenda Trium Sociorum,* as we know it today, is only a fragment; and, in his characteristic way, he said that the minister general Crescentius of Jesi was responsible for deleting what is missing because he was not in sympathy with the thought of Brother Leo and his companions. Two Franciscans, Marcellino da Civezza and Teofilo Domenichelli, pursued the thought of Sabatier that the legend was only a fragment. They took Melchiorri's Italian text, translated it into Latin, added the Latin texts from the other authors mentioned (Celano, Bonaventure, Bartholomew of Pisa, the *Speculum Vitae*), and published the whole as the complete *Legenda Trium Sociorum.*

In 1900 Franciscus Van Ortroy, writing in the *Analecta Bollandiana,* showed that the *Legenda Trium Sociorum* contains passages borrowed from later writings, like St. Bonaventure's *Legenda Major Sancti Francisci* and Bernard of Bessa's *Liber de Laudibus S. Francisci.*[49] He argued therefore rather conclusively that it was necessarily a later work, probably of the latter part of the thirteenth century or of the early part of the fourteenth century, and could not therefore be the work of the three companions of St. Francis. The letter prefaced to the work accordingly belongs elsewhere. The discussion has continued, but today the opinion is rather general that the *Legenda Trium Sociorum,* though it may derive some of its material from the contributions of the three companions in 1246, is a work of the early fourteenth century and that the letter of the three companions is very probably the covering letter for the material they sent to the minister general in 1246. The material itself, however, is lost, probably for good.[50]

Meanwhile Sabatier happened upon a manuscript that bore the title *Speculum vitae S. Francisci et sociorum ejus* and dated back to about 1445. It was a rather formless collection of material, first issued in Venice in 1504. Sabatier extracted from this mass of material whatever seemed to harmonize with the style of the *Legenda Trium Sociorum,* believing that here he had found the missing part of the *Legenda.* He was especially struck by the rather frequent occurrence of the phrase, "we who were with him," a phrase that is very similar to the phrase used by the three companions in their letter to the minister general, "we who, though unworthy, lived with him for a long time." However, just about this time he came upon another manuscript in the Mazarin Library, Paris, that contained the very same material he had culled from the *Speculum Vitae* manuscript, but bearing the title *Speculum Perfectionis Fratris Minoris.*

Sabatier, however, was misled by an error in the dating of this manuscript into thinking that it was the oldest of all the legends about St. Francis. The date given was *anno domini MCCXXVIII,* that is, 1228, or, according to the old Pisan reckoning of the years, 1227. He therefore published his material as a separate work under the title *Speculum Perfectionis, legenda antiquissima auctore fratre Leone*. But the fact that he was in error about the date seemed obvious to others, and their surmise was confirmed shortly thereafter by the discovery of another manuscript of the *Speculum Perfectionis* which bore the correct date of 1318.[51]

A little later Fr. Leonard Lemmens O.F.M. edited a manuscript of the *Speculum Perfectionis* that was found in the archives of the Franciscan convent of St. Isidore in Rome, dating back to the fourteenth century.[52] This is a comparatively short work as compared to the *Speculum Perfectionis* edited by Sabatier; it has only forty-five numbered paragraphs as against 124 chapters in the latter. This manuscript opens with these words: "In the name of the Lord begins the Mirror of Perfection, of the rule and profession, the life and vocation of the true Friar Minor according to the will of Christ and the intention of Blessed Francis, composed from certain things found in the writings of Brother Leo, the companion of Blessed Francis, and of other of his companions, which are not in the common legend."

Some saw in this comparatively short work the original material sent to the minister general in 1246 by the three companions. This is not the case; but, as the manuscript says, it was compiled from this same material. Fr. Lemmens, taking note of the opening words just quoted, concluded that it was compiled after the *Legenda Major* of St. Bonaventure had become, by decree, the *legenda communis,* the common or standard legend for the order; and, as is indicated in those opening words, that it was written as a kind of supplement to that legend. Since therefore it precedes in time the *Speculum Perfectionis* published by Sabatier, it is often referred to as the *first redaction,* or, as some prefer, the *earlier red-*

action, considering the original material of the three companions to be the *first redaction*. Sabatier's edition, therefore, is a later redaction and is primarily an expansion of the earlier *Speculum Perfectionis* by the addition of material that had come to light during the intervening years.

As is to be expected, the *Speculum Perfectionis* in both redactions contains much material that was contained in the *Second Life* of Brother Thomas of Celano, for all of these writings derive at least in some part from the original material given to the minister general by the three companions in 1246. Thus all but the very last paragraph of the earlier redaction is found in the second redaction; and forty-four of the 124 chapters of the second redaction are contained in the Second Life of Celano. This, of course, has reference to substance, not to precise wording.

In summary, this can be said. The three companions named in the letter to the minister general, namely, Brothers Leo, Rufino, and Angelo, forwarded to Crescentius of Jesi the material they were able to gather between the general chapter of Genoa in 1244 and the date of their letter, August 11, 1246. This material was then used by Brother Thomas of Celano for his *Second Life of St. Francis*. It was again used by later writers for the separate redactions of the *Speculum Perfectionis*. The *Legenda Trium Sociorum* does not belong with the letter with which it is generally associated, but is a later compilation, probably of the early fourteenth century.[53]

The *Treatise on the Miracles of Blessed Francis*

In the *Second Life of St. Francis* Brother Thomas of Celano had included only a few miracles, inserting them here and there as occasion presented itself; and these were only such miracles as were performed through St. Francis while he was yet alive.[54] In this, the *Second Life* was considered deficient, for even the *First Life* had included a special section on the miracles that had been accepted and read for the process of canonization. Consequently, John of Parma, minister general 1247-1257, commanded Brother Thomas of Celano to correct this defect. The *Chronica XXIV Generalium* tells of this command: "This general [John of Parma] commanded Brother Thomas of Celano in repeated letters to complete the *Life of Blessed Francis,* which was called the *Ancient Legend,*[55] because mention had been made in the first treatise,[56] compiled at the order of the minister general Crescentius, only of his life and words, the miracles being omitted"[57]

The *Treatise on the Miracles of Blessed Francis* (*Tractatus de Miraculis B. Francisci*) was written, therefore, by Thomas of Celano during the term of office of John of Parma, and most probably during the middle years of that term, 1250-1253.[58] When the work was completed, Brother Thomas sent it to the minister general together with a letter that began with the words: *Religiosa vestra sollicitudo,*[59] a letter, however, that has not come down to us. The treatise was accepted and approved in the next general chapter, most probably, at Metz in 1254.

The *Treatise on the Miracles of the Blessed Francis* is not divided into books, as were both the *First* and *Second Life,* but the 198 numbered paragraphs of the work are distributed over nineteen chapters, the last of which is an epilogue. The opening chapter treats of the miraculous beginnings of the order. The second chapter treats of the stigmata of St. Francis and of the miracles related to these wounds. The rest of the chapters, with the exception of Chapter VI, recount the various miracles wrought through St. Francis, some of them during his life, but most of them after his death. Chapter VI, however, concerns itself with the visit of Lady Jacoba of Settesoli to Francis just before the death of the saint.

Much of the *Treatise on the Miracles* is not new material; about one third of it is contained already in the earlier *Lives*.[60] Nevertheless, and despite the fact that most of the miracles narrated are miracles that were wrought after St. Francis' death, the *Treatise on the Miracles* has a value for the biography of the saint. Forty-one of its 198 numbered paragraphs refer to things that happened while Francis was still alive. Although most of these paragraphs are contained already in the two *Lives*, thirteen contain material that is new. These thirteen paragraphs are of special value for the biography of St. Francis. They are included in Part III of this English volume.

Other Works

1   The *Legenda Sanctae Clarae Assisiensis.* — St. Clare of Assisi was the founder, under St. Francis, of the Order of Poor Clares. Born in 1194, she left her home in 1212 and was given a habit and a way of life by St. Francis.[61] All her life, however, she had to carry on a struggle to maintain her ideal of highest or absolute poverty. Pope Innocent III had confirmed for her this "privilege of seraphic poverty" in 1215 or 1216. But in 1218 or 1219 Cardinal Hugolino prepared a new rule of life for St. Clare and her followers, in which the rule of absolute poverty was softened. St. Clare insisted, however, that the highest poverty would be observed at least in the convent at St. Damian's church.

In 1245 Pope Innocent IV[62] confirmed this rule of Cardinal Hugolino for all the monasteries of the Poor

Clares; but two years later he wrote a new rule for them, which he hoped would prove more satisfactory. This new rule, however, was even more lenient than Cardinal Hugolino's and St. Clare refused to accept it. Instead, she set herself the task of writing her own rule. This rule was approved orally by Pope Innocent IV when he visited her on her deathbed, and it was approved by papal Bull August 9, 1253, just two days before her death.

Pope Innocent IV died December 7, 1254. One of the early acts of the new pope, Alexander IV,[63] was the canonization of St. Clare, August 15, 1255. In accordance with custom, he commissioned a biography or legend to be written to celebrate the new saint. For many years it had been thought that St. Bonaventure was the author of this legend, the *Legenda Sanctae Clarae Assisiensis*. Now, however, it is quite generally accepted that Brother Thomas of Celano was the author of this legend too. The work indeed has all the characteristics of style that the earlier works of Celano have, and there is no longer any reason to doubt his authorship.

The life opens with a Prologue that has the form of a letter addressed to the pope, Alexander IV. In it the author recalls the fact that he had been asked to write the life: "It has pleased Your Holiness to enjoin on my lowliness to review the *Acta* of Saint Clare and form therefrom a Legend."[64] It may be noted that Brother Thomas is also indicating here his chief source for this life, namely, the official *Acta*, that is, the acts of the canonical process of canonization and the Bull of canonization. The author adds that he "deemed it unwise to rely on incomplete records, and had recourse to the companions of Blessed Francis and even to the community of the virgins of Christ," for "none should write history save those who had seen for themselves or who had received their knowledge from eyewitnesses."[65]

The *Legenda Sanctae Clarae Assisiensis* was therefore started by Brother Thomas of Celano in 1255 and finished probably within a year or so.

2   The *Legenda ad Usum Chori* (Legend for Use in Choir). In the opening paragraph of this brief legend the author addresses himself to a certain Brother Benedict who had asked for a shortened form of the *First Life of St. Francis* for use in choir service: "You asked me, Brother Benedict, to excerpt some things from the legend of our most blessed father Francis and to arrange them in a series of nine lessons, so that they might be placed in our breviaries and be had by all by reason of their brevity."[66]

It is not known definitely who this Brother Benedict was, but some think it may have been Brother Benedict of Arezzo, a rather noteworthy person who was minister provincial in Greece from 1221 to 1237.[67] It is possible that he met Brother Thomas at the general chapter held at Assisi in 1230 on the occasion of the translation of St. Francis' remains to the new basilica and made his request at that time for a brief condensation of the *First Life*.

While the author of this brief legend does not identify himself by name, nevertheless the opening words (quoted above) give much the same impression as would the words *"de Legenda mea,"* from *my* legend, and therefore point to Brother Thomas as the author. Furthermore, almost the entire legend is based upon the *First Life;* it is literally excerpted from it, words, phrases, clauses taken over and tied together to make a very compact and concise summary of that *First Life*.[68] The style too has the same artistic touches as the two *Lives*.

There are, however, several new items in this short *Legenda ad Usum Chori*. In the first place, the day of Francis' death is more precisely indicated by adding these several words: *die sabbati in sero,* Saturday evening.[69] Moreover, the translation of Francis' remains from the church of St. George to the new basilica is given.[70] This was not contained in the *First Life* in as much as that life had been completed before this event. Likewise, some new miracles are added that were not known to the author at the time of the writing of the *First Life.* These miracles are further expanded in the later *Treatise on the Miracles of Blessed Francis.*

Brother Thomas is undoubtedly the author of this brief legend which was written quite certainly in 1230 or immediately thereafter.

3   The liturgical sequence, *Dies Irae.* — According to a long standing tradition that goes back at least to the fourteenth century, Thomas of Celano was the author of this well known and highly poetic sequence of the Requiem Mass, the *Dies Irae.*[71] That Brother Thomas was the author also of the two other sequences, *Sanctitatis nova signa* and *Fregit victor,* is very doubtful.[72]

3
THE LITERARY CHARACTER OF THE *LIVES*

Brother Thomas of Celano had no intention, of course, of writing a biography of St. Francis in the way we understand that term today. Neither did he intend to write an exhaustive study of the saint. In the Prologue of the *First Life* he says: "No one can retain fully in his memory all the things that Francis did and taught." And a little later in that same life:[73] "Many more things happened too which we could not tell adequately even at great length."

What Brother Thomas did intend to write was a *legenda* or legend in the medieval understanding of that term, namely, a book or record of the deeds of a saint. The emphasis was upon the word *saint*, and accordingly the supernatural elements in the life of the subject were emphasized, often at the expense of the human side of his life. The medieval writer of a legend was careful to avoid any purely human detail that might in any way lessen the estimate of the sanctity of the saint, while at the same time he played up strongly what might be considered a supernatural explanation of something that actually could be explained naturally. This does not mean that the writers of the middle ages were poor and unreliable biographers. They wrote the truth as they saw and understood it, but they also followed the practice of their times and were inclined to stress the supernatural and often to suppress the natural and distinctly human. It may well be, for all of that, that they were more reliable than some modern biographers who only too often tend to stress the natural and human at the expense of the supernatural.

It is readily apparent from a study of Brother Thomas' two lives of St. Francis that the author was a skilled literary craftsman and a painstaking artist. His style is vigorous and forceful, elegant, and even poetic. He makes use of figurative language freely, metaphors, similes, plays on words.[74] He uses contrast and antithesis to good effect.[75] He quotes countless passages from Holy Scripture[76] and now and then he inserts a passage from classical writers[77] and from early Christian writers.[78]

One artistic device in particular that Brother Thomas uses deserves a little more extended treatment since it is such a constant factor of his writing. This is the device known as the *cursus*, or periodic cadence, or end-pattern. Both ancient and medieval Latin writers strove to follow a certain rhythmic pattern, particularly at the end of each sentence.

This practice was governed by the laws of the so-called *cursus* or end-pattern. In the course of time these end-patterns came to be reduced to the three that Brother Thomas uses throughout his works, namely:[79]

a. the *cursus planus*: a u / u a u
b. the *cursus tardus*: a u / u a u u
c. the *cursus velox*: a u u / u u a u

To illustrate Brother Thomas' use of these end-patterns, we might take as an example the first paragraph of Chapter I of the *First Life*. The words given below are the final words of each sentence of that paragraph. The syllables not in italics indicate the position of the word accent; the letter following each phrase indicates which *cursus* is being used in each case.

*insolen*tior *est ef*fectus — c.
stu*deant edu*care — c.
*ope*rari *co*guntur — a.
sub*jacet disci*plinis — c.
ma*la se*quuntur — a.
*ces*sere *fe*licius — b.
op*era di*labuntur — c.
re*gulam ae*quitatis — c.
fi*eri arbi*traris — c.
*flagi*tiis de*servire — c.
no*mine* se *tu*entur — c.
*innocentiores e*xistunt — a.

The painstaking care with which Brother Thomas observes these patterns is evidence in itself that he was a true artist.

4

THE HISTORICAL VALUE OF THE *LIVES*

During the past seventy years or so there has been much discussion as to the historical value of Brother Thomas' lives of St. Francis. Opinions have varied, but the harshest have been the opinions of Paul Sabatier and those who have followed his lead.[80] Sabatier noted, in the first place, that Brother Thomas made no mention in his *First Life* of the general chapters of the order or of the fact that St. Francis was opposed to the friars seeking privileges at the Roman curia. Sabatier concluded that Celano deliberately omitted these things because he was dominated by Brother Elias and wanted to gain favor with him; and Elias had no use for general chapters[81] and was at the time seeking privileges from the Pope for the new basilica of St. Francis that was then under construction. Some add to this also that Brother Thomas was dominated similarly by Pope Gregory IX who more or less told him what he was to include in the life and what he was to omit. There is, however, no evidence of any of this either in the *First Life* or in any contemporary sources, and the omission of such things can very readily be explained by the fact that Brother Thomas's whole intent was to present to a reading audience that extended far beyond the order itself a picture of Francis, the saint, not a history of the order. The things omitted were simply not relevant to that picture.[82]

Another accusation leveled against Brother Thomas is that of inconsistency and, as a consequence, of unreliability as an historian and biographer.[83] This accusation grows out of Brother Thomas' handling of the case of Brother Elias in the *First Life* and again later in the *Second Life*. The situation is as follows. By actual count Elias is mentioned by name in six paragraphs of the *First Life*.[84] Each time he is mentioned, the wording of the narrative is such that it has a ring of good feeling about it concerning Elias. To give but one example, six months before Francis' death, when he was staying at Siena to get some much needed medical care, "Brother Elias hurried to him with great haste from a distant place."[85] Almost immediately, Francis began to improve and soon was well enough to go with Brother Elias to Le Celle near Cortona. But there his illness took a turn for the worse again, and Francis asked Elias to take him back to Assisi. Brother Thomas says, "this good son did what his gracious father asked."[86] There is a kindly feeling on the part of Brother Thomas throughout the telling of this incident. The same is true wherever Elias is mentioned in this *First Life*.

Unquestionably, however, there is a difference in the way Brother Elias is treated in the *Second Life*. Not once is he mentioned by name there. Twice he is referred to as the *vicar* of Francis.[87] Once there is a veiled reference to him.[88] Once he is simply referred to as "another of the brothers."[89] In this last instance Brother Thomas tells how Elias artfully managed to satisfy his curiosity about the wound in Francis' side and how by a bit of maneuvering he became the only brother to see that wound while Francis was yet alive. The telling of the incident is in sharp contrast to the brief note about it in the *First Life* where it was simply said: "But happy was Elias who, while the saint lived, merited to see this wound."[90] In the *Second Life* the words and the whole tone of the narrative are cold and almost contemptuous.

It is not difficult to understand the changed attitude of Brother Thomas in the *Second Life* and the changed tone of his writing about Brother Elias. When he wrote the *First Life*, Brother Elias was still in good standing with his confreres and with the Church. He had been an efficient vicar for Francis and, as a matter of fact, had been highly regarded by Francis, as Francis was by him. Francis relied heavily upon him during the last years of his life, and Elias in turn had a deep regard and a deep concern for his father. These things are evident from the *First Life*.[91]

But after Francis' death, Elias was entrusted by Pope Gregory IX with the task of building a new basilica to honor St. Francis, a work that was carried out under papal auspices. But Elias angered the rest of the friars by insisting that the various provinces supply funds for the new building.[92] However, had this been the only thing, it is quite likely that it would have been overlooked, for the brothers as such were undoubtedly in sympathy with the goal for which the funds were being collected.

Of even more serious concern to the friars was Brother Elias' personal conduct as minister general.[93] He lived in luxury, maintained two residences for himself,[94] rode horseback, kept a private cook to serve his tastes at table, ate but seldom with other friars, and so on. Furthermore, he apparently refused to hold any general chapters. In the end, the friars, led by such outstanding brothers as Alexander of Hales, John of La Rochelle, and Haymo of Faversham, moved against him and succeeded in having him deposed from his office of minister general in 1239. Shortly thereafter Elias joined the excommunicated emperor Frederick II and was himself excommunicated. In 1244 he was summoned to appear at the general chapter of Genoa, but when he failed to appear, he was again excommunicated.[95]

In the light of these circumstances of Elias' life, Brother Thomas' attitude toward him is not at all surprising. When he wrote the *First Life*, Elias was in good standing, had been a friend and confidant of St. Francis, had been Francis' vicar for about six years, and had been known for his kindness and consideration toward Francis as well as for his efficiency as an administrator. Why then should Thomas have felt anything but sympathy and kindliness toward him? But by the time he wrote the *Second Life* Elias had fallen from grace, and proved himself a tyrannical ruler, had abandoned the order, and had been excommunicated. Should he have continued his sympathetic attitude toward him? As a matter of fact, the only proper attitude he could have taken toward him was the attitude he did in reality take. True, that attitude did of necessity weaken the picture of Elias' relationship toward Francis in the *Second Life*. That, however, could not matter. Elias had fallen, as all the friars knew; and to depict him with the same sympathy with which he had depicted him in the *First Life* would have been a scandal to all.

Of particular concern to some writers is the way Brother Thomas handled the blessing that St. Francis imparted to those about him on his deathbed. That there is considerable difference between the narrative of the *First Life* and that of the *Second Life* on this matter will be readily apparent from a comparison of the relevant passages.

In the *First Life* Francis is presented as imparting his blessing twice to his brothers. The first blessing was given while Francis was staying at the palace of the bishop of Assisi. He summoned some of his brothers about him and, like the patriarch Jacob of old, blessed them. Elias was seated at the left of Francis and Francis reached over and put his right hand on Elias' head and spoke the following blessing:

> You, my son, I bless *above all and throughout all;*[96] and, just as the Most High has multiplied my brothers and sons in your hands, so also I bless them all upon you and

in you. May God, the King of all, bless you in heaven and upon earth. I bless you as much as I can and more than I can, and what I cannot, may He who can do all things do in you. May the Lord be mindful of your work and of your labor, and may a share be reserved for you in the reward of the just. May you find every blessing you desire, and may whatever you ask worthily be granted to you.[97]

Then to the rest of the brothers Francis said:

Farewell, all you my sons, *in the fear of God*,[98] and may you remain in him always, for a very great trial will come upon you and a great tribulation is approaching. Happy will they be who will persevere in the things they have begun; from them future scandals will separate some. I am hastening to the Lord and I am confident that I will go to my God *whom I serve* devoutly *in my spirit*.[99]

Francis then asked the brothers to take him to St. Mary's of the Portiuncula. There, on the day of his death, he was asked by Brother Elias to bless all the brothers present and absent. And Francis did so, saying:

Behold, my son, I am called by God; I forgive my brothers, both present and absent, all their offenses and faults, and, in as far as I am able, I absolve them; I want you to announce this to them and to bless them all on my behalf.[100]

In the *Second Life*, however, there is only one blessing, and while it is not clear just where it took place, the supposition is that it was at the Portiuncula. Brother Thomas relates that Francis placed his right hand upon the head of each one present, beginning with his vicar, and then said:

> Farewell, all you my sons, *in the fear of the
> Lord*,[101] and may you remain in him al-
> ways! And because a future temptation and
> tribulation is approaching, happy will they
> be who will persevere in the things they
> have begun. I am hastening to the Lord,
> to whose grace I commend you all.[102]

Then Francis blessed them, we are told, those present
and all his brothers who were in the world and who
would come after them unto the end of the world.
He then took bread and broke it and gave to each a
share. Then he had a portion of the Gospel of St.
John read to him and thereafter spent the remaining
days in praising Christ.

Apart from the fact that in the *First Life* two dis-
tinct occasions are indicated upon which Francis
gave the brothers a blessing and in the *Second Life*
no such distinction is made, the only essential difference between the two narratives is the omission in
the *Second Life* of the special blessing imparted to
Brother Elias.[103] The same facts indicated above
apply here, namely, that it is the changed circumstances surrounding Elias that account for Brother
Thomas' handling the same blessings in a different
manner in the *Second Life*. Again, because of the
scandals that accompanied Elias' actions, he wants
to keep Elias in the background, and again too, there
was nothing else for him to do. Of course it should
also be kept in mind that the *Second Life* was written
as a complement to the *First Life* and accordingly
Brother Thomas was in no way obliged to repeat all
the details that were given already in the *First Life*.

In it all, however, there is no reason to blame
Brother Thomas or to call into question either his
honesty or his reliability as an historian. He acted
as anyone else would act under similar circumstances.

His *Second Life,* like the first, was about St. Francis; and, while it was necessary that Brother Elias should come into the narrative, there was no need to include details of a relationship with St. Francis that had become tarnished by Elias' subsequent defection and excommunication. The fact that he allowed touches of his personal feelings toward Elias to enter in does not lessen in any way his reputation as an historian. On the contrary, to anyone who reads the *Lives* with a mind unprejudiced by what some critics have said the legends have a ring of truthfulness and accuracy about them that makes one sure that here are reliable accounts of the life of St. Francis, and of the early days of the Franciscan Order as well; in fact, accounts so reliable that they are indispensable to both the biographer of St. Francis and the historian of the Franciscan Order.

5

THE LATER FATE OF THE *LIVES*

By the time St. Bonaventure came to be minister general of the order,[104] there were in existence the three major writings of Brother Thomas of Celano: the *First Life of St. Francis,* the *Second Life of St. Francis,* and the *Treatise on the Miracles of Blessed Francis.* In addition there were several short legends in existence, principally: Brother Thomas' *Legend for Use in Choir;* Julian of Speyer's short *Life of St. Francis* based on Brother Thomas' *First Life;* a very short life of St. Francis by a certain Bartholomew of Trent, a Dominican; and a life of St. Francis in verse (*Legenda Versificata*) by Henry of Avranches.

The short treatises served a purpose, but they could not be considered in any way an adequate narrative of the life of St. Francis. On the other hand, the three main works of Brother Thomas of Celano were separate works, none of which was complete in itself; and even taken together, they did not constitute a unified whole. As a result of these many legends, there was a growing confusion over the life and deeds of the founder of the order among the friars of the later generation, and these men were finding it difficult to come to know St. Francis as he should be known. The superiors of the order recognized these facts and in due time took action to remedy the situation.

In the general chapter of the order held at Narbonne in 1260, the minister general, St. Bonaventure, was asked by the members of the chapter to prepare a new life of St. Francis to take the place of the existing *legendae* as the official life of the saint. Bonaventure himself refers to this request in the Prologue of his life where he says that he "would not by any means have attempted the task of describing the life of St. Francis"[105] had not the insistence of the general chapter induced him to do so, for he considered himself unworthy and incapable of the task.[106]

Bonaventure, however, despite his feelings of inadequacy, carried out the wishes of the general chapter and completed the *Vita B. Francisci* by 1262 or 1263.[107] The Quaracchi editors think that it was then presented to the general chapter of Pisa in 1263, where it was received with enthusiasm, and that then some thirty-four copies were ordered made, a copy for each of the ministers provincial of the order.[108]

Three years later, at the general chapter at Paris, 1266, the new *legenda* was again discussed; and at this time there was issued that much discussed decree, under obedience, that "all the *legendae* about St. Francis that had been made in the past should be destroyed." Likewise, the decree went on to say, that wherever these *legendae* could be located outside of the order, they should be given the same treatment.

Thereafter, "that *Legenda* that had been made by the minister general," since it had been compiled in accordance with what he could learn from the mouths of those who had been close to St. Francis,[109] was to be henceforth the standard biography of St. Francis.[110]

The results of this decree of the general chapter of Paris, whatever may have been the motivation behind it,[111] were catastrophic as far as the works of Brother Thomas of Celano were concerned. These were lost sight of almost completely for many years thereafter. Gradually, however, manuscripts of these works have been rediscovered. In all, twenty manuscripts of the *First Life* have been found, five of which are complete, and four others fairly complete. Eight of these manuscripts were found in Cistercian monasteries, three in Benedictine monasteries, but only one among the Franciscans themselves. It is perhaps not too surprising that so many were found among the Cistericans, for in 1259, at the request of St. Bonaventure, their general chapter accepted the feast of St. Francis for their whole order, and St. Bonaventure gave them a copy of the *First Life*. Apparently this life was copied many times by the Cistercians for their various monasteries, and since they were outside the Franciscan Order, these copies more easily escaped the effects of the decree of the general chapter of Paris. The Benedictines, too, used the *First Life* in their liturgy. The friars themselves, however, seem to have done a rather complete job of carrying out the decree of the general chapter. The *Second Life* and the *Treatise on the Miracles* did not fare as well as the *First Life*. Only two complete copies of the former have survived,[112] and only one of the latter.[113]

Since the middle of the eighteenth century there have been a number of editions of these works of

Brother Thomas. In 1768 the *First Life* was published for the first time in the *Acta Sanctorum* by Constantine Suysken S.J. In 1806 the *First* and *Second Life* were published together by Stephen Rinaldi O.F.M. Conv. In 1904 H. G. Rosedale published an edition of all three works, which, however, was very imperfect and uncritical. In 1906 Edward d'Alencon published a much better edition of these works. But the best edition of all is that of the Fathers of St. Bonaventure's College, Quaracchi, published in the *Analecta Franciscana*, X. It is this edition that was used for this present English translation.

PART I

The First Life of St. Francis
by
Thomas of Celano

PROLOGUE

In the Name of the Lord. Amen

HERE BEGINS THE PROLOGUE OF
THE LIFE OF BLESSED FRANCIS

1 It is my desire to relate in an orderly manner, with pious devotion and with truth as my first consideration and guide, the acts and the life of our most blessed father Francis. But in as much as no one can retain fully in his memory all the things that Francis *did and taught,*[1] I have tried, at the command of our lord, the gloriously reigning Pope Gregory,[2] to set forth as well as I can, though indeed with unskilled words, at least those things that I have heard from his own mouth or that I have gathered from faithful and trustworthy witnesses. I wish, however, that I might truly deserve to be a disciple of him who always avoided enigmatic ways of saying things and who knew nothing of the ornaments of language!

2 I have divided the things I have been able to gather concerning the blessed Francis into three books, arranging everything in separate chapters, so that the many occasions when these things were done will not confuse the order and lead to doubt about their truth. The first book follows the historical order and is given over, for the most part, to the purity of his conduct and life,[3] to his holy striving after virtue, and to his salutary teachings. In it, too, are inserted a few of the many miracles which the Lord our God deigned to perform through him while he was *in the flesh.*[4] — The second book tells what happened from the second last year of his life until his happy death.[5] The third book relates many of the miracles this most glorious saint worked here upon earth while reigning with Christ in heaven,

though it omits many more. It also records the reverence, honor, praise, and glory which the happy Pope Gregory, along with the cardinals of the holy Roman Church, heaped upon him when they enrolled him in the catalogue of saints.[6] Thanks be to Almighty God, who shows himself in his saints always worthy of admiration and love.

THUS ENDS THE PROLOGUE

BOOK ONE

*To the Praise and Glory of Almighty God,
the Father, Son, and Holy Spirit. Amen*

HERE BEGINS THE LIFE
OF OUR MOST BLESSED FATHER FRANCIS

CHAPTER I

How Francis lived in the world before his conversion

1   In the city of Assisi, which lies at the edge of
the Spoleto valley,[1] *there was a man*[2] by the name of
Francis, who from his earliest years was brought up
by his parents proud of spirit, in accordance with
the vanity of the world; and imitating their wretched
life and habits for a long time, he became even more
vain and proud. For this very evil custom has grown
up everywhere among those who are considered
Christians in name, and this pernicious teaching has
become so established and prescribed, as though by
public law, that people seek to educate their children
from the cradle on very negligently and dissolutely.
For, indeed, when they first begin to speak or stammer, children, just hardly born, are taught by signs
and words to do certain wicked and detestable things;
and when they come to be weaned, they are forced
not only to speak but also to do certain things full of
lust and wantonness. Impelled by a fear that is
natural to their age, none of them dares to conduct
himself in an upright manner, for if he were to do so
he would be subjected to severe punishments. Therefore, a secular poet says well: "Because we have
grown up amid the practices of our parents, we therefore pursue all evil things from our childhood on."[3]
This testimony is true, for so much the more in-
jurious to their children are the desires of the parents, the more successfully they work out. But when
the children have progressed a little in age, they always sink into worse deeds, following their own

impulses. For from a corrupt root a corrupt tree will grow,[4] and what has once become wickedly depraved can hardly ever be brought into harmony with the norms of uprightness. But when they begin to enter the portals of adolescence, how do you think they will turn out? Then, indeed, tossed about amid every kind of debauchery, they give themselves over completely to shameful practices, in as much as they are permitted to do as they please. For once they have become the slaves of sin by a voluntary servitude, they give over all their members to be instruments of wickedness;[5] and showing forth in themselves nothing of the Christian religion either in their lives or in their conduct, they take refuge under the mere name of Christianity. These miserable people very often pretend that they have done even worse things than they have actually done, lest they seem more despicable the more innocent they are.

2   These are the wretched circumstances among which the man whom we venerate today as a saint, for he is truly a saint, lived in his youth; and almost up to the twenty-fifth year of his age, he squandered and wasted his time miserably.[6] Indeed, he outdid all his contemporaries in vanities and he came to be a promoter of evil[7] and was more abundantly zealous for all kinds of foolishness.[8] He was the admiration of all and strove to outdo the rest in the pomp of vainglory, in jokes, in strange doings, in idle and useless talk, in songs, in soft and flowing garments, for he was very rich, not however avaricious but prodigal, not a hoarder of money but a squanderer of his possessions, a cautious business man but a very unreliable steward. On the other hand, he was a very kindly person, easy and affable, even making himself foolish because of it; for because of these qualities many ran after him, doers of evil and promoters of crime. And thus overwhelmed by a host of evil com-

6

panions, proud and high-minded, he walked about the streets of Babylon[9] until the *Lord looked down from heaven*[10] and for his own name's sake removed his *wrath far off* and for his praise bridled Francis lest he should perish.[11] *The hand of the Lord* therefore came *upon him*[12] and a change was wrought by the right hand of the Most High, that through him an assurance might be granted to sinners that they had been restored to grace and that he might become an example to all of conversion to God.[13]

CHAPTER II

How God touched the heart of Francis by sickness and by a vision

3   For, indeed, while this man was still in the glow of youthful passion, and the age of wantonness was urging him on immoderately to fulfill the demands of youth; and while, not knowing how to restrain himself, he was stirred by the venom of the serpent of old, suddenly the divine vengeance, or, perhaps better, the divine unction, came upon him and sought first to recall his erring senses by visiting upon him mental distress and bodily suffering, according to the saying of the prophet: *Behold I will hedge up thy way with thorns, and I will stop it up with a wall.*[14] Thus, worn down by a long illness, as man's stubbornness deserves when it can hardly be corrected except by punishments, he began to think of things other than he was used to thinking upon. When he had recovered somewhat and had begun to walk about the house with the support of a cane to speed the recovery of his health, he went outside one day and began to look about at the surrounding landscape with great interest. But the beauty of the fields, the pleasantness of the vineyards, and whatever else was beautiful to look upon, could stir in him no de-

light. He wondered therefore at the sudden change that had come over him, and those who took delight in such things he considered very foolish.

4 From that day on, therefore, he began to despise himself and to hold in some contempt the things he had admired and loved before. But not fully or truly, for he was not yet freed from the *cords of vanity*[15] nor had he shaken off from his neck the yoke of evil servitude.[16] It is indeed very hard to give up things one is accustomed to, and things that once enter into the mind are not easily eradicated; the mind, even though it has been kept away from them for a long time, returns to the things it once learned; and by constant repetition vice generally becomes second nature.[17] So Francis still tried to flee the hand of God, and, forgetting for a while his paternal correction, he thought, amid the smiles of prosperity, of *the things of the world;*[18] and, ignorant of the *counsel of God,*[19] he still looked forward to accomplishing great deeds of worldly glory and vanity. For a certain nobleman of the city of Assisi was preparing himself in no mean way with military arms, and, puffed up by a gust of vainglory, vowed that he would go to Apulia[20] to increase his wealth and fame. Upon hearing this, Francis, who was flighty and not a little rash, arranged to go with him; he was inferior to him in nobility of birth, but superior in generosity, poorer in the matter of wealth, but more lavish in giving things away.

5 On a certain night, therefore, after he had given himself with all deliberation to the accomplishment of these things, and while, burning with desire, he longed greatly to set about the journey, he who had struck him with the rod of justice visited him in the sweetness of grace by means of a nocturnal vision; and because Francis was eager for glory, he

enticed him and raised his spirits with a vision of the heights of glory. For it seemed to Francis that his whole home was filled with the trappings of war, namely, saddles, shields, lances, and other things; rejoicing greatly, he wondered silently within himself what this should mean. For he was not accustomed to see such things in his home, but rather piles of cloth to be sold. When, accordingly, he was not a little astonished at this sudden turn of events, the answer was given him that all these arms would belong to him and to his soldiers. When he awoke, he arose in the morning with a glad heart, and considering the vision an omen of great success, he felt sure that his journey to Apulia would come out well. *He did not know what to say*[21] and he did not as yet recognize the task given him from heaven. Nevertheless, he might have understood that his interpretation of the vision was not correct, for while the vision bore some resemblance to things pertaining to war, his heart was not filled with his usual happiness over such things. He had to use some force on himself to carry out his designs and to complete the proposed journey. It is indeed quite fitting that mention be made of arms in the beginning and it is quite opportune that arms should be offered to the soldier about to engage one strongly armed, that like another David he might free Israel from the long-standing reproach of its enemies[22] in *the name of the Lord God of hosts.*[23]

CHAPTER III

How, changed in mind but not in body, Francis spoke of the treasure he had found and of his spouse in allegory

6   Changed, therefore, but in mind, not in body, he refused to go to Apulia and he strove to bend his

9

own will to the will of God. Accordingly, he withdrew for a while from the bustle and the business of the world and tried to establish Jesus Christ dwelling within himself.[24] Like a prudent business man, he hid the treasure he had found from the eyes of the deluded, and, having sold all his possessions, he tried to buy it secretly.[25] Now since there was a certain man in the city of Assisi whom he loved more than any other because he was of the same age as the other, and since the great familiarity of their mutual affection led him to share his secrets with him,[26] he often took him to remote places, places well-suited for counsel, telling him that he had found a certain precious and great treasure. This one rejoiced and, concerned about what he heard, he willingly accompanied Francis whenever he was asked. There was a certain grotto near the city where they frequently went and talked about this treasure. The man of God, who was already holy by reason of his holy purpose, would enter the grotto, while his companion would wait for him outside; and filled with a new and singular spirit, he would pray to his Father in secret. He wanted no one to know what he did within, and taking the occasion of the good to wisely conceal the better, he took counsel with God alone concerning his holy proposal. He prayed devoutly that the eternal and true God would direct his way and teach him to do his will. He bore the greatest sufferings in mind and was not able to rest until he should have completed in deed what he had conceived in his heart; various thoughts succeeded one another and their importunity disturbed him greatly. He was afire within himself with a divine fire and he was not able to hide outwardly the ardor of his mind; he repented that he had sinned so grievously and had offended *the eyes of God's majesty*,[27] and neither the past evils nor those present gave him any delight. Still he had not as yet won full confidence that he would be able to guard himself against them in the future. Consequently, when he came out again to his companion, he was so exhausted with the strain, that one person seemed to have entered, and another to have come out.

7   One day, however, when he had begged for the mercy of God most earnestly, it was shown to him by God what he was to do. Accordingly, he was so filled with joy that he could not contain himself, and, though he did not want to, he uttered some things to the ears of men. But, though he could not keep silent because of the greatness of the joy that filled him, he nevertheless spoke cautiously and *in an obscure manner*.[28] For, while he spoke to his special friend of a hidden treasure, as was said, he tried to speak to others only figuratively; he said that he did not want to go to Apulia, but he promised that he would do noble and great things in his native place. People thought he wished to take to himself a wife, and they asked him, saying: "Francis, do you wish to get married?" But he answered them, saying: "I shall take a more noble and more beautiful spouse than you have ever seen; she will surpass all others in beauty and will excel all others in wisdom." Indeed, the immaculate spouse of God is the true religion which he embraced; and the hidden treasure is the kingdom of heaven, which he sought with such great desire; for it was extremely necessary that the Gospel calling be fulfilled in him who was to be the minister of the Gospel in faith and in truth.

CHAPTER IV

Francis sold all his goods and despised the money given him

8   Behold, when the blessed servant of the Most

11

High was thus disposed and strengthened by the Holy Spirit, now that the opportune time had come, he followed the blessed impulse of his soul, by which he would come to the highest things, trampling worldly things under foot. He could not delay any longer, because a deadly disease had grown up everywhere to such an extent and had so taken hold of all the limbs of many that, were the physician to delay even a little, it would snatch away life, shutting off the life-giving spirit. He rose up, therefore, fortified himself with the sign of the cross, got his horse ready and mounted it, and taking with him some fine cloth to sell, he hastened to the city called Foligno.[29] There, as usual, he sold everything he had with him, and, successful as a merchant, he left behind even the horse he was riding, after he had received payment for it; and, free of all luggage, he started back, wondering with a religious mind what he should do with the money. Soon, turned toward God's work in a wondrous manner, and accordingly feeling that it would be a great burden to him to carry that money even for an hour, he hastened to get rid of it, considering the advantage he might get from it as so much sand. When, therefore, he neared the city of Assisi, he discovered a certain church along the way that had been built of old in honor of St. Damian but which was now threatening to collapse because it was so old.[30]

9   When this new soldier of Christ came up to this church, moved with pity over such great need, he entered it with fear and reverence. And when he found there a certain poor priest, he kissed his sacred hands with great faith, and offered him the money he had with him, telling him in order what he proposed to do. The priest was astonished and, wondering over a conversion so incredibly sudden, he refused to believe what he heard. And because he

thought he was being deceived, he refused to keep the money offered him. For he had seen him just the day before, so to say, living in a riotous way *among his relatives and acquaintances*[31] and showing greater foolishness than the rest. But Francis persisted obstinately and tried to gain credence for what he said, asking earnestly and begging the priest to suffer him to remain with him for the sake of the Lord. In the end the priest acquiesced to his remaining there, but out of fear of the young man's parents, he did not accept the money; whereupon this true contemner of money threw it upon a window sill, for he cared no more for it than for the dust. He wanted to possess that wisdom that is better than gold and to acquire that prudence that is more precious than silver.[32]

CHAPTER V

How his father persecuted Francis and put him in chains

10   So while the servant of the most high God was staying in the aforesaid place, his father[33] went about everywhere, like a persistent spy, wanting to learn what had happened to his son. And when he learned that he was living in such a way at that place, *being touched inwardly with sorrow of heart*,[34] he was *troubled exceedingly*[35] at the sudden turn of events, and calling together his friends and neighbors, he hurried to the place where the servant of God was staying. But he, the new athlete of Christ, when he heard of the threats of those who were pursuing him and when he got knowledge of their coming, wanting to *give place to wrath*,[36] hid himself in a certain secret pit which he himself had prepared for just such an emergency. That pit was in that house and was known probably to one person alone; in it he hid so continuously for one month that he hardly dared

leave it to provide for his human needs. Food, when it was given to him, he ate in the secrecy of the pit, and every service was rendered to him by stealth. Praying, he prayed always with a torrent of tears that the Lord would deliver him from the hands of those who were persecuting his soul,[37] and that he would fulfill his pious wishes in his loving kindness; *in fasting and in weeping*[38] he begged for the clemency of the Savior, and, distrusting his own efforts, he *cast* his whole *care upon the Lord*.[39] And though he was in a pit and *in darkness*,[40] he was nevertheless filled with a certain exquisite joy of which till then he had had no experience; and catching fire therefrom, he left the pit and exposed himself openly to the curses of his persecutors.

11   He arose, therefore, immediately, active, eager, and lively; and, bearing the shield of faith to fight for the Lord, armed with a great confidence, he took the way toward the city; aglow with a divine fire, he began to accuse himself severely of laziness and cowardice. When those who knew him saw this, they compared what he was now with what he had been; and they began to revile him miserably. Shouting out that he was mad and demented, they threw the mud of the streets and stones at him. They saw that he was changed from his former ways and greatly worn down by mortification of the flesh, and they therefore set down everything he did to exhaustion and madness. But since a patient man is better than a proud man, the servant of God showed himself deaf to all these things and, neither broken nor changed by any of these injuries, he gave thanks to God for all of them. In vain does the wicked man persecute one striving after virtue, for the more he is buffeted, the more strongly will he triumph. As someone says, indignity strengthens a generous spirit.[41]

12   Now when the noise and the shouting of this kind concerning Francis had been going on for a long time through the streets and quarters of the city, and the sound of it all was echoing here and there, among the many to whose ears the report of these things came was finally his father. When he heard the name of his son mentioned, and understood that the commotion among the citizens turned about his son, he immediately arose, not indeed to free him but rather to destroy him; and, with no regard for moderation, he rushed upon him like a wolf upon a sheep, and looking upon him with a fierce and savage countenance, he laid hands upon him and dragged him shamelessly and disgracefully to his home. Thus, without mercy, he shut him up in a dark place for several days, and thinking to bend his spirit to his own will, he first used words and then blows and chains. But Francis became only the more ready and more strong to carry out his purpose; but he did not abandon his patience either because he was insulted by words or worn out by chains. For he who is commanded to rejoice in tribulation[42] cannot swerve from the right intention and position of his mind or be led away from Christ's flock, not even by scourgings and chains; neither does he waver *in a flood of many waters*,[43] whose refuge from oppression is the Son of God, who, lest our troubles seem hard to us, showed always that those he bore were greater.

CHAPTER VI

How Francis' mother freed him, and how he stripped himself before the bishop of Assisi

13   It happened, however, when Francis' father had left home for a while on business and the man of God remained bound in the basement of the house, his mother, who was alone with him and who did

15

not approve of what her husband had done, spoke kindly to her son. But when she saw that he could not be persuaded away from his purpose, she was moved by motherly compassion for him, and loosening his chains, she let him go free. He, however, giving thanks to Almighty God, returned quickly to the place where he had been before. But now, after he had been proved by temptations, he allowed himself greater liberty, and he took on a more cheerful aspect because of the many struggles he had gone through. From the wrongs done him he acquired a more confident spirit, and he went about everywhere freely with higher spirits than before. Meanwhile his father returned, and not finding Francis, he turned to upbraid his wife, heaping sins upon sins. Then, raging and blustering, he ran to that place hoping that if he could not recall him from his ways, he might at least drive him from the province. But, because it is true that *in the fear of the Lord is confidence*,[44] when this child of grace heard his carnally minded[45] father coming to him, confident and joyful he went to meet him, exclaiming in a clear voice that he cared nothing for his chains and blows. Moreover, he stated that he would gladly undergo evils for the name of Christ.

14   But when his father saw that he could not bring him back from the way he had undertaken, he was roused by all means to get his money back. The man of God had desired to offer it and expend it to feed the poor and to repair the buildings of that place. But he who had no love for money could not be mislead by any aspect of good in it; and he who was not held back by any affection for it was in no way disturbed by its loss. Therefore, when the money was found, which he who hated the things of this world so greatly and desired the riches of heaven so much had thrown aside in the dust, of the window

16

sill, the fury of his raging father was extinguished a little, and the thirst of his avarice was somewhat allayed by the warmth of discovery. He then brought his son before the bishop of the city,[46] so that, renouncing all his possessions into his hands, he might give up everything he had. Francis not only did not refuse to do this, but he hastened with great joy to do what was demanded of him.

15   When he was brought before the bishop, he would suffer no delay or hesitation in anything; indeed, he did not wait for any words nor did he speak any, but immediately putting off his clothes and casting them aside, he gave them back to his father. Moreover, not even retaining his trousers, he stripped himself completely naked before all. The bishop, however, sensing his disposition and admiring greatly his fervor and constancy, arose and drew him within his arms and covered him with the mantle he was wearing. He understood clearly that the counsel was of God, and he understood that the actions of the man of God that he had personally witnessed contained a mystery. He immediately, therefore, became his helper and cherishing him and encouraging him, he embraced him in the bowels of charity. Behold, now he wrestles naked with his naked adversary,[47] and having put off everything that is of this world, he thinks only *about the things of the Lord.*[48] He seeks now so to despise his own life, putting off all solicitude for it, that he might find peace in his harassed ways,[49] and that meanwhile only the wall of flesh should separate him from the vision of God.

CHAPTER VII

How Francis was seized by robbers and cast into the snow, and how he served the lepers

16   He who once wore fine garments now went

about clad only in scanty garments. As he went through a certain woods singing praises to the Lord in the French language, robbers suddenly rushed out upon him. When they asked him in a ferocious tone who he was, the man of God replied confidently in a loud voice: "I am the herald of the great King. What is that to you?" But they struck him and cast him into a ditch filled with deep snow, saying: "Lie there, foolish herald of God!" But he rolled himself about and shook off the snow; and when they had gone away, he jumped out of the ditch, and, glad with great joy, he began to call out the praises of God in a loud voice throughout the grove. At length, coming to a certain cloister of monks,[50] he spent several days there as a scullion, wearing a ragged shirt and being satisfied to be filled only with broth. But, when all pity was withdrawn from him and he could not get even an old garment, he left the place, not moved by anger, but forced by necessity; and he went to the city of Gubbio,[51] where he obtained a small tunic from a certain man who once had been his friend.[52] Then, after some time had elapsed, when the fame of the man of God was beginning to grow and *his name was spread abroad*[53] among the people, the prior of the aforementioned monastery recalled and realised how the man of God had been treated and he came to him and begged pardon for himself and for his monks out of reverence for the Savior.

17   Then the holy lover of complete humility went to the lepers and lived with them, serving them most diligently for God's sake; and washing all foulness from them, he wiped away also the corruption of the ulcers, just as he said in his *Testament*: "When I was in sins, it seemed extremely bitter to me to look at lepers, and the Lord himself led me among them and I practiced mercy with them."[54] So greatly loathsome was the sight of lepers to him at one time, he used to

say, that, in the days of his vanity, he would look at their houses only from a distance of two miles and he would hold his nostrils with his hands. But now, when by the grace and the power of the Most High he was beginning to think of holy and useful things, while he was still clad in secular garments, he met a leper one day and, made stronger than himself, he kissed him. From then on he began to despise himself more and more, until, by the mercy of the Redeemer, he came to perfect victory over himself. Of other poor, too, while he yet remained in the world and still followed the world, he was the helper, stretching forth a hand of mercy to those who had nothing, and showing compassion to the afflicted. For when one day, contrary to his custom, for he was a most courteous person, he upbraided a certain poor man who had asked an alms of him, he was immediately sorry; and he began to say to himself that it was a great reproach and a shame to withhold what was asked from one who had asked in the name of so great a King. He therefore resolved in his heart never in the future to refuse any one, if at all possible, who asked for the love of God. This he most diligently did and carried out, until he sacrificed himself entirely and in every way; and thus he became first a practicer before he became a teacher of the evangelical counsel: *To him who asks of thee,* he said, *give; and from him who would borrow of thee, do not turn away.*[55]

CHAPTER VIII

How Francis built the church of St. Damian; and of the life of the Ladies who dwelt in that place

18   The first work that blessed Francis undertook after he had gained his freedom from the hand of his carnally minded father was to build a house of God.

He did not try to build one anew, but he repaired an old one, restored an ancient one. He did not tear out the foundation, but he built upon it, ever reserving to Christ his prerogative, though he was not aware of it, *for other foundation no one can lay, but that which has been laid, which is Christ Jesus.*[56] When he had returned to the place where, as has been said, the church of St. Damian had been built in ancient times, he repaired it zealously within a short time with the help of the grace of the Most High. This is the blessed and holy place, where the glorious religion and most excellent order of Poor Ladies and holy virgins had its blessed origin about six years after the conversion of St. Francis and through that same blessed man. Of it, the Lady Clare,[57] a native of the city of Assisi, the most precious and the firmest stone of the whole structure, was the foundation. For when, after the beginning of the Order of Brothers, the said lady was converted to God through the counsel of the holy man, she lived unto the advantage of many and as an example to a countless multitude. She was of noble parentage, but she was more noble by grace; she was a virgin in body, most chaste in mind; a youth in age, but mature in spirit; steadfast in purpose and most ardent in her desire for divine love; endowed with wisdom and excelling in humility; Clare by name,[58] brighter in life, and brightest in character.

19   Over her arose a noble structure of most precious pearls, whose *praise is not from men but from God,*[59] since neither is our limited understanding sufficient to imagine it, nor our scanty vocabulary to utter it. For above everything else there flourishes among them that excelling virtue of mutual and continual charity, which so binds their wills into one that, though forty or fifty of them dwell together in one place, agreement in likes and dislikes moulds one spirit in them out of many.[60] Secondly, in each one there glows the gem of humility, which so preserves the gifts and good things bestowed from heaven,[61] that they merit other virtues too. Thirdly, the lily of virginity and chastity so sprinkles them with a wondrous odor that, forgetful of earthly thoughts, they desire to meditate only on heavenly things; and so great a love for their eternal Spouse arises in their hearts from the fragrance of that lily that the integrity of that holy affection excludes from them every habit of their former life. Fourthly, they have all become so conspicuous by the title of the highest poverty that their food and clothing hardly at all or never come together to satisfy extreme necessity.

20   Fifthly, they have so attained the singular grace of abstinence and silence that they need exert hardly any effort to check the movements of the flesh and to restrain their tongues; some of them have become so unaccustomed to speak that when necessity demands that they speak, they can hardly remember how to form the words as they should. Sixthly, with all these things, they are adorned so admirably with the virtue of patience, that no adversity of tribulations or injury of vexations ever breaks their spirit or changes it. Seventhly, and finally, they have so merited the height of contemplation that in it they learn everything they should do or avoid; and happily they know how to be *out of mind for God,*[62] persevering night and day in praising him and in praying to him. May the eternal God deign by his holy grace to bring so holy a beginning to an even more holy end. And let this suffice for the present concerning these virgins dedicated to God and the most devout handmaids of Christ, for their wondrous life and their glorious institutions, which they received from the lord Pope Gregory, at that time Bishop of Ostia,[63] requires a work of its

own and leisure in which to write it.[64]

CHAPTER IX

How Francis, having changed his habit, rebuilt the church of St. Mary of the Portiuncula, and how, upon hearing the Gospel, he left all things, and how he designed and made the habit the brothers wear

21   Meanwhile the holy man of God, having put on a new kind of habit and having repaired the aforesaid church, went to another place near the city of Assisi, where he began to rebuild a certain dilapidated and well-nigh destroyed church, and he did not leave off from his good purpose until he had brought it to completion.[65] Then he went to another place, which is called the Portiuncula,[66] where there stood a church of the Blessed Virgin Mother of God that had been built in ancient times, but was now deserted and cared for by no one. When the holy man of God saw how it was thus in ruins, he was moved to pity, because he burned with devotion toward the mother of all good; and he began to live there in great zeal. It was the third year of his conversion when he began to repair this church. At this time he wore a kind of hermit's dress, with a leather girdle about his waist; he carried a staff in his hands and wore shoes on his feet.

22   But when on a certain day the Gospel was read in that church,[67] how the Lord sent his disciples out to preach, the holy man of God, assisting there, understood somewhat the words of the Gospel; after Mass he humbly asked the priest to explain the Gospel to him more fully. When he had set forth for him in order all these things, the holy Francis, hearing that the disciples of Christ should not possess gold or silver or money; nor carry along the way scrip, or wallet, or bread, or a staff; that they should

not have shoes, or two tunics;[68] but that they should preach the kingdom of God and penance,[69] immediately cried out exultingly: "This is what I wish, this is what I seek, this is what I long to do with all my heart."[70] Then the holy father, *overflowing with joy,*[71] hastened to fulfill that salutary word he had heard, and he did not suffer any delay to intervene before beginning devoutly to perform what he had heard. He immediately put off his shoes from his feet, put aside the staff from his hands, was content with one tunic, and exchanged his leather girdle for a small cord. He designed for himself a tunic that bore a likeness to the cross, that by means of it he might beat off all temptations of the devil; he designed a very rough tunic so that by it he might crucify the flesh with all its vices and sins;[72] he designed a very poor and mean tunic, one that would not excite the covetousness of the world. The other things that he had heard, however, he longed with the greatest diligence and the greatest reverence to perform. For he was not a deaf hearer of the Gospel, but committing all that he had heard to praiseworthy memory, he tried diligently to carry it out to the letter.

CHAPTER X

Of his preaching of the Gospel and his announcing peace and of the conversion of the first six brothers

23   From then on he began to preach penance to all with great fervor of spirit and joy of mind, edifying his hearers with his simple words and his greatness of heart. His words was like a *burning fire,*[73] penetrating the inmost reaches of the heart, and it filled the minds of all the hearers with admiration. He seemed completely different from what he had been, and, looking up to the heavens, he disdained to look upon the earth. This indeed is wonderful,

that he first began to preach where as a child he had first learned to read and where for a time he was buried amid great honor,[74] so that the happy beginning might be commended by a still happier ending. Where he had learned he also taught, and where he began he also ended. In all his preaching, before he proposed the word of God to those gathered about, he first prayed for peace for them, saying: "The Lord give you peace."[75] He always most devoutly announced peace to men and women, to all he met and overtook. For this reason many who had hated peace and had hated also salvation embraced peace, through the cooperation of the Lord, with all their heart and were made children of peace and seekers after eternal salvation.

24   Among these, a certain man from Assisi, of pious and simple spirit, was the first to devoutly follow the man of God.[76] After him, Brother Bernard,[77] embracing the delegation of peace,[78] ran eagerly after the holy man of God to purchase the kingdom of heaven.[79] He had often given the blessed father hospitality, and, having had experience of his life and conduct and having been refreshed by the fragrance of his holiness, he conceived a fear and brought forth the spirit of salvation.[80] He noticed that Francis would pray all night, sleeping but rarely, praising God and the glorious Virgin Mother of God, and he wondered and said: "In all truth, this man is from God." He hastened therefore to sell all his goods and gave the money to the poor, though not to his parents; and laying hold of the title to the way of perfection, he carried out the counsel of the holy Gospel: *If thou wilt be perfect, go, sell what thou hast, and give to the poor, and thou shalt have treasure in heaven; and come, follow me.*[81] When he had done this, he was associated with St. Francis by his life and by his habit, and he was always with him

until, after the number of the brothers had increased, he was sent to other regions by obedience to his kind father.[82] His conversion to God was a model to others in the manner of selling one's possessions and giving them to the poor. St. Francis rejoiced with very great joy over the coming and conversion of so great a man, in that the Lord was seen to have a care for him by giving him a needed companion and a faithful friend.[83]

25   But immediately another man of the city of Assisi followed him; he deserves to be greatly praised for his conduct, and what he began in a holy way, he completed after a short time in a more holy way.[84] After a not very long time, Brother Giles followed him; he was *a simple and upright man,* and one *fearing* God.[85] He lived a long time, leading a holy life, *justly and piously,*[86] and giving us examples of perfect obedience, manual labor, solitary life, and holy contemplation.[87] After another one had been added to these, Brother Philip brought the number to seven.[88] The Lord touched his lips with a purifying coal,[89] that he might speak pleasing things of him and utter sweet things. Understanding and interpreting the sacred Scriptures, though he had not studied,[90] he became an imitator of those whom the leaders of the Jews alleged to be ignorant and unlearned.[91]

CHAPTER XI

Of the spirit of prophecy of St. Francis and of his admonitions

26   Therefore the blessed father Francis was being daily filled with the consolation and the grace of the Holy Spirit; and with all vigilance and solicitude he was forming his new sons with new learning, teach-

ing them to walk with undeviating steps the way of
holy poverty and blessed simplicity. One day, when
he was wondering over the mercy of the Lord with
regard to the gifts bestowed upon him, he wished
that the course of his own life and that of his brothers
might be shown him by the Lord; he sought out a
place of prayer, as he had done so often, and he
persevered there for a long time *with fear and trem-*
bling[92] standing *before the Lord of the whole earth,*[93]
and he thought *in the bitterness of his soul*[94] of the
years he had spent wretchedly, frequently repeating
this word: *O God, be merciful to me the sinner.*[95]
Little by little a certain unspeakable joy and very
great sweetness began to flood his innermost heart.
He began also to stand aloof from himself, and, as
his feelings were checked and the darkness that had
gathered in his heart because of his fear of sin dispelled, there was poured into him a certainty that all
his sins had been forgiven and a confidence of his
restoration to grace was given him. He was then
caught up above himself, and absorbed in a certain
light; the capacity of his mind was enlarged and he
could see clearly what was to come to pass. When this
sweetness finally passed, along with the light, renewed in spirit, he seemed changed into another man.

27   And then, coming back, he said with joy to his
brothers: *"Be strengthened,* dear brothers, *and re-*
joice in the Lord,[96] and do not be sad because you
seem so few; and do not let either my simplicity or
your own dismay you, for, as it has been shown me
in truth by the Lord, God will make us grow into
a very great multitude and will make us increase to
the ends of the world. For your profit I am compelled
to tell you what I have seen, though I would much
rather remain silent, were it not that charity urges
me to tell you. I saw a great multitude of men coming
to us and wanting to live with us in the habit of our

way of life and under the rule of our blessed religion. And behold, the sound of them is in my ears as they go and come according to the command of holy obedience. I have seen, as it were, the roads filled with their great numbers coming together in these parts from almost every nation. Frenchmen are coming, Spaniards are hastening, Germans and Englishmen are running, and a very great multitude of others speaking various tongues are hurrying." When the brothers had heard this, they were filled with a salutary joy, both because of the grace the Lord God gave to his holy one and because they were ardently thirsting for the advantages to be gained by their neighbors, whom they wished to grow daily in numbers and to be saved thereby.

28   And the holy one said to them: "Brothers, in order that we may give thanks to the Lord our God faithfully and devoutly for all his gifts, and that you may know what kind of life the present and future brothers are to live, understand the truth of the things that are to come. We will find now, at the beginning of our life, fruits that are extremely sweet and pleasant to eat; but a little later some that are less sweet and less pleasant will be offered; and lastly, some that are full of bitterness will be given, which we will not be able to eat, for because of their bitterness they will be inedible to all, though they will manifest some external fragrance and beauty. And, in truth, as I have told you, the Lord will give us increase unto *a great nation.*[97] In the end, however, it will so happen just as though a man were to cast his nets into the sea or into some lake and *enclose a great number of fishes,*[98] and, when he has put them all into his boat, not liking to carry them all because of their great number, he gathers the bigger ones and those that please him into his vessels and throws the rest away."[99] It is apparent to those who, in the spirit

27

of truth, consider all these things which the holy man of God predicted, how greatly they shine forth for their truth and how manifestly they were fulfilled. Behold how the spirit of prophecy rested on St. Francis.

CHAPTER XII

How Francis sent them into the world two by two, and how they came together again after a short time

29 At this same time also, when another good man had entered their religion, their number rose to eight.[100] Then the blessed Francis called them all together, and telling them many things concerning the kingdom of God, the contempt of the world, the renunciation of their own will, and the subduing of their own body, he separated them into four groups of two each and said to them: "Go, my dearest brothers, two by two into the various parts of the world, announcing to men peace and repentance unto the forgiveness of sins;[101] and *be patient in tribulation,*[102] confident that the Lord will fulfill his purpose and his promise. To those who put questions to you, reply humbly; bless those who persecute you; give thanks to those who injure you and calumniate you; because for these things there is prepared for you an eternal kingdom."[103] But they, accepting the command of holy obedience *with joy* and great *gladness,*[104] cast themselves upon the ground before St. Francis. But he embraced them and said to each one with sweetness and affection: "Cast thy thought upon the Lord, and he will nourish you."[105] This word he spoke whenever he transferred any brothers in obedience.

30 Then Brother Bernard made a journey with Brother Giles to St. James.[106] St. Francis, however, with one companion chose another part of the world; the four others went two by two to other regions.

But, after a short time had elapsed, St. Francis, wanting to see them all, prayed to the Lord, who *gathers the dispersed of Israel*,[107] that he would deign to bring them together within a short time. And thus it happened that within a short time they came together as he wished and without any human intervention, and they gave thanks to God. When they had gathered together, they rejoiced greatly at seeing their kind shepherd; and they wondered that they had thus come together by a common desire. They then gave an account of the good things the merciful Lord had done for them; and, if they had been negligent and ungrateful in any way, they humbly begged and willingly received correction and punishment from their holy father. For thus they had always been accustomed to act when they came to him, and they did not hide from him the least thought or the first impulses of their hearts; and when they had fulfilled all things that had been commanded them, they considered themselves unprofitable servants.[108] For the spirit of purity so filled that first school of the blessed Francis that, though they knew how to do useful, holy, and just works, they knew not at all how to rejoice vainly over them. But the blessed father, embracing his sons with exceedingly great love, began to make known to them his purpose and to show them what the Lord had revealed to him.[109]

31   Immediately, however, four other good and suitable men were numbered among them and they followed the holy man of God.[110] Then a great stir arose among the people and the fame of the man of God began to be spread farther about. There was indeed at that time a great rejoicing and a singular joy among St. Francis and his brothers whenever one of the faithful, no matter who he might be or of what quality, rich or poor, noble or ignoble, despised or valued, prudent or simple, cleric or unlettered or lay,

led on by the spirit of God, came to put on the habit of holy religion. There was also great wonder among the people of the world over all these things and the example of humility led them to amend their way of life and to do penance for their sins. Not even lowness of birth or any condition of poverty stood in the way of building up the work of God in those in whom God wished to build it up, God who delights to be with the outcasts of the world and with the simple.

CHAPTER XIII

How Francis first wrote a rule when he had eleven brothers, and how the lord pope confirmed it; and how he had a vision of a great tree

32   When Blessed Francis saw that the Lord God was daily adding to their number,[111] he wrote for himself and his brothers, present and to come, simply and with few words,[112] a form of life and rule, using for the most part the words of the holy Gospel, for the perfection of which alone he yearned. But he did insert a few other things that were necessary to provide for a holy way of life. He then came to Rome with all the aforementioned brothers, desiring very much that what he had written should be confirmed by the Lord Pope Innocent III.[113] At that time the venerable bishop of Assisi was at Rome, Guido by name,[114] who honored Francis and all his brothers in all things and venerated them with special affection. When he saw St. Francis and his brothers, he was grievously annoyed at their coming, not knowing the reason for it; for he feared that they might wish to leave their native region where the Lord had already begun to work very great things through his servants. He rejoiced greatly to have such great men in his diocese, on whose life and conduct he was relying greatly. But when he had heard the reason for their coming and understood their purpose, he rejoiced greatly in the Lord, promising to give them his advice and help in these things. St. Francis also approached the lord bishop of Sabina, John of St. Paul by name,[115] who of all the other princes and great ones at the Roman curia was seen to despise earthly things and love heavenly things. He received Francis kindly and charitably, and praised highly his will and purpose.

33   Indeed, because he was a prudent and discreet man, he began to ask Francis about many things and urged him to turn to the life of a monk or hermit.[116] But St. Francis refused his counsel, as humbly as he could, not despising what was counselled, but in his pious leaning toward another life, he was inspired by a higher desire. The lord bishop wondered at his fervor, and, fearing that he might decline from so great a purpose, he showed him ways that would be easier to follow. In the end, overcome by Francis' constancy, he acquiesced to his petition and strove from then on to further his aims before the lord pope. It was Pope Innocent III who was at that time at the head of the Church, a famous man, greatly learned, renowned in discourse, burning with zeal for justice in the things that the cause of the Christian faith demanded. When he had come to know the wishes of these men of God, he first examined the matter, then gave assent to their request and carried out all that had to be done;[117] exhorting them concerning many things and admonishing them, he blessed St. Francis and his brothers and said to them: "Go with the Lord, brothers, and as the Lord will deign to inspire you, preach penance to all. Then, when the almighty Lord shall give you increase in number and in grace, return to me with joy, and I will add many more things to these and entrust greater things to you with greater confidence."

In all truth the Lord was with St. Francis wherever

he went, cheering him with revelations and encouraging him by his gifts. For one night after he had given himself to sleep, it seemed to him that he was walking along a certain road, at the side of which stood a tree of great height. The tree was beautiful and strong, thick and exceedingly high. It happened as he drew near to it, and was standing beneath it, admiring its beauty and its height, that suddenly the holy man himself grew to so great a height that he touched the top of the tree, and taking hold of it with his hand, he bent it to the ground. And so indeed it happened, for the lord Innocent, the highest and loftiest tree in the world, graciously stooped to Francis' petition and desire.

CHAPTER XIV

Concerning Francis' return from the city of Rome to the Spoleto valley and how he stopped along the way

34　　Greatly rejoicing over the gift and the grace of so great a father and lord, St. Francis gave thanks with his brothers to Almighty God, who *setteth up the humble on high* and *comforteth with health those that mourn*.[118] Immediately he went to visit the shrine of St. Peter; and, when he had finished his prayer, he left the city, and taking up his journey, he proceeded toward the Spoleto valley.

While they were going along the way, they talked with one another about the number and the quality of the gifts the most kind God had bestowed upon them, and about how they had been received most kindly by the vicar of Christ, the lord and father of the whole Christian world; about how they might be able to fulfill his admonitions and commands; about how they could sincerely observe the rule they had taken upon themselves and keep it without failure; about how they should walk in all sanctity and religion before the Most High; and finally, about how their life and conduct might be an example to their neighbors by an increase of holy virtues.

By the time the new disciples of Christ had sufficiently discussed these things in the school of humility, the day was far spent and the *hour* was *already late*. They came then to a *desert place*[119] greatly fatigued from their journey and hungry, but they could find no refreshment because that place was far removed from any dwelling of men. Immediately, the grace of God providing, a man met them bearing in his hand some bread, which he gave them and departed. But they did not know him and they wondered in their hearts and devoutly admonished one another to place even greater trust in the divine mercy. After they had eaten the food and were strengthened not a little, they went to a certain place near the city of Orte[120] and stayed there for fifteen days. Some of them would go into the city and get the necessary food, and what little they could get by begging from door to door, they would bring back to the other brothers; and they all ate *with all thankfulness*[121] and *joy of heart*.[122] If anything was left over, since they could not give it to anyone, they stowed it away in a certain sepulcher that had at one time held the bodies of the dead, that they might eat of it again. That place was deserted and abandoned and visited by few or no people at all.[123]

35 There was great rejoicing among them when they saw and had nothing that might give them vain or carnal pleasure. They began therefore to have in that place commerce with holy poverty; and comforted exceedingly in the absence of all things that are of this world, they resolved to cling to poverty everywhere just as they were doing here. And because once they had put aside solicitude for earthly things, only the divine consolation gave them joy,

they decreed and confirmed that they would not depart from its embraces no matter by what tribulations they might be shaken or by what temptations they might be led on. But, though the pleasantness of that place, which could contribute not a little toward a weakening of their true strength of mind, did not detain their affections, they nevertheless withdrew from it, lest a longer stay might entangle them even in some outward show of ownership; and, following their happy father, they went at that time to the Spoleto valley. They all conferred together, as true followers of justice, whether they should dwell among men or go to solitary places. But St. Francis, who did not trust in his own skill, but had recourse to holy prayer before all transactions, chose not to live for himself alone, but for him *who died for all*,[124] knowing that he was sent for this that he might win for God the souls the devil was trying to snatch away.

CHAPTER XV

Concerning the fame of the blessed Francis and the conversion of many to God; how the order was called the Order of Friars Minor, and how Blessed Francis formed those entering religion

36   Francis, therefore, the most valiant knight of Christ, went about *the towns and villages*[125] announcing the kingdom of God, preaching peace, teaching salvation and penance unto the remission of sins, *not in the persuasive words of* human *wisdom*,[126] but with the learning and power of the Spirit. He *acted boldly* in all things,[127] because of the apostolic authority granted to him, using no words of flattery or seductive blandishments. He did not know how to make light of the faults of others, but he knew well how to cut them out; neither did he encourage the life of sinners, but he struck hard at them with sharp

reproof, for he had first convinced himself by practicing himself what he wished to persuade others to do by his words; and fearing not the censurer, he spoke the truth boldly, so that even the most learned men, men enjoying renown and dignity, wondered at his words and were struck with wholesome fear by his presence. Men ran, and women too ran, clerics hurried, and religious hastened that they might see and hear the holy man of God who seemed to all to be a man of another world. Every age and every sex hurried to see the wonderful things that the Lord was newly working in the world through his servant. It seemed at that time, whether because of the presence of St. Francis or through his reputation, that a new light had been sent from heaven upon this earth, shattering the widespread darkness that had so filled almost the whole region that hardly anyone knew where to go. For so profound was the forgetfulness of God and the sleep of neglect of his commandments oppressing almost everyone that they could hardly be aroused even a little from their old and deeply rooted sins.

37   Francis shone forth like a brilliant star in the *obscurity of the night*[128] and *like the morning spread upon the* darkness.[129] And thus it happened that in a short time the face of the region was changed, and it took on a more cheerful aspect everywhere, once the former foulness had been laid aside. The former dryness was routed and the crops sprang up quickly in the neglected field. Even the untended vine began to sprout shoots of the fragrance of the Lord and, after producing blossoms of sweetness, it brought forth fruits of *honor and riches.*[130] *Thanksgiving and voice of praise*[131] resounded everywhere so that many put aside wordly cares and gained knowledge of themselves from the life and teaching of the most blessed Francis, and they longed to attain love and reverence

for their Creator.¹³² Many of the people, both noble and ignoble, cleric and lay, impelled by divine inspiration, began to come to St. Francis, wanting to carry on the battle constantly under his discipline and under his leadership. All of these the holy man of God, like a plenteous river of heavenly grace, watered with streams of gifts; he enriched the field of their hearts with flowers of virtue, for he was an excellent craftsman; and, according to his plan, rule, and teaching, proclaimed before all, the Church is being renewed in both sexes, and the threefold army of those to be served is triumphing.¹³³ To all he gave a norm of life, and he showed in truth the way of salvation in every walk of life.

38 But our first concern here is with the order of which he was the founder and preserver both by charity and by profession. What shall we say? He himself first planted the Order of Friars Minor and accordingly gave it this name. For he wrote in the rule, "and let them be lesser brothers," and when these words were spoken, indeed in that same hour, he said: "I wish that this fraternity should be called the Order of Friars Minor."¹³⁴ And indeed they were lesser brothers, who, being subject to all, always sought a place that was lowly and sought to perform a duty that seemed in some way to be burdensome to them so that they might merit to be founded solidly in true humility and that through their fruitful disposition a spiritual structure of all virtues might arise in them. Truly, upon the foundation of constancy a noble structure of charity arose, in which the living stones, gathered from all parts of the world, were erected into a dwelling place of the Holy Spirit. O with what ardor of charity the new disciples of Christ burned! How great was the love that flourished in the members of this pious society! For whenever they came together anywhere, or met one another along the way, as the custom is, there a shoot of spiritual love sprang up, sprinkling over all love the seed of true affection. What more shall I say? Chaste embraces, gentle feelings, a holy kiss, pleasing conversation, modest laughter, joyous looks, a *single eye*,[135] a submissive spirit, a *peacable tongue*,[136] a *mild answer*,[137] oneness of purpose, ready obedience, unwearied hand, all these were found in them.

39   And indeed, since they despised all earthly things and did not love themselves with a selfish love, pouring out their whole affection on all the brothers, they strove to give themselves as the price of helping one another in their needs. They came together with great desire; they remained together with joy; but separation from one another was sad on both sides, a bitter divorce, a cruel estrangement. But these most obedient knights dared put nothing before holy obedience; before the command of obedience was even uttered, they prepared themselves to fulfill the order; knowing not how to misinterpret the commands, they put aside every objection and hastened to fulfill what was commanded. Followers of most holy poverty, because they had nothing, loved nothing, they feared in no way to lose anything. They were content with one tunic, patched at times within and without;[138] in it was seen no refinement, but rather abjectness and cheapness, so that they might seem to be completely crucified to the world. Girt with a cord, they wore poor trousers, and they had the pious intention of remaining like this, and they wished to have nothing more. They were, therefore, everywhere secure, kept in no suspense by fear; distracted by no care, they awaited the next day without solicitude,[139] nor were they in anxiety about the night's lodging, though in their journeyings they were often placed in great danger. For, when they frequently lacked the necessary lodging amid the cold-

est weather, an oven sheltered them, or at least they lay hid for the night humbly in grottos or caves. During the day, those who knew how labored with their hands,[140] staying in the houses of lepers, or in other decent places, serving all humbly and devotedly. They did not wish to exercise any position from which scandal might arise,[141] but always doing what is holy and just, honest and useful, they led all with whom they came into contact to follow their example of humility and patience.

40   The virtue of patience so took hold of them that they sought rather to be where they might suffer persecution of their bodies than where they might be lifted up by the favor of the world, when their holiness was known or praised. For many times when they were insulted and ridiculed, stripped naked, beaten, bound, imprisoned, they did not protect themselves by means of anyone's patronage, but they bore all things so courageously that nothing but the voice of praise and thanksgiving resounded in their mouths. Scarcely at all, or really never, did they let up in their praise of God and in their prayers; but recalling by constant discussion what they had done, they gave thanks to God for what they had done well; for what they had neglected or incautiously committed, they poured forth groans and tears. They thought they were forsaken by God if they did not find themselves to be constantly visited in their devotions by their accustomed piety. For when they wanted to give themselves to prayer, they made use of certain means lest sleep should take hold of them: some were held erect by hanging ropes lest their prayers should be disturbed by sleep stealing over them; others put instruments of iron about their bodies, and others wore wooden girdles of penance. If, as it can happen, their sobriety were disturbed by an abundance of food or drink, or if because they

were tired from a journey, they surpassed even a little the bounds of necessity, they mortified themselves very sharply by an abstinence of many days. Lastly, they tried to repress the promptings of the flesh with such great mortification that often they did not refrain from stripping themselves naked in the coldest weather and from piercing their bodies all over with the points of thorns, even to causing the blood to flow.

41   They despised all wordly things so keenly that they hardly permitted themselves to receive even the necessaries of life; and they were separated from bodily comforts for so long a time that they did not shrink from anything difficult. Amid all these things they strove for *peace* and gentleness *with all men*,[142] and always conducting themselves modestly and peaceably, they avoided all scandals with the greatest zeal. They hardly spoke even when necessary; neither did anything scurrilous or idle proceed from their mouths, in order that nothing immodest or unbecoming might be found in their life and conversation. Their every action was disciplined, their every movement modest; all their senses were so mortified that they would hardly permit themselves to hear or see anything except what their purpose demanded. With their eyes directed toward the ground, they clung to heaven with their minds. No envy, no malice, no rancor, no abusive speech, no suspicion, no bitterness found any place in them; but great concord, continual quiet, thanksgiving, and the voice of praise were in them. These were the teachings of their beloved father, by which he formed his new sons, not by words alone and tongue, but above all *in deeds and in truth*.[143]

CHAPTER XVI

Of Francis' stay at Rivo Torto and of the observance of poverty

42   Blessed Francis betook himself with the rest of his brothers to a place near Assisi called Rivo Torto.[144] In that place there was a certain abandoned hovel in the shelter of which these most ardent despisers of great and beautiful homes lived; and there they kept themselves safe from the rains. For, as a certain saint said,[145] from a hovel one ascends more quickly to heaven than from a palace. All his sons and brothers lived in this same place with their blessed father, working much, lacking everything; very often they were entirely deprived of the comfort of bread, and they were content with turnips which they begged here and there over the plain of Assisi. That place was so very cramped that they could hardly sit down or rest in it. But no murmur was heard over these things, no complaint; but with a serene heart and a mind filled with joy they kept their patience.[146] St. Francis most diligently examined himself and his brothers daily, even continually; and, suffering nothing in them of wantonness, he drove every negligence from their hearts. Strict in discipline, he was watchful of his trust at all hours. For if, as happens, a temptation of the flesh at times assailed him, he would hurl himself into a ditch full of ice, when it was winter, and remain in it until every vestige of anything carnal had departed. And indeed the others most fervently followed his example of such great mortification.

43   He taught them not only to mortify vices and repress carnal movements, but also to restrain the exterior senses themselves, for through them death enters the soul. When at that time the Emperor Otto was passing through the place with much clamor and pomp to receive the crown of his earthly empire,[147] the most holy father, who was living with his brothers in that hovel close to the road on which the emperor would pass, did not even go out to watch; and he did not let any one else do so except one who continuously called out to the emperor that his glory would last but a short time.[148] for the glorious saint, withdrawn within himself and walking in the broadness of his heart, had prepared within himself a dwelling fit for God, and therefore the outward clamor did not catch his ears, nor could any sound drive out or interrupt the great business he had at hand. The apostolic authority[149] was strong in him, and he therefore refused entirely to offer flattery to kings and princes.

44 He attended always to holy simplicity and he did not permit the straitened circumstances of that place to impede the greatness of his heart. He therefore wrote the names of his brothers on the beams of their dwelling so that each one, if he wished to pray or to rest, would know his place, and that the smallness of the place might not disturb the silence of the mind. While they were dwelling there, it happened that one day a certain man came leading an ass to the shelter where the man of God was staying with his brothers; and lest he suffer repulse, the man, exhorting his ass to enter, spoke these words: "Go in, for we will do well for this place."[150] When St. Francis heard this, he took it very ill, knowing what the man's intention was; for the man thought the brothers wanted to stay there to enlarge the place and to *join house to house*.[151] Immediately St. Francis went away from there, and abandoning the hovel because of what the peasant had said, he went to another place not far from there, which is called the Portiuncula, where, as was said above,[152] the church of St. Mary had been built and had been re-

41

paired by him. He wanted to have nothing to do with ownership, in order that he might possess all things more fully in God.

CHAPTER XVII

How Blessed Francis taught his brothers to pray; and of the obedience and purity of the brothers

45   At that time, *walking in simplicity* of spirit,[153] they did not know as yet the ecclesiastical office.[154] He said to them:*"When you pray, say Our Father,[155] and We adore thee, Christ, here and in all thy churches which are in the whole world, and we bless thee, because by thy holy cross thou hast redeemed the world."*[156] But this the brothers strove to observe with the greatest diligence as disciples of their beloved master, for they strove to carry out most efficaciously not only those things which the blessed father Francis said to them in fraternal advice or fatherly command, but also the things that were in his mind or on which he was meditating, if in some way they would come to know them. For the blessed father himself said to them that true obedience consists not only in doing things that are commanded in word, but even those merely thought of; not only in doing things commanded, but even things desired; for, "if a brother, subject to a brother superior, not only hears his voice, but even understands his will, he must immediately give himself entirely to obedience and do what he understands him to will by some sign or other."[157]

Moreover, if a church were standing in any place whatsoever, even though the brothers were not present there but could only see it from some distance, they were to prostrate themselves upon the ground in its direction and, having bowed low with body and soul,[158] they were to adore Almighty God, saying,

We adore thee, Christ, here and in all thy churches, as the holy father had taught them. And, what is no less to be admired, wherever they saw a crucifix or the mark of a cross, whether upon the ground, or upon a wall, or on trees, or in the hedges along the way, they were to do the same thing.

46   For holy simplicity had so filled them, innocence of life was so instructing them, purity of heart so possessed them, that they knew nothing of duplicity of mind. For, as there was one faith in them, so was there one spirit in them, one will, one love; there was unity of souls among them, harmony of behavior, the practice of virtues, conformity of minds, and piety of actions.

At one time, when they were often confessing their sins to a certain secular priest who was very infamous, as he deserved, and was despised by all because of the enormity of his crimes, and they were made aware of his iniquity by many people, they did not want to believe it and they did not on that account omit confessing their sins to him as usual; and they did not refuse him the reverence due him.[159] Indeed, when one day, he, or another priest, said to a certain one of the brothers, "See, Brother, that you be not a hypocrite," that brother immediately believed that he was a hypocrite, because of the word of the priest. Because of this he wept day and night, moved by excessive grief. When, however, the brothers asked him why he was so filled with grief and why he mourned in such an unusual way, he replied: "A certain priest spoke such a word to me and it caused me so much grief I can hardly think of anything else." The brothers consoled him and admonished him not to believe such a thing. But he said to them: "What is this you say, brothers? It was a priest who spoke this word to me. Can a priest lie? Since therefore a priest cannot lie, we must believe that what he said is true." And then he continued for a long time in this simplicity; but at last he gave in at the words of the most blessed father, who explained to him the word of the priest and wisely excused the priest's intention.[160] It was hardly possible for any of the brothers to be troubled to such an extent in mind that every cloud would not be dispersed at Francis' glowing words and serenity return.

CHAPTER XVIII

Of the fiery chariot, and of the knowledge the blessed Francis had of those who were absent

47   Walking in simplicity before God and in confidence before men, the brothers merited at this time to be filled with gladness by means of a divine revelation.[161] For while, kindled by the fire of the Holy Spirit, they chanted the *Pater Noster*, not only at the appointed hours, but at all hours, with suppliant and melodious voice, being little occupied with earthly solicitude and troublesome anxiety of cares, the most blessed father Francis absented himself one night from them in body. And behold, about midnight, when some of the brothers were resting and some were praying in silence with great devotion, a most splendid fiery chariot entered through the door of the house and turned around two or three times here and there inside the house; a huge globe of light rested above it, much like the sun, and it lit up the night. The watchers were dazed, and those who had been asleep were frightened; and they felt no less a lighting up of the heart than a lighting up of the body. Gathering together, they began to ask one another what it was; but by the strength and grace of that great light each one's conscience was revealed to the others. Finally they understood and knew that it was the soul of their holy father that

was shining with such great brilliance and that, on account of the grace of his understanding purity and his great tenderness for his sons, he merited to receive such a blessing from God.

48 And indeed they had found proof of this by manifest tokens and had experienced that the secrets of their hearts were not hidden from their most holy father. O how often, without any man telling him, but by means of a revelation of the Holy Spirit, Francis knew the actions of his absent brothers, laid open the secrets of their hearts, and explored their consciences! O how many he admonished in their sleep, commanded them things to be done, forbade things not to be done! Of how many did he not predict future evils, though their present conduct seemed good! Thus, knowing in many cases that certain brothers would end their evil ways, he foretold the future grace of salvation for them. Even more, if anyone merited to be distinguished by his spirit of purity and simplicity, he enjoyed the singular consolation of seeing Francis in a way not experienced by the rest. I will give one example from among many, which I know from reliable witnesses. When at one time Brother John of Florence,[162] who had been appointed by St. Francis minister of the brothers in the Provence,[163] was celebrating a chapter of the brothers in that same province,[164] the Lord God, in his customary mercy, opened unto him the door of speech[165] and he made all the brothers well disposed and attentive to his words. Among the brothers was one, a priest of great renown but of more splendid life, Monaldo by name;[166] his virtue was grounded in humility, aided by frequent prayer, and preserved by the shield of patience. Brother Anthony[167] was also present at this chapter, he whose mind the Lord opened[168] that he might understand the Scriptures and speak among all the people words about Jesus that were sweeter than syrup or honey from the comb.[169] While he was preaching very fervently and devoutly to the brothers on this topic, *"Jesus of Nazareth, King of the Jews,"*[170] the aforementioned Brother Monaldo looked toward the door of the house in which there were many other brothers gathered and he saw there with his bodily eyes Blessed Francis raised up into the air, his arms extended as though upon a cross, and blessing the brothers. And they all were seen to be filled *with the consolation of the Holy Spirit,*[171] and, from the joy of salvation they felt, what they were told concerning the vision and the presence of their most glorious father seemed entirely believable.

49   To show that Francis knew the secrets of the hearts of others, I will mention from among the many cases experienced by many one case about which no doubt can arise. A certain brother, Riccerio by name,[172] a noble by birth but even more noble in his conduct, one who loved God and despised himself, was led by a pious spirit and a great desire to attain and possess perfectly the favor of holy father Francis; but he feared greatly that St. Francis despised him for some secret reason and therefore made him a stranger to the favor of his affection. That brother thought, in as much as he was a God-fearing man, that whomever St. Francis loved with an intimate love would merit to be worthy of the divine favor; but, on the other hand, he to whom St. Francis did not show himself well disposed and kind would, he thought, incur the anger of the heavenly judge. These things that brother revolved in his mind and spoke about frequently within himself, but he did not reveal the secret of his thoughts to anyone.

50   For the rest, when on a certain day the blessed father was praying in his cell and Brother Riccerio had come to that place, disturbed by his usual thoughts, the holy man of God became aware of his coming and of what was going on in his mind. Immediately he sent for him and said to him: "Let no temptation disturb you, son; let no thought exasperate you; for you are very dear to me. Know that among those who are especially dear to me you are worthy of my affection and intimacy. Come to me with confidence whenever you wish and talk with me with great familiarity." The brother was filled with the greatest admiration at this; and as a result was even more reverent; and, as he grew in the favor of his father, so did he begin to *open wide*[173] in his trust in the mercy of God.

How sadly, holy father, must not they take your absence who despair of ever finding anyone like you upon earth. Help, we pray, by your intercession those whom you see mired in the harmful contagion of sin. Though you were already filled with the spirit of all the just, foreseeing the future and knowing the present, you always kept before you the image of holy simplicity in order that you might shun all boastfulness.

But now let us return to what we were speaking of above and observe again the historical order.

CHAPTER XIX

Of the watchfulness of Francis over his brothers; and of his contempt of self and of his true humility

51 The most blessed Francis returned to his brothers in body, from whom, as has been said, he never withdrew in spirit. Scrutinizing the actions of all his brothers with cautious and diligent examination, he was concerned about his subjects out of a kindly curiosity; and he left nothing unpunished if he found something done that was less than good. He first

settled spiritual failings, then he judged concerning bodily things, and lastly he rooted out all occasions that open the way to sins.

With all zeal, with all solicitude, he guarded holy Lady Poverty, not permitting any vessel of any kind [174] to be in the house, lest it lead to superfluous things, when he could in some way avoid being subject to extreme necessity without it. For, he used to say, it is impossible to satisfy necessity and not give in to pleasure. Cooked foods he permitted himself scarcely at all or very rarely; and if he did allow them, he either mixed them with ashes or destroyed their flavor with cold water. O how often, when he was going about the world preaching the *Gospel of God*,[175] if he were invited to dinner by great princes who venerated him with wonderful affection, he would taste a bit of the meat in observance of the holy Gospel[176] and then, making a pretense of eating by raising his hand to his mouth, lest anyone should perceive what he was doing, he would drop the rest in his lap. But what can I say of his drinking of wine, when he would not allow himself to drink enough water to quench his thirst?

52   Francis would not allow his resting place to be laid over with covers or garments when he received hospitality, but the bare ground received his bare limbs, with only a tunic between. When at times he refreshed his small body with sleep, he very often slept sitting up, and in no other position, using a piece of wood or a stone as a pillow. When his appetite for something particular was aroused, as often happens, he seldom ate that thing afterwards. Once, when in an infirmity he had eaten a little chicken, after he regained his strength of body he entered the city of Assisi; and when he had come to the gate of the city, he commanded a certain brother who was with him to tie a rope about his neck and to drag

him in this way like a robber through the entire city and to shout in the voice of a herald, saying: "Behold the glutton who has grown fat on the meat of chickens which he ate without your knowing about it." Many therefore ran to see so great a spectacle, and weeping together with great sighs, they said: "Woe to us miserable ones, whose whole life is spent in blood and who nourish our hearts and bodies with uncleanness and drunkenness." And thus, *pierced to the heart*,[177] they were moved to a better way of life by so great an example.

53 Many other things like these he did very often that he might learn to despise himself perfectly and that he might entice others to seek eternal honor. He had become to himself *like a vessel that is destroyed*,[178] and, burdened by no fear or solicitude for his body, he most zealously subjected it to affronts, lest he be driven by love of his body to desire eagerly some temporal things. Despising himself in all truth, he taught others by his word and example to despise themselves.

What then? He was *honored by all*[179] and extolled by all, with praiseworthy judgment; and he alone considered himself the most vile among men, he alone despised himself most severely. For often, when he was honored by all, he suffered the deepest sorrow; and rejecting the favor of men, he would see to it that he would be rebuked by some one. He would call some brother to him, saying to him: "In obedience, I say to you, revile me harshly and speak the truth against the lies of these others." And when that brother, though unwilling, would say he was a boor, a hired servant, a worthless being, Francis, smiling and applauding very much, would reply: "May the Lord bless you, for you have spoken most truly; it is becoming that the son of Peter of Bernardone[180] should hear such things." So saying, he would recall the conditions of his humble origin.

54   That he might show himself in every way contemptible and give an example to the rest of true confession, Francis was not ashamed, when he had failed in something, to confess his failing in his preaching before all the people. Indeed, if it happened that he had had an evil thought about anyone, or if he had on occasion spoken an angry word, he would immediately confess his sins with all humility to the one about whom he had had the evil thought and beg his pardon. His conscience, which was a witness to his complete innocence, guarding itself with all solicitude, would not let him rest until it had gently healed the wound in his heart. Certainly he wanted to make progress in every kind of good deed, but he did not want to be looked up to on that account, but he fled admiration in every way, lest he ever become vain. But woe to us, who have lost you, worthy father, model of every good deed and of humility. By a just judgment, in truth, we have lost him whom we did not care to know when we had him.

CHAPTER XX

Of Francis' desire for martyrdom and his trip first to Spain, then to Syria; and how God delivered the sailors from peril through him by multiplying the provisions

55   Glowing with love for God, the most blessed father Francis sought always to put his hand to courageous deeds; and walking the way of the commandments of God with a generous heart, he longed to attain the height of perfection. In the sixth year of his conversion,[181] burning intensely with the desire for holy martydrom, he wanted to take ship for the regions of Syria to preach the Christian faith and penance to the Saracens and infidels. When he had

gone on board a certain ship to go there, contrary winds arose and he found himself with the rest of his shipmates in the region of Slavonia.[182] But when he saw that he was deprived of attaining his great desire, after a short period of time he begged some sailors who were going to Ancona[183] to take him with them, because it would hardly be possible for any other ship to sail for Syria that year. But they obstinately refused since Francis could not pay the expenses; the holy man of God, however, trusting very·much in the goodness of the Lord, stowed away on the boat with his companion. However, by Divine Providence, there was a certain man who had come on board without anyone knowing it and who carried with him the necessary provisions; and he called one of the crew members who feared God and said to him: "Take these things with you and give them faithfully to those poor men hiding on your boat when they have need of them." And thus it happened that, when a great storm arose and the men had been working hard at rowing for many days, they consumed all the food, and only the provisions of the poor Francis were left. These, by divine grace and power, were multiplied to such an extent that, though the voyage was to last through several more days, they had enough to take care of their needs generously all the way to the port of Ancona. Therefore, when the sailors saw that they had escaped the dangers of the sea through the servant of God Francis, they thanked Almighty God who always shows himself wonderful and lovable in his servants.

56   The servant of the most high God, Francis, leaving the sea, walked over the land, and ploughing it up with the word, he sowed the seed of life and brought forth blessed fruit. For immediately quite a few good and suitable men, clerics and lay, fleeing from the world and manfully crushing the devil, fol-

lowed Francis devoutly in his life and purpose through the grace and the will of the Most High. Still, though the branch of the Gospel[184] produced an abundance of the choicest fruits, the sublime purpose of attaining martyrdom and the ardent desire for it in no way grew cold in him. After a not very long time he started on a journey toward Morocco, to preach the Gospel of Christ to Miramamolin and his people.[185] He was carried along by so great a desire, that at times he left his companion on the trip behind and hurried to accomplish his purpose, drunk, as it were, in spirit. But the good God, whom it pleased in his kindness to be mindful of me and of many others, *withstood him to his face*[186] when he had traveled as far as Spain; and, that he might not go any farther, he recalled him from the journey he had begun by a prolonged illness.

57   Not long after he had returned to the church of St. Mary of the Portiuncula,[187] some educated and noble men very gratifyingly joined him. These, since Francis was a most noble and discreet man in spirit, he treated with honor and dignity and he most generously gave each one his due. In truth, since he was endowed with outstanding discretion, he prudently considered in all the dignity of each one's station. But he was not able to rest without following even more fervently the impulse of his soul. Accordingly, in the thirteenth year of his conversion[188] he set out for Syria, at a time when great and severe battles were raging daily between the Christians and the pagans; he took with him a companion,[189] and he did not fear to present himself before the sultan of the Saracens.[190] But who can narrate with what great steadfastness of mind he stood before him, with what strength of spirit he spoke to him, with what eloquence and confidence he replied to those who insulted the Christian law? For before he gained access

to the sultan, though he was captured by the sultan's soldiers, was insulted and beaten, still he was not frightened; he did not fear the threats of torture and, when death was threatened, he did not grow pale. But though he was treated shamefully by many who were quite hostile and hateful toward him, he was nevertheless received very honorably by the sultan. The sultan honored him as much as he was able, and having given him many gifts, he tried to bend Francis' mind toward the riches of the world. But when he saw that Francis most vigorously despised all these things as so much dung, he was filled with the greatest admiration, and he looked upon him as a man different from all others. He was deeply moved by his words and he listened to him very willingly. Still, in all these things the Lord did not fulfill Francis' desire for martyrdom, reserving for him the prerogative of a singular grace.[191]

CHAPTER XXI

How Francis preached to the birds and of the obedience of creatures

58   Meanwhile, while many were joining the brothers, as was said, the most blessed father Francis was making a trip through the Spoleto valley. He came to a certain place near Bevagna[192] where a very great number of birds of various kinds had congregated, namely, doves, crows, and some others popularly called daws.[193] When the most blessed servant of God, Francis, saw them, being a man of very great fervor and great tenderness toward lower and irrational creatures, he left his companions in the road and ran eagerly toward the birds. When he was close enough to them, seeing that they were waiting expectantly for him, he greeted them in his usual way. But, not a little surprised that the birds did not rise in flight, as they usually do, he was filled with great

joy and humbly begged them to listen to the word of God. Among the many things he spoke to them were these words that he added: "My brothers, birds, you should praise your Creator very much and always love him; he gave you feathers to clothe you, wings so that you can fly, and whatever else was necessary for you. God made you noble among his creatures, and he gave you a home in the purity of the air; though you neither sow nor reap, he nevertheless protects and governs you without any solicitude on your part."[194] At these words, as Francis himself used to say and those too who were with him, the birds, rejoicing in a wonderful way according to their nature, began to stretch their necks, extend their wings, open their mouths and gaze at him. And Francis, *passing through their midst, went on his way*[195] and returned, touching their heads and bodies with his tunic. Finally he blessed them, and then, after he had made the sign of the cross over them, he gave them permission to fly away to some other place. But the blessed father went his way with his companions, rejoicing and giving thanks to God, whom all creatures venerate with humble acknowledgement. But now that he had become simple by grace, not by nature, he began to blame himself for negligence in not having preached to the birds before, seeing that they had listened to the word of God with such great reverence. And so it happened that, from that day on, he solicitously admonished all birds, all animals and reptiles, and even creatures that have no feeling, to praise and love their Creator, for daily, when the name of the Savior had been invoked, he saw their obedience by personal experience.

59   When he came one day to a city called Alviano[196] to preach the word of God, he went up *to a higher place*[197] so that he could be seen by all and he began to ask for silence. But when all the

people had fallen silent and were standing reverently at attention, a flock of swallows, chattering and making a loud noise, were building nests in that same place. Since the blessed Francis could not be heard by the people over the chattering of the birds, he spoke to them saying: "My sisters, swallows, it is now time for me to speak, for you have already spoken enough. Listen to the word of the Lord and be silent and quiet until the word of the Lord is finished." And those little birds, to the astonishment and wonder of the people standing by, immediately fell silent, and they did not move from that place until the sermon was finished. When these men therefore saw this miracle, they were filled with the greatest admiration and said: "Truly this man is a saint and a friend of the Most High." And they hastened with the greatest devotion to at least touch his clothing, *praising and blessing God.*[198] It is indeed wonderful how even irrational creatures recognized his affection for them and felt his tender love for them.

60   Once when he was staying at the town of Greccio,[199] a little rabbit[200] that had been caught in a trap was brought alive to him by a certain brother. When the most blessed man saw it, he was moved to pity and said: "Brother rabbit, come to me. Why did you allow yourself to be deceived like this?" And as soon as the rabbit had been let go by the brother who held it, it fled to the saint, and, without being forced by anyone, it lay quiet in his bosom as the safest place possible. After he had rested there a little while, the holy father, caressing it with motherly affection, released it so it could return free to the woods. But when it had been placed upon the ground several times and had returned each time to the saint's bosom, he finally commanded it to be carried by the brothers to the nearby woods. Something similar happened with a certain rabbit, by nature a very

wild creature, when he was on an island in the lake of Perugia.[201]

61   He was moved by the same tender affection toward fish, too, which, when they were caught, and he had the chance, he threw back into the water, commanding them to be careful lest they be caught again.[202] Once when he was sitting in a boat near a port in the lake of Rieti,[203] a certain fisherman, who had caught a big fish popularly called a *tinca*,[204] offered it kindly to him. He accepted it joyfully and kindly and began to call it *brother;* then placing it in the water outside the boat, he began devoutly to bless the name of the Lord. And while he continued in prayer for some time, the fish played in the water beside the boat and did not go away from the place where it had been put until his prayer was finished and the holy man of God gave it permission to leave. For thus did the glorious father Francis, walking in the way of obedience and embracing perfectly the yoke of obedience to God, acquire great dignity in the sight of God in that creatures obeyed him. For even water was turned into wine for him, when on one occasion he was grievously ill at the hermitage of St. Urban.[205] At the taste of it he became well so easily that it was thought to be a miracle by all, as it really was. And truly he is a saint whom creatures obey in this way,[206] and at whose nod the elements change themselves to other uses.

CHAPTER XXII

Of Francis' preaching at Ascoli; and how the sick were healed by touching things his hand had touched, though he himself was absent

62   At that time, when, as has been said, the venerable father Francis preached to the birds,[207] going about the cities and towns and everywhere scattering

the seeds of his blessings, he came to the city of Ascoli.[208] There, when he preached the word of God very fervently, as was his custom, almost all the people were filled with such great grace and devotion, through a change brought about by the right hand of the Most High, that they trampled on one another in their eagerness to hear and see him. For at that time thirty men, clerics and lay, received the habit of religion from him.

So great was the faith of the men and women, so great their devotion toward the holy man of God, that he pronounced himself happy who could but touch his garment. When he entered any city, the clergy rejoiced, the bells were rung, the men were filled with happiness, the women rejoiced together, the children clapped their hands; and often, taking branches from the trees, they went to meet him singing. The wickedness of heretics was confounded, the faith of the Church exalted; and while the faithful rejoiced, the heretics slipped secretly away. For such great signs of sanctity were evident in him that no one dared to oppose his words, while the great assembly of people looked only upon him. In the midst of all these things and above everything else, Francis thought that the faith of the holy Roman Church was by all means to be preserved, honored, and imitated, that faith in which alone is found the salvation of all who are to be saved. He revered priests and he had a great affection for every ecclesiastical order.

63   The people would offer Francis bread to bless, which they would then keep for a long time; and upon eating it, they were cured of various illnesses. So also they very often cut off parts of his tunic in their very great faith, so much so that he sometimes was left almost naked. And what is even more wonderful, if the holy father would touch any object with his hand, health returned to many by means of that

object. Thus when a certain woman from a little village near Arezzo was pregnant[209] and the time had come for her to be delivered, she was in labor through several days and thereby in incredible suffering, hanging between life and death. Her neighbors and her relatives heard that the blessed Francis was going to pass through that village on his way to a certain hermitage. But, while they were waiting for him, it happened that Francis went to that place by another way. He was riding a horse because he was weak and ill. When he had come to that place, he sent the horse back by a certain brother, Peter by name, to the man who had let him have it out of charity. Brother Peter, bringing the horse back, passed through that village where the suffering woman lay. When the men of the village saw him, they ran quickly to him, thinking he was the blessed Francis himself; when they saw it was not Francis, they were exceedingly sad. Finally, they began to ask each other if they might be able to find something that Francis had touched with his hand. After looking for a long time, they found the reins which he had held in his hands while riding. And taking the bit from the mouth of the horse upon which Francis had sat, they put the reins he had touched with his hands upon the woman; immediately the danger was gone and she bore her child with joy in safety.

64   Walfried, who lived in Città della Pieve,[210] *a devout and God-fearing man, as was all his household*,[211] had a cord with which the blessed Francis had been girded at one time. It happened that in this place many men and not a few women were afflicted with various illnesses and fevers. This man, after dipping the cord in water or mixing some strands of the cord with the water, would give the water to the sick to drink; and thus all of them were healed in Christ's name. These things took place in the absence

of Blessed Francis, and many more things happened too which we could not tell adaquately even at great length. Now we will insert in this work a few things that the Lord Our God deigned to work through his presence.

CHAPTER XXIII

How Francis healed a cripple at Toscanella and a paralytic at Narni

65   Once when the holy man of God Francis was going about through various regions to preach the kingdom of God, he came to a certain city called Toscanella.[212] There, when he was sowing the seed of life[213] in his usual way, a certain soldier of that city gave him hospitality; he had an only son who was lame and weak of body. Though he was a young child, he had passed the years of weaning; still he remained in a cradle. When the father of the boy saw the great sanctity of the man of God, he humbly cast himself at his feet, begging from him health for his son. But Francis, who considered himself useless and unworthy of such great power and grace, refused for a long time to do this. But finally overcome by the insistence of his petitions, he prayed and then put his hand upon the boy and, blessing him, raised him up. Immediately, with all present looking on and rejoicing, the boy arose completely restored and began to walk here and there about the house.

66   Once when the man of God Francis had come to Narni[214] and was staying there for a number of days, a certain man of that city, Peter by name, lay in bed paralyzed. For a period of five months he had been so deprived of the use of all his limbs that he could not rise at all or move himself even a little; and thus having completely lost the use of his feet and hands and head, he could only move his tongue and

open his eyes. When he heard that Francis had come to Narni, he sent a messenger to the bishop of that city to ask him for the love of God to send the servant of the most high God to him, confident that he would be freed from the illness from which he suffered at the sight and presence of Francis. And it so happened that, when the blessed Francis had come to him and had made the sign of the cross over him from his head to his feet, he was immediately healed and restored to his former health.

CHAPTER XXIV

How Francis gave sight to a blind woman; and how at Gubbio he straightened the hands of a crippled woman

67 A certain woman from the city mentioned just above,[215] who had been struck blind, merited to receive immediately the sight she desired when the blessed Francis drew the sign of the cross upon her eyes. At Gubbio there was a woman both of whose hands were so crippled that she could do no work at all with them. When she learned that St. Francis had entered the city, she immediately ran to him; and with her face covered with misery and sadness, she showed her crippled hands to him and began to ask him to touch them. Moved to pity he touched her and healed her. Immediately the woman went home full of joy, made a kind of cheese cake with her own hands, and offered it to the holy man. He took a little of it in his kindness and commanded the woman to eat the rest of it with her family.

CHAPTER XXV

How Francis freed one of the brothers from the falling sickness or from a devil; and how he freed a possessed woman at the city of San Gemini

68 One of the brothers suffered frequently from a very serious infirmity and one horrible to see; I do not know by what name it is called, though some think it is an evil spirit. Frequently he was cast upon the ground and he turned about foaming at the mouth and with a terrible look upon his face; at times his limbs were drawn up, at other times they were extended; now they were folded up and twisted, again they were rigid and hard. Sometimes, when he was stretched out and rigid, he would be raised up into the air to the height of a man's stature, with his feet even with his head, and then would fall back to the ground. Pitying his grievous illness the holy father Francis went to him and, after praying, signed him and blessed him. Suddenly he was cured and he did not again suffer in the least from the tortures of this illness.

69 One day when the most blessed father Francis was passing through the diocese of Narni, he came to a certain city called San Gemini,[216] and preaching there the kingdom of God, he was entertained along with three of his brothers by a certain man of good repute in that region who feared and worshipped God. But his wife was *beset by a devil*,[217] as was known to all who lived in that town. Her husband interceded with St. Francis for her, confident that she could be freed by his merits. But because Francis preferred in his simplicity to be held in contempt rather than be praised by the world because of a demonstration of his sanctity, he refused firmly to do this. Finally, because God was concerned in the case, and because so many were begging him to do it, he consented, overcome by their prayers. He called the three brothers who were with him and, placing each one in a corner of the house, he said to them: "Let us pray to the Lord, brothers, for this woman that God may strike the yoke of the devil from her unto his own praise and glory. Let us stand separately in the corners of the house lest that evil spirit be able to escape us or deceive us by getting into the hiding places of the corners." When the prayer was finished, blessed Francis went up to the woman, who was being miserably tormented and who was clamoring horribly, and, with the power of the Holy Spirit, he said: "In the name of the Lord Jesus Christ, I command you in holy obedience, evil spirit, to go out of her and never dare to hinder her again." He had hardly finished the words when the devil left that woman so very quickly and with such anger and racket that, because of the sudden healing of the woman and the very quick obedience of the devil, the holy father thought he perhaps had been deceived. He immediately left that place in shame, divine providence so arranging things that he would not be able to glory vainly in any way. Whence it happened that blessed Francis was passing through the same place on another occasion, and Brother Elias was with him; and behold, that woman, when she heard of his coming, immediately arose; and running through the street, she cried out after him that he should deign to speak to her. But he did not want to speak to her, knowing that she was the woman from whom he had once cast out a devil by the power of God. But she *kissed the steps of his feet*,[218] giving thanks to God and to his servant St. Francis who had freed her *out of the hand of death.*[219] Finally, Brother Elias urged the saint by his prayers, and he spoke to her after he had been assured by the people of her illness, as was said, and of her cure.

CHAPTER XXVI

How Francis also cast out a devil at Città di Castello

70 Also at Citta di Castello[220] there was a woman obsessed by the devil. When the most blessed father Francis was in this city, the woman was brought to the house where he was staying. That woman, standing outside, began to gnash her teeth and, her face twisted, she began to set up a great howl, as unclean spirits do. Many people of both sexes from that city came and pleaded with St. Francis in her behalf, for that evil spirit had long tormented and tortured her and had disturbed them with his loud cries. The holy father then sent to her a brother who was with him, wishing to discover whether it was really a devil or deception on the part of the woman. When that woman saw him, she began to deride him, knowing that it was not Francis who had come out. The holy father was inside praying. He came out when he had finished his prayer. But the woman, unable to stand his power, began to tremble and roll about on the ground. St. Francis called to her and said: "In virtue of obedience, I command you, unclean spirit, to go out of her." Immediately he left her, without injuring her, but departing in great anger. Thanks be to God, who does everything according to his will.

But since we have not undertaken to narrate miracles, which indeed do not make sanctity, but only manifest it, but rather to speak of the excellence of Francis' life and his most pure conduct, we will omit the miracles because of their great number and tell of his works for eternal salvation.

CHAPTER XXVII

Of the clarity and constancy of Francis' mind, and of his preaching before Pope Honorius; and how he committed himself and his brothers to the lord Hugo, Bishop of Ostia

71   The man of God Francis had been taught not to seek his own,[221] but to seek especially what in his eyes would be helpful toward the salvation of others; but above everything else he desired *to depart and to be with Christ.*[222] Therefore, his greatest concern was to be free from everything of this world, lest the serenity of his mind be disturbed even for an hour by the taint of anything that was mere dust. He made himself insensible to all external noise, and, bridling his external senses with all his strength and repressing the movements of his nature, he occupied himself with God alone. *In the clefts of the rock* he would build his nest and *in the hollow places of the wall* his dwelling.[223] With fruitful devotion he frequented only heavenly dwellings,[224] and he who had totally emptied himself remained so much the longer in the wounds of the Savior. He therefore frequently chose solitary places so that he could direct his mind completely to God; yet he was not slothful about entering into the affairs of his neighbors, when he saw the time was opportune, and he willingly took care of things pertaining to their salvation. For his safest haven was prayer; not prayer of a single moment, or idle or presumptuous prayer, but prayer of long duration, full of devotion, serene in humility. If he began late, he would scarcely finish before morning. Walking, sitting, eating, or drinking, he was always intent upon prayer. He would go alone to pray at night in churches abandoned and located in deserted places, where, under the protection of divine grace, he overcame many fears and many dis-

turbances of mind.

72   He fought hand to hand with the devil, for in
such places the devil not only struck at him with
temptations but discouraged him by ruining and
destroying things. But the most valiant soldier of
God, knowing that his Lord can do all things everywhere, did not give in to fright, but said within his
heart: "You can no more rattle the weapons of your
wickedness against me here, O evil one, than if we
were in public before all the people." Indeed, he was
extremely steadfast, and he paid no attention to anything except what pertained to the Lord. For when
he so very often preached the word of God to thousands of people, he was as sure of himself as though
he were speaking with a familiar companion. He
looked upon the greatest multitude of people as one
person and he preached to one as he would to a multitude. Out of the purity of his mind he provided for
himself security in preaching a sermon and, without
thinking about it beforehand, he spoke wonderful
things to all and things not heard before. When he
did give some time to meditation before a sermon,
he at times forgot what he had meditated upon when
the people had come together, and he knew nothing
else to say. Without embarrassment he would confess
to the people that he had thought of many things
but could remember nothing at all of them; and
suddenly he would be filled with such great eloquence that he would move the souls of the hearers
to admiration. At times, however, knowing nothing to
say, he would give a blessing and dismiss the people
feeling that from this alone they had received a great
sermon.

73   But when at one time he had come to Rome
because the interests of his order demanded it, he
longed greatly to speak before Pope Honorius and

the venerable cardinals.²²⁵ When the lord Hugo,²²⁶ the glorious bishop of Ostia, who venerated the holy man of God with a special affection, understood this, he was filled with both fear and joy, admiring the fervor of the holy man but conscious of his simple purity. But confident of the mercy of the Almighty, which in the time of need never fails those who trust in it, the bishop brought Francis before the lord pope and the reverend cardinals; and standing before such great princes, after receiving their permission and blessing, he began to speak fearlessly. Indeed, he spoke with such great fervor of spirit, that, not being able to contain himself for joy, when he spoke the words with his mouth, he moved his feet as though he were dancing, not indeed lustfully, but as one burning with the fire of divine love, not provoking laughter, but drawing forth tears of grief. For many of them were *pierced to the heart*²²⁷ in admiration of divine grace and of such great constancy in man. But the venerable lord bishop of Ostia was kept in suspense by fear and he prayed with all his strength to the Lord that the simplicity of the blessed man would not be despised, since the glory of the saint would reflect upon himself as would his disgrace, in as much as he had been placed over Francis' family as a father.²²⁸

74   For St. Francis had clung to him as a son to his father and as an only son to his mother, sleeping and resting securely upon the bosom of his kindness. In truth, the bishop held the place and did the work of a shepherd, but he left the name of shepherd to the holy man. The blessed father provided what provisions were necessary, but the kindly lord bishop carried them into effect. O how many, above all when these things were first taking place, were plotting to destroy the new Order that had been planted! O how many were trying to choke off this new *chosen vine-*

yard[229] that the hand of the Lord had so kindly planted in the world! How many there were who were trying to steal and consume its first and purest fruits! But they were all *slain by the sword*[230] of the reverend father and lord who *brought* them to *nothing.*[231] For he was a river of eloquence, a wall of the Church, a champion of truth, and a lover of the humble. Blessed that day, therefore, and memorable, on which the holy man of God committed himself to such a venerable lord. For once when that lord was exercising the office of legate for the holy see, as he often did, in Tuscany,[232] Blessed Francis, who as yet did not have many brothers but wanted to go to France, came to Florence where the aforementioned bishop was staying at the time. As yet they were not joined in that extraordinary familiarity, but only the fame of Francis' blessed life joined them in mutual affection and charity.

75 For the rest, because it was blessed Francis' custom upon entering any city or country to go to the bishops or priests, hearing of the presence of so great a bishop, he presented himself to his clemency with great reverence. When the lord bishop saw him, he received him with humble devotion, as he always did those who professed holy religion, those particularly who loved the noble insignia of blessed poverty and holy simplicity. And because he was solicitous in providing for the wants of the poor and in handling their business with special care, he diligently asked Francis the reason for his coming and listened to his proposal with great kindness. When he saw that Francis despised all earthly things more than the rest and that he was alight with that fire that Jesus had sent upon earth,[233] his soul was from that moment knit with the soul of Francis and he devoutly asked his prayers and most graciously offered his protection to him in all things. Then he ad-

monished Francis not to finish the journey he had begun but to give himself solicitously to the care of and watchfulness over those whom the Lord had committed to him. But St. Francis, seeing such a venerable lord conducting himself so kindly, giving such warm affection and such efficacious advice, rejoiced with a very great joy; and then, *falling at his feet*,[234] he handed himself over and entrusted himself and his brothers to him with a devout mind.[235]

CHAPTER XXVIII

Concerning Francis' spirit of charity and compassion toward the poor; and how he treated a sheep and some lambs

76 The father of the poor, the poor Francis, conforming himself to the poor in all things, was grieved when he saw some one poorer than himself, not because he longed for vainglory, but only from a feeling of compassion. And, though he was content with a tunic that was quite poor and rough, he very frequently longed to divide it with some poor person.[236] But that this very rich poor man, drawn on by a great feeling of affection, might be able to help the poor in some way, he would ask the rich of this world, when the weather was cold, to give him a mantle or some furs. And when, out of devotion, they willingly did what the most blessed father asked of them, he would say to them: "I will accept this from you with this understanding that you do not expect ever to have it back again." And when he met the first poor man, he would clothe him with what he had received with joy and gladness.[237] He bore it very ill if he saw a poor person reproached or if he heard a curse hurled upon any creature by anyone.

Once it happened that a certain brother uttered a word of invective against a certain poor man who had asked for an alms, saying to him: "See, perhaps you are a rich man and pretending to be poor." Hearing this, the father of the poor, St. Francis, was greatly saddened, and he severely rebuked the brother who had said such a thing and commanded him to strip himself before the poor man and, kissing his feet, beg pardon of him. For, he was accustomed to say: "Who curses a poor man does an injury to Christ, whose noble image he wears, the image of him who made himself poor for us in this world." Frequently, therefore, when he found the poor burdened down with wood or other things, he offered his own shoulders to help them, though his shoulders were very weak.

77   Francis abounded in the spirit of charity; he was filled with compassion not only toward men in need, but even toward dumb animals, reptiles, birds, and other creatures, sensible and insensible. But, among all the various kinds of animals, he loved little lambs with a special predilection and more ready affection, because in the sacred scriptures the humility of our Lord Jesus Christ is more frequently likened to that of the lamb and best illustrated by the simile of a lamb.[238] So, all things, especially those in which some allegorical similarity to the Son of God could be found, he would embrace more fondly and look upon more willingly. Once, when he made a trip through the Marches of Ancona[239] and had preached the word of God in that same city and had taken up his journey toward Osimo[240] with a certain Brother Paul whom he had appointed minister of all the brothers in that province,[241] he found a certain shepherd feeding a herd of she-goats and he-goats in the fields. Among the great number of these goats there was one little lamb going along and feeding humbly and quietly. When blessed Francis saw it, he stopped and, *touched inwardly with sorrow of*

heart[242] and groaning deeply, he said to the brother who was with him: "Do you not see this sheep that walks so meekly among the goats? I tell you that our Lord Jesus Christ walked in the same way meekly and humbly among the pharisees and chief priests. Therefore I ask you, my son, for love of him, to have pity with me on this little sheep. Let us pay the price and lead her away from among these goats."

78   Brother Paul, wondering over Francis' grief, began himself to be filled with sorrow. But since they had nothing but the poor tunics with which they were clothed and while they were worrying about the price of buying the sheep, immediately a certain merchant on a journey was there and offered the price desired. Thanking God, they took the sheep and went on to Osimo. There, entering the house of the bishop of the city, they were received by him with great reverence. But the lord bishop wondered about the sheep which the man of God was leading and about his affection for it. But when the servant of Christ had recounted the long parable of the sheep of the Gospel, touched to the heart the bishop gave thanks to God for the purity of the man of God. The next day, however, when he was leaving the city and wondering what he should do with the sheep, he took the advice of his companion and brother and gave it over to a certain monastery of handmaids of Christ at San Severino[243] to be cared for. The venerable handmaids of Christ accepted the sheep with joy as a great gift to them by God. They watched over it carefully for a long time, and they made a tunic out of its wool and sent it to the blessed father Francis at St. Mary of the Portiuncula at the time of a certain chapter. The holy man of God took it with great reverence and joy of spirit, and, embracing it, he kissed it and invited all who stood by to share his happiness.

79   Another time when he was passing through the same marches, with the same brother serving gladly as his companion, he met a certain man who had two little lambs hanging bound over his shoulder, taking them to the market to sell them. When blessed Francis heard them bleating, he was filled with pity; and, coming close, he touched them and showed his compassion for them like a mother over her weeping child. And he said to the man: "Why are you torturing my brother lambs tied up and hanging like this?" Answering, he said: "I am taking them to the market to sell them, because I need the money." The saint said: "What will happen to them then?" He answered: "Those who buy them will kill them and eat them." "God forbid," replied the saint; "this must not happen. Take the mantle I am wearing as their price and give the lambs to me." He quickly gave him the lambs and took the mantle, for the mantle was of much greater value. Now the saint had borrowed the mantle that day from a certain faithful man to ward off the cold. For the rest, the saint, after receiving the lambs, considered carefully what he should do with them; and, at the advice of his companion, he gave them to that man to take care of them; and he commanded him not to sell them at any time, nor to do them any harm, but to keep them, feed them, and take care of them conscientiously.

CHAPTER XXIX

Of the love Francis bore all creatures on account of their Creator; a description of the inner and outer man[244]

80   It would take too long and it would be impossible to enumerate and gather together all the things the glorious Francis did and taught while he was living in the flesh. For who could ever give expression to the very great affection he bore for all things that are God's? Who would be able to narrate the sweetness he enjoyed while contemplating in creatures the wisdom of their Creator, his power and his goodness? Indeed, he was very often filled with a wonderful and ineffable joy from this consideration while he looked upon the sun, while he beheld the moon, and while he gazed upon the stars and the firmament. O simple piety and pious simplicity! Toward little worms even he glowed with a very great love, for he had read this saying about the Savior: *I am a worm, not a man.*[245] Therefore he picked them up from the road and placed them in a safe place, lest they be crushed by the feet of the passersby. What shall I say of the lower creatures, when he would see to it that the bees would be provided with honey in the winter, or the best wine, lest they should die from the cold? He used to praise in public the perfection of their works and the excellence of their skill, for the glory of God, with such encomiums that he would often spend a whole day in praising them and the rest of creatures. For as of old the three youths in the fiery furnace[246] invited all the elements to praise and glorify the Creator of the universe, so also this man, filled with the spirit of God, never ceased to glorify, praise, and bless the Creator and Ruler of all things in all the elements and creatures.[247]

81   How great a gladness do you think the beauty of the flowers brought to his mind[248] when he saw the shape of their beauty and perceived the odor of their sweetness? He used to turn the eye of consideration immediately to the beauty of that flower that comes *from the root of Jesse*[249] and gives light *in the days of spring*[250] and by its fragrance has raised innumerable thousands from the dead. When he found

an abundance of flowers, he preached to them and invited them to praise the Lord as though they were endowed with reason. In the same way he exhorted with the sincerest purity cornfields and vineyards, stones and forests and all the beautiful things of the fields, fountains of water and the green things of the gardens, earth and fire, air and wind, to love God and serve him willingly. Finally, he called all creatures *brother,* and in a most extraordinary manner, a manner never experienced by others, he discerned the hidden things of nature with his sensitive heart, as one who had already escaped *into the freedom of the glory of the sons of God.*[251] O good Jesus, he is now praising you as admirable in heaven with all the angels, he who on earth preached you as lovable to every creature.

82 For he was filled with love that surpasses all human understanding when he pronounced your holy name, O holy Lord; and carried away with joy and purest gladness, he seemed like a new man, one from another world. Therefore, whenever he would find anything written, whether about God or about man,[252] along the way, or in a house, or on the floor, he would pick it up with the greatest reverence and put it in a sacred or decent place, so that the name of the Lord would not remain there or anything else pertaining to it. One day when he was asked by a certain brother why he so diligently picked up writings even of pagans or writings in which there was no mention of the name of the Lord, he replied: "Son, because the letters are there out of which the most glorious name of the Lord God could be put together. Whatever is good there does not pertain to the pagans, nor to any other men, but to God alone, to whom belongs every good." And what is no less to be admired, when he had caused some letters of greeting or admonition to be written, he would not allow even a single letter or syllable to be deleted, even though they had often been placed there superfluously or in error.

83 O how beautiful, how splendid, how glorious did he appear in the innocence of his life, in the simplicity of his words, in the purity of his heart, in his love for God, in his fraternal charity, in his ardent obedience, in his peaceful submission, in his angelic countenance![253] He was charming in his manners, serene by nature, affable in his conversation, most opportune in his exhortations, most faithful in what was entrusted to him, cautious in counsel, effective in business, gracious in all things. He was serene of mind, sweet of disposition, sober in spirit, raised up in contemplation, zealous in prayer, and in all things fervent. He was constant in purpose, stable in virtue, persevering in grace, and unchanging in all things. He was quick to pardon, slow to become angry, ready of wit, tenacious of memory, subtle in discussion, circumspect in choosing, and in all things simple. He was unbending with himself, understanding toward others, and discreet in all things.

He was a most eloquent man, a man of cheerful countenance, of kindly aspect; he was immune to cowardice, free of insolence. [He was of medium height, closer to shortness; his head was moderate in size and round, his face a bit long and prominent, his forehead smooth and low; his eyes were of moderate size, black and sound;[254] his hair was black, his eyebrows straight, his nose symmetrical, thin and straight; his ears were upright, but small; his temples smooth. His speech was peaceable,[255] fiery and sharp; his voice was strong, sweet, clear, and sonorous. His teeth were set close together, even, and white; his lips were small and thin; his beard black, but not bushy. His neck was slender, his shoulders straight, his arms short, his hands slender, his fingers long, his

nails extended; his legs were thin, his feet small. His skin was delicate, his flesh very spare. He wore rough garments, he slept but very briefly, he gave most generously. And because he was very humble, he showed *all mildness to all men*,[256] adapting himself usefully to the behavior of all. The more holy amongst the holy, among sinners he was as one of them. Therefore, most holy father, help the sinners, you who loved sinners, and deign, we beg of you, most kindly to raise up by your most glorious intercession those whom you see lying in the mire of their sins.

CHAPTER XXX

Of the manger Francis made on the day of the Lord's birth

84 Francis' highest intention, his chief desire, his uppermost purpose was to observe the holy Gospel in all things and through all things and, with perfect vigilance, with all zeal, with all the longing of his mind and all the fervor of his heart, "to follow the teaching and the footsteps of our Lord Jesus Christ."[257] He would recall Christ's words through persistent meditation and bring to mind his deeds through the most penetrating consideration. The humility of the incarnation and the charity of the passion occupied his memory particularly, to the extent that he wanted to think of hardly anything else. What he did on the birthday of our Lord Jesus Christ near the little town called Greccio[258] in the third year before his glorious death[259] should especially be noted and recalled with reverent memory. In that place there was a certain man by the name of John, of good reputation and an even better life, whom blessed Francis loved with a special love, for in the place where he lived he held a noble and honorable position in as much as he had trampled upon the nobility of his birth and pursued nobility of soul. Blessed Francis sent for this man, as he often did, about fifteen days before the birth of the Lord, and he said to him: "If you want us to celebrate the present feast of our Lord at Greccio, go with haste and diligently prepare what I tell you. For I wish to do something that will recall to memory the little Child who was born in Bethlehem and set before our bodily eyes in some way the inconveniences of his infant needs, how he lay in a manger, how, with an ox and an ass standing by, he lay upon the hay where he had been placed." When the good and faithful man heard these things, he ran with haste and prepared in that place all the things the saint had told him.

85   But the day of joy drew near, the time of great rejoicing came. The brothers were called from their various places. Men and women of that neighborhood prepared with glad hearts, according to their means, candles and torches to light up that night that has lighted up all the days and years with its gleaming star. At length the saint of God came, and finding all things prepared, *he saw it and was glad.*[260] The manger was prepared, the hay had been brought, the ox and ass were led in. There simplicity was honored, poverty was exhalted, humility was commended, and Greccio was made, as it were, a new Bethlehem. The night was lighted up like the day, and it delighted men and beasts. The people came and were filled with new joy over the new mystery. The woods rang with the voices of the crowd and the rocks made answer to their jubilation. The brothers sang, paying their debt of praise to the Lord, and the whole night resounded with their rejoicing. The saint of God stood before the manger, uttering sighs, overcome with love, and filled with a wonderful happiness. The solemnities of the Mass were celebrated over the manger and the priest experienced a new

76

consolation.

86   The saint of God was clothed with the vestments of the deacon, for he was a deacon, and he sang the holy Gospel in a sonorous voice. And his voice was a strong voice, a sweet voice, a clear voice, a sonorous voice,[261] inviting all to the highest rewards. Then he preached to the people standing about, and he spoke charming words concerning the nativity of the poor King and the little town of Bethlehem. Frequently too, when he wished to call Christ *Jesus,* he would call him simply the *Child of Bethlehem,* aglow with overflowing love for him; and speaking the word *Bethlehem,* his voice was more like the bleating of a sheep. His mouth was filled more with sweet affection than with words. Besides, when he spoke the name *Child of Bethlehem* or *Jesus,* his tongue licked his lips, as it were, relishing and savoring with pleased palate the sweetness of the words. The gifts of the Almighty were multiplied there, and a wonderful vision was seen by a certain virtuous man. For he saw a little child lying in the manger lifeless, and he saw the holy man of God go up to it and rouse the child as from a deep sleep. This vision was not unfitting, for the Child Jesus had been forgotten in the hearts of many; but, by the working of his grace, he was brought to life again through his servant St. Francis and stamped upon their fervent memory. At length the solemn night celebration was brought to a close, and each one returned to his home with holy joy.

87   The hay that had been placed in the manger was kept, so that the Lord might save the beasts of burden and other animals through it as he multiplied his holy mercy.[262] And in truth it so happened that many animals throughout the surrounding region that had various illnesses were freed from their ill-

nesses after eating of this hay. Indeed, even women laboring for a long time in a difficult birth, were delivered safely when some of this hay was placed upon them; and a large number of persons of both sexes of that place, suffering from various illnesses, obtained the health they sought. Later, the place on which the manger had stood was made sacred by a *temple of the Lord,*[263] and an altar was built in honor of the most blessed father Francis over the manger and a church was built, so that where once the animals had eaten the hay, there in the future men would eat unto health of soul and body the flesh of the *lamb without blemish and without spot,*[264] our Lord Jesus Christ,[265] who in highest and ineffable love gave himself to us, who lives and reigns with the Father and the Holy Spirit, God, eternally glorious, forever and ever. Amen. Alleluja, Alleluja.

HERE ENDS THE FIRST BOOK ABOUT THE LIFE AND ACTS OF BLESSED FRANCIS

BOOK TWO

HERE BEGINS THE SECOND BOOK WHICH TELLS OF THE LAST TWO YEARS OF THE LIFE OF OUR MOST BLESSED FATHER FRANCIS AND ABOUT HIS HAPPY DEATH

CHAPTER I

[About the contents of this book, about the time of Francis' death, and about his progress in perfection][1]

88   In the first part of this work, which, with the help of the grace of the Savior, we have brought to a fitting conclusion, we wrote about the life and acts of our most blessed father Francis up to the eighteenth year of his conversion.[2] We will now add to this work briefly the rest of the things he did from the second last year of his life on, in so far as we have been able to get proper knowledge of them; and at present we intend to note down only those things which were of greater importance, so that they who wish to say more about them may always be able to find something they can add.

In the year of our Lord's incarnation 1226, in the fourteenth indiction,[3] on Sunday, October 4,[4] our blessed father Francis went forth from the prison of the flesh and took flight most happily to the mansions of the heavenly spirits, consummating perfectly what he had begun. He died in the city of Assisi, where he was born and at St. Mary of the Portiuncula where he first planted the Order of Friars Minor, twenty years after he had given himself perfectly to Christ, following the life and the footsteps of the Apostles. His sacred and holy body was laid to rest and honorably buried with hymns and praises in that city, and there, by reason of many miracles, it shines radiantly unto the glory of Almighty God. Amen.

89   Since this man had received little or no instruction in the way of God and in knowledge of him when he was young, he remained for no short time in his natural simplicity and under the sway of vices; but *he was justified from sin*[5] *by a change of the right hand of the Most High,*[6] and by the grace and *power of the Most High*[7] he was filled with divine wisdom above all others of his time. For when the teachings of the Gospel, not indeed in every respect, but taken generally, had everywhere failed to be put into practice, this man was sent by God to bear *witness to the truth*[8] throughout the whole world in accordance with the example of the Apostles. And thus it came to pass that his teaching showed that *the wisdom of this world* is most evidently *turned to foolishness,*[9] and within a short period of time brought it, under the guidance of Christ, to the true wisdom of God *by the foolishness of* his *preaching.*[10] For in this *last time*[11] this new evangelist, like one of the rivers that flowed out of paradise, diffused the waters of the Gospel over the whole world by his tender watering, and preached by his deeds the way of the Son of God and the doctrine of truth. Accordingly, in him and through him there arose throughout the world an unlooked for happiness and a holy newness, and a shoot of the ancient religion suddenly brought a great renewal to those who had grown calloused and to the very old. A new spirit was born in the hearts of the elect, and a saving unction was poured out in their midst, when the servant and holy man of Christ, like one of the lights of the heavens, shone brilliantly with a new rite and with new signs. Through him the miracles of ancient times were renewed, while there was planted in the desert of this world, by a new order but in an ancient way, a fruitful vine bearing flowers of sweetness unto the odor of holy virtues by extending everywhere the branches of a sacred religion

90   For, though he was a man *subject to the same infirmities* as we ourselves,[12] he was not content with observing the common precepts, but overflowing with the most ardent charity, he set out upon the way of total perfection; he aimed at the heights of perfect sanctity, and he saw the *end of all perfection.*[13] Therefore, every order, every sex, every age has in him a visible pattern of the way of salvation and has outstanding examples of holy works. If any propose to set their hand to difficult things and to *strive after the greater gifts*[14] of the more excellent way, let them look into the mirror of his life and learn every perfection. If any take to the lower and easier way, fearing to walk the difficult way and fearing the ascent to the top of the mountain, on this plain too they will find in him suitable guidance. If any, finally, seek signs and wonders, let them petition his sanctity and they will get what they seek. And indeed the glorious life of this man sheds a more brilliant light upon the perfection of the saints who preceded him. The passion of Jesus Christ proves this and his cross shows it most clearly. For in truth, the venerable father was marked in five parts of his body with the marks of the passion and of the cross as though he had hung upon the cross with the Son of God. *This is a great mystery*[15] and shows forth the majesty of the prerogative of love. But a secret counsel lies hidden therein and therein is concealed an awe-inspiring mystery which we believe is known to God alone and revealed only in part by the saint himself to a certain person. Therefore it is not expedient to attempt much in praise of him whose praise is from him who is the praise of all, the source and highest honor, giving the rewards of light. Blessing, therefore, the holy, true, and glorious God, let us return to our narrative.

CHAPTER II

Concerning Blessed Francis' greatest desire; and how he understood the Lord's will in his regard through the opening of a book

91   At a certain time the blessed and venerable father Francis left behind the crowds of the world that were coming together daily with the greatest devotion to hear and see him, and he sought out a quiet and secret place of solitude, desiring to spend his time there with God and to cleanse himself of any dust that may have clung to him from his association with men.[16] It was his custom to divide up the time given him to merit grace, and, as seemed necessary to him, to give part of it to working for the good of his neighbors and the rest to the blessed retirement of contemplation. He therefore took with him just the very few companions to whom his holy life was better known than it was to the rest, so that they might protect him from the invasion and *disturbance of men*[17] and respect and preserve his quiet in all things. After he had remained there for a while and had acquired in an inexpressible way familiarity with God by his constant prayer and frequent contemplation, he longed to know what might be more acceptable to the eternal King concerning himself or in himself or what might happen. Most carefully he sought out and most piously longed to know in what manner, by what way, and by what desire he might cling perfectly to the Lord God according to his counsel and according to the good pleasure of his will. This was always his highest philosophy; this very great desire always flamed in him while he lived, namely, to seek out from the simple, from the wise, from the perfect and imperfect, how he might attain the way of truth and come to his highest good.

92   For, though he was the most perfect of the

perfect, he denied that he was perfect and considered himself entirely imperfect. For he had tasted and seen how sweet,[18] how delightful and *how good is God to Israel, to them who are of a right heart*[19] and who seek him in pure *simplicity*[20] and true purity. The infused sweetness and serenity, which he felt had been given him from on high, such as is but rarely given even to the very rarest of men, compelled him to renounce himself completely, and, filled with great joyfulness, he wished to pass over completely to that state to which, going beyond his own strength, he had already gone in part. Filled with *the Spirit of God,*[21] he was ready to suffer every distress of mind and to bear every bodily torment, if only his wish might be granted, that the will of the Father in heaven might be mercifully fulfilled in him. One day therefore he went before the holy altar which was erected in the hermitage where he was staying, and taking the book in which the holy Gospel was written, he reverently placed it upon the altar. Then he prostrated himself in prayer to God, not less in heart than in body, and he asked in humble prayer that the good God, *the Father of mercies and the God of all comfort,*[22] would deign to make known his will to him, and that he might be able to carry out what he had earlier begun simply and devoutly; and he prayed that it might be shown to him at the first opening of the book what was more fitting for him to do. For he was led by the spirit of the saints and of the most perfect men, who, we read, did the same thing with pious devotion in their desire for sanctity.[23]

93   Then rising from his prayer, in a spirit of humility and with a contrite heart[24] and signing himself with the sign of the holy cross, he took the book from the altar and opened it with reverence and fear. But it happened that when he had opened the book

the passion of our Lord Jesus Christ was the first thing that met his eye, and that part of it that said he would suffer tribulation.[25] But that there could be no suspicion that this had happened by chance, he opened the book a second and a third time, and each time he found the same passage or a similar one written there. Then the man filled with the Spirit of God understood that it was for him *to enter the kingdom of God*[26] through many tribulations, many trials, and many struggles. But the very strong soldier of the Lord was not disturbed at the struggles at hand, nor was he shaken, he who was about to fight the battles of the Lord on the battlefields of this world. It is not likely that a man would succumb to an enemy who has labored long, even beyond the measure of human strength, not to give in to himself. In truth, he was most fervent, and if in the past centuries there had been anyone who equaled him in his purpose, there was no one who was superior to him in his desire. For since he knew it was easier for him to do perfect things than to talk about them, he always put his zeal and his efforts not in words, which do not accomplish good but only give evidence of it, but in holy deeds. He remained therefore unshaken and happy, and he sang songs of happiness in his heart to himself and to God. Accordingly, he was considered worthy of a greater revelation who had so rejoiced over the least, and *faithful in a very little,*[27] he was *set over many.*[28]

CHAPTER III

Concerning the vision of the man in the likeness of a crucified seraph

94 Two years before Francis gave his soul back to heaven, while he was living in the hermitage which was called Alverna,[29] after the place on which it stood, he saw *in the vision of God*[30] a man standing above him, like a seraph with six wings, his hands extended and his feet joined together and fixed to a cross. Two of the wings were extended above his head, two were extended as if for flight, and two were wrapped around the whole body.[31] When the blessed servant of the Most High saw these things, he was filled with the greatest wonder, but he could not understand what this vision should mean. Still, he was filled with happiness and he rejoiced very greatly because of the kind and gracious look with which he saw himself regarded by the seraph, whose beauty was beyond estimation; but the fact that the seraph was fixed to a cross and the sharpness of his suffering filled Francis with fear. And so he arose, if I may so speak, sorrowful and joyful, and joy and grief were in him alternately. Solicitously he thought what this vision could mean, and his soul was in great anxiety to find its meaning. And while he was thus unable to come to any understanding of it and the strangeness of the vision perplexed his heart, the marks of the nails began to appear in his hands and feet, just as he had seen them a little before in the crucified man above him.

95 His hands and feet seemed to be pierced through the middle by nails, with the heads of the nails appearing in the inner side of the hands and on the upper sides of the feet and their pointed ends on the opposite sides. The marks in the hands were round on the inner side, but on the outer side they were elongated; and some small pieces of flesh took on the appearance of the ends of the nails, bent and driven back and rising above the rest of the flesh. In the same way the marks of the nails were impressed upon the feet and raised in a similar way above the rest of the flesh. Furthermore, his right side was as though it had been pierced by a lance and had a wound in it that frequently bled so that his tunic and trousers were very often covered with his sacred blood. Alas, how few indeed merited to see the wound in his side while this crucified servant of the crucified Lord lived! But happy was Elias who, while the saint lived, merited to see this wound;[32] and no less happy was Rufino who touched the wound with his own hands.[33] For when this Brother Rufino once put his hand upon the bosom of this most holy man to rub him, his hand fell down to the right side of Francis, as it can happen; and it happened to touch the precious wound. The holy man of God was not a little grieved at this touch, and pushing his hand away, he cried out to the Lord to forgive Rufino. For he made every effort to hide this wound from those outside the order, and he hid it with such great care from those close to him that even the brothers who were always at his side and his most devoted followers did not know of this wound for a long time. And though the servant and friend of the Most High saw himself adorned with so many and such great pearls, as with the most precious gems, and endowed in a wonderful manner above the glory and honor of all other men,[34] he did not become vain in heart nor did he seek to please anyone out of thirst for vainglory; but, lest human favor should steal any of the grace given him, he strove in every way he could to hide it.

96   It was Francis' custom to reveal his great secret but rarely or to no one at all, for he feared that his revealing it to anyone might have the appearance of a special affection for him, in the way in which special friends act, and that he would thereby suffer some loss in the grace that was given him. He therefore carried about in his heart and frequently had on his lips this saying of the prophet: *Thy words have I hidden in my heart, that I may not sin against thee.*[35] Francis had given a sign to his brothers and sons who

lived with him, that whenever any lay people would come to him and he wanted to refrain from speaking with them, he would recite the aforementioned verse and immediately they were to dismiss with courtesy those who had come to him. For he had experienced that it is a great evil to make known all things to every one, and that he cannot be a spiritual man whose secrets are not more perfect and more numerous than the things that can be read on his face and completely understood by men. For he had found some who outwardly agreed with him but inwardly disagreed with him, who applauded him to his face, but ridiculed him behind his back, who acquired credit for themselves, but made the upright suspect to him. For wickedness often tries to blacken purity, and because of a lie that is familiar to many, the truth spoken by a few is not believed.

CHAPTER IV

Of the fervor of Blessed Francis and of the infirmity of his eyes

97   During the course of this same period of time Francis' body began to be burdened with various and more serious sicknesses than before. For he suffered frequent infirmities in as much as he had chastised his body and brought it into subjection[36] during the many years that had preceded. For during the space of eighteen years, which was now completed,[37] his body had had little or no rest while he traveled through various very large regions so that that willing spirit,[38] that devoted spirit, that fervent spirit that dwelt within him might scatter everywhere the seeds of the word of God.[39] He filled the whole earth with the Gospel of Christ, so that often in one day *he made a circuit of*[40] four or five villages and even cities, *preaching the kingdom of God*[41] to every one;

and edifying his hearers not less by his example than by his word, he made a tongue out of his whole body. For so great was the harmony of his body toward his spirit, so great its obedience, that while his spirit tried to lay hold of all sanctity, his body nevertheless did not only not resist, but tried even to outrun his spirit, according to what was written: *For thee my soul hath thirsted; for thee my flesh, O how many ways.*[42] Persistence in subjection had made the flesh willing, and he attained his position of such great virtue by daily conquering himself, for custom is often turned into second nature.[43]

98 But since according to the laws of nature and the constitution of man it is necessary that our outer man decay day by day, though the inner man is being renewed,[44] that most precious vessel in which the heavenly treasure was hidden began to break up and to suffer the loss of all its powers. Because indeed, *when a man hath done, then shall he begin*: *and when he leaveth off,*[45] then shall he work, his spirit became more willing as his flesh became weak.[46] So much did he value the salvation of souls and thirst for the advancement of his neighbors that, since he could no longer walk, he went about the country riding on an ass.

Frequently the brothers admonished him, suggesting to him with great urgency in their entreaties, that he should seek to restore his infirm and greatly weakened body in some measure with the help of doctors. But Francis, with his noble spirit fixed on heaven and wanting only *to depart and to be with Christ,*[47] refused entirely to do this. In truth, because he had not yet filled *up in his flesh what* was *lacking of the suffering of Christ,*[48] though he bore *the marks of the Lord Jesus in* his *body,*[49] he incurred a very severe infirmity of the eyes, according as God had multiplied his mercy to him.[50] But when the infirmity increased day by day and seemed to be aggravated daily from a lack of care, Brother Elias, whom Francis had chosen to take the place of a mother in his own regard and to take the place of a father for the rest of the brothers,[51] finally compelled him not to abhor medicine but to accept it *in the name of the Son of God*[52] by whom it was created, as it is written: *The Most High hath created medicines out of the earth, and a wise man will not abhor them.*[53] The holy father then graciously acquiesced and humbly complied with the words of his adviser.

CHAPTER V

How Francis was received at Rieti by the lord Hugo, bishop of Ostia, and how the saint foretold that Hugo would be bishop of the whole world

99   But it happened that, when many were coming to help Francis with their medicines and no remedy was found, he went to the city of Rieti where a man was said to live who was very skilful in curing this disease. When he arrived there, he was received quite kindly and respectfully by the whole Roman curia, which was staying at that time in that city,[54] and especially by the lord Hugo, bishop of Ostia, who was greatly conspicuous for his virtue and holiness.

The blessed father Francis had chosen him, with the consent and at the will of the lord Pope Honorius,[55] to be father and lord over the whole religion and order of his brothers in as much as blessed poverty was very pleasing to him and holy simplicity was held in great reverence by him.[56] This lord conformed himself to the ways of the brothers, and in his desire for sanctity he was simple with the simple, humble with the humble, poor with the poor. He was a brother among the brothers, the least among the lesser brothers; and he strove to conduct himself in his life and manners, in so far as it was permissible for him, as though he were one of the brothers. He was solicitous about planting this holy religion everywhere and the widespread fame of his renowned life greatly enlarged the Order in remote places.

The Lord gave him *a learned tongue*,[57] with which he confounded adversaries of truth, refuted *the enemies of the cross of Christ*,[58] brought back to the right way those who had gone astray, made peace with those in discord, and bound together with the bond of charity those who lived in concord. He was a *lamp burning and shining*[59] in the Church of God and a *chosen arrow*[60] prepared *in a seasonable time*.[61] O how often, having put aside his expensive garments and having put on mean ones, and with his feet unshod, he would go about like one of the brothers and ask *the terms of peace*.[62] This he did solicitously *between a man and his neighbor*[63] as often as was necessary and between God and man always. Therefore, a little later God chose him shepherd in his whole holy Church and lifted up his head among the tribes of the people.

100   And that it might be known that this was brought about through the inspiration of God and by the will of Christ Jesus, the blessed father Francis predicted it in words and foretold it by a sign long before it came about. For when the Order and religion of the brothers was beginning to be spread about through the operation of divine grace and was raising its crown of merits to the heavens like a cedar *in the paradise of God*,[64] and, like a *chosen vineyard*[65] was stretching forth its sacred branches to the limits of the world,[66] St. Francis went to the lord Pope Honorius, who was then the head of the Roman Church, and asked him with humble prayer to appoint the lord Hugo, bishop of Ostia, to be the father and lord of himself and all his brothers.[67] The lord pope granted

the prayers of the saint and graciously made over his own authority over the order of brothers to Hugo. And, accepting it reverently and devoutly, he sought in every way to administer the food of eternal life opportunely to those committed to him, like a *faithful and prudent servant*[68] set over the family of the Lord. Therefore the holy father Francis submitted himself to him in all things and revered him with a wonderful and respectful affection.

Francis was led on by the spirit of God with which he was filled, and therefore he saw long before what in the future would be before the eyes of all. For whenever he wished to write to the bishop with regard to some urgent business on behalf of his religious family, or rather because he was constrained by the charity of Christ with which he burned toward him, he never allowed him to be called in his letters *Bishop of Ostia* or *of Velletri*,[69] as others called him in their customary salutations; but, using this formula, he would say: *To the Most Reverend Father, or the Lord Hugo, Bishop of the Whole World*. Often too he would greet him with unusual blessings; and, though he was a son by reason of his devoted submission, at the inspiration of the Holy Spirit, he would at times comfort him with a fatherly colloquy that he might strengthen upon him *the blessings of his fathers, until the desire of the everlasting hills should come*.[70]

101 The lord bishop too was afire with love for the holy man and therefore whatever the blessed man said, whatever he did, pleased the bishop, and he was often deeply affected even by the mere sight of him. He himself testified that he was never so greatly disturbed or upset but that, upon seeing St. Francis or talking with him, every mental cloud would be dispersed and serenity return, melancholy would be put to flight and joy breathed upon him from above. He ministered to the blessed Francis as a servant to his master; and as often as he saw him, he showed reverence to him as to an apostle of Christ, and bowing down both the inner and the outer man, he would often kiss his hand with his consecrated mouth.

Solicitously and devotedly he sought a way for the blessed father to recover the former health of his eyes, knowing him to be a holy and just man and a man very necessary and very useful to the Church of God. He had compassion on the whole congregation of brothers because of him and he pitied the sons on account of the father. He therefore admonished the holy father to take care of himself and not to discard what was necessary in his infirmity, lest his neglect should be imputed to him as something sinful rather than as something meritorious. St. Francis, however, humbly listened to what was told him by so venerable a lord and so dear a father, and he acted more cautiously thereafter and with less fear regarding things necessary for his cure. But because the disease had already increased so much, for any remedy at all there was required the most skilful advice and the harshest treatment. Thus it happened that his head was cauterized in several places, his veins opened, plasters put on, and eye-salves applied; but he made no progress and seemed only to get constantly worse.

CHAPTER VI

Of the way the brothers who attended St. Francis conducted themselves; and how he disposed himself to live

102   These things St. Francis bore for almost two years with all patience and humility, *giving thanks to God*[71] in all things. But that he might direct his intention more freely to God and, in frequent ecstasy, wander about and enter the workshops of the blessed mansions of heaven and present himself with an

abundance of grace *on high*[72] before the most kind and serene *Lord of all things*,[73] he committed the care of himself to certain brothers who were deservedly very dear to him. For these were men of virtue, devoted to God, pleasing to the saints, acceptable to men, upon whom the blessed father Francis leaned, like a house upon its four columns. Their names, however, I will not mention to spare their modesty, which is a familiar friend to them since they are spiritual men. For modesty is an ornament of all ages, the witness of innocence, the sign of a virtuous mind, *the rod of correction*,[74] the special glory of conscience, the guardian of reputation, and the badge of all uprightness. This virtue adorned all these brothers and made them lovable and kind to men; this grace was common to all of them, but a special virtue adorned each one. One was known for his outstanding discretion,[75] another for his extraordinary patience,[76] the third for his great simplicity,[77] and the last was robust of body and gentle of disposition.[78] These tried with all vigilance, with all zeal, with all their will to foster the peace of mind of their blessed father, and they cared for the infirmity of his body, shunning no distress, no labors, that they might give themselves entirely to serving the saint.

103 But, though the glorious father had been brought to the fulness of grace before God and shone among men of this world by his good works, he nevertheless thought always to begin more perfect works and, like the most skilled soldier in the *camps of God*,[79] the enemy having been challenged, to stir up new wars. He proposed, under *Christ the prince*,[80] to do great things, and, with his limbs failing and his body dying, he hoped for a victory over the enemy in a new struggle. For true virtue knows not a limit of time, since the expectation of a reward is eternal. Therefore he was afire with a very great desire to

return to the first beginnings of humility and, by reason of the immensity of his love, *rejoicing in hope*,[81] he thought to recall his body to its former subjection, even though it had already come to such an extremity. He removed from himself completely the obstacles of all cares, and he fully silenced the clamorings of all anxieties. Though he found it necessary to moderate his early rigor because of his infirmity, he would still say: "Let us begin, brothers, to serve the Lord God, for up to now we have made little or no progress." He did not consider that he had laid hold of his goal as yet,[82] and persevering untiringly in his purpose of attaining holy *newness of life*,[83] he hoped always to make a beginning. He wished to go back again to serving lepers, to be held in contempt, as he once had been. He proposed to shun companionship with men and to retire to the most remote places, so that, having thus put off all cares and laid aside all solicitude for others, only the wall of the flesh would stand between him and God.

104   For he saw many pursuing offices of authority, and despising their rashness, he sought to recall them from this pestilence by his example. He used to say that it was a good and acceptable thing before God to exercise the care of others and that it was becoming that they should undertake the care of souls who would seek in it nothing of themselves but who would attend always to the divine will in all things. Those, namely, who would put nothing ahead of their own salvation and who would pay no heed to the applause of their subjects but only to their advancement; who would seek not display before men, but glory before God; who do not strive after a prelacy, but who fear it; who are not puffed up by such a thing when they have it, but are humbled, and who are not dejected when it is taken away, but are filled with joy. But he said that it was dangerous to

rule, especially at this time when wickedness had grown so greatly and increased so abundantly; and he said that it was better to be ruled. He was filled with sorrow that some had left their *former works*[84] and had forgotten their earlier simplicity after they had found new things. Wherefore he grieved over those who were once intent upon higher things with their whole desire but who had descended to base and vile things, and had left the true joys to roam and wander amid frivolous and inane things in the field of empty freedom. He prayed therefore that God's mercy might free these sons and asked most earnestly that they might be kept in the grace *that had been given to them.*[85]

CHAPTER VII

How Francis came from Siena to Assisi, and of the church of St. Mary of the Portiuncula and of the blessing he gave to the brothers

105   But in the sixth month before the day of his death,[86] while he was at Siena[87] for treatment of the infirmity of his eyes, Francis began to be gravely ill in all the rest of his body; and, with his stomach racked by a long-standing illness and his liver infected, he vomited much blood, so that he appeared to be approaching death. Upon hearing this, Brother Elias hurried to him with great haste from a distant place. Upon his arrival, the holy father recovered so much that, leaving that city, he went with Elias to Le Celle near Cortona.[88] Arriving there, he remained there for some time; and while he was there, his abdomen began to swell, and his legs and feet too, and the ailment of his stomach began to grow worse and worse, so that he could take hardly any food. He then asked Brother Elias to have him brought to Assisi. This good son did what his gracious father asked, and,

when everything had been prepared, he took him to the place he longed for. *All the city rejoiced*[89] at the coming of the blessed father and the mouths of all the people praised God; for *the whole multitude of the people*[90] hoped that the *holy one of God*[91] would die close by, and this was the reason for their great joy.

106   And at the will of God it happened that his holy soul was released from his body and passed to the kingdom of heaven at that place, where, while he was still *in the flesh*,[92] the knowledge of heavenly things was first given to him and the saving unction poured upon him.[93] For though he knew that the kingdom of heaven was set up *in all the habitations of the land*[94] and believed that the grace of God was given to the *elect of God*[95] in every place, he had however experienced that the place of the church of St. Mary of the Portiuncula was endowed with more fruitful graces and visited by heavenly spirits.[96] Therefore he often said to his brothers: "See to it, my sons, that you never abandon this place. If you are driven out from one side, go back in at the other. For this place is truly holy and is the dwelling place of God. Here, when we were but a few, the Most High gave us increase; here he enlightened the hearts of his poor ones by the light of his wisdom; here he set our wills afire with the fire of his love. Here he who prays with a devout heart will obtain what he prays for and he who offends will be punished more severely. Wherefore, my sons, consider this dwelling place of God to be worthy of all honor, and with all your heart, *with the voice of joy and praise*,[97] give glory to God in this place."

107   Meanwhile, as his infirmity increased, all his bodily strength failed and, destitute of all his powers, he could not move himself at all. Still when he was asked by a certain brother what he would prefer to bear, this lingering and long illness or the suffering of a severe martyrdom at the hands of an executioner, he replied: "My son, that has always been and still is most dear to me and more sweet and more acceptable which pleases the Lord my God most to let happen in me and with me, for I desire always only to be found conformed and obedient to his will in all things. Yet, this infirmity is harder for me to bear even for three days than any martyrdom. I am not speaking of the reward, but only of the intensity of suffering it causes." O martyr and martyr, who smiling and rejoicing most willingly put up with what was most bitter and most difficult to bear! In all truth, not a single member in him remained free of the greatest suffering and, as the natural warmth was gradually lost, he approached nearer to the end each day. The doctors were amazed, the brothers astonished, that his soul could live in flesh so dead, for, the flesh having been consumed, nothing but skin clung to his bones.

108   Now when he saw that his last day was at hand, a fact that had been made known to him by a revelation from God two years earlier,[98] Francis called to him the brothers he wanted and, as it was given to him from above, he blessed each one just as the patriarch Jacob of old had blessed his sons;[99] indeed, like another Moses who, when he was about to ascend the mountain appointed by God, enriched the children of Israel with blessings.[100] Since Brother Elias was sitting at his left side, with the other brothers standing about, Francis, crossing his right hand over his left, placed his right hand upon Elias' head; and, deprived as he was of the light of his bodily eyes and of their use, he said: "On whom am I holding my hand?" "On Brother Elias," they said. "That is what I wish," said Francis; "you, my son, I bless *above all and throughout all*;[101] and, just as the Most High

has multiplied my brothers and sons in your hands, so also I bless them all upon you and in you. May God, the King of all, bless you in heaven and upon earth. I bless you as much as I can and more than I can, and what I cannot, may He who can do all things do in you. May the Lord be mindful of your work and of your labor, and may a share be reserved for you in the reward of the just. May you find every blessing you desire, and may whatever you ask worthily be granted to you." "Farewell, all you my sons, *in the fear of God,*[102] and may you remain in him always, for a very great trial will come upon you and a great tribulation is approaching. Happy will they be who will persevere in the things they have begun; from them future scandals will separate some. I am hastening to the Lord and I am confident that I will go to my God *whom I serve* devoutly *in my spirit.*"[103]

At this time he was staying in the palace of the bishop of Assisi,[104] and he therefore asked the brothers to take him as quickly as possible to the place of St. Mary of the Portiuncula. For he wished to give back his soul to God in that place where, as has been said, he first knew the way of truth perfectly.

CHAPTER VIII

What Francis did and said when he died happily

109   The space of twenty years had now passed since Francis' conversion,[105] according to what had been made known to him by the will of God. For when the blessed father and Brother Elias were staying at one time at Foligno, one night when they had given themselves to sleep a certain white-garbed priest of a very great and advanced age and of venerable appearance stood before Brother Elias and said: "Arise, Brother, and say to Brother Francis that eighteen years are now completed since he renounced

the world and gave himself to Christ, and that he will remain in this life for only two more years; then the Lord will call him to himself and he will go the way of all flesh." And thus it happened that the word of the Lord that had been made known long before was fulfilled at the appointed time.

When therefore he had rested for a few days in a place he greatly longed to be in and realized that the time of his death was at hand, he called to him two of his brothers and spiritual sons[106] and commanded them to sing in a loud voice with joy of spirit the Praises of the Lord[107] over his approaching death, or rather, over the life that was so near. He himself, in as far as he was able, broke forth in that psalm of David: *I cried to the Lord with my voice: with my voice I made supplication to the Lord.*[108] A certain brother, however, from among those standing about,[109] whom the saint loved with a great affection, in his anxiety for all the brothers, said to him, when he saw these things and recognized that Francis was approaching his end: "Kind Father, alas, your sons are now without a father and are deprived of the true light of their eyes. Remember therefore your orphan sons whom you are now leaving;[110] forgive them all their faults and give joy to those present and absent with your holy blessing." And the saint said to him: "Behold, my son, I am called by God; I forgive my brothers, both present and absent, all their offenses and faults, and, in as far as I am able, I absolve them; I want you to announce this to them and to bless them all on my behalf."

110   Finally he ordered the book of the Gospels to be brought and commanded that the Gospel according to St. John be read from that place where it begins: *Six days before the Passover, Jesus, knowing that the hour had come for him to pass from this world to the Father.*[111] The minister general[112] had

intended to read this Gospel, even before he had been commanded to do so; this passage had also appeared at the first opening of the book earlier,[113] although the book was the whole and complete Bible in which this Gospel was contained. Francis then commanded that a hair shirt be put upon him and that he be sprinkled with ashes, for he was soon to become dust and ashes. Then, when many brothers had gathered about, whose father and leader he was, and while they were standing reverently at his side awaiting his blessed death and happy end, his most holy soul was freed from his body and received into the abyss of light, and his body *fell asleep*[114] in the Lord. One of his brothers and disciples, a man of some renown, whose name I think I should withhold here because while he lives in the flesh, he prefers not to glory in so great a privilege,[115] saw the soul of the most holy father ascend over many waters directly to heaven. For it was like a star, having in some way the immensity of the moon, but to a certain extent the brightness of the sun, and it was borne upward on a little white cloud.

111   Therefore I cry out concerning him: O how glorious is this saint, whose soul a disciple saw *ascend into heaven*,[116] *fair as the moon, bright as the sun*,[117] and as he ascended upon a white cloud he was shining most gloriously! O truly you are a light of the world, shining in the Church of Christ more splendidly than the sun; behold, you have withdrawn the rays of your light now and, withdrawing into the kingdom of light, you have exchanged company with us miserable ones for company with the angels and saints! O glorious kindness of singular renown, do not put aside the care of your sons though you have now put off your flesh like unto theirs! Know, O know indeed, in what great distress you have left them whose innumerable labors and frequent anxieties merely your presence

always mercifully relieved. O truly merciful and most holy father, you who were always ready to show mercy to your sinning sons and to kindly forgive them! We therefore bless you, worthy father, whom the Most High has blessed, who is *over all things, God blessed forever, amen.*[118]

CHAPTER IX

The sorrowing of the brothers and their joy when they saw Francis bearing the marks of the cross; and of the wings of the seraphim

112 There was therefore a concourse of many people *praising God and saying:*[119] "Praised and blessed be you, our Lord, God, who have entrusted so precious a treasure to us who are unworthy! Praise and glory be to you, ineffable Trinity." The whole city of Assisi rushed in a body and the whole region hastened to see the wonderful things of God which the Lord of Majesty had made manifest in his holy servant. Every one sang a canticle of joy, as their heartfelt gladness prompted them; and all blessed the omnipotence of the Savior for the fulfillment of their desire. However, Francis' sons were filled with sorrow at being deprived of so great a father and they showed the pious affection of their hearts by tears and sighs.

But an unheard of joy tempered their grief and the newness of a miracle threw their minds into great amazement.[120] Their mourning was turned to song and their weeping to jubilation. For they had never heard or read in the Scriptures what was set before their eyes, what they could hardly be persuaded to believe if it had not been proved to them by such evident testimony. For in truth there appeared in him a true image of the cross and of the passion of the *lamb without blemish*[121] who washed away the sins of the world, for he seemed as though he had been recently taken down from the cross, his hands and feet were pierced as though by nails and his side wounded as though by a lance.

They saw his flesh, which before had been dark, now gleaming with a dazzling whiteness and giving promise of the rewards of the blessed resurrection by reason of its beauty. They saw, finally, that his face was like the face of an angel, as though he were living and not dead; and the rest of his members had taken on the softness and pliability of an innocent child's members. His sinews were not contracted, as they generally are in the dead; his skin had not become hard; his members were not rigid, but they could be turned this way and that, however one wished.

113   And because he glowed with such wondrous beauty before all who looked upon him and his flesh had become even more white, it was wonderful to see in the middle of his hands and feet, not indeed the holes made by the nails, but the nails themselves formed out of his flesh and retaining the blackness of iron, and his right side was red with blood. These signs of martyrdom did not arouse horror in the minds of those who looked upon them, but they gave his body much beauty and grace, just as little black stones do when they are set in a white pavement.

His brothers and sons came hurriedly, and weeping, they kissed the hands and feet of their beloved father who was leaving them, and also his right side, in the wound of which was presented a remarkable memorial of him who in pouring forth both *blood and water*[122] from that same place reconciled the world to his Father. Not only those who were permitted to kiss the sacred stigmata of Jesus Christ which St. Francis bore on his body, but even those who were permitted only to see them, thought they had been granted a very great gift. For who, seeing this thing, would give himself to weeping rather than to joy? Or if he wept, would he not do so rather from joy than from sorrow? Whose breast is so much like iron that it would not be moved to sighs? Whose heart so much like stone that it would not be broken to compunction, that it would not be fired to love of God, that it would not be strengthened to good will? Who is so dull, so unfeeling, that he would not realize in truth that as this saint was honored upon earth with so singular a gift, so would he also be magnified in heaven by an ineffable glory?

114 Singular gift and mark of special love, that a soldier should be adorned with the same arms of glory that were suitable for the son of the King by reason of their most excellent dignity! O miracle worthy of everlasting memory, and memorable sacrament worthy of admirable and unceasing reverence, which represents to the eyes of faith that mystery in which the blood of the *lamb without blemish*[123] flowed from five outlets to wash away the sins of the world! O sublime splendor of the living cross that gives life to the dead, the burden of which presses so gently and pricks so delicately that by it dead flesh is made to live and the weak spirit is made strong! He loved you much, whom you adorned so very gloriously. Glory and blessing be *to the only wise God*[124] who renews *signs* and works *new miracles*[125] that he might console the minds of the weak with new revelations and that by means of a wonderful work in things visible their hearts might be caught up to a love of things invisible. O wonderful and lovable disposition of God, which, that no suspicion might arise concerning this new miracle, first mercifully displayed in him who *descended from heaven*[126] what a little later was to be wonderfully wrought in him who dwelt upon earth! And indeed the true Father of mercies[127] wanted to show how great a re-

ward he is worthy of who tried to love him with all his heart, namely, to be placed in the highest order of celestial spirits and indeed in the order nearest to himself.[128]

We can without a doubt attain this reward, if, after the manner of the seraphim,[129] we extend two wings above our head, that is, if we have, after the example of the blessed Francis, a pure intention in all our works and if our actions are upright, and if, directing these to God, we strive tirelessly to please him alone in all our works. These two wings must be joined together to cover the head, because the Father of lights will by no means accept either the uprightness of a work without purity of intention or vice versa, for he says: *If thy eye be sound, thy whole body will be full of light. But if thy eye be evil, thy whole body will be full of darkness.*[130] The eye is not sound if it does not see what is to be seen, lacking the knowledge of truth, or if it looks upon what it should not see, not having a pure intention. In the first case, simple reasoning will show that the eye is not sound, but blind; in the second, that it is evil. The feathers of these wings are love of the Father, who saves us in his mercy, and fear of the Lord, who judges us terribly. These feathers must raise the souls of the elect from earthly things by repressing evil impulses and properly ordering chaste affections. With two wings for flying one is to extend a twofold charity to one's neighbor, namely, by refreshing his soul with the word of God and by sustaining his body with earthly help. These two wings, however, are rarely joined together, for both can hardly be fulfilled by anyone. The feathers of these wings are the various works which must be shown to one's neighbor to advise and help him. Lastly, with two wings the body that is bare of merits must be covered, and this is properly done when as often as sin has intervened it is again clothed with innocence through contrition and confession. The feathers of these wings are the many various affections which are born of hatred for sin and hunger for justice.

115 These things the most blessed father Francis fulfilled most perfectly; he bore the image and form of a seraph and, persevering upon the cross, merited to rise to the ranks of the heavenly spirits. For he was always on the cross, fleeing no labor or suffering, if only he could fulfill the will of the Lord in himself and concerning himself.

The brothers, moreover, who lived with him knew how his daily and continuous talk was of Jesus and how sweet and tender his conversation was, how kind and filled with love his talk with them. His mouth spoke *out of the abundance of* his *heart*,[131] and the fountain of enlightened love that filled his whole being bubbled forth outwardly. Indeed, he was always occupied with Jesus; Jesus he bore in his heart, Jesus in his mouth, Jesus in his ears, Jesus in his eyes, Jesus in his hands, Jesus in the rest of his members. O how often, when he sat down to eat, hearing or speaking or thinking of Jesus, he forgot bodily food, as we read of the holy one: "Seeing, he did not see, and hearing he did not hear."[132] Indeed, many times, as he went along the way meditating on and singing of Jesus, he would forget his journey and invite all the elements to praise Jesus.[133] And because he always bore and preserved *Christ Jesus and him crucified*[134] in his heart with a wonderful love, he was marked in a most glorious way above all others with the seal of him whom in a rapture of mind he contemplated sitting in inexpressible and incomprehensible glory at the right hand of the Father, with whom he, the co-equal and most high Son of the Most High, lives and reigns, conquers and governs in union with the Holy Spirit, God eternally glorious through all ages forever. Amen.

CHAPTER X
Concerning the grief of the ladies at St. Damian's;
and how St. Francis was buried with praise and glory

116 Francis' brothers and sons, therefore, who
gathered together with a great multitude of people
from the cities nearby and rejoiced to be present at
such great solemnities, spent the whole night in
which the holy father had died singing the praises
of God, so much so that, because of the charm of the
jubilation and the brightness of the lights, it seemed
to be a wake of the angels. But when morning had
come, a great multitude from the city of Assisi as-
sembled with all the clergy, and, taking the sacred
body from the place where Francis had died,[135] they
carried it amid great honor to the city, with hymns
and praises and sounding trumpets. They all took up
branches of olive trees and of other trees, and, carrying out the obsequies with solemnity, they discharged
the duties of praise with many lights and with loud
voices. When, with the sons carrying their father,
and the flock following their shepherd who was hastening to meet the Shepherd of all, they came to the
place where he had himself first planted the religion
and order of holy virgins and poor ladies,[136] they
placed him in the church of St. Damian, where these
same daughters whom he had won for the Lord dwelt;
there they paused and the little window through
which the handmaids of Christ were accustomed to
receive at the appointed time the sacrament of the
body of the Lord was opened. The coffin was opened,
in which lay hidden the treasure of supercelestial
virtues and in which he was being borne by a few
who was accustomed to bear many.[137] And behold,
the Lady Clare, who was truly illustrious[138] by the
holiness of her merits and was the first mother of the

106

rest since she was the very first plant of this holy Order, came with the rest of her daughters to see their father who would no longer speak to them or return to them but was hastening elsewhere.

117 And redoubling their sighs and looking upon him with great sorrow of heart and many tears, they *began to proclaim*[139] in a restrained voice: "Father, Father, what shall we do? Why do you forsake us in our misery, or to whom do you leave us who are so desolate? Why did you not send us rejoicing ahead of you to the place where you are going, us whom you leave here in sorrow? What do you bid us do, shut up in this prison, us whom you will never again visit as you used to? All our consolation departs with you and no solace like it remains to us buried to the world. Who will comfort us in our great poverty no less of merit than of goods? O Father of the poor, lover of poverty! Who will strengthen us in temptation, O you who experienced innumerable temptations and who knew how to overcome them? Who will console us in our trials, O you who were our *helper in troubles which found us exceedingly?*[140] O most bitter separation, O unfriendly leave-taking! O most dreadful death, that slays thousands of sons and daughters bereft of so great a father, by hastening to remove beyond recall him through whom mainly our efforts, such as they were, were made to flourish!" But their virginal modesty restrained their great weeping; and it was not fitting to mourn too much for him at whose passing a host of the army of angels had come together *and the citizens with the saints and members of God's household* rejoiced.[141] And so, divided between sorrow and joy, they kissed his most radiant hands, adorned with the most precious gems and shining pearls; and, when he had been taken away, the door was closed to them which will hardly again be opened for such great sorrow. O how great

107

was the sorrow of all over the woeful and pitiable outcry of these poor ladies! How great in particular were the lamentations of his grieving sons! Their special grief was shared by all, so much so that hardly anyone could refrain from weeping when the angels of peace wept so bitterly.[142]

118   Finally, when all had come to the city, they placed the most holy body, amid great rejoicing and exultation, in a sacred place,[143] a place that was to be even more scared in the future; there, to the glory of the supreme Almighty God, he illumines the world by a multiplicity of new miracles, just as up to then he had enlightened it in a wonderful way by the teachings of his holy preaching. Thanks be to God. Amen.

Behold, most holy and blessed Father, I have attended you with praises that are your due and of which you are worthy, though indeed they are insufficient, and I have to some extent set down your deeds in narrative form. Grant me, therefore, miserable as I am, that I may follow you so worthily in the present life that I may mercifully merit to be with you in the future life. Remember, O gracious Father, your poor sons, to whom there remains hardly any comfort after you, their only and one solace. For, though you, their best and first portion, are now joined with the choirs of angels and placed with the apostles on a throne of glory, they, however, still lie in the *mire of dregs*,[144] shut up in a dark prison, crying thus sadly to you: "Present, Father, to Jesus Christ, the Son of the most high Father, his sacred stigmata, and let him see the marks of the cross in your side, feet, and hands, that he may mercifully deign to show his own wounds to the Father, who because of them will indeed be ever gracious to us miserable ones. Amen." So be it. So be it.

HERE ENDS THE SECOND BOOK

BOOK THREE

HERE BEGINS THE THIRD BOOK,
CONCERNING THE CANONIZATION OF
OUR BLESSED FATHER FRANCIS AND
CONCERNING HIS MIRACLES

CHAPTER I

The canonization of our blessed father Francis

119   Therefore the most glorious father Francis,
adding an even more happy end to a happy beginning, most happily commended his spirit to heaven
in the twentieth year of his conversion, and there,
crowned with glory and honor[1] and having attained
a place *in the midst of the stones of fire,*[2] he stands
at the throne of God and devotes himself to further-
ing effectually the concerns of those he left behind
upon earth. What indeed can be denied to him in
the imprint of whose stigmata appears the form of
him who, being equal to the Father, *has taken his
seat at the right hand of the majesty on high, the
brightness of his glory and the image of his substance,*
and *has effected man's purgation from sin?*[3] What
else should there be but that he be heard who has
been made comformable unto the death of Christ
Jesus in *the fellowship of his sufferings*[4] which the
sacred wounds in his hands and feet and side show
forth?

Actually, he is already giving joy to the whole
world that has been gladdened by a new joy, and he is
offering to all the advantages of true salvation. He is
brightening the world with the very bright light of his
miracles and illuminating the whole world with the
brilliance of a new star. Once the world was saddened
when it was deprived of his presence, and it saw
itself overwhelmed in a pit of darkness, as it were,
at his setting. But now, lighted up as the noonday
with more refulgent beams by the rising of this new

light, it feels that it has lost this universal darkness. All its complaining, *blessed be God*,[5] has now ceased, since every day and everywhere it is filled most abundantly through him with new rejoicing over the abundance of his virtues. *From the east and from the west*,[6] from the south and from the north those come who have been helped through his intercession; thus these things are proved by the testimony of truth. Indeed, while he lived in the flesh, that extraordinary lover of heavenly things accepted nothing of ownership in the world so that he might possess more fully and more joyfully the universal good. It therefore came about that he received in its entirety what he had declined in part, and he exchanged eternity for time. Everywhere he is helping everyone; everywhere he is at the behest of everyone; and, truly a lover of unity, he knows no loss because of such division.[7]

120 While he was still living among sinners, Francis went about through the whole world preaching; reigning now with the angels in heaven, he flies more swiftly than thought as the messenger of the most high King and bestows generous gifts upon all. Therefore all the world honors him, venerates, glorifies, and praises him. In truth, all share in the common good. Who can tell what great miracles and who can tell what kind of miracles God deigns to work everywhere through him? What great miracles is not Francis working in France alone, where the king and queen[8] and all the great ones run to kiss and venerate[9] the pillow Francis used in his sickness? Where also the wise and most learned men of the world, of whom Paris[10] is accustomed to produce a greater abundance than the rest of the world, humbly and most devoutly venerate, admire, and honor Francis, an unlettered man and the friend of true simplicity and complete sincerity. Truly Francis had a free[11]

and noble heart. Those who have experienced his magnanimity know how free, how liberal he was in all things; how confident and fearless he was in all things; with what great virtue, with what great fervor he trampled under foot all wordly things. What indeed shall I say of the other parts of the world, where, by means of his clothing, diseases depart, illnesses leave, and crowds of both sexes are delivered from their troubles by merely invoking his name?

121　　At his tomb, too, new miracles are constantly occurring, and, the number of petitions greatly increasing, great benefits for body and for soul are sought at that same place. Sight is given to the blind, hearing is restored to the deaf, the ability to walk is given to the lame, the mute speak, he who has the gout leaps, the leper is healed, he who suffers from a swelling has it reduced, and those who suffer diverse and various infirmities obtain health, so that his dead body heals living bodies just as his living body had raised up dead souls.

The Roman pontiff, the highest of all bishops, the leader of the Christians, the lord of the world, the pastor of the Church, the anointed of the Lord, the vicar of Christ, heard and understood all this. He rejoiced and was happy, he danced with joy and was glad, when he saw the Church of God renewed in his own day by new mysteries but ancient wonders, and that in his own son, whom he bore in his holy womb, cherished in his bosom, nursed with his words, and nourished with the food of salvation. The rest of the guardians of the Church too heard it, the shepherds of the flock, the defenders of the faith, *the friends of the bridegroom*,[12] those who are at his side, the hinges of the world,[13] the venerable cardinals. They congratulated the Church, they rejoiced with the pope, they glorified the Savior, who with the highest and ineffable wisdom, the highest and incomprehensible grace, the highest and immeasurable goodness chooses the foolish and base things of this world[14] that he might thus draw the strong things to himself.[15] The whole world heard and applauded, and the entire realm that was subject to the Catholic faith superabounded in joy and overflowed with holy consolation.

122   But there was a sudden change in things and new dangers arose meanwhile in the world. Suddenly the joy of peace was disturbed and the torch of envy was lighted and the Church was torn by domestic and civil war. The Romans, a rebellious and ferocious race of men, raged against their neighbors, as was their custom, and, being rash, they stretched *forth their hands against* the *holy places*.[16] The distinguished Pope Gregory tried to curb their growing wickedness, to repress their savagery, to temper their violence; and, like a tower of great strength, he protected the Church of Christ. Many dangers assailed her, destruction became more frequent, and in the rest of the world *the necks of sinners*[17] were raised against God. What then? Measuring the future by his very great experience and weighing the present circumstances, he abandoned the city to the rebels,[18] so that he might free the world from rebellions and defend it. He came therefore to the city of Rieti,[19] where he was received with honor, as was befitting. From there he went to Spoleto where he was honored with great respect by all. He remained there a few days, and, after the affairs of the Church had been provided for, he kindly visited, in the company of the venerable cardinals, the Poor Ladies of Christ, who were dead and buried to the world.[20] The holy life of these Poor Ladies, their highest poverty, and their glorious way of life moved him and the others to tears, stirred them to contempt of the world, and kindled in them a desire for the life of retirement. O lovable humility,

nurse of all graces! The prince of the world, the successor of the prince of the apostles, visits these poor women, comes to them lowly and humble in their seclusion; and, though this humility is worthy of just approbation, it was nevertheless an unusual example and one that had not been seen for many ages past.

123 Then he hastened on, hastened to Assisi,[21] where a glorious treasure awaited him, that through it the universal suffering and imminent tribulation might be extinguished. At his approach, the whole region rejoiced, the city was filled with exultation, the great throng of people celebrated their happiness, and the already bright day was further illuminated by brighter lights. Every one went out to meet him and solemn watches were kept by all. The pious fraternity of Poor Brothers went out to meet him, and they all sang sweet songs to Christ the Lord. The vicar of Christ arrived at the place and going first to the grave of St. Francis, he greeted it reverently and eagerly. He sighed deeply, struck his breast, shed tears, and bowed his venerable head with great devotion. While he was there a solemn discussion was held concerning the canonization of the holy man, and the noble assembly of cardinals met often concerning this business. From all sides many came together who had been freed from their illnesses through the holy man of God, and from every side a very great number of miracles gave forth their luster: these were approved, verified, heard, accepted. Meanwhile, the urgency of the affairs of his office pressed upon the pope, a new emergency threatened, and the holy father went to Perugia[22] that by a superabounding and singular grace he might return again to Assisi in the interests of this very great business. Then they met again at Perugia, and a sacred assembly of cardinals was held concerning this matter in the room of the lord pope. They were all in agreement and they spoke unanimously; they read the miracles and regarded them with great reverence, and they commended the life and conduct of the blessed father with the highest praises.

124 "The most holy life of this most holy man," they said, "needs no attestation of miracles; *what we have seen with our eyes, what our hands have handled,*[23] we have proved with the light of truth." They were all transported with joy, they rejoiced, they wept, and indeed in those tears there was a great blessing. They immediately appointed the happy day on which they would fill the whole world with saving happiness. The solemn day came, a day to be held in reverence by every age, a day that shed its sublime rapture not only upon the earth but even upon the heavenly mansions. Bishops came together, abbots arrived, prelates of the Church were present from even the most remote parts of the world; a king too was present,[24] and a noble multitude of counts and princes. They then escorted the lord of all the world and entered the city of Assisi with him amid great pomp. He reached the place prepared for so solemn an event[25] and the whole multitude of glorious cardinals, bishops, and abbots gathered around the blessed pope. A most distinguished gathering of priests and clerics was there; a happy and sacred company of religious men was there; the more bashful habit of the sacred veil was there too; a great crowd of all the people was there and an almost innumerable multitude of both sexes. They hurried there from all sides, and every age came to the concourse of people with the greatest eagerness. *The small and great* were *there,*[26] the servant and they who were free of a master.

125 The supreme pontiff was there, the spouse of the Church of Christ, surrounded by a variety of his great children and with a crown of glory on his head,

an ornament of honor.[27] He stood there adorned with the pontifical robes and clad in holy vestments ornamented with *jewels set in gold and graven by the work of a lapidary.*[28] The anointed of the Lord stood there, resplendent in *magnificence and glory*[29] *in gilded clothing;*[30] and covered with engraven jewels sparkling with the radiance of spring, he caught the attention of all. Cardinals and bishops stood around him; decked with splendid necklaces and clad in garments as white as snow they showed forth the image of super-celestial beauties and displayed the joy of the glorified. All the people stood in expectation of *the voice of mirth, the voice of gladness,*[31] a new voice, a voice full of all sweetness, a voice of praise, a voice of constant blessing. First Pope Gregory preached to all the people, and with a sweetly flowing and sonorous voice he spoke the praises of God. He also praised the holy father Francis in a noble eulogy, and recalling and speaking of the purity of his life, he was bathed in tears. His sermon had this text: *He shone in his days as the morning star in the midst of a cloud, and as the moon at the full. And as the sun when it shineth, so did he shine in the temple of God.*[32] When the *faithful saying and worthy of all acceptation*[33] was completed, one of the lord pope's subdeacons, Octavian by name,[34] read the miracles of the saint before all in a very loud voice, and the lord Raynerius, a cardinal deacon,[35] a man of penetrating intellect and renowned for his piety and life, spoke about them with holy words and with an abundance of tears. The Shepherd of the Church was carried away with joy, and sighing from the very depths of his being and sobbing, he shed torrents of tears. So too the other prelates of the Church poured out floods of tears, and their sacred vestments were moistened with their abundance. All the people too wept, and with the suspense of their longing expectation, they became wearied.

126   Then the happy pope spoke with a loud voice, and extending his hands to heaven, he said: "To the praise and glory of Almighty God, the Father, Son, and Holy Spirit, and of the glorious Virgin Mary and of the blessed apostles Peter and Paul, and to the honor of the glorious Roman Church, at the advice of our brothers and of the other prelates, we decree that the most blessed father Francis, whom the Lord has glorified in heaven and whom we venerate on earth, shall be enrolled in the catalogue of saints and that his feast shall be celebrated on the day of his death."[36] At this decree, the venerable cardinals began to sing in a loud voice along with the pope the *Te Deum Laudamus*. Then there was raised a clamor among the many people praising God; the earth resounded with their mighty voices, the air was filled with their rejoicings, and the ground was moistened with their tears. New songs were sung,[37] and the servants of God gave expression to their joy in melody of spirit. Sweet sounding organs were heard there and spiritual hymns were sung with well modulated voices. There a very sweet odor was breathed, and a more joyous melody that stirred the emotions resounded there. The day was bright and colored with more splendid rays than usual. There were green olive branches there and fresh branches of other trees. Brightly glittering festive attire adorned all the people, and the blessing of peace filled the minds of those who had come there with joy. Then the happy Pope Gregory descended from his lofty throne, and going by way of the lower steps, he entered the sanctuary to offer *the vows and voluntary oblations;*[38] he kissed with his happy lips the tomb that contained the body that was sacred and consecrated to God. He offered and multiplied his prayers and celebrated the sacred mysteries.[39] A *ring of his brethren*[40] stood

116

about him, praising, adoring, and blessing Almighty God who had done *great things in all the earth.*[41] All the people increased the praises of God and they paid due thanksgiving to St. Francis in honor of the most holy Trinity. Amen.

These things took place in the city of Assisi in the second year[42] of the pontificate of the lord pope Gregory on the seventeenth day of the calends of the month of August.[43]

CHAPTER II

The Miracles of St. Francis

IN THE NAME OF CHRIST, HERE BEGINS THE ACCOUNT OF THE MIRACLES OF OUR MOST HOLY FATHER FRANCIS

127   Humbly imploring the grace of our Lord Jesus Christ, we will set down briefly, but accurately, under the guidance of Christ, certain miracles, which, as was said, were read before the lord pope Gregory and announced to the people, to excite and promote the devotion of the people now alive and to strengthen the faith of those who are to come.

THE HEALING OF THE CRIPPLED

On the very day on which the sacred and holy body of the most blessed father Francis was laid away like a most precious treasure, anointed with heavenly spices rather than with earthly ointments, a certain girl was brought to the grave; for a year already her neck had been monstrously bent and her head had grown down to her shoulders so that she could look up only sideways. When however she had placed her head for a little while upon the tomb in which lay the precious body of the saint, immediately she raised up her neck through the merits of this most holy man and her head was restored to its proper position, so that the girl was greatly dumbfounded at the sudden change in herself and she began to run away and weep. For now a kind of pit appeared in her shoulder where her head had touched it before, caused by the position which the long illness had brought about.[44]

128　　In the region of Narni there was a certain boy whose leg was so bent back that he could not walk at all without the help of two sticks. He was a beggar, and burdened with this infirmity for several years, he did not know his own father and mother. But by the merits of our most blessed father Francis he was freed from this difficulty to the extent that he could walk about freely wherever he wished without the help of the sticks, praising and blessing the Lord and his holy one.[45]

129　　A certain Nicholas, a citizen of Foligno, had a crippled left leg and suffered very great pain; he spent such great sums on physicians in an attempt to recover his former health that he incurred indebtedness beyond his wishes and beyond what he could afford. At last, when their help had done him no good at all and his suffering was so great that his cries kept his neighbors from sleeping at night, he vowed himself to God and St. Francis and had himself brought to the tomb of the saint. After he had spent a whole night in prayer before the tomb of the saint, his leg was stretched out and he returned home with great joy without a cane.[46]

130　　A boy, too, who had his leg so bent that his knee clung to his chest and his heel to his hips, came to the tomb of St. Francis. His father wore a cilice next to his flesh and his mother mortified herself severely for the sake of the child. The boy was suddenly cured so completely that he was able to run about the streets full of health and happiness, giving thanks to God and St. Francis.[47]

131   In the city of Fano[48] there was a certain crippled man whose legs were full of sores and clung to his hips; they gave off such a stench that those in charge of the hospital would not receive him in the hospital or keep him there. But by the merits of the most blessed father Francis, whose mercy he implored, he was soon made happy in being cured.[49]

132   A certain girl from Gubbio had hands so crippled that she had lost the use of all her members for a year already. Her nurse carried her with a waxen image to the tomb of the most blessed father Francis to obtain the grace of health. After she had been there for about eight days, one day all her limbs were restored to their proper use, so that she was considered fit again for her former tasks.[50]

133   Another boy, too, from Montenero,[51] lay for several days before the doors of the church where the body of St. Francis lies at rest.[52] He was unable to walk or sit down, for from the waist down he was deprived of all his powers and of the use of his limbs. But one day he entered the church, and upon touching the tomb of the most blessed father Francis he came out completely healthy and sound. The little boy himself used to say that while he lay at the tomb of the glorious saint, a certain young man stood before him above the tomb clothed in the habit of the brothers and carrying some pears in his hands. The young man called to him and offered him one of the pears and encouraged him to rise. He took the pear from his hand and said: "See, I am crippled and cannot rise." But then he ate the pear that had been given him and he began to extend his hand for another pear that was offered him by the same young man. The latter urged him again to rise, but feeling the weight of his infirmity upon him, he did not get up. But as he was reaching out his hand toward the pear, the young man, after giving him the pear, took his hand and led him out. He then disappeared from his sight. But seeing that he was made well and whole again, the boy began to call out in a loud voice, showing everyone what had happened to him.[53]

134   A certain woman from the city called Coccorano[54] was brought to the tomb of the glorious father on a stretcher; she could not use any of her members except her tongue. But after remaining a little while at the tomb of this most holy man, she arose completely cured. Another citizen of Gubbio who had brought his crippled son to the tomb of the holy father received him back healthy and wholly restored. He had been so crippled up that his legs clung to his hips and were almost completely withered.[55]

135   Bartholomew, of the city of Narni, was an extremely poor and needy man. He fell asleep once under the shade of a certain walnut tree, and when he awoke, he found himself so crippled up that he could not walk. The infirmity gradually increased and his leg and foot became emaciated, crooked, and withered, so that he could not feel an incision made by a knife nor did he fear a burning with fire. But that true lover of the poor and the father of all needy people, the most holy Francis, showed himself one night in a dream to this man, commanding him to go to a certain bath, where he, moved by great compassion for him, wished to free him from his illness. But when the man awoke and did not know what to do, he told the dream, as it had happened, to the bishop of the city. The bishop, however, exhorted him to go to the bath as he had been told to do, and he made the sign of the cross over him and blessed him. The man then began to drag himself to the place as best he could with the aid of a cane. While he was going along his way in sorrow and with great effort, he heard a voice saying to him: "Go with the peace of the Lord; I am he to whom you vowed yourself." Then, as he approached the bath, he missed the way, for it was night; and again he heard the voice saying to him that he was not walking along the right way, and it directed him to the bath. And when he had come to the place and had entered the bath, he felt one hand placed upon his foot and another on his leg, gently stretching it out. Immediately he was cured, and he jumped from the bath praising and blessing the omnipotence of the Creator and blessed Francis, his servant, who had shown him such favor and power. For the man had been crippled and had been a beggar for the space of six years, and he was advanced in age.[56]

OF THE BLIND WHO RECEIVED THEIR SIGHT

136 A certain woman named Sibyl, who had suffered for many years from blindness, was brought sorrowing to the grave of the man of God. But after she had recovered her sight, she returned home rejoicing and full of gladness.[57] A certain blind man from Spello[58] recovered his sight that had been lost for a long time at the tomb of that sacred body.[59] Another woman from Camerino[60] had lost entirely the sight of her right eye. Her parents laid a piece of cloth that the blessed Francis had touched upon that eye, and after they had made a vow, they gave thanks to the Lord God and to St. Francis for the recovery of the sight of that eye.[61] A similar thing happened to a certain woman from Gubbio, who, after she had made a vow, was able to rejoice in the recovery of the sight she had once had.[62] A certain citizen of Assisi too had lost the light of his eyes for five years. Now since, while the blessed Francis was still alive, this man had been very friendly with him, he always recalled that friendship when he prayed to the blessed man, and, upon touching the tomb of the saint, he was healed.[63] A certain Albertino of Narni had completely lost the light of his eyes for about a year so that his eyelids hung down to his cheeks. He made a vow to blessed Francis, and immediately upon recovering his sight, he prepared to visit the glorious tomb of Francis and he went there.[64]

OF THOSE POSSESSED BY DEMONS

137   There was a man in the city of Foligno, Peter by name, who, when he was once on his way to visit the shrine of Blessed Michael the Archangel,[65] either because of a vow or because of a penance imposed upon him for his sins, came to a certain spring. Because he was thirsty after the tiresomeness of the journey, he tasted the water of the spring. But it seemed to him that he drank devils. And so, obsessed by them for three years, he did some most wicked things, horrible to see and horrible to speak of. But coming to the tomb of the most holy father, with the devils raging and torturing him cruelly, he was wonderfully freed from them by a clear and manifest miracle when he touched the sepulcher.[66]

138   There was a certain woman in the city of Narni who was subject to a terrible frenzy, and having lost her mind, she did horrible things and spoke unseemly words. But the blessed Francis appeared to her in a vision, saying: "Make the sign of the cross." And she said: "I cannot." Then the saint himself made the sign of the cross upon her and drove out all her madness and every deceit of the devil.[67] In the same way, many men and women who were tormented in various ways by the designs of the devils and deluded by their deceits were snatched away from their power through the great merits of the holy and glorious father. But because such people are often the

victims of delusions, we will go on to more important things with just a mention of these things.

139   A certain boy, Matthew by name, from the city of Todi,[68] lay in his bed for eight days as though dead; his mouth was closed tight and the light of his eyes was gone; the skin of his face and hands and feet had turned black as a pot, and all despaired of his life. But at his mother's vow he recovered with remarkable speed. He discharged foul blood from his mouth and it was thought that he was vomiting up his intestines too. Immediately his mother fell to her knees and humbly called upon the name of St. Francis; and as she arose from prayer, the boy began to open his eyes, to see light, and to suck the breasts. A little while later the black skin fell off and the flesh became as it had been at first. He got well and recovered his strength. As soon as he began to get well, his mother asked him, saying: "Who delivered you, son?" And lisping, he answered: "Ciccu, Ciccu."[69] Again he was asked "Whose servant are you?" And he answered again: "Ciccu, Ciccu." He could not speak plainly because he was an infant, and therefore he shortened the name of blessed Francis in this way.[70]

140   A certain young man who was on a certain very high place fell down from that place and lost his speech and the use of all his limbs. And not eating for three days, nor drinking anything, nor giving any signs of life, he was thought to be dead. His mother, however, did not seek the aid of doctors, but she begged health for him from blessed Francis. And so, after she had made a vow, she received him back alive and whole; and she began to praise the omnipo-

tence of the Savior.[71] Another boy named Mancinus was sick unto death and all despaired of any cure for him. But he invoked the name of blessed Francis and recovered instantly. Another boy from Arezzo, Walter by name, who was suffering from a continuous fever and was tormented by a double abscess, was given up by all the doctors; but when the parents made a vow to blessed Francis, he was restored to the health he desired.[72] Another one who was near death made a waxen image, and even before it was finished, he was freed from all his sufferings.

141   A certain woman who had been confined to a sickbed for several years and could neither turn nor move made a vow to God and to blessed Francis and was freed from her sickness completely, and she carried out the necessary duties of her life.[73] In the city of Narni there was a certain woman who for eight years had a hand that was so withered that she could do nothing with it. Finally the most blessed father Francis appeared to her in a vision and stretching her hand made it just as useful as the other.[74] In the same city there was a certain young man who had been afflicted for ten years with a most severe illness; he had become so swollen that no medicine could do him any good at all. But after his mother had made a vow, he immediately recovered his health through the merits of blessed Francis.[75] In the city of Fano there was a certain man afflicted with dropsy. His limbs were swollen horribly. He merited to be freed completely from his illness through the instrumentality of blessed Francis.[76] A certain inhabitant of Todi suffered so much from arthritis in his joints that he could not sit or rest at all. The intensity of his suffering gave him such chills that he seemed reduced to nothing. He called in doctors, used more and more baths, took many medicines, but he could be helped by none of these remedies. One day, however, he

made a vow in the presence of a priest in the hope that St. Francis would give him back his health. And so, after praying to the saint, he soon saw himself restored to his former health.[77]

142 A certain woman who lay paralyzed in the city of Gubbio was freed from her infirmity and made well after calling upon the name of blessed Francis three times.[78] A certain man named Bontadosus suffered such severe pain in his feet and hands that he could not move or turn in any direction. When he could no longer eat or sleep, a certain woman came to him one day urging and suggesting that, if he wanted to be freed very quickly from his infirmity, he should vow himself very devoutly to blessed Francis. Amid great pain that man replied: "I do not believe that he is a saint." But the woman continued persistently in her suggestion, and at last the man vowed himself in this way: "I vow myself," he said, "to St. Francis and I will believe him to be a saint, if he will free me from this illness within three days." By the merits of God's saint he was soon delivered, and he walked, ate, and rested, giving glory to Almighty God.[79]

143 There was a man who had been wounded severely in the head with an iron arrow; the arrow had entered through the socket of his eye and remained in his head, and he could not be helped by the skill of the doctors. Then he vowed himself with humble devotion to Francis, the saint of God, hoping that he could be healed through his intercession. While he was resting and sleeping a little, he was told in a dream by St. Francis that he should have the arrow drawn out through the back of his head. And this was done the next day, just as he saw it in his dream, and he was delivered without any great difficulty.[80]

144 A certain man of Spello, named Imperator, suffered such a severe rupture for two years that all his intestines were descending outwardly through his lower parts. For a long time he had not been able to put them back inside or keep them in place, so that he had to have a truss to keep them inside. He went to doctors over and over, begging them to give him some relief; but they demanded from him a price that he could not pay since he did not have the means or even food for a single day; and so he despaired completely of their help. Finally he turned to God for help and began humbly to call upon the merits of blessed Francis along the way, in the house, or wherever he might be. And thus it came about that within a short space of time he was restored to complete health through God's grace and the merits of blessed Francis.[81]

145 A certain brother who was living under the obedience of our order in the Marches of Ancona was suffering from a very serious infection in the lumbar region or in the region of the ribs, so much so that he had already been given up by the doctors because of the severity of his disease. He then begged the minister provincial under whose obedience he was living to grant him permission to go visit the place where the body of our most blessed father is buried, trusting that he would obtain the grace of a cure through the merits of the saint. But his minister forbade him to go, fearing that he would suffer greater harm from the fatigue of the journey on account of the snow and rain at that time. But while the brother felt a little disturbed over the refusal of permission, one night the holy father Francis stood at his side, saying: "Son, be not disturbed any more about this, but take off the fur coat you are wearing and throw away the plaster and the bandage that is over the plaster and observe your Rule, and you will be delivered." Rising in the morning, he did everything according to Francis' command, and he gave thanks to God for a sudden deliverance.[82]

OF THE CLEANSING OF LEPERS

146   At San Severino in the Marches of Ancona a certain young man named Acto, who was covered all over with leprosy, was considered a leper by all in accordance with the verdict of the doctors. All his limbs were swollen and enlarged, and because of the distention and puffed up condition of his veins he saw everything awry. He could not walk, but lying as he did continuously in his sickbed, he caused his parents sorrow and grief. His father, tortured daily as he was with his son's suffering, did not know what to do about him. At length it came into his heart to commend his son by all means to blessed Francis, and he said to his son: "Son, do you wish to vow yourself to St. Francis, who everywhere is renowned for his miracles, that it might please him to free you from your illness?" He replied: "I want to, father." The father immediately had paper brought and, after he had measured his son's stature in height and girth, he said: "Raise yourself up, son, and vow yourself to blessed Francis, and after he has cured you, you shall bring him a candle as tall as you are every year as long as you live." At the command of his father he rose up as well as he could, and joining his hands, he began humbly to invoke blessed Francis' compassion. Accordingly, after he had taken up the paper measure and completed his prayer, he was immediately cured of his leprosy; and getting up and giving glory to God and to blessed Francis, he began to walk with joy.[83] In the city of Fano, a certain young man named Bonushomo, who was considered paralyzed and leprous by all the doctors, was devoutly offered to blessed Francis by his parents. He was cleansed from the leprosy and cured of his paralysis and made completely well.[84]

OF THE CURING OF THE DUMB AND THE DEAF

147   At Città della Pieve there was a very poor beggar boy who was completely dumb and deaf from his birth. He had a tongue that was very short and mutilated, so much so that it seemed to those who had examined it many times that it had been cut off. One evening he came to the house of a certain man of the city who was called Mark, and by means of signs, as is customary with the mute, he begged shelter from him. He leaned his head sideways, his jaw against his hand, so that it could be understood that he wanted to be sheltered with him for the night. But the man took him into his house with great happiness and willingly kept him with him, for the boy knew how to be a competent servant. He was an ingenious young man, for, though he had been deaf and dumb from the cradle, he understood by signs what was commanded him. One night when the man was at supper with his wife and the boy was waiting on them, the man said to his wife: "I would consider it the greatest miracle if the blessed Francis would give hearing and speech to this boy."

148   And he added: "I vow to the Lord God that if the blessed Francis should deign to work this miracle, I will, for love of him, hold this boy most dear and provide for him as long as he lives." Wonderful indeed! When the vow had been made, the boy immediately spoke and said: "St. Francis lives." And then looking about, he again said: "I see St. Francis standing on high and he is coming to give me speech." And the boy added: "What therefore shall I say to the people?" Then that man arose, rejoicing and exulting greatly, and he made known to all the people what had happened. All those who had seen the boy

before when he could not speak came running, and, filled with admiration and wonder, they humbly gave praise to God and to blessed Francis. The boy's tongue grew and became adapted for speech, and he began to utter properly formed words as though he had always been speaking.[85]

149 Another boy, by the name of Villa, could not speak or walk. His mother made a waxen image in fulfillment of a vow and took it with reverence to the place where the blessed father Francis is buried. When she returned home, she found her son walking and speaking.[86] A certain man, in the diocese of Perugia, had lost completely the faculty of speech. He always kept his mouth open, gaping horribly and in great distress, for his throat was much swollen and puffed up. When he had come to the place where the most holy body is buried and wished to go up the steps to the tomb, he vomited much blood, and completely relieved, he began to speak and to close and open his mouth as was necessary.[87]

150 A certain woman suffered such great pain in her throat that from the excessive burning her tongue clung dried to her palate. She could not speak, nor eat, nor drink. Plasters were applied and medicines used, but she felt no relief from her infirmity with all these things. Finally, she vowed herself in her heart to St. Francis, for she could not speak, and suddenly her flesh broke open and there came from her throat a small round stone which she took in her hand and showed to everyone nearby, and she was soon completely healed.[88] In the city of Greccio there was a certain young man who had lost his hearing, his memory, and his speech, and he could not understand or perceive anything. But his parents, who had great faith in St. Francis, vowed the young man to him with humble devotion; when the vow had been fulfilled, he was most abundantly endowed with the senses he had lacked through the favor of the most holy and glorious father Francis.

To the praise, glory, and honor
of Jesus Christ our Lord,
whose kingdom and empire endure
firm and immoveable forever and ever
Amen

EPILOGUE

151   We have said a few things about the miracles of our most blessed father Francis and have omitted many more things, leaving to those who wish to follow in his footsteps the task of seeking out the grace of a new blessing so that he who has most gloriously renewed the whole world by his word and example, his life and teaching, may always deign to water with new showers of super-celestial gifts the minds of those who love the name of the Lord. I beg, for the love of the poor crucified one and through his sacred wounds, which the blessed father Francis bore in his body, that all who read these things, who see and hear them, may be mindful of me, a sinner, before God. Amen.

> *Benediction and honor*[89] and all praise be *to the only wise God*[90] who always works most wisely *all things in all*[91] unto his glory. Amen. Amen. Amen.[92]

PART II

The Second Life of St. Francis
by
Thomas of Celano

THE SECOND LIFE OF ST. FRANCIS

PROLOGUE

In the Name of our Lord Jesus Christ. Amen

To the Minister General of
the Order of Friars Minor

HERE BEGINS THE PROLOGUE

1   It has pleased the entire holy assembly of the past general chapter[1] and you, Most Reverend Father,[2] not without the dispensation of divine wisdom, to enjoin upon our littleness that we set down in writing for the consolation of those living and for a remembrance for those to come the deeds and also the words of our glorious father Francis, in as much as they were better known to us than to the rest because of our close association with him and our mutual intimacy.[3] We hasten therefore to obey with humble devotion the holy injunctions which we may not pass by; but we are struck with just fear when we consider more seriously the weakness of our abilities, lest so worthy a matter, in not being treated by us as it deserves, may derive from us what may be displeasing to the rest. For we fear that things that are worthy of all sweetness of taste may be rendered insipid by the unworthiness of those who dispense them, and so our efforts will be attributed to our presumption rather than to obedience. For if the examination of the result of our great labor pertained only to your good pleasure, blessed father, and it were not opportune for it to be made public, we would very gratefully accept instruction from your correction or happiness from your confirmation. For who, amid such diversity of words and actions, would be able to so weigh everything on the scales of a pre-

cise examination that all who hear them would be *of one mind*[4] concerning the single points? But since we are seeking with a single heart the benefit of all and of each one, we suggest that they who read these things interpret them kindly and bear with the simplicity of the narration or properly direct it so that reverence for him about whom these things tell may be preserved intact. Our memory, dulled as it is by length of time, like that of untrained men, cannot reach the flights of his subtle words and the wonders of his deeds, for the agility of a practiced mind could hardly comprehend these things if it were confronted with them. Therefore, let the authority of him who has repeatedly commanded us excuse before all the faults of our lack of skill.

2   This little work contains in the first place certain wonderful facts about the conversion of St. Francis that were not included in the legends that were composed some time earlier because they had not come to the notice of the author. Then we intend to portray and to declare with careful zeal what was *the good and acceptable and perfect will*[5] of Francis both for himself and for his followers in every practice of heavenly discipline and in zeal for the highest perfection which he ever had toward God in his sacred affections, and toward men in his examples. Certain miracles are inserted, as occasion for inserting them presents itself. We describe in a plain and simple way the things that occur to us, wishing to accommodate ourselves to the slower ones and also to please the more learned, if we can.[6]

We beg, therefore, kindest father, that you will not despise the small gift of this work which we have put together with no little effort,[7] but will deign to consecrate it by your blessing, correcting what is in error and removing what is superfluous, so that the things that are approved as well said by your learned judgment may indeed grow together with your name *Crescentius* and be multiplied in Christ. Amen.

THUS ENDS THE PROLOGUE

BOOK ONE

OF FRANCIS' CONVERSION

CHAPTER I

*How he was first called John and afterwards Francis;
how his mother prophecied concerning him, and he
himself also foretold what would come to pass in his
regard; and of his patience in imprisonment*

3   Francis, the servant and friend of the Most
High, to whom divine providence gave this name so
that by means of this singular and unusual name[2]
the knowledge of his ministry might become known
to the whole world, was called John by his mother,
when, being *born again of water and the Holy Spirit*,[3]
he was made a child of grace from a child of wrath.[4]

This woman, a friend of all goodness, bore about
her a certain image in her conduct of the virtue of
that holy Elizabeth, enjoying as she did a certain
privilege of resemblance to her both in the giving of
a name to her son[5] and in her spirit of prophecy.[6]
For while her neighbors were wondering at the nobility of soul and the modesty of Francis, she would say,
as though prompted by divine guidance: "What do
you think this my son will turn out to be? Know that
he will be a son of God by the grace of his merits."

This indeed was the opinion of not a few whom the
youthful Francis pleased by reason of his good incli-
nations. He always put away from himself everything
that could be regarded as evil by anyone and in his
youth his manners were so refined that it seemed
that he was not born of the parents from whom he

was said to have been born. The name *John* referred to the work of the ministry which he would undertake;[7] the name *Francis* referred to the spread of his fame, which, after he had been fully converted to God, quickly spread everywhere. He considered the feast of John the Baptist to be more illustrious than the feasts of all the other saints,[8] for the dignity of his name left a mark of mystic virtue upon him. *Among those born of women there has not arisen a greater than John;*[9] among the founders of religious orders there has not arisen a more perfect one than Francis. This is an observation that is worthy to be heralded about.

4   John prophecied enclosed within the hidden places of his mother's womb;[10] Francis prophecied future events enclosed within the prison of this world while he was still ignorant of the divine counsel. Indeed, once when there was a bloody battle between the citizens of Perugia and those of Assisi, Francis was made captive with several others and endured the squalors of a prison.[11] His fellow captives were consumed with sorrow, bemoaning miserably their imprisonment; Francis rejoiced in the Lord, laughed at his chains and despised them. His grieving companions resented his happiness and considered him insane and mad. Francis replied prophetically: "Why do you think I rejoice? There is another consideration, for I will yet be venerated as a saint throughout the whole world." And so it has truly come about; everything he said has been fulfilled.

There was at that time among his fellow prisoners a certain proud and completely unbearable knight whom the rest were determined to shun, but Francis' patience was not disturbed. He put up with the unbearable knight and brought the others to peace with him. Capable of every grace, a chosen vessel of virtues, he poured out his gifts on all sides.

CHAPTER II

Of a poor knight whom Francis clothed; and of the vision of his call which he had while he was in the world

5   Freed from his chains a short time later, he became more kindly toward the needy. He now resolved not to turn his face away from any poor man,[12] who in begging asked for the love of God.[13] One day he met a knight who was poor and well nigh naked; moved by pity he gave him for Christ's sake the costly garments he was wearing. How did he conduct himself any differently from the way the most holy Martin conducted himself,[14] except that, while both had the same purpose and both did the same deed, they differed in the way they acted. Francis first gave his garments before the rest of his things; Martin first gave up the rest of his things and then finally his garments. Both lived poor and feeble[15] in this world; both entered heaven rich.[16] The latter, a knight, but poor, cut his garment in two to clothe a poor man; the former, not a knight, but rich, clothed a poor knight with his whole garment. Both, having fulfilled the command of Christ,[17] merited to be visited by Christ in a vision; one was praised for his perfection, the other was graciously invited to fulfill what was yet lacking.

6   Now Francis was soon shown in a vision a splendid palace in which he saw various military apparatus and a most beautiful bride.[18] In the dream Francis was called by name and enticed by the promise of all these things. He attempted, therefore, to go to Apulia to win knighthood; and after he had made the necessary preparations in a lavish manner, he hurried on to gain that degree of military honors. A carnal spirit prompted him to make a carnal interpretation of the dream he had had, while a far

more glorious interpretation lay hidden in the treasures of God's wisdom.

Accordingly, while he was sleeping one night, someone addressed him a second time in a vision and questioned him solicitously as to whether he intended to go. When he had told his purpose to him who was asking and said that he was going to Apulia[19] to fight, he was asked earnestly who could do better for him, the servant or the Lord. And Francis said: "The Lord." The other answered: "Why then are you seeking the servant in place of the Lord?" And Francis said: "Lord, what do you want me to do?" And the Lord said to him: "Go back to the place of your birth for through me your vision will have a spiritual fulfillment." He went back without delay, for he had already become a model of obedience and, giving up his own will, he became a Paul in place of a Saul. Saul is thrown to the ground and heavy blows beget sweet words. Francis, however, changes his carnal weapons into spiritual ones and in place of military glory he receives the knighthood of God. Therefore to the many who were astounded at his unusual happiness he said that he was going to be a great prince.[20]

CHAPTER III

How a band of youths made him their leader, so that he might feed them; and of the change that came over him

7 Francis began to be changed into a perfect man and to become other than his former self. After he had returned home, *the sons of Babylon*[21] followed him and dragged him unwilling to other pursuits than those he intended to follow. For a band of young people of Assisi, who had formerly considered him their leader in their vain pursuits,[22] came

to him now to invite him to their social banquets which always served their wantonness and buffoonery. He was chosen by them to be their leader, for, since they had often experienced his liberality, they knew without a doubt that he would pay the expenses for them all. They gave him obedience so that they might fill their bellies and they endured being subject so that they might be filled. He did not spurn the honor, lest he be thought avaricious, and amid his holy meditations he was mindful of the obligations of courtesy. He prepared a sumptuous banquet, doubled the dainty foods; filled to vomiting with these things, they defiled the streets of the city with drunken singing. Francis followed them, carrying a *staff in his hands*[23] as the master of revels; but little by little he withdrew himself bodily from them, for he was already totally deaf to all these things and was singing in his heart to the Lord.

He was then filled with such divine sweetness, as he himself said, that he became speechless and was totally unable to move from the place. Then a certain spiritual affection took hold of him and carried him away to things invisible, by virtue of which he judged all earthly things to be of no importance but entirely worthless. Stupendous indeed is the condescension of Christ, which gives the greatest gifts to those who are doing the least and *in a flood of many waters*[24] preserves and advances the things that are his. For Christ fed the multitudes with bread and fishes,[25] neither did he repel sinners from his banquet. When they sought him to make him king, he took to flight and *went up to the mountain to pray.*[26] These were the mysteries of God Francis was learning; and ignorant as he was he was being led unto perfect knowledge.

CHAPTER IV

How Francis, clad in a poor man's garments, ate with the poor at St. Peter's; and of his offering there

8   But already he was the chief lover of the poor, already his holy beginnings gave indication of what he was to be perfectly. Accordingly, frequently stripping himself, he clothed the poor, like unto whom he was striving with his whole heart to become, though as yet he had not put his desire into execution.

When he was on a pilgrimage to Rome, he put off his fine garments out of love of poverty, clothed himself with the garments of a certain poor man, and joyfully sat among the poor in the vestibule before the church of St. Peter, where there were many poor, and considering himself one of them, he ate eagerly with them. Many times he would have done a similar thing had he not been held back by shame before those who knew him. Astounded when he came to the altar of the prince of the apostles that the offerings of those who came there were so meager, he threw down a handful of coins at that place, thus indicating that he whom God honored above the rest should be honored by all in a special way.

Several times he also gave poor priests church ornaments, and he showed due honor to all clerics even down to the lowest grade. For, as one about to take upon himself the apostolic mission[27] and one wholly and entirely Catholic, he was filled from the beginning with reverence toward the ministers and the ministry of God.[28]

CHAPTER V

How, while Francis was praying, the devil showed him a woman; and of the answer God gave him and of his treatment of the lepers

9 Thus already beneath his secular garb he wore a religious spirit and, withdrawing from public to solitary places, he was often admonished by a visitation of the Holy Spirit.[29] For he was carried away and enticed by that perfect sweetness which poured over him with such abundance from the very beginning that it never departed from him as long as he lived.

But while he frequented hidden places as more suitable to prayer, the devil tried to drive him away from such places by an evil suggestion. He put into his mind a certain woman who was monstrously hunchbacked, an inhabitant of his city, and who was a hideous sight to all. He threatened to make him like her if he did not leave off what he had begun. But *strengthened in the Lord*,[30] he rejoiced to hear a reply of salvation and grace: "Francis," God said to him in spirit, "what you have loved carnally and vainly you should now exchange for spiritual things, and taking the *bitter for sweet*,[31] despise yourself, if you wish to acknowledge me; for you will have a taste for what I speak of even if the order is reversed." Immediately he was compelled to obey the divine command and was led to actual experience.[32]

For among all the unhappy spectacles of the world Francis naturally abhorred lepers; but one day he met a leper while he was riding near Assisi. Though the leper caused him no small disgust and horror, nevertheless, lest like a transgressor of a commandment he should break his given word, he got off the horse and prepared to kiss the leper. But when the leper put out his hand as though to receive something, he received money along with a kiss. And immediately mounting his horse, Francis looked here and there about him; but though the plain lay open and clear on all sides, and there were no obstacles about, he could not see the leper anywhere.

Filled with wonder and joy as a result, after a few days he took care to do the same thing again. He went to the dwelling places of the lepers, and after he had given each leper some money, he kissed his hand and his mouth. Thus he exchanged the bitter for the sweet, and manfully prepared himself to carry out the rest.

CHAPTER VI

Of the image of the crucified that spoke to him, and of the honor he paid it

10   Changed now perfectly in heart and soon to be changed in body too, he was walking one day near the church of St. Damian, which had nearly fallen to ruin and was abandoned by everyone. Led by the Spirit, he went in and fell down before the crucifix in devout and humble supplication; and smitten by unusual visitations, he found himself other than he had been when he entered. While he was thus affected, something unheard of before happened to him: the painted image of Christ[33] crucified moved its lips and spoke. Calling him by name it said: "Francis, go, repair my house, which, as you see, is falling completely to ruin." Trembling, Francis was not a little amazed and became almost deranged by these words. He prepared himself to obey and gave himself completely to the fulfillment of this command. But since he felt that the change he had undergone was beyond expression, it is becoming that we should be silent about what he could not express. From then on compassion for the crucified was rooted in

144

his holy soul, and, as it can be piously supposed, the stigmata of the venerable passion were deeply imprinted in his heart, though not as yet upon his flesh.

11   What a wonderful thing and a thing unheard of in our times! Who is not astonished at these things? Who has ever heard like things? Who would doubt that Francis, returning now to his native city,[34] appeared crucified, when, though he had not yet outwardly completely renounced the world, Christ had spoken to him from the wood of the cross in a new and unheard of miracle? From that hour on, his *soul was melted* when his beloved *spoke* to him.[35] A little later,[36] the love of his heart made itself manifest by the wounds of his body. And from then on he could never keep himself from weeping, even bewailing in a loud voice the passion of Christ which was always, as it were, before his mind. He filled the ways with his sighs. He permitted himself no consolation, remembering the wounds of Christ. He met a certain intimate friend, to whom he made known the cause of his grief, and immediately his friend was moved to tears.

Indeed, he never forgot to be concerned about that holy image, and he never passed over its command with negligence. Right away he gave a certain priest some money that he might buy a lamp and oil, lest the sacred image should be deprived of the due honor of a light even for a moment. Then he diligently hastened to do the rest and devoted his untiring efforts toward repairing that church. For, though the divine command concerned itself with the church that Christ had *purchased with his own blood*,[37] Francis would not suddenly become perfect, but he was to pass gradually from the flesh to the spirit.

CHAPTER VII

Of his father's persecution and of that of his brother according to the flesh

12   But now that Francis was giving himself to works of piety, his carnally minded father[38] persecuted him and judging his service of Christ to be madness, he hurled curses at him everywhere. Therefore the servant of God called to his aid a certain low-born and quite simple man, and putting him in the place of his father, he begged him that when his father hurled curses at him he should on the contrary bless him. In truth he turned the word of the prophet to action and showed by deeds what was the meaning of that saying: *They will curse and thou wilt bless.*[39]

At the urging of the bishop of the city, a very pious man, who informed him that it was not lawful to spend anything for sacred uses that had been gotten unlawfully, the man of God gave up to his father the money he had wanted to spend for restoring the church mentioned above.[40] In the hearing of many who had come together, he said: "From now on I can freely say *Our Father who art in heaven,* not *father Peter Bernardone,*[41] to whom, behold, I give up not only the money, but all my clothes too. I will therefore go naked to the Lord." O generous spirit, to whom Christ alone is sufficient! The man of God was then found to be wearing a hair shirt beneath his clothing, rejoicing in the reality of virtues rather than in mere appearances.

His brother according to the flesh,[42] after the manner of his father, pursued him with venomous words. On a certain morning in winter time, that perverse man saw Francis at prayer clothed in poor garments and shivering with the cold; and he said to a certain fellow townsman: "Tell Francis to sell

146

you a pennysworth of sweat." But hearing this, the man of God was filled with gladness and answered smiling: "Indeed, I will sell my sweat more dearly to my Lord." There is nothing more true, for he received not only a hundredfold but even more than a thousandfold in this life, and he won not only for himself but for many others too eternal life hereafter.

CHAPTER VIII

Of the bashfulness Francis conquered and of his prophecy concerning the Poor Virgins

13   Francis strove then to change completely his former delicate way of living and to bring his body, used to luxury, back to the goodness of nature. One day the man of God went through Assisi to beg oil to light up the lamps of the church of St. Damian which he was repairing at that time. And seeing a large group of men playing before the house he wanted to enter, he was filled with bashfulness and retraced his steps. But after he had directed his noble spirit to heaven, he rebuked himself for cowardice and passed judgment upon himself. Immediately he returned to the house and freely explained the cause of his bashfulness; and, in a kind of spiritual intoxication, he begged in French for oil and got it. Most fervently he stirred up everyone for the work of that church and speaking in a loud voice in French, he prophecied before all that there would be a monastery there of holy virgins of Christ. For always when he was filled with the ardor of the Holy Spirit, he burst forth in French to speak his ardent words, foreknowing that he would be especially honored by that people and venerated with a special reverence by them.[43]

CHAPTER IX

How Francis begged food from door to door

14   From the time when he began to serve the common Lord of all, Francis always loved to do common things, shunning in all things singularity, which is soiled with the foulness of all vices. For, while he was pouring out his sweat in the work at that church concerning which he had received a command from Christ, and when he had been changed from a person of extreme delicacy to a lowly and patient laborer, the priest to whose care the church pertained, seeing that Francis was worn down by constant labor and moved to pity, began to give him daily some special food, though it was not dainty since he was poor. Commending the discretion of the priest and welcoming his kindness, Francis nevertheless said to himself: "You will not find a priest everywhere to provide these things always for you. This is not the life of a man who professes poverty. It is not proper for you to get accustomed to such things; gradually you will return to the things you have despised, and you will run again after delicacies. Arise now without delay, and beg from door to door for foods of mixed kinds." He therefore begged for prepared foods from door to door throughout Assisi, and when he saw his bowl full of all kinds of scraps, he was struck with horror; but mindful of God and conquering himself, he ate the food with joy of spirit. Love softens all things[44] and makes every bitter thing sweet.

CHAPTER X

Of Brother Bernard's renunciation of his goods

15   A certain Bernard of the city of Assisi, who was afterwards a son of perfection,[45] since he was

planning to perfectly despise the world after the example of the man of God, humbly sought his advice. He therefore consulted him, saying: "If some one, father, possessed for a long time the goods of some lord and did not want to keep them any longer, what would be the more perfect thing to do with them?" The man of God answered that all of them should be given back to the lord from whom he had received them. And Bernard said to him: "Everything I have, I recognize as having been given me by God, and at your advice I stand ready to give them back to him." "If you wish to prove what you say by deeds," the holy man said, "let us go early in the morning to the church and taking the book of the Gospel, let us seek counsel from Christ."[46] They therefore entered the church early in the morning, and after offering up a prayer, they opened the book of the Gospel, proposing to follow what counsel should first appear. They opened the book and Christ showed them his counsel in it: *If thou wilt be perfect, go, sell what thou hast, and give to the poor.*[47] A second time they did this and *Take nothing for your journey* occurred.[48] They did the same thing a third time and they found: *If anyone wishes to come after me, let him deny himself.*[49] Without delay Bernard fulfilled all these things and he did not transgress any of this advice, not even a single iota of it.

In a short time many others were converted from the corroding cares of the world and returned *into their country*[50] under the guidance of Francis, unto infinite good. It would be long to tell of each one how they all attained *the prize* of their *heavenly call.*[51]

CHAPTER XI

Of the parable Francis spoke before the pope

16   At the time when Francis presented himself along with his followers before Pope Innocent to ask for a rule of life,[52] the pope, a man endowed with the greatest discretion, seeing that his proposed way of life was beyond his powers, said to him: "Pray, son, to Christ, that he may show us his will through you, so that, knowing his will, we may more securely give assent to your pious desires." The holy man agreed to the command of the supreme shepherd and hastened confidently to Christ; he prayed earnestly and devoutly exhorted his companions to pray to God. But why should we speak at length? He obtained an answer by prayer and reported the news of salvation to his sons. The familiar talk of Christ is made known in parables. "Francis," he said, "speak thus to the pope. A certain woman who was poor but very beautiful lived in a certain desert. A certain king loved her because of her very great beauty; he gladly married her and begot very handsome sons by her. When they had grown to adulthood and been brought up nobly, their mother said to them: 'Do not be ashamed, my loved ones, in that you are poor, for you are all sons of that king. Go gladly to his court and ask him for whatever you need.' Hearing this they were in admiration and rejoiced, and buoyed up by the assurance of their royal origin, they regarded want as riches, knowing that they would be heirs. They boldly presented themselves to the king and they did not fear the face of him whose likeness they bore. Recognizing his own likeness in them, the king wondered and asked whose sons they were. When they said they were the sons of that poor woman living in the desert, the king embraced them and said: 'You are

my sons and heirs; fear not. For if strangers are fed at my table, it is all the more just that I see to it that those be fed to whom my entire heritage is reserved by right.' The king then ordered the woman to send all the sons he had begotten to the court to be provided for." The saint was made happy and glad by the parable and reported the holy message to the pope.

17   This woman was Francis, because he was fruitful in many sons, not because of any softness in his actions. The desert was the world, untilled and barren at that time in the teaching of virtues.[53] The handsome and numerous progeny of sons was the great multitude of brothers adorned with every virtue. The king was the Son of God, to whom they bore a resemblance by their holy poverty. And they received nourishment at the table of the king, despising all shame over their meanness; for, content with imitating Christ and living by alms, they knew they would be happy amid the reproaches of the world.

The lord pope wondered at the parable proposed to him and recognized without doubting that Christ had spoken in man. He recalled a certain vision he had had a few days before, which, he affirmed, under the guidance of the Holy Spirit, would be fulfilled in this man. He had seen in his sleep the Lateran basilica about to fall to ruin, when a certain religious, small and despised, propped it up by putting his own back under it lest it fall. "Surely," he said, "this is that man who, by his works and by the teaching of Christ, will give support to the Church." For this reason the lord pope readily gave in to the petition of Francis. Therefore, filled with love of God he always showed a special love toward the servant of Christ. And therefore he quickly granted what had been asked, and he promised to grant even greater things than these.[54] Francis, therefore, by reason of the authority granted him,[55] began to scatter the seeds of virtue, going about *the towns and villages*[56] preaching fervently.

CHAPTER XII

Of Francis' love for the Portiuncula, of the life of the brothers there, and of the love of the Blessed Mother for it

18 The servant of God Francis, a person small in stature, humble in mind, a *minor* by profession, while yet in the world chose out of the world for himself and his followers a *little portion,* in as much as he could not serve Christ without having something of the world. For it was not without the foreknowledge of a divine disposition that from ancient times that place was called the *Portiuncula*[57] which was to fall to the lot of those who wished to have nothing whatsoever of the world. For there had also been built in that place a church of the virgin mother who merited by her singular humility to be, after her son, the head of all the saints. In this church the Order of Friars Minor had its beginning;[58] there, as on a firm foundation, when their number had grown, the noble fabric of the order arose.[59] The holy man loved this place above all others; this place he commanded his brothers to venerate with a special reverence;[60] this place he willed to be preserved as a model of humility and highest poverty for their order, reserving the ownership of it to others, and keeping only the use of it for himself and his brothers.[61]

19 The most rigid discipline was observed there in all things, both as to silence and work and as to the other ordinances of the rule.⁶² To no one was admittance there granted except to specially appointed brothers who, coming from all parts of the world, the holy man wanted to be devoted to God and perfect in every way. So too admittance was prohibited to every secular person. He did not want the brothers dwelling there, who were restricted severely as to number, to have *itching ears*⁶³ for news of worldly things, lest, with their meditation on heavenly things interrupted, they should be drawn to the business of inferior things through those who spread rumors. It was not permitted to anyone there to utter idle words or repeat those uttered by others. If anyone at any time did this, he was taught through punishment to be careful not to let it happen again. Those who dwelt in this place were occupied with the divine praises without interruption day and night, and fragrant with a wonderful odor, they led an angelic life.

This was as it should be. For, according to what the old inhabitants use to say, the place was also called St. Mary of the Angels. The happy father used to say that it had been revealed to him by God that the Blessed Mother loved this church, among all the other churches built in her honor throughout the world, with a special love; for this reason the holy man loved it above all others.

CHAPTER XIII

Of a certain vision

20 A certain brother, given to God, had a certain vision before his conversion about this church which is worth mentioning. He saw a whole host of men in his vision who had been struck blind kneeling about in this church, their faces turned toward heaven. They were all stretching their hands upwards and crying with tearful voices to God, asking for mercy and light. And behold, a great splendor from heaven approached and spread itself over them all, giving light to each one and the healing they sought.

CHAPTER XIV

Of the rigor of discipline

21   The zealous knight of Christ never spared his body, but exposed it to every hurt both in deed and in word, as though it were something separate from himself. If someone were to count the things this man suffered, he would find that they exceed what is told in that passage of the Apostle where the sufferings of the holy ones are recounted.[64] But that whole first school so subjected themselves to every inconvenience that it was thought an evil thing if someone refreshed himself in anything except in the consolation of the Holy Spirit. For since they girded themselves and clothed themselves with iron hoops and corslets and tried themselves with many vigils and fasts, they would very often have succumbed had they not relaxed the rigor of such abstinence at the earnest advice of their kind shepherd.[65]

CHAPTER XV

Of the discretion of St. Francis

22   One night one of the sheep cried out while the rest were sleeping: "I am dying, brothers, I am dying of hunger." Immediately the good shepherd got up and hastened to give the ailing sheep the proper remedy. He commanded the table to be set, though it was filled with poor things, and, as is often the case, where wine was lacking water took its place.

First he himself began to eat, and then he invited the rest of the brothers to share this duty of charity, lest that brother should waste away from shame. When they had eaten the food with fear of the Lord, the father wove a long parable for his sons about the virtue of discretion, lest something should be lacking in the offices of charity. He commanded them always to give to the Lord a sacrifice seasoned with salt, and carefully admonished each one to consider his own strength in the service of God. He said that to deprive the body indiscreetly of what it needs was a sin just the same as it is a sin to give it superfluous things at the prompting of gluttony. And he added: "Know, dearest brothers, that what I have done in eating, I have done by dispensation, not by desire, because fraternal charity commanded it. Let this charity be an example to you, not the food, for the latter ministers to gluttony, the former to the spirit."

CHAPTER XVI

How Francis foresaw the future and how he committed his order to the Church of Rome; and of a certain vision

23 The holy father, making progress continually in the merits of life and in virtue, while the tree of his order was everywhere spreading by a multiplying of its members and was stretching its branches laden wonderfully with fruits to the ends of the earth, began to meditate alone more often how that new plant might be preserved and how it might increase, bound together by the bond of unity. He then saw many raging savagely against his little flock, like wolves, and men *grown old in evil days*[66] taking occasion from its mere youthfulness to cause it harm.[67] He foresaw that even among his own sons

certain things contrary to holy peace and unity would occur and he did not doubt that, as often happens among the elect, some would rebel, *puffed up by* their *mere human mind*[68] and in spirit would be prepared for quarrelling and prone to scandals.

24   While the man of God revolved these and similar things in his mind more often, one night while he was asleep he saw this vision. He saw a little black hen, much like a tame dove, whose legs and feet were covered with feathers. She had innumerable chicks which pressed close around her, but they could not all get under her wings. The man of God, *arising from sleep,*[69] took to heart what he had meditated on, and became his own interpreter of his vision. "The hen," he said, "is I, small as I am in stature and naturally dark, who ought to be attended through innocence of life by dove-like simplicity, which easily wings its way to heaven, as is most rare in this world. The chicks are my brothers, multiplied in number and in grace,[70] whom Francis' strength does not suffice to defend from the disturbances of men and from *the contradiction of tongues.*[71]

"I will go, therefore, and I will commend them to the holy Roman church, by the rod of whose power those of ill-will will be struck down and the children of God will enjoy full freedom everywhere unto the increase of eternal salvation. From this the sons will acknowledge the kind gifts of their mother and always embrace her venerable footsteps with special devotion. Under her protection, no evil will befall the order, nor will the *son of Belial*[72] pass with impunity over the vineyard of the Lord. Our holy mother herself will emulate the glory of our poverty and will not permit the fame of our humility to be clouded over by the mist of pride. She will keep unbroken in us the bonds of charity and peace, striking the dissenters with her strictest censure. The holy observance of Gospel purity will constantly flourish in her sight, and she will not permit the fragrance of their life to vanish even for an hour." This was the whole intention of the holy man of God in commending himself to the Church; these were the most holy testimonies to the foresight of the man of God in commending himself against the time to come.

CHAPTER XVII

How he asked for the Lord of Ostia as his pope

25   Coming therefore to Rome, the man of God was received with great devotedness by the lord pope Honorius[73] and all the cardinals. For what had been reported of him shone forth in his life and resounded on his tongue; under such conditions there is no room for disrespect. He preached before the pope and the cardinals with ready and fervent foresight, speaking without restraint whatever the spirit suggested. The mountains[74] were moved at his word, and great sighs rose from their innermost depths and bathed the inner man with tears.

When the sermon was finished and a few words spoken familiarly with the lord pope, Francis presented his petition thus: "As you know, my lord, access to such majesty as yours is not easily given to poor and despised men. You indeed hold the world in your hands and business of great importance does not permit you to attend to little afairs. Therefore I beg of the kindness of your holiness that you give me the lord of Ostia[75] as my pope, so that, saving always the dignity of your pre-eminence, the brothers may go to him in the time of need and obtain from him the benefits of his protection and rule."[76] Such a holy petition found favor in the eyes of the pope and soon he appointed the lord Hugo, bishop of Ostia at the time, over the order, as the man of God had asked. That holy cardinal accepted the flock committed to him, became its diligent guardian, its shepherd and its foster-child until his happy death.[77] To·this special subjection is due the prerogative of love and care which the holy Roman Church has never ceased to show to the Order of Friars Minor.[78]

THUS ENDS THE FIRST PART

BOOK TWO

26 To preserve the record of the outstanding accomplishments of our forefathers for the memory of their children is a mark of honor to the former and of love for the latter. For truly, those who have not seen the bodily presence of their forefathers are spurred on to good at least by their deeds and moved to better things when their memorable deeds bring back to mind their fathers separated from them by the passing of time. But the first and not the least fruit we derive therefrom is a knowledge of our own littleness, seeing how great was the abundance of their merits and how great the lack of our own. But I think Blessed Francis was a most holy mirror of the sanctity of the Lord and an image of his perfection.[1] All his words, I say, as well as his deeds are redolent of the divine, and if they be diligently examined by a humble disciple, they will imbue him with a wholesome discipline and make him docile to that highest philosophy.[2] Therefore, now that I have set down in humble style[3] and, as it were in passing, some things concerning him, I think it not superfluous to add a few things from the many whereby the saint may be commended and our slumbering affections stirred anew.[4]

CHAPTER I

27   The blessed father, borne up as he was above the things of this world by a certain exaltation, brought whatever is in the world into subjection by a wondrous power, for, always directing the eye of his intellect to the Supreme Light, he not only knew by divine revelation what was to be done, but he also foretold many things *in the spirit of prophecy,*[5] peered into the secrets of hearts, knew things from which he was absent, foresaw and foretold things that were yet to happen. Examples give proof of what we say.[6]

CHAPTER II

How Francis knew that one who was reputed holy was a fraud

28   There was a certain brother of extraordinary sanctity, as far as could be seen outwardly, outstanding in his life, yet quite singular. He spent all his time in prayer and he observed silence with such strictness that he was accustomed to confess not with words but with signs. He derived great ardor from the words of Scripture, and, after hearing them, he relished them with wonderful sweetness. Why should we give many details? He was considered thrice holy by all. The blessed father happened to come to that place and happened to see that brother and hear him called a saint. But when all were commending him and praising him, the father replied: "Leave off, brothers, and do not praise the things the

devil has fashioned in him. Know in truth that it is a temptation of the devil and a fraudulent deception. I am convinced of this and the greatest proof of it is that he does not want to confess." The brothers took this ill, especially the vicar of the saint.[7] "And how could it be true," they inquired, "that the workings of fraud could be concealed under so many signs of perfection?" The father said to them: "Let him be admonished to confess twice or once a week; if he does not do this, you will know that what I have said is true." The vicar took him aside and first joked familiarly with him, then commanded him to confess. He refused, and putting his finger into his ear and shaking his head, he indicated that he would not by any means confess. The brothers were silent, fearing the scandal of a false saint. After not many days, he left religion of his own accord, went back to the world, returned *to his vomit*.[8] Finally, redoubling his crimes, he was deprived at the same time of repentance and of life. Singularity is always to be avoided, for it is nothing else but a lovely precipice. Many singular persons have learned by experience that from singularity *they mount up to heaven, and they go down to the depths.*[9] Attend, on the other hand, to the power of devout confession, which not only makes a person holy, but also manifests his holiness.

CHAPTER III

A similar case in another brother. Against singularity

29   Something similar happened to another brother, Thomas of Spoleto by name. The opinion and firm conviction of all concerning him was that he was a saint. But his apostasy eventually proved the soundness of the judgment of the holy father about

him, namely, that he was a wicked man. He did not persevere long, for virtue sought by fraud does not last long. He left religion and died outside of it, and now he knows what he did.

CHAPTER IV

How Francis foretold the defeat of the Christians at Damietta

30   At the time when the Christian army was besieging Damietta[10] the holy man of God was present with some companions,[11] for they had crossed the sea in a desire for martyrdom. When therefore our soldiers were preparing to go into the fight on the day of the battle, hearing about it, the saint was deeply grieved. He said to his companion: "The Lord has showed me that if the battle takes place on such a day, it will not go well with the Christians. But if I tell them this, I will be considered a fool; if I am silent, I will not escape my conscience. What therefore seems best to you?" His companion answered, saying: "Consider it as nothing to be judged by men, for it is not only now that you will begin to be thought a fool.[12] Keep your conscience free from blame and fear God rather than men." The holy man therefore arose and approached the Christians with salutary warnings, forbidding the war, denouncing the reason for it. But truth was turned to ridicule, and they hardened their hearts and refused to be guided. They went, they joined battle, they fought, and our army was pressed hard by the enemy. In the very time of the battle, the holy man, in great suspense, made his companion go and watch the battle; and when he saw nothing the first or second time, he made him look a third time. And behold, the whole Christian army was turned to flight, and the battle ended in shame, not triumph.

So great was the number of soldiers lost in the disaster that six thousand were among the dead and captured. Compassion pressed upon the holy man over them, nor were they less regretful over the deed. But he mourned especially over the Spaniards, when he saw that their greater impetuosity in the battle had left but a few of them remaining.[13] Let the princes of the world know these things and let them know that *it is not easy to fight against God,*[14] that is, against the will of the Lord. Rashness generally ends in disaster, for since it relies on its own powers, it does not deserve help from heaven. But if victory is to be hoped for from on high, battles must be entrusted to the Spirit of God.

CHAPTER V

Of a brother whose secrets of heart Francis knew

31   At that time when the holy Francis returned from beyond the sea with Brother Leonard of Assisi as his companion, it happened that, weary and fatigued from the journey, he was riding on a donkey for a while. But his companion was following behind him, and not a little tired, he began to say within himself, giving way to a bit of humanness: "This man's parents and mine were not accustomed to play together as equals. Yet he is riding and I on foot am leading the donkey." While he was thinking this, the holy man got down from the donkey and said: "Brother, it is not right that I should ride, and you go on foot, for you were more noble and more powerful than I in the world." That brother was astounded at this and, filled with shame, he knew that he had been found out by the holy man. He cast himself at his feet and, bathed in tears, he made known his thought to him and begged his pardon.

CHAPTER VI

Of the brother over whom Francis saw a devil, and against those who withdraw themselves from the community

32   There was another brother who was quite celebrated before man and even more celebrated through grace before God. The father of all envy envied this man because of his virtues and plotted to cut down this tree that had already reached the heavens and to snatch away the crown from his hands; he went about, overturned, battered, and sifted what belonged to the brother to see if he could put some suitable obstacle before him. And so he put into his mind a desire for solitude, under the appearance of greater perfection, so that he might in the end rush upon him when he was alone and make him fall more quickly, and that, falling alone, he would have no one to lift him up.[15] Why add more details? The brother separated himself from the religion of his brothers and wandered about the world as a stranger and pilgrim. From the tunic of his habit he made a small tunic, with the capuch not sewed to the tunic, and went about thus throughout the region, despising himself in all things. But it happened that when he was going about in this way God's consolation was withdrawn from him and he was assailed with a storm of temptations. *The waters* came *in even unto* his *soul*[16] and both the inner and the outer man were made desolate, and he went about like *a bird* that makes *haste to the snare.*[17] And now he was brought close to the abyss and was being borne along to a precipice, as it were, when the eye of a fatherly providence, pitying the wretched man, *looked upon him for good.*[18] Thus he recovered his understanding through affliction, and returning to himself, he said: "Return, miserable

one, to religion, for there is your salvation." He did not wait, but immediately arose and hurried back to the bosom of his mother.

33   But when that brother came to Siena to the place of the brothers, St. Francis was there. Astonishing to say, as soon as the saint saw him, he fled from him and hurriedly shut himself up in his cell. The brothers, excited, inquired the reason for his flight. He said to them: "Why do you wonder at my flight, paying no attention to the cause? I fled to the protection of prayer to deliver the erring one. I saw in my son what rightly displeased me; but behold, now, by the grace of my Christ, all delusion has departed." The brother knelt down and admitted his guilt with shame. The holy man said to him: "May the Lord forgive you, Brother. But beware for the future that you do not separate yourself from your order and from your brothers under the plea of holiness." That brother then became a friend of the congregation and of the community, being especially attached to those communities where regular observance was more in evidence. O how great are the works of the Lord *in the council of the just and in the congregation!*[19] Indeed, in it those who are troubled are restrained, the crushed lifted up, the tepid spurred on; in it *iron sharpeneth iron,*[20] and *a brother that is helped by his brother* is set up *like a strong city;*[21] and, though you cannot see Jesus because of the worldly throng, the throng of heavenly spirits does not in any way hinder you. Only do not flee, and, faithful unto death, you *will receive the crown of life.*[22]

34   Not long thereafter something not dissimilar happened with another brother. One of the brothers would not submit himself to the vicar of St. Francis, but followed another brother as his own particular

superior. But after he had been admonished by the saint, who was present, through an intermediary person, he immediately threw himself at the feet of the vicar and, spurning his first superior, he submitted himself to the one the saint had appointed as his prelate. But the saint sighed deeply and said to his companion whom he had sent as intermediary: "I saw a devil, Brother, on the back of that disobedient brother, clutching him by the neck. Subdued by such a one sitting on his back, he had spurned the curb of obedience and was following the pulling of the reins by his rider. And," he went on, "when I prayed to the Lord for the brother, the devil suddenly left him in confusion." Such was this man's vision that, though his eyes were weak toward bodily things, they were sharp for spiritual things. And what wonder that a man who does not want to bear the Lord of majesty should be weighed down by a shameful burden? There is no middle way, I say: either you will bear a light burden, which, rather, bears you, or wickedness will sit upon you like a millstone hung around your neck,[23] heavier than a *talent of lead*.[24]

CHAPTER VII

How Francis freed the people of Greccio from wolves and hail

35 Francis liked to stay at the brothers' place at Greccio, both because he saw that it was rich by reason of its poverty and because he could give himself more freely to heavenly things in a more secluded cell hewn from a projecting rock. Here is that place where he brought back to memory the birthday of the Child of Bethlehem,[25] becoming a child with that Child. It happened, however, that the inhabitants were being annoyed by many evils, for a pack of ravening wolves was devouring not only animals but even men, and every year hail storms were devastating the fields and vineyards. One day, while he was preaching to them, Francis said: "To the honor and glory of Almighty God, hear the truth I announce to you. If every one of you confesses his sins and brings forth *fruits befitting repentance*,[26] I give you my word that every pestilence will depart and the Lord, looking kindly upon you, will grant you an increase of temporal goods. But hear this also: again I announce to you that if you are ungrateful for his gifts and *return to your vomit*,[27] the plague will be renewed, your punishment will be doubled, and even greater wrath will be let loose against you."

36   It happened, therefore, by the merits and prayers of the holy father, that from that hour the destruction ceased, the dangers passed, and neither the wolves nor the hailstorms caused any further damage. Moreover, what is greater still, if any hail came over the fields of their neighbors, it either stopped short when it got near the borders of their lands or turned aside to some other region. Now that they had peace, they were *multiplied exceedingly*[28] and filled beyond measure with temporal goods. But prosperity did what it usually does: their faces were covered with grossness and the fat of temporal things; or rather, they were blinded with dung. In the end, relapsing into even worse things, *they forgot God who saved them*.[29] But not with impunity, for the censure of divine justice punishes those who lapse into sin less severely than those who relapse. The anger of God was aroused against them and the evils that had departed returned, and over and above, there was added the sword of man and a heaven-sent sickness consumed very many of them; eventually the whole town was burned up in avenging flames.[30] Of a truth, it is just that they who turn their backs upon the benefits they have received come to destruction.

CHAPTER VIII

How in his preaching to the Perugians Francis foretold a sedition that was to come among them; and of the praise of unity

37   After some days, when Francis was coming down once from the cell mentioned earlier,[31] he said in a complaining tone to the brothers who were there: "The men of Perugia have done many evil things to their neighbors[32] and their hearts are lifted up unto ignominy. However, the revenge of the Lord is approaching and his hand is on his sword." After a few days had passed, therefore, he arose in fervor of spirit and turned his steps toward the city of Perugia. The brothers could understand clearly that he had seen some vision in his cell. Coming therefore to Perugia, he began to preach to the people who had gathered about; but when some knights rode up on their horses, as is their custom, and crossing their weapons in a military exercise, interfered with his words, the saint turned toward them and sighing, said: "O miserable folly of wretched men who do not consider nor fear the judgment of God! But listen to what the Lord announces to you through me, poor little one. The Lord," he said, "has exalted you above all others around you; for this reason you should be kinder to your neighbors and you should live in a way more pleasing to God. But, ungrateful for God's grace, you attack your neighbors with arms, kill and plunder them. I say to you: this will not go unpunished; but, for your greater punishment, God will cause you to fall into civil war, so that one will rise against the other in mutual sedition. Wrath will teach you, for kindness has not

169

taught you." Not many days after this an altercation arose among them, arms were taken up against those close to them, the citizens fought against the knights, and the nobles attacked the ordinary people; the battle was fought with such unrestrained fury and slaughter that the neighbors who had been wronged grieved with them.[33] This judgment is worthy of praise, for since they had withdrawn from the One and Highest Good, it would follow necessarily that unity would not remain in them. There can be no more powerful bond in a state than pious love of God, sincere and unfeigned faith.[34]

CHAPTER IX

Of the woman to whom Francis foretold that her husband would change from bad to good

38   In those days when the man of God was going to Le Celle near Cortona,[25] a certain noble woman of the city called Volusiano[36] heard of it and hastened to him. Fatigued after a long journey, in as much as she was very *tender and delicate,*[37] she at length came to the saint. When the most holy father saw her exhaustion and heavy breathing, he pitied her and said: "What is your pleasure, lady?" But she said: "Father, bless me." And the saint said: "Are you married or unmarried?" She answered, saying: "Father, I have a husband who is very cruel and whom I must put up with as an opponent to my serving Jesus Christ; this is my chief sorrow that I cannot fulfill the good resolve that the Lord inspired in me, because my husband prevents me: therefore, I beg of you, holy man, pray for him that the divine mercy may humble his heart." The father wondered at such a virile spirit in a woman and at the spirit of an older person in a girl; and moved to pity, he said: "Go, blessed daughter, and know that you will soon have consolation because of your husband." And he added: "Say to him on the part of God and on my own part that now is the time of salvation, and afterwards, of justice." After she had received his blessing, she went home, found her husband, and told him these things. Suddenly the Holy Spirit came upon him and he became a changed man and answered with gentleness: "Lady, let us serve God and save our souls in our home." His wife replied: "It seems to me that continence should be established in the soul as a kind of foundation and that the rest of the virtues should be built upon it." "And this," he said, "pleases me as it pleases you." For many years thereafter they lived a celibate life, and they both departed from this life happily on the same day, one as a *morning holocaust,* the other as an *evening sacrifice.*[38] Happy woman, who thus could soften her lord unto eternal life! In her is fulfilled the words of the Apostle: *The unbelieving husband is sanctified by the believing wife.*[39] But such people, if I may use a popular expression, can be counted on one's fingers today.

CHAPTER X

How Francis knew through the Spirit that one brother had given scandal to another, and how he foretold that the former would quit the order

39 Once two brothers came from the Terra di Lavoro,[40] of whom the older gave much scandal to the younger. He was not, I say, a companion, but he was a tyrant. The younger, however, bore it all with admirable silence out of love for God. But when they had come to Assisi and the younger brother had gone to St. Francis (for he was a friend of the saint), the saint said to him among other things: "How did your companion behave toward you on this journ-

171

ey?" He replied: "Quite well, dearest Father." But the saint said to him: "Beware, Brother, lest under the pretext of humility you should lie. For I know how he conducted himself toward you. But wait a little and you will see." The brother was very much surprised that Francis could have known through the Spirit things that had happened in his absence. After not many days, therefore, the brother who had given scandal to his brother, despising the order, was cast out into the world. Without a doubt, it is a sign of perverseness and an evident proof of a failing spiritual sense not to be of one mind with a good companion when on a journey with him.

CHAPTER XI

Of a young man who came to enter religion, but who the saint knew was not led by the Spirit of God

40   At this same time a certain young man of noble birth from Lucca[41] came to Assisi, wanting to enter the order. When he was presented to St. Francis, he begged him on bended knees and with tears to receive him. But looking upon him, the man of God immediately knew through the Spirit that he was not led by the Spirit. And he said to him: "Wretched and carnal man, why have you had the courage to lie to the Holy Spirit and to me? You weep from a carnal spirit and your heart is not with God. Go, for you have no taste for spiritual things." After he had said these things, he was told that the young man's parents were at the door seeking their son to take him home with them; and going out to them, the young man at length went away of his own will. Then the brothers wondered, praising the Lord in his holy servant.

CHAPTER XII

Of a certain cleric who was healed by Francis and of whom Francis foretold that he would suffer worse things because of his sins

41   At the time when the holy father lay ill in the palace of the bishop of Rieti,[42] a certain canon by the name of Gedeon,[43] a dissolute and worldly man, was taken ill and lay in bed amid many pains. He had himself carried before St. Francis and begged with tears to be blessed with the sign of the cross by him. The saint said to him: "Since you lived in the past according to the desires of the flesh, not according to the judgments of God, why should I sign you with the sign of the cross?" But he went on: "I sign you in the name of Christ; but know that you will suffer worse things if after you are delivered, you return to your vomit." And he added: "Because of the sin of ingratitude worse things than the first are inflicted." Therefore, after he had made the sign of the cross over him, the man who had lain there crippled arose healthy, and breaking forth in praise, he said: "I am freed." The bones of his loins, however, made a noise that many heard, as though sticks of dry wood were broken with the hand. But after a short time had elapsed, forgetful of God, he gave his body again to impurity. One evening after he had dined in the home of another of his fellow canons and was sleeping there that night, suddenly the roof of the house fell upon all of them. But the rest escaped death and only that wretched man was cut off and perished. No wonder, that, as the saint said, worse evils than the first followed, for one should be grateful over the forgiveness he has received, and a crime that is repeated displeases doubly.

CHAPTER XIII

Of a certain brother who was tempted

42   While the saint was staying at that same place, a certain spiritual brother from the custody of Marsica[44] who was troubled grievously with temptations said in his heart: "Oh, if I but had something that belonged to St. Francis with me, if only some bits of his fingernails, I believe indeed that this whole storm of temptations would disperse and peace would return, God willing." Therefore, after he had obtained permission, he went to that place and explained the situation to one of the holy father's companions. The brother answered him: "I think it would not be possible for me to give you any of his nails, because, though we cut them for him at times, he orders that they be thrown away and forbids us to keep them." But immediately the brother was called and ordered to go to the saint who was asking for him. Francis said to him: "Find a scissors for me, son, so you may cut my nails." He gave him the iron instrument which he had already taken into his hands for that purpose, and getting the parings, he brought them to the brother who had asked for them; and he, receiving them devoutly, kept them more devoutly, and he was immediately freed from every assault.

CHAPTER XIV

Of a man who offered cloth of the kind the saint had asked for before

43   In that same place the father of the poor, clad in an old tunic, said once to one of his companions whom he had appointed his guardian:[45] "I would like, Brother, that, if you can, you would find some cloth for me for a tunic." The brother, upon hearing this, thought it over in his mind how he might obtain the cloth that was so necessary and so humbly asked for. The next morning early he went to the door intending to go to the village for the cloth; and behold, a certain man was sitting at the door, wanting to speak to him. He said to the brother: "For the love of God, accept this cloth from me for six tunics; and, keeping one for yourself, distribute the rest as it pleases you for the good of my soul." Filled with joy the brother returned to Brother Francis and made known to him the gift from heaven. The father said to him: "Accept the tunics, for the man was sent for this purpose that he might help me in this way in my necessity. Thanks be to Him," he added, "who alone seems to be solicitous for us."

CHAPTER XV

How Francis invited his doctor to dinner at a time when the brothers had nothing to eat; and how the Lord suddenly supplied them abundantly; and of God's providence with regard to his own

44 When Francis was staying in a certain hermitage near Rieti, a doctor[46] visited him daily to take care of his eyes. But one day the saint said to the brothers: "Invite the doctor and give him something very good to eat." The guardian answered him, saying: "Father, we blush to say that we are ashamed to invite him, because we are now so poor." The saint replied, saying: "Do you want me to tell you again?" The doctor, who was standing by, said: "Dearest brothers, I will consider your poverty a real delicacy." The brothers hurried and placed upon the table all they had in their storeroom, namely, a little bread, not much wine, and, that they might eat a bit more sumptuously, the kitchen provided some vegetables. Meanwhile the table of the Lord had compassion on the table of his servants. There was a knock at the door and it was answered quickly. Behold, a certain woman offered them a basket full of fine bread, fishes and lobster pies, honey and grapes. The table of the poor brothers rejoiced at the sight of these things, and keeping the common things for the next day, they ate the better things that day. With a sigh the doctor spoke, saying: "Brothers, neither you nor we of the world know this man's sanctity as we should." At length they were satisfied, but the miracle gave them greater satisfaction than the banquet. Thus the eye of the Father never despises his children, but rather, the more poor they are, the more richly does providence provide for them. The poor man is provided with a more abundant table than the tyrant, in as much as God is more generous in his gifts than man.

How Francis freed Brother Riccerio from a temptation[47]

44a   A certain brother, Riccerio by name, a noble both in his conduct and by his birth, thought so much of the merits of the blessed Francis that he believed that anyone would merit divine grace if he enjoyed the favor of the saint, and that if he lacked it, he would merit the anger of God. And while he aspired so vehemently to obtain the favor of his friendship, he feared greatly lest the saint would see some hidden vice in him on account of which it would happen that he would not show him his favor. Therefore, while this fear daily weighed heavily upon him and he did not reveal his thoughts to anyone, it happened that he came one day, disturbed as usual, to the cell where the blessed Francis was praying. The man of God knew both of his coming and of his disposition, and calling the brother to him, he spoke thus: "Let no fear disturb you in the future, let no temptation upset you, son; for you are very dear to me, and among those who are especially dear to me I love you with a special affection. Come to me with confidence whenever it suits you, and feel free to leave me whenever it suits you." That brother was astonished not a little at this and he rejoiced over the words of the holy father; and thereafter he felt sure of his affection, and he grew, as he had believed, in the grace of the Savior.

CHAPTER XVI

Of the two brothers whom Francis came out of his cell to bless, knowing their wish through the Spirit

45 St. Francis had the custom of spending the whole day alone in his cell, and he did not come among the brothers unless the need for food forced him to come. But he did not come out to eat at the fixed times, for a greater hunger for contemplation more often claimed him. It happened once that two brothers who were leading lives pleasing to God came from afar to the place at Greccio. Their whole reason for coming was to see the saint and to receive from him a blessing they had long desired. Therefore when they came and did not find him because he had already withdrawn and gone to his cell, they were very greatly saddened; and because the uncertainty concerning his return would cause them a long delay, they left, attributing the whole thing to their lack of worthiness. But Francis' companions followed them and consoled them in their desolation. When they had advanced about a stone's throw from the place, the saint suddenly called after them and said to one of his companions: "Tell my brothers who came here to look back at me." Now when these brothers turned their faces to him, he signed them with the sign of the cross and blessed them with the greatest affection. They then went on their way, praising and blessing the Lord, for they were made more joyful the more they realized that they had gotten what they wanted and had very usefully obtained a miracle.

CHAPTER XVII

How Francis brought water out of a rock by his prayer and gave it to a thirsty peasant

46 Once when the blessed Francis wanted to go to a certain hermitage that he might devote himself more freely to contemplation there, he obtained an ass from a certain poor man to ride on, because he was not a little weak. Since it was summer, the peasant, following the man of God up the mountain, became fatigued from the difficulty and the length of the trip; and before they had reached the place, he collapsed exhausted by a burning thirst. He called after the saint and begged him to have pity on him; he said he would die unless he would be refreshed by some drink. The holy man of God, who always had compassion on those who were suffering, got down without delay from the ass and kneeling upon the ground, he stretched his hands toward heaven; and he did not let up in his prayers until he felt he had been heard. "Hurry," he said to the peasant, "and you will find living water over there, which Christ has just now mercifully brought from the rock for you to drink." O how astounding is the condescension of God which readily inclines him to help his servants! The peasant drank the water that came from the rock by the power of him who had prayed, and he drew drink from the hardest rock. There had never been a flow of water there before,

and, as diligent search has proved, none could be found there afterwards. Why should we wonder that a man who is full of the Holy Spirit should show forth in himself the wonderful deeds of all the just? For, for a man who is joined with Christ by the gift of a special grace it is not something great if he does things similar to the things that have been done by other saints.

CHAPTER XVIII

Of the birds Francis fed, and how one of them perished through greed

47 One day the blessed Francis was sitting at the table with his brothers. Two little birds, one male, the other female, came up, and, solicitous about the bringing up of their newly born little ones, they took the crumbs from the table of the saint as they pleased and as they had been doing day by day. The holy man rejoiced in creatures like these and he coaxed them, as was his custom, and offered them grain solicitously. One day the father and the mother offered their little ones to the brothers, as having been reared at their expense, and after they had given their little ones to the brothers, they did not appear in that place again. The little birds grew tame among the brothers and they perched on their hands, not indeed as guests, but as belonging to that house. They avoided the sight of secular people and professed themselves foster children only of the brothers. The saint observed this and was astonished, and he invited the brothers to rejoice. "See," he said, "what our brothers with the red breasts do, as though they were endowed with reason. For they have said: 'Behold, brothers, we present to you our little ones who have been nourished with your crumbs. Do with them what you wish. We are going to another home." They became completely tame among the brothers and took their food together with them. But greed broke up the peace, in that the greed of the larger bird persecuted the smaller ones. For when the bigger one had had his fill as he wished, he drove the rest away from the food. "See," said the father, "see what this greedy one is doing. Even though he is full and satisfied, he envies his hungry brothers. He will come to a bad end yet." The revenge followed quickly upon the words of the saint. The disturber of his brothers got up on a vessel of water to drink and immediately fell into the water and suffocating, died. No cat was found nor any beast that would touch the bird that had been cursed by the saint. Greed in men is surely a horrible evil if it is punished in such a way in birds. The words of the saints too are to be feared if punishment follows upon them with such ease.

CHAPTER XIX

How all Francis' predictions about Brother Bernard were fulfilled

48   Another time Francis spoke prophetically in the following way about Brother Bernard who had been the second brother in the order:[48] "I tell you that the most subtle demons and the worst among all the other spirits have been assigned to Brother Bernard to try him; but though they are constantly on watch to make this star fall from heaven, there will be a different end to the affair. He will indeed be troubled, tormented, afflicted; but in the end he will come out of all these things triumphant." And he added: "About the time of his death, all the disturbances will be removed, every temptation will have been overcome, and he will enjoy a wonderful tranquillity and peace; and having run his course, he will go happily to Christ." Of a truth it happened this way; his death was made bright by miracles and what the man of God had predicted was fulfilled to the letter. For which reason the brothers said at his death: "Truly, this brother was not known while he lived." But we leave to others the singing of the praises of this Bernard.

CHAPTER XX

Of a brother who was tempted and who wanted to have something written in the saint's own hand

49   While the saint was living on Mount Alverna alone in a cell, one of his companions[49] longed with a great desire to have something encouraging from the words of the Lord noted down briefly in the hand of St. Francis. For he believed he would escape by this means a serious temptation that troubled him, not indeed of the flesh but of the spirit, or at least that he would be able to resist it more easily. Languishing with such a desire, he nevertheless was afraid to make known the matter to the most holy father. But what man did not tell Francis, the Spirit revealed to him. One day Blessed Francis called this brother and said: "Bring me some paper and ink, for I want to write down the words of the Lord and his praises which I have meditated upon in my heart." After these things he had asked for were quickly brought to him, he wrote down with his own hand the *Praises of God* and the words he wanted, and lastly a blessing for that brother, saying: "Take this paper and guard it carefully till the day of your death." Immediately every temptation was put to flight, and the writing was kept and afterwards it worked wonderful things.[50]

CHAPTER XXI

Of that same brother whose desire Francis fulfilled by giving him his tunic

50   For that same brother another remarkable thing was done by the holy father. For at the time when Francis lay ill in the palace at Assisi,[51] the aforementioned brother thought to himself, saying: "See, the father is approaching death and my soul would be greatly comforted if I could have the tunic of my father after his death." As though the desire of his heart had been a petition by word of mouth, the blessed Francis called him after a little while, saying: "I give you this tunic; take it that it may be yours for the future. Though I wear it while I am alive, it will be yours at my death." Astounded at such great insight on the part of his father, the brother was comforted at length in receiving the tunic, and holy devotion afterwards carried it into France.[52]

CHAPTER XXII

Of the parsley that was found at night among the wild herbs at Francis' command

51   One night during his last illness Francis wanted to eat some parsley and he humbly asked for it. But when the cook had been called to bring some, he replied that he could not gather any in the garden at that time, saying: "I have picked parsley every day and I have cut so much of it that I can hardly distinguish any even in the daylight; how would I be able to tell it from the other herbs in the dark?" The saint said to him: "Go, Brother, and do not worry, but bring back the first herbs you lay your hands on." The brother went into the garden and picked the wild herbs which he first happened on

though he could not see them, and he brought them into the house. The brothers looked at the wild herbs, turned them about carefully, and found among them some leafy and tender parsley. The saint ate a little of it and was much comforted. The father said to his brothers: "My brothers, obey a command at the very first word, and do not wait for what has been said to be repeated. Do not say that something is impossible, for, if I should command something that is beyond your strength, obedience would not lack strength." To this extent did the Spirit entrust to him the privilege of the spirit of prophecy.

CHAPTER XXIII

Of the famine Francis foretold would come after his death

52   At times holy men are impelled by an impulse of the Holy Spirit to speak certain wonderful things about themselves, when, for example, either the glory of God demands that they reveal something or the law of charity demands it for the edification of their neighbor. Hence it was that one day the blessed father made known to a certain brother whom he loved a great deal this word which he brought from the secret chamber of the Divine Majesty to which he was admitted familiarly: "Today," he said, "there is upon earth a servant of God for whose sake, as long as he lives, the Lord will not permit famine to rage among men." There was no vanity about this, but it was a holy recital which that holy charity that *is not self-seeking*[53] uttered unto our edification in holy and modest words; nor is that privilege of such wonderful love on the part of Christ toward his servant to be passed over in useless silence. For all of us who saw it know what quiet

and peaceful times passed while the servant of Christ lived and how they were filled with such an abundance of all good things. For there was no *famine of the word of God*,[54] since the words of preachers were greatly filled with power and the hearts of all the hearers were so approved before God. Examples of holiness shone forth in religious life; the hypocrisy of *whited sepulchres*[55] had not yet infected so many holy men, nor had the learning of those *disguising themselves*[56] brought in such curiosity. Deservedly, therefore, did temporal goods abound, since eternal things were so truly loved by all.

53   But after he had been taken away, the order of things was completely reversed and everything was changed; for *wars and insurrections*[57] prevailed everywhere, and a carnage of many deaths suddenly passed through several kingdoms.[58] The horror of famine too spread far and wide, and the cruelty of it, which exceeds the bitterness of everything else, consumed very many.[59] Necessity then turned everything into food and compelled human teeth to chew things that were not even customarily eaten by animals. Bread was made from the shells of nuts and the bark of trees; and, to put it mildly, paternal piety, under the compulsion of famine, did not mourn the death of a child, as became clear from the confession of a certain man.[60] But that it might be made clearly manifest who that faithful servant was, for the love of whom the divine chastisement suspended the hand of its vengeance, the blessed father Francis, just a few days after his death, clearly revealed to that brother to whom he had predicted while he was alive the destruction to come that he himself was that servant of God. For one night, while that brother slept, he called to him in a clear voice, saying: "Brother, a famine is coming which, while I was alive, the Lord did not permit to come upon the earth." The brother awoke at the sound of the voice and later related everything in order as it had happened. On the third night after this the saint appeared again to him and spoke like words.

CHAPTER XXIV

Of the saint's splendor and of our ignorance

54   It should not appear strange to anyone that the prophet of our time should stand forth with such privileges; in fact, freed from the darkness of earthly things and having brought into subjection the pleasures of the flesh, his mind was free to fly to the greatest heights and pure enough to enter into the light. Thus, illumined by the rays of eternal light, he drew from the Word what resounded in his words. Indeed, how different we are today, we who are wrapped in darkness and do not know the necessary things! What do you think is the reason, except that we, being friends of the flesh, are bogged down in the dust of worldliness? For, if *we lift up our hearts with our hands*[61] to heaven, if we would choose to be inclined to eternal things, we would perhaps know what we are ignorant of, namely, God and ourselves. Bogged down in the mire, we can only see the mire; but with our eyes fixed on heaven, we cannot possibly not see heavenly things.

OF POVERTY

CHAPTER XXV

Of the praise of poverty

55   While he was in this valley of tears, that blessed father considered the common wealth of the sons of men as trifles, and, ambitious for higher things, he longed for poverty with all his heart. Looking upon poverty as especially dear to the Son of God, though it was spurned throughout the whole world, he sought to espouse it in perpetual charity. Therefore, after he had become a lover of her beauty, he not only left his father and mother, but even put aside all things, that he might cling to her more closely as his spouse and that *they might be two in one* spirit.[62] Therefore he gathered her to himself with chaste embraces and not even for an hour did he allow himself not to be her husband. This, he would tell his sons, is the way to perfection, this the pledge and earnest of eternal riches.[63] There was no one so desirous of gold as he was desirous of poverty, and no one so solicitous in guarding his treasure as he was solicitous in guarding this pearl of the Gospel. In this, above all, would his sight be offended, if he saw anything contrary to poverty in his brothers either at home or away from home. Indeed, from the very beginning of his religious life unto his death he was rich in having only a tunic, a cord, and drawers, and he had nothing else.[64] His poor habit showed where he was laying up his riches. With this he went his way happy, secure, and confident; he rejoiced to exchange a perishable treasure for the hundredfold.[65]

OF THE POVERTY OF HOUSES

CHAPTER XXVI

56 He taught his brothers to make poor dwellings, of wood, not of stone, and to erect small places according to a humble plan. Often, indeed, speaking of poverty, he would propose to his brothers this saying of the Gospel: *The foxes have dens and the birds of the air have nests; but the Son of Man has nowhere to lay his head.*[66]

CHAPTER XXVII

Of the house at the Portiuncula which he started to destroy

57 Once when a chapter had to be held at St. Mary of the Portiuncula and the time was already at hand, the people of Assisi, seeing that there was no house there, very quickly built a house for the chapter, without the knowledge and in the absence of the man of God. Upon his return, the father looked at the house and took it ill and bewailed it in no gentle tones. Then he himself went up first to destroy the house; he got up on the roof and with strong hands tore off the slates and tiles. He also commanded the brothers to come up and to tear down completely this monstrous thing contrary to poverty. For he used to say that whatever might have the appearance of arrogance in that place would quickly spread throughout the order and be accepted as a model by all. He therefore would have destroyed the house to its very foundations, except that a knight who was standing by cooled the ardor of his spirit when he said that the house belonged to the commune and not to the brothers.

CHAPTER XXVIII

Of the house at Bologna from which Francis drove out even the sick

58 Once when he was returning from Verona and wanted to pass through Bologna, Francis heard that a house had been built there recently. In as much as it was said that it was "the brothers' house," he turned aside and not going on to Bologna, he went another way. But he ordered the brothers to leave that house with haste. Wherefore they abandoned the house and not even the sick remained but were cast out with the others. Neither was permission given to go back in, until the lord Hugo, who was at that time bishop of Ostia[67] and legate in Lombardy,[68] proclaimed publicly that the house belonged to him. He who at that time was turned out of the house sick gives testimony and writes it down.[69]

CHAPTER XXIX

How Francis refused to enter a cell to which his name had been attached

59   Francis did not want his brothers to live in any place unless there was a definite patron to whom the ownership pertained. For he always wanted the laws for strangers to be observed by his sons, namely, to be gathered under a roof that belongs to another, to go about peaceably, to thirst after their fatherland. Now in the hermitage at Sarteano,[70] when a brother was asked by another brother where he was coming from, he said that he was coming from the cell of Brother Francis. Upon hearing this, the saint said: "Since you have attached my name to a cell, appropriating it thereby to me, look for another one for me to live in, for I will not stay in it any more. The Lord," he said, "when he was in the desert[71] where he prayed and fasted for forty days, did not set up a cell for himself there, nor any house, but he lived beneath the rock of the mountain. We can do without ownership according to the form prescribed,[72] even though we cannot live without the use of houses."

CHAPTER XXX

60   This man not only despised arrogance with

regard to houses, but he also had a great horror of many and exquisite furnishings in the houses. He wanted nothing on the table, nothing in the utensils, that would bring back memories of the world. Everything should show forth our state as pilgrims, everything bespeak our exile.

CHAPTER XXXI

An instance where the table at Greccio was prepared on Easter day, and of how Francis showed himself a pilgrim after the example of Christ

61   It happened one Easter that the brothers at the hermitage of Greccio prepared the table more carefully than they usually did with white linens and glassware. Coming down from his cell, the father came to the table and saw that it was placed high and decorated extravagantly. But he did not smile at the smiling table. Stealthily and little by little he retraced his steps, put on the hat of a poor man who was there, and taking a staff in his hand, he went outside. He waited outside at the door until the brothers began to eat; for they were in the habit of not waiting for him when he did not come at the signal. When they had begun to eat, this truly poor man cried out at the door: "For the love of the Lord God," he said, "give an alms to this poor, sick wanderer." The brothers answered: "Come in, man, for love of him whom you have invoked." He immediately entered and appeared before them as they were eating. But what astonishment, do you think, the beggar caused these inhabitants? The beggar was given a dish, and sitting alone, he put the dish in the ashes. "Now I am sitting as a Friar Minor should sit," he said. And to the brothers he said: "We should be moved by the examples of poverty of the Son of God more than other religious. I saw the table prepared and decorated, and I knew it was not the table of poor men who beg from door to door."

This series of actions proves that he was like that other pilgrim who was alone in Jerusalem that day.[73] But he made the hearts of the disciples burn when he spoke to them.[74]

CHAPTER XXXII

Against curiosity of books

62   Francis taught that the testimony of God should be sought in books, not something precious; edification, not beauty. However, he wanted only a few to be had, such as would be suited to the needs of poor brothers. Wherefore, when a certain minister asked that some magnificent and very valuable books be kept with his permission, he heard this from him: "I do not want to lose the book of the Gospel, which we have promised, for your books. You may do as you please, but my permission will not be made a trap."

ON POVERTY IN BEDS

CHAPTER XXXIII

An instance concerning the lord of Ostia, and praise of him

63   Finally in couches and beds such abundant poverty reigned that he who had a few half-torn rags over some straw considered that he had a wedding bed. Whence it happened at the time a chapter was being held at St. Mary of the Portiuncula, that the lord of Ostia,[75] together with a crowd of knights and clerics, came to visit the brothers. Seeing how the brothers lay upon the ground and noticing that their beds might be taken for the lairs of wild beasts, he wept bitterly and said before all present: "See, here the brothers sleep." And he added: "What will become of us, miserable as we are, who make use of such superfluity?" All who were present were

moved to tears and departed greatly edified. This was that lord of Ostia who after he was eventually made the greatest door in the Church resisted always her foes until he returned his blessed soul to heaven as a sacred victim.[76] O pious breast, O bowels of mercy! Placed on high, he grieved that he had no high merits, when, as a matter of fact, he was higher in virtue than in position.[77]

CHAPTER XXXIV

What happened to St. Francis one night when he used a feather pillow

64   Since we have made mention of beds, something else occurred that might be useful to tell. From the time this saint was converted to Christ, he forgot the things of the world and he would not lie on a mattress nor would he have a feather pillow under his head. Neither sickness nor hospitality from outsiders lifted this restriction. But it happened at the hermitage at Greccio, when he was suffering more than usual with the infirmity of his eyes, that he was forced against his will to use a little pillow. On the first night, at an early morning hour, the saint called his companion and said to him: "I have not been able to sleep tonight, Brother, nor could I remain erect at prayer. My head shakes, my knees grow weak and my whole body is shaking as though I had eaten bread made out of darnel.[78] I believe," he said, "that the devil dwells in this pillow that I have under my head. Take it away, because I do not want the devil at my head any longer." The brother sympathized with the complaint of his father and caught the pillow as it was thrown to him to take it away. Therefore going out, he suddenly lost his speech and was oppressed and bound up with such horror that he could neither move his feet from the place nor move his arms in any way. After a while, he was called by the saint, who knew these things,

191

and he was set free and came back and narrated what he had suffered. The saint said to him: "In the evening, while I was saying Compline, I knew clearly that the devil was coming to my cell." And again: "Our enemy is very clever and deeply subtle; when he cannot do us harm inwardly in our soul, he gives the body at least something to murmur about." Let those hear who everywhere are preparing little pillows, so that, wherever they may fall, they may be caught on something soft. The devil willingly follows wealth of things; he likes to stand at expensive beds, especially where necessity does not demand such and profession forbids such. No less does the ancient serpent flee the man who is naked, either because he despises association with the poor, or because he fears the heights of poverty. If a brother gives heed to this that the devil lurks in feathers, his head will be satisfied with straw.

CHAPTER XXXV

A sharp correction of a brother who touched money with his hand

65   That friend of God despised very greatly all the things of this world, but he cursed money more than all other things. Consequently, from the beginning of his conversion he held it in special contempt and always said it was to be shunned as the devil himself. This saying was given by him to his followers that they should value dung and money at the same price of love.[79] It happened, therefore, one day that a certain secular person entered the church of St. Mary of the Portiuncula to pray, and he left some money near the cross as an offering. When he had gone, one of the brothers simply touched it with his hand and threw it on the window sill. The saint heard what the brother had done, and the

brother, seeing that he was found out, hurried to ask pardon, and casting himself upon the ground, he offered himself to stripes. The saint rebuked him and upbraided him most severely because he had touched the money. He commanded him to lift the money from the window sill with his mouth and to place it with his mouth on the asses' dung outside the walls of the place. While that brother gladly fulfilled the command, fear filled the hearts of all who heard of it. All held in greater contempt for the future what was put on the level of dung and they were spurred on daily to contempt by fresh examples.

CHAPTER XXXVI

The punishment of a brother who picked up money

66   Two brothers were once going along the way together and they drew near to the hospital of the lepers. They found a coin on the road and they stopped and discussed between them what was to be done with the dung. One of them, laughing at the conscience of the other brother, tried to take the coin to offer it to the lepers greedy for money.[80] His companion forbade him, lest he be deceived by false piety, and quoted to the rash brother the words of the rule from which it is very clear that a coin that is found is to be trampled on as though it were dust.[81] But he hardened his mind against the admonitions, for by custom he was always a stiff-necked person. He spurned the rule, bent down and took the coin. But he did not escape divine judgment. Immediately he lost his speech; he ground his teeth, but he could not speak. Thus does punishment show up the empty headed; thus does punishment teach the proud to obey the commands of our father. Finally, after he had thrown the foul stuff away, he washed his besoiled lips with the waters of repen-

tance and they were loosed to offer praise. There is an old proverb that says: *Correct the fool and he will be your friend.*[82]

CHAPTER XXXVII

The rebuke of a brother who wanted to keep money on the plea of necessity

67   At one time the vicar of the holy father, Peter of Catania,[83] seeing that St. Mary of the Portiuncula was visited by a great number of brothers from afar and that there were not sufficient alms to provide for their needs, said to St. Francis: "Brother, I do not know what I will do, for with these brothers who have come here in such masses from all over, I do not have enough to provide for them properly. May it please you, I beg of you, that some of the goods of the entering novices be kept aside so that we might have recourse to them at the opportune time." The saint answered: "Away with kindness of this kind, dearest Brother, that would act wrongly against the rule for anyone's sake."[84] And the former said: "What then shall I do?" Francis said: "Strip the altar of the Blessed Virgin and take away its many ornaments, since you cannot otherwise come to the help of the needy. Believe me, she would be more pleased to have the Gospel of her son kept and her altar stripped than that the altar should be ornamented and her son despised. The Lord will send someone who will give back to our mother the ornaments he has lent to us."

CHAPTER XXXVIII

Of money that was turned into a snake

68   Once when the man of God was passing through Apulia near Bari, he found a large purse in

the road, full of money, such as is called in the vocabulary of merchants a money belt.[85] The saint was admonished by his companion and urgently persuaded that the purse should be taken from the ground and the money given to the poor. His pity for the poor was aroused and the mercy that could be shown to the poor men by giving the money to them was praised. The saint refused absolutely to do this and he said it was a trick of the devil. "It is not lawful, son," he said, "to take something that belongs to another; and to give away what belongs to another merits the punishment of sin, not the glory of merit." They withdrew from the place and hastened to complete the journey they had begun. But the brother was not yet satisfied, deluded as he was by empty pity; he continued to suggest transgression. The saint consented to return to the place, not to fulfill the brother's wish, but to demonstrate to a fool the divine mystery. He called a certain young man, who was sitting on a well along the way, so that *in the mouth of two or three witnesses*[86] the mystery of the Trinity might be made clear. When the three had come to the purse, they saw it filled with money. The saint forbade any of them to go near, so that the deceit of the devil might be made known by the power of prayer. Withdrawing to the distance *of about a stone's throw,*[87] he gave himself to holy prayer. Coming back from his prayer, he commanded the brother to lift the purse, which, as he had prayed, contained a snake instead of the money. The brother shook all over and was astounded, and I know not what he was expecting; something unusual was in his mind. Driving away the hesitation in his heart by his fear of obedience, he took the purse in his hands. And behold, a not very small serpent jumped out of the purse and showed the brother the deception of the devil. The saint said to him: "Money to God's servants, Brother, is nothing else but a devil and a poisonous snake."

CHAPTER XXXIX

How the saint rebuked those clothed in soft and fine garments by his word and example

69   This man, endowed with 'power from on high, was warmed inwardly by a divine fire much more than outwardly by bodily clothing. He cursed those in the order who were clothed with three garments or who, without necessity, used soft garments. Such a necessity, however, that was created by pleasure rather than by reason he would say was a sign of an extinguished spirit. "When the spirit becomes tepid," he said, "and gradually grows cold toward grace, flesh and blood necessarily *seek their own interests.*[88] For what remains," he said, "if the soul does not find its delight, but that the flesh should turn to its delights? And then the animal appetite satisfies the craving of necessity, then carnal feeling forms the conscience." And he would add: "Suppose a real necessity comes upon my brother, or some want takes hold of him; if he is quick to satisfy it and thereby to put it a long way away from him, what reward will he receive? He had indeed an opportunity of gaining merit, but he deliberately proved that it did not please him." With these and like words he would strike through to those unfamiliar with necessities, since not to put up with necessities patiently is nothing more than to turn back to Egypt.[89]

Finally, under no circumstances did he want the brothers to have more than two tunics,[90] which, however, he granted might have patches sewn to them.[91] He commanded them to despise fine clothing and those who did not do so he rebuked very sharply before all; and that such might be confounded by his own example, he sewed some rough sackcloth over his own tunic. He asked too that at his death the tunic he would be buried in be covered with sackcloth.[92]

But he permitted the brothers who were forced by sickness or other necessity to have a soft tunic against the skin, in such a way, however, that outwardly the roughness and poorness of the habit be preserved. For he would say: "So much yet will rigor be relaxed and lukewarmness hold sway that the sons of the poor father will not even be ashamed to wear scarlet garments, the color alone being changed." For this reason, we *your children that are strayed,*[93] do not lie to you, father; much more our *iniquity hath lied to itself.*[94] For see, it is now clearer than the light and it grows with each day.

CHAPTER XL

Francis said that those who depart from Poverty must be brought back by experiencing need

70   At times the saint would repeat: "In as far as the brothers depart from poverty, in so much will the world depart from them, and they will seek," he said, "and not find. But if they embrace my Lady Poverty, the world will provide for them, because they have been given to the world unto its salvation." And again: "There is a contract between the world and the brothers: the brothers must give the world a good example, the world must provide for their needs. When they break faith and withdraw their good example, the world will withdraw its hand in a just censure."

The man of God feared a multitude in his solicitude for poverty, for a multitude has the appearance of wealth, if indeed it is not in fact wealth. Hence he used to say: "Oh, if it were possible, my wish would be that the world would see the Friars Minor but rarely and be filled with wonder at the smallness of their number!" Therefore, bound to the Lady Poverty by an indissoluble bond, he looked for her dowry not in the present life, but in the future. He used to chant with more fervent affections and greater rejoicing those psalms that speak of poverty, for instance: *The patience of the poor shall not perish forever*,[95] and *Let the poor see and rejoice.*[96]

CHAPTER XLI

How Francis praised the seeking of alms

71   The holy father made use of alms begged from door to door[97] much more willingly than those offered spontaneously. He would say that shame in begging is the enemy of salvation, and he affirmed that that kind of shame in begging which does not withdraw the foot is holy. He praised the blush that mounts the modest forehead, but not one who allows himself to be confused by shame. At times exhorting his brothers to go begging for alms, he would use these words: "Go," he said, "for at this last hour the Friars Minor have been lent to the world, that the elect might fulfill in them what will be commended by the Judge: Because *as long as you did it for one of these, the least of my brethren, you did it for me.*"[98] Wherefore he said that the order had been privileged by the Great Prophet,[99] who spoke its name so plainly.[100] Therefore he wanted his brothers to live not only in the cities, but also in

hermitages where all might be given the opportunity to gain merit and the veil of excuse might be stripped from wicked ones.[101]

CHAPTER XLII

Francis' example in begging alms

72   So that he might not offend even once that holy spouse,[102] the servant of the Most High used to do this: if he was invited by lords and was to be honored with a more lavish table, he would first beg some scraps of bread from the houses of neighbors, and thus enriched by want, he would hasten to the table. Asked now and then why he did this, he would say that he would not give up a permanent inheritance for a fief loaned to him for an hour.[103] "It is poverty," he said, "that makes us heirs and kings of the kingdom of heaven, not your false riches."[104]

CHAPTER XLIII

The example Francis gave in the court of the lord of Ostia

73   Once when St. Francis visited Pope Gregory of happy memory, when the latter was still placed in a lower station, and the hour of dinner was at hand, he went out for alms, and returning, placed some of the scraps of black bread on the bishop's table. When the bishop saw this, he was somewhat ashamed, above all because of the newly invited guests. The father, however, with a joyous countenance distributed the alms he had received to the knights and the chaplains gathered about the table; all of them accepted the alms with wonderful devotion, and some of them ate them, others kept them out of reverence. When the dinner was finished, the bishop arose and taking the man of God to

an inner room, he raised his arms and embraced him. "My Brother," he said, "why did you bring shame on me in the house that is yours and your brothers by going out for alms?" The saint said to him: "Rather I have shown you honor, for I have honored a greater lord. For the Lord is well pleased with poverty, and above all with that poverty that is voluntary. For I have a royal dignity and a special nobility, namely, to follow the Lord who, *being rich, became poor for us.*"[105] And he added: "I get more delight from a poor table that is furnished with small alms than from great tables on which dainty foods are placed almost without number." Then, greatly edified, the bishop said to the saint: "Son, do what seems good in your eyes, for the Lord is with you."

CHAPTER XLIV

Francis' exhortation by example and by precept to seek alms

74   In the beginning Francis would at times go out alone for alms to discipline himself and to spare the bashfulness of his brothers. But when he saw that some were not attending to their vocation as they should, he once said: "Dearest brothers, the Son of God was more noble than we and he made himself poor for us in this world. We have chosen the way of poverty out of love for him; we should not be ashamed to go out to beg for alms. It is not right for the heirs of the kingdom to be ashamed of their heavenly inheritance. I say to you, there will be many noble and wise men who will join our order and who will consider it an honor to beg for alms. You, therefore, who are the first fruits among them, should rejoice and be glad and not refuse to do what you are handing down for these holy men to do."

CHAPTER XLV

How Francis rebuked a brother who refused to beg

75   The blessed Francis frequently said that a true Friar Minor should not be long without going out to beg alms. "And the more noble my son is," he said, "the more ready should he be to go, for in this way will merits be heaped up for him." There was a certain brother in a certain place who never went out for alms but always ate more than several together at table. When the saint observed that he was a friend of the belly, one who shared the fruits without sharing the labor, he once said to him: "Go your way, brother fly, for you want to eat the sweat of your brothers and to do nothing in God's work. You are like brother drone who wants to be first to eat the honey, though he does not do the work of the bees." When that carnal man saw that his gluttony was discovered, he went back to the world that he had not as yet given up. For he left the order, and he who was a nothing at begging is no longer a brother; and he who ate more than several together has become a devil in many different ways.

CHAPTER XLVI

How Francis met a brother carrying alms and kissed his shoulder

76   Another time, at the Portiuncula, when a certain brother returned from Assisi with an alms, he began to break forth in song as he neared the place and to praise the Lord in a loud voice. Upon hearing this, the saint jumped up quickly and ran out and kissed the shoulder of the brother; he then put the sack on his own shoulder. "Blessed be my brother," he said, "who goes out readily, begs humbly, and returns rejoicing."

CHAPTER XLVII

How Francis persuaded some knights to seek alms

77 When the blessed Francis was full of infirmities and already approaching his end, he was at the place at Nocera.[106] The people of Assisi sent messengers there and demanded to get him back, lest they give their glory in the body of the man of God to another. As the knights were bringing him reverently on horseback, they came to a certain very poor village, Satriano by name.[107] Here, since hunger and the hour demanded food, they went out, but found nothing for sale; coming back to the blessed Francis, they said: "You must give us something from your alms, for we could find nothing to buy." The saint replied and said: "You find nothing because you trust more in your flies than in God." For he called money flies. "Go back," he said, "to the houses which you visited and offering God's love in place of money, beg humbly for an alms. Do not be ashamed, for all things have been given to us as an alms after sin, and that great Almsgiver bestows his gifts with loving kindness to the worthy and the unworthy." The knights put aside their shame and asking for an alms with readiness, they bought more with the love of God than with money. All gave gladly, and hunger had no power where abundant poverty prevailed.

CHAPTER XLVIII

How a piece of capon was changed into a fish at Alessandria

78 In giving alms Francis was concerned with the profit of souls rather than with aid to the body, and he made himself an example to the rest no less in giving than in receiving. For when he came to Alessandria in Lombardy to preach the word of God and was given hospitality by a certain God-fearing man of praiseworthy reputation, he was asked by him for the sake of observing the holy Gospel to eat of everything put before him.[108] Overcome by the devotion of his host, Francis graciously consented to do so. The host went in haste and carefully prepared a capon seven years old for the man of God to eat. While the patriarch of the poor was sitting at the table and the family was rejoicing, suddenly there appeared at the door *a son of Belial,*[109] poor in all grace, pretending poverty in all necessary things. He proposed craftily the love of God in his asking for alms and in a tearful voice demanded that he be helped for God's sake. The saint held that name blessed above all things and sweeter than honey. Very agreeably he took up a piece of the bird that had been set before him and putting it on some bread, he gave it to the beggar. Why add more? That unhappy man kept the gift to bring reproach upon the saint.

79   The next day, the saint preached the word of God to the gathered people, as was his custom. Suddenly that wicked man began to grumble and tried to show that piece of capon to all the people. "Behold," he cried out, "what kind of man this Francis is who preaches and whom you honor as a saint. Look at the meat he gave me yesterday evening while he was eating." All the people cried out against that wicked man and they reproached him as being possessed by the devil. As a matter of fact, what he was trying to tell them was a piece of capon appeared to the people to be a fish. The wretched man himself, astounded by the miracle, was forced to admit what the rest were saying. That unhappy man finally blushed with shame and washed away the exposed crime by his penitence. Before all the

people he begged pardon from the saint, making known to him his evil intention. The meat was changed back to its proper species again after that deceitful man had returned to his right mind.

CHAPTER XLIX

An instance of one whom the saint rebuked for giving away his property to his relatives and not to the poor

80   The saint instructed those who came to the order that first they should give a *notice of dismissal*[110] to the world by offering first their outward possessions to God and then themselves inwardly. Only those who had given away all their goods and retained absolutely nothing did he admit to the order, both on account of the word of the holy Gospel[111] and in order that no scandal would arise over any treasures kept back.

81   It happened in the Marches of Ancona that after Francis had preached there a certain man came humbly asking to be admitted into the order. The saint said to him: "If you wish to be joined with the poor, first distribute your possessions to the poor of the world." When he heard this, the man left, and, impelled by a carnal love, he distributed his goods to his relatives and gave nothing to the poor. It happened that when he came back and told the saint of his generous liberality, the father laughed at him and said: "Go on your way, brother fly, for you have not yet left your home and your relatives. You gave your goods to your relatives and you have defrauded the poor; you are not worthy to be numbered among the holy poor. You have begun with the flesh, you have laid an unsound foundation on

which to build a spiritual structure." That carnal man returned to his own and got back his goods which he did not want to give to the poor and for that reason he abandoned very quickly his virtuous purpose. That same kind of pitiful distribution deceives many today who seek a blessed life with a worldly beginning. For no one consecrates himself to God for the purpose of making his relatives rich, but to acquire life by the fruit of his good works, redeeming his sins with the price of compassion.

For Francis often taught that if the brothers were in want they should rather have recourse to others than to those who are entering the order, first of all for the sake of example, then to avoid all appearance of base advantage.

OF A VISION FRANCIS HAD ABOUT POVERTY

CHAPTER L

82   It pleases me to tell here of a vision the saint had that is worthy to be remembered. One night, after he had prayed for a long time, sleep gradually overtook him. That holy soul was taken into *the sanctuary of God*[112] and he saw *in a dream,*[113] among other things, a certain woman that looked like this: her head seemed to be of gold, her bosom and arms of silver, her abdomen of crystal, and the rest from there on down of iron. She was tall of stature, delicately and symmetrically framed. But this woman of such beautiful form was covered over with a soiled mantle. Getting up in the morning, the blessed father told the vision to that holy man Brother Pacificus,[114] but he did not explain what it meant.

Although many have interpreted this vision as they saw fit, I believe it would not be amiss to hold to the interpretation of Brother Pacificus, which the Holy Spirit suggested to him while he listened. "This beautiful woman," he said, "is the beautiful soul of St. Francis. The golden head is his contemplation and his wisdom regarding eternal things. The bosom and arms of silver are the *words of the Lord*,[115] which he meditated on in his heart and fulfilled in his actions. The crystal, because of its rigidity, signifies sobriety, and because of its brightness, chastity. Iron is the greatest perseverance. But take the soiled mantle to be his despised little body with which his precious soul is covered."

Many, however, having the spirit of God, understand this woman to represent poverty, the spouse of our father. "The reward of glory," they say, "made her golden; the praise of her fame made her silver; the profession of poverty both outward and inward and without treasures made her crystal; final perseverance, iron. But the judgment of carnal men wove a sordid mantle for this renowned woman."

Many adapt this vision to the order, following Daniel's succession of periods of time.[116] But that the vision refers to our father is apparent especially from this fact that, avoiding any arrogance, he refused absolutely to interpret it. Indeed, if it had pertained to the order, he would not have passed over it with complete silence.

OF ST. FRANCIS' COMPASSION FOR THE POOR

CHAPTER LI

Of his compassion for the poor and how he envied those poorer than himself

83   What tongue can tell how great was this man's compassion toward the poor? Truly, he had an inborn kindness which was doubled by a kindness given him from on high. Therefore the soul of Fran-

cis melted toward the poor, and to those to whom he could not extend a helping hand, he at least showed his affection. Whatever he saw in anyone of want, whatever of penury, he transferred in his mind, by a quick change, to Christ. Thus in all the poor he saw the Son of the poor lady,[117] and he bore naked in his heart him whom she bore naked in her hands. But though he had laid aside all envy, he could not be without envy of poverty. If indeed he saw someone poorer than himself, he was immediately envious, and in the struggle for complete poverty he feared to be outdone by another.

84 It happened one day when the man of God was going about preaching that he met a certain poor man along the way. When he saw his nakedness, he was struck with compunction, and he turned to his companion, saying: "This man's want brings great shame to us and rebukes our poverty severely." His companion replied: "For what reason, Brother?" And the saint replied with a sad voice: "For my wealth, for my spouse, I chose poverty; but see, poverty shines forth more brightly in this man. Are you ignorant of the fact that the word has gone about the world that we are the poorest of men for Christ's sake? But this poor man proves that the fact is otherwise." O enviable envy! O emulation to be emulated by his sons! This is not that envy that is grieved over the goods of others; it is not that envy that is darkened by the rays of the sun; not that envy that is opposed to kindness; not that envy that is tortured by spite. Do you think that evangelical poverty has nothing about it to be envied? It has Christ and through him it has *all things in all.*[118] Why do you pant after revenues, modern cleric? Tomorrow you will know that Francis was rich, when you will find in your hand the revenues of torments.

CHAPTER LII

How Francis corrected a brother who spoke ill of a poor man

85　Another day when Francis was preaching, a certain poor and infirm man came to the place. Pitying his double affliction, namely, his want and his feebleness, Francis began to speak with his companion about poverty. And when, suffering with the sufferer, Francis' heart had become deeply afflicted, the companion of the saint said to him: "Brother, it is true that this man is poor, but it may also be true that nowhere in the whole province is there a man who is richer in his desires." Immediately the saint rebuked him and said to him when he admitted his guilt: "Hurry quickly and take off your tunic and cast yourself down at the feet of this poor man and acknowledge your guilt. And do not only ask for forgiveness, but ask him also to pray for you." He obeyed and went to make satisfaction and he came back. The saint said to him: "When you see a poor man, Brother, an image is placed before you of the Lord and his poor mother. So too in the sick consider the infirmities which the Lord took upon himself for us." Indeed, there was always *a bundle of myrrh* with Francis;[119] he always looked *on the face* of his *Christ*,[120] always touched *the man of sorrows* who was *acquainted with infirmity*.[121]

CHAPTER LIII

Of the mantle that was given to an old woman at Celano

86　It happened in the winter at Celano[122] that St. Francis was wearing a cloth folded after the manner of a mantle which a certain man from Tivoli,[123] a friend of the brothers, had lent him.

And when he was in the palace of the bishop of the diocese of Marsica,[124] an old woman came up to him begging an alms. Immediately he loosened the cloth from his neck, and though it belonged to someone else, he gave it to the poor woman, saying: "Go, make yourself a dress, for you are greatly in need of one." The old woman smiled, and rather overcome, I know not whether with fear or with joy, she took the cloth from his hands. Quickly she ran away, and lest a delay should bring on the danger of its being asked back again, she cut it with her scissors. But when she found that the cut cloth would not be enough for a dress, encouraged by her first success, she returned to the saint, indicating to him that there was not enough cloth. The saint turned his eyes to his companion, who had the same kind of cloth on his back. "Did you hear, Brother," he said, "what this poor woman said? Let us put up with the cold for the love of God and give the cloth to the old woman so that she may complete her dress." As Francis had given his mantle, so too did his companion give his, and both remained naked so that the old woman might be clothed.

CHAPTER LIV

Of another poor man to whom Francis gave his mantle

87   Another time, when Francis was returning from Siena, he met a certain poor man and said to his companion: "Brother, we must return this mantle to that poor man to whom it belongs. We borrowed it from him until we should meet someone poorer than ourselves." His companion, thinking about his father's need, obstinately refused, lest Francis provide for another by neglecting himself. The saint said to him: " I do not want to be a thief;

for it would be considered a theft in us if we did not give to someone who is in greater need than we." The other gave in, and Francis gave over his mantle.

CHAPTER LV

How he did the same thing for another poor man

88 Something similar occurred at Le Celle near Cortona. Blessed Francis was wearing a new mantle which the brothers had solicitously sought for him. A poor man came to the place loudly bemoaning his dead wife and his family that had been left desolate. The saint said to him: "I give you this mantle for the love of God with this understanding that you do not give it to anyone else unless he pays you well for it." The brothers ran immediately to take back the mantle and prevent the gift of it. But taking courage at the look of the holy father, the poor man hung on to the mantle with both hands and defended it as his own. Finally the brothers redeemed the mantle and the poor man, after receiving the price of it, went away.

CHAPTER LVI

How Francis gave his mantle to a certain man so that he would not hate his lord

89 Once at Collestrada,[125] near Perugia, St. Francis found a certain poor man whom he had known earlier in the world. And he said to him: "Brother, how does it go with you?" But he began with ill will to heap curses upon his lord who had taken all his goods away from him. "Thanks to my lord," he said, "whom I pray the Almighty Lord to curse, I am in a bad way." The blessed Francis, pitying his soul more than his body, since he was persisting in such hatred, said to him: "Brother, forgive your lord out of love for God, so that you may free your soul, and it could be that he will give back what he has taken away from you. Otherwise, you will lose both your possessions and your soul." And he said: "I cannot forgive him completely unless he first give back what he has taken." Blessed Francis, since he had a mantle on his back, said to him: "Behold, I give you this mantle, and I beg you to forgive your lord out of love for the Lord God." Softened and moved by this kindness, he took the gift and forgave the wrongs that had been done him.

CHAPTER LVII

How Francis gave a poor man a part of his tunic

90   Once when Francis was asked by a poor man for something and he had nothing at hand, he unsewed the border of his tunic[126] and gave it to the poor man. At times, too, in similar circumstances, he gave away his trousers. Such was his compassion toward the poor and such the sincerity with which he followed in the footsteps of the poor Christ.

CHAPTER LVIII

How Francis caused the first New Testament in the order to be given to the poor mother of two of the brothers

91   Once the mother of two of the brothers came to the saint confidently asking an alms. The holy father had pity on her and said to his vicar, Brother Peter of Catania:[127] "Can we give some alms to our mother?" Francis was accustomed to call the mother of any brother his mother and the mother of all the brothers. Brother Peter answered him: "There is nothing left in the house that could be given her." And he added: "We have one New Testament from

211

which we read the lessons at Matins since we do not have a breviary." Blessed Francis said to him: "Give the New Testament to our mother that she might sell it to take care of her needs, since we are admonished by it to help the poor.[128] I believe indeed that the gift of it will be more pleasing to God than our reading from it." The book, therefore, was given to the woman, and thus the first Testament that was in the order was given away through this holy kindness.

CHAPTER LIX

How Francis gave his mantle to a poor woman suffering from an eye disease

92   When St. Francis was living in the palace of the bishop of Rieti trying to get a cure for the infirmity of his eyes,[129] a certain poor woman from Machilone,[130] who had an infirmity similar to that of the saint, came to the doctor. The saint, therefore, addressing his guardian familiarly, said something like this: "Brother guardian, we must give back what belongs to another." He replied: "Let it be given back, Father, if there is such a thing here." "This mantle," he said, "which we borrowed from that poor woman; let us give it back to her, for she has nothing in her purse to take care of her expenses." The guardian answered: "Brother, this mantle is mine and it was not lent to me by anyone. But use it as long as it pleases you; when you no longer want to use it, give it back to me." Actually, the guardian had bought it a little earlier for St. Francis' need. The saint said to him: "Brother guardian, you have always been courteous to me, and I beg of you to show me the same courtesy now." The guardian replied: "Do as you wish, Father, whatever the Spirit suggests to you." Therefore calling a certain secular person, a very devout man, he said to him: "Take this mantle and twelve loaves of bread and go and say to that poor woman: 'The poor man to whom you lent this mantle thanks you for its loan; but now take back what belongs to you.'" The man went and spoke what he had heard. The woman, thinking she was being mocked, said to him with shame: "Let me alone with your mantle; I don't know what you are talking about." The man insisted and placed the mantle in her hands. When she saw that she was not being deceived and fearing that what she had gotten so easily might be taken away from her, she got up during the night and, not caring about a cure for her eyes, returned home with the mantle.

CHAPTER LX

How three women appeared to Francis along the road and then disappeared again after giving him a new greeting

93   I will narrate in a few words something that is of doubtful interpretation but most certain as regards the fact. When the poor man of Christ, Francis, was hurrying from Rieti to Siena[131] to find a remedy for his eye trouble, he crossed a plain near the town of Campiglia[132] in the company of a certain doctor deeply attached to the order. And behold, three poor women appeared beside the road when Francis was passing. They were all so similar in stature, age, and appearance that you might think that a threefold matter had been perfected by a single form. When Francis approached, they reverently bowed their heads and praised him with this new greeting: "Welcome," they said, "Lady Poverty."[133] Immediately the saint was filled with exquisite joy, in as much as there was nothing in him that he would rather have men salute than what

213

these women had chosen. And at first Francis thought they were really poor women and he turned to the doctor who accompanied him and said: " I ask you, for God's sake, give me something that I might give it to these poor women." Very quickly the doctor got out some money and leaping from his horse, he gave some to each of the women. They, therefore, proceeded a little farther along their way, and when the brothers and the doctor looked around immediately, they saw that the plain was completely empty of any women. They were greatly surprised and they then considered the happening among the miracles of the Lord, knowing that these were not women who had flown away more quickly than birds.

CHAPTER LXI

Of the time and place of Francis' prayers and of his disposition in prayer

94   Although the man of God, Francis, was *exiled from the Lord* while *in the body*,[134] he strove constantly to have his spirit present in heaven and thus he was already a *citizen with* the angels[135] and only a wall of flesh separated him from them.[136] His whole soul thirsted after Christ, and he dedicated not only his whole heart, but his whole body as well, to him.

We give here a few of the great things about his prayers that may be imitated by those who come after him, in so far as we have seen them with our own eyes and in so far as it is possible to convey them to human ears.[137] He made his whole time a holy leisure in which to inscribe wisdom in his heart, lest he would be seen to fall back if he did not constantly advance. When visits of secular persons or any other business disturbed him, he would interrupt his prayers rather than end them and return to them again in his innermost being.[138] The world was tasteless to him who was fed with heavenly sweetness, and the delights he found in God made him too delicate for the gross concerns of men.

He always sought a hidden place where he could adapt not only his soul but also all his members to God. When he suddenly felt himself visited by the Lord in public, lest he be without a cell he made a cell of his mantle. At times, when he did not have a mantle, he would cover his face with his sleeve so that he would not disclose the *hidden manna*.[139] Always he put something between himself and the bystanders, lest they should become aware of the bridegroom's touch. Thus he could pray unseen even among many people in the narrow confines of a ship.[140] Finally, when he could not do any of these things, he would make a temple of his breast. Because he was forgetful of himself, there were no sobs or sighs; because he was absorbed in God, there was no hard breathing or external movement.

95   Thus was it at home. But when he prayed in the woods and in solitary places, he would fill the woods with sighs, water the places with his tears, strike his breast with his hand; and discovering there a kind of secret hiding place, he would often speak with his Lord with words. There he would give answer to his judge; there he would offer his petitions to his father; there he would talk to his friend; there he would rejoice with the bridegroom. Indeed, that he might make his whole being a holocaust in many ways, he would set before his eyes in many ways him who is simple to the greatest degree. Often, without moving his lips, he would meditate within himself and drawing external things within himself, he would lift his spirit to higher things. All his attention and affection he directed with his whole

215

being to the one thing which he was asking of the Lord, not so much praying as becoming himself a prayer. With what sweetness of heart do you think he was pervaded when he became accustomed to such things? He knows, but I can only wonder. To him who has experienced it knowledge is given, not to him who has not experienced it. Thus, filled with a glowing fervor of spirit and his whole appearance and his whole soul melted, he dwelt already in the highest realms of the heavenly kingdom.

The blessed father was accustomed not to pass over any visitation of the Spirit with negligence. When indeed such was offered, he followed it, and as long as the Lord would permit, he would enjoy the sweetness thus offered him. When, therefore, while he was pressed by some business or was intent upon a journey, he felt little by little certain touches of grace, he would taste the sweetest manna in frequent snatches. For also along the way, with his companions going on ahead, he would stand still, and turning the new inspiration to fruitfulness, he would not *receive the grace in vain.*[141]

CHAPTER LXII

How Francis devoutly recited the canonical hours

96 Francis recited the canonical hours no less reverently than devoutly. For, though he suffered from infirmity of the eyes, stomach, spleen, and liver,[142] he did not want to lean against a wall or a partition when he chanted, but he always said the hours standing erect and without a capuche,[143] without letting his eyes roam about and without interruption.

When he went through the world on foot, he always stopped to say the hours; when he was on horseback, he got down upon the ground. Wherefore, when he was returning one day from Rome and it was raining steadily, he got down from his horse, and standing there a long time, he was completely soaked with the rain. For he used to say at times: "If the body takes its food in quiet, which, along with itself, will become the food of worms, with what great peace and tranquillity should not the soul take its food, which is God himself."

CHAPTER LXIII

How Francis drove away the imaginings of the heart at prayer

97   Francis thought he had seriously offended, if, when he was at prayer, he would be disturbed by vain imaginings. If something of the kind happened, he did not spare himself the confession of the fault, so that he could atone for it completely. Thus he turned his zeal to immediate use so that but very rarely did he suffer flies of this kind.

One Lent he had made a little vase, using just the little time he had to spare, so that he would not be completely taken up with it. One day, while he was devoutly saying Tierce, his eyes turned to look at the vessel, and he felt that the interior man was thereby impeded in its fervor. Sorrowful therefore that the voice of his heart had been interrupted in its speaking to the ears of God, when Tierce was finished he said before the listening brothers: "Alas, what a worthless work that has such power over me that it can twist my mind to itself! I will sacrifice it to the Lord, whose sacrifice it has impeded." When he said these words, he took the little vase and threw it into the fire to be burned. "Let us be ashamed," he said, "to be caught up by worthless imaginings, for at the time of prayer we speak to the *great King*."[144]

CHAPTER LXIV

Of Francis' Contemplation

98 Francis was often suspended in such sweetness of contemplation that, caught up out of himself, he could not reveal what he had experienced because it went beyond all human comprehension. Through one instance that once became known, it is clear to us how frequently he was absorbed in heavenly sweetness. Once he was riding on an ass when he had to pass through Borgo San Sepolcro.[145] And since he wanted to rest at a certain house of lepers, many found out that the man of God was to pass by. From all sides men and women came to see him, wanting to touch him out of devotion to him. What then? They touched him and pulled him about and cut off little pieces of his tunic to keep. The man seemed insensible to all these things, and paid no attention to the things that happened, as though he were a lifeless corpse. At length they came to the place and, though they had long left the city behind, that contemplator of heavenly things, as though returning to himself from some other place, solicitously inquired when they would come to the city.

CHAPTER LXV

Francis' behavior after prayer

99 When Francis returned from his private prayers, through which he was changed almost into another man, he tried with all his strength to conform himself to others, lest, if the inner fire were apparent to others, he should lose what he had gained under the glow of human favor. Often too he spoke things like these to his familiar friends: "When a servant of God is praying and is visited by a new consolation from the Lord, he should, before he comes away from his prayer, raise his eyes to heaven and with hands joined say to the Lord: 'This consolation and sweetness you have sent from heaven, Lord, to me, an unworthy sinner, and I return it to you so you may keep it for me, for I am a robber of your treasure.' And again: 'Lord, take your good things away from me in this world and keep them for me in the life to come.' Thus," he said, "he ought to speak. And when he comes away from prayer, he should show himself to others as poor and as a sinner, as though he had attained no new grace." For he would say: "It happens that a person loses something precious for the sake of some trifling reward and easily provokes him, who gives, not to give again."

Finally, it was his habit to rise so furtively and so gently to pray that none of his companions would notice him getting up or praying. But when he went to bed late at night, he would make a noise, and even a great noise, so that his going to rest might be noticed by all.

CHAPTER LXVI

How a bishop was deprived of his speech when he came upon Francis at prayer

100   When St. Francis was praying at the place of the Portiuncula, it happened that the bishop of Assisi came to him on a friendly visit, as was his custom.[146] As soon as he entered the place, he went unceremoniously to Francis' cell without being called, and after knocking at the door, was about to enter. But behold, when he put his head in and saw the saint praying, a trembling took hold of him suddenly and his limbs became rigid, and he also lost his speech. Suddenly, by the will of God, he was driven out by force and pushed backward some distance. I believe that he was either unworthy to look upon

this secret thing or that the saint was worthy to keep his secret longer. The astonished bishop returned to the brothers, and with the first word he uttered in confessing his fault, he recovered his speech.

CHAPTER LXVII

How an abbot felt the power of St. Francis' prayer

101   Another time it happened that the abbot of the monastery of St. Justin, in the diocese of Perugia, met Francis.[147] The abbot got down quickly from his horse, exchanged a few words with St. Francis about the welfare of his soul, and then, as he was leaving, he humbly asked St. Francis to pray for him. St. Francis answered him: "I will willingly pray, my lord." When the abbot had gone a little way from St. Francis, the saint said to his companion: "Wait a bit, Brother, because I want to discharge the debt I incurred by my promise." For it was always his custom that, when he had been asked for prayers, he would not postpone the matter, but would quickly fulfill a promise of this kind. Therefore, while the saint was praying to God, the abbot suddenly felt in his soul an unusual warmth and sweetness, such as he had never experienced before in his soul, so much so that he seemed to be completely carried out of himself in ecstasy. He paused for a moment and when he came to himself, he recognized the power of St. Francis' prayer. Thereafter he always burned with a greater love for the order and related the happening to many as a miracle. It is becoming that servants of God bestow upon one another little gifts like this; and it is fitting that there be a *partnership* between them *in the matter of giving and receiving.*[148] That holy love, which is at times called spiritual, is content with the fruit of prayer; charity makes little earthly gifts. To help and to be helped in the

spiritual conflict, to commend and to be commended *before the tribunal of Christ*,[149] this I think is the mark of holy love. But to what great heights in prayer do you think he rose who could thus raise up another by his merits?

CHAPTER LXVIII

The knowledge and the memory of St. Francis

102   Although this blessed man had been educated in none of the branches of learning,[150] still, grasping the wisdom that is of God from above and enlightened by the rays of eternal light, he had a deep understanding of the Scriptures. For his genius, free from all stain, penetrated the hidden things of mysteries, and where the knowledge of the masters is something external, the affection of one who loves enters within the thing itself. At times he would read the sacred books and what he put into his mind once he wrote indelibly in his heart. His memory substituted for books, for he did not hear a thing once in vain, for his love meditated on it with constant devotion. This he would say was a fruitful way of learning and reading, not by wandering about through thousands of treatises. Him he considered a true philosopher who put nothing before his desire for eternal life. But he often said that that man would easily move from knowledge of himself to a knowledge of God who would set himself to study the Scriptures humbly, not presumptuously. He often explained doubtful questions word for word, and though he was unskilled in words, he set forth the sense and meaning admirably.

CHAPTER LXIX

Of the prophetic word Francis expounded at the prayers of a Friar Preacher

103   While Francis was staying at Siena, it happened that a certain friar of the Order of Preachers came there; he was a spiritual man and a doctor of Sacred Theology. Since he had come to visit the blessed Francis, that learned man and the saint enjoyed a long and pleasant conversation about the words of God. The aforesaid master[151] questioned Francis about that saying of Ezechiel: *If thou proclaim not to the wicked man his wickedness, I will require his soul at thy hand.*[152] For he said: "Good Father, I know many who, to the best of my knowledge, are in the state of mortal sin, but I do not always proclaim their wickedness. Will the souls of such men be required at my hand?" The blessed Francis said that he was unlettered and therefore it would be more fitting for him to be taught by that master than for him to interpret the meaning of Scripture. And the humble master said: "Brother, though I have heard these words interpreted by learned men, I would be glad to hear your understanding of the passage." The blessed Francis said to him: "If the passage is to be understood in a general meaning, I would take it that the servant of God should be so aflame in his life and his holiness that he would reprove all wicked men by the light of his example and by the words of his conversation. So, I say, the splendor of his life and the renown of his fame will proclaim to all their wickedness." That man, therefore, went away much edified, and he said to the companions of the blessed Francis: "My brothers, the theology of this man, based upon purity of life and contemplation, is a soaring eagle; but our learning crawls on its belly on the ground.

CHAPTER LXX

Of the things Francis made clear when he was questioned by a cardinal

104   Another time when Francis was in Rome at the home of a certain cardinal, he was asked about some obscure words and brought such profound things to light that you would think he had always dwelt among the Scriptures. The lord cardinal said to him: "I do not ask you as a learned man, but as a man having the Spirit of God, and I therefore willingly accept the word of your reply, for I know it has proceeded from God alone."

CHAPTER LXXI

How Francis answered a brother who urged him to apply himself to reading

105   When Francis was ill and filled throughout with pains, his companion once said: "Father, you have always sought refuge in the Scriptures, and they have always given you remedies for your pains. I pray you to have something read to you now from the prophets; perhaps your spirit will rejoice in the Lord." The saint said to him: "It is good to read the testimonies of Scripture; it is good to seek the Lord our God in them. As for me, however, I have already made so much of Scripture my own that I have more than enough to meditate on and revolve in my mind. I need no more, son; I know Christ, the poor crucified one."

CHAPTER LXXII

Of the swords that Brother Pacificus saw glittering in the mouth of the saint[153]

106   In the Marches of Ancona there was a certain

223

secular person who, forgetful of himself and not knowing God, gave himself completely to vanity. He was called *The King of Verses,* because he was the most outstanding of those who sang impure songs and he was a composer of worldly songs. To put it briefly, so high had worldly glory raised him that he had been crowned with the greatest pomp by the emperor.[154] While he was thus walking in darkness and drawing *iniquity with cords of vanity,*[155] the merciful kindness of God thought to call him back *that he that is cast off should not altogether perish.*[156] By the providence of God the blessed Francis and this man met each other at a certain monastery of cloistered poor nuns.[157] The blessed father had come there with his companions to visit his daughters; that other man had come there with many of his companions to visit a certain relative of his.

The hand of the Lord was laid upon him and he saw with his bodily eyes St. Francis signed in the manner of a cross with two greatly glittering swords, one of which went from his head to his feet, the other from one hand to the other across his breast. He did not know the blessed Francis; but when Francis had been shown to him in so great a miracle, he soon recognized him. But astonished at the vision, he began to resolve to do better things, though only for some future time. But the blessed father, after he had first preached to all in common, turned the sword of God's word upon this man. For, taking him aside, he gently admonished him concerning the vanity of the world and concerning contempt of the world, and then he touched his heart deeply by threatening him with God's judgments. Immediately that man answered: "What need is there for more words? Let us come to deeds. Take me from among men and give me back to the great Emperor." The next day the saint invested him and gave him the name Pacificus, in as much as he had been brought back to the peace of God. The conversion of this man was so much the more edifying to many in that the circle of his vain companions had been so large.

Rejoicing in the company of the blessed father, Brother Pacificus began to experience favors that he had not known before. For he was permitted to see a second time what was hidden from others. Not long afterwards, he saw the great sign *Tau* on the forehead of the blessed Francis, which gave off from many-colored circles the beauty of a peacock.[158]

CHAPTER LXXIII

Of the efficacy of Francis' sermons and a certain doctor's tesimony about it

107   Although the evangelist Francis preached to the unlearned people through visible and simple things, in as much as he knew that virtue is more necessary than words, nevertheless among spiritual men and men of greater capacity he spoke enlivening and profound words. He would suggest in a few words what was beyond expression, and using fervent gestures and nods, he would transport his hearers wholly to heavenly things.[159] He did not make use of the keys of philosophical distinctions; he did not put order to his sermons, for he did not compose them ahead of time. Christ, the true Power and Wisdom, gave *to his voice the voice of power*.[160] A certain doctor,[161] a learned and eloquent man, once said: "While I can retain the preaching of others word for word, only the things that St. Francis speaks elude me. If I commit any of them to memory, they do not seem to be the same that dropped from his lips before."

CHAPTER LXXIV

How by the power of his words he drove out devils from Arezzo through the instrumentality of Brother Sylvester

108   Not only were Francis' words effective when he was present in person, but at times when they were transmitted through others they did *not return to him void.*[162] It happened once that he came to the city of Arezzo, when behold, the whole city was shaken by civil war to the extent that destruction seemed very close. The man of God therefore lodged in a town outside the city and he saw devils rejoicing over that place and stirring up the citizens to each other's destruction. But calling a brother, Sylvester by name, a man of God of worthy simplicity,[163] he commanded him saying: "Go before the gate of the city, and on the part of Almighty God command the devils to leave the city as quickly as they can." Pious simplicity hastened to carry out the command and speaking psalms of praise before the face of the Lord, he cried out loudly before the gate: "On the part of Almighty God and at the command of our father Francis, depart from here, all you devils." Soon thereafter the city returned to peace and the people preserved their civic rights in great tranquility. Wherefore afterwards blessed Francis, when preaching to them, said at the beginning of his sermon: "I speak to you as men who were once subjected to the devil and in the bonds of the devils, but I know that you have been set free by the prayers of a certain poor man."

CHAPTER LXXV

Of the conversion of that same Brother Sylvester and of a vision he had

109   I think it would not be amiss to join to the present narration the conversion of the afore-mentioned Sylvester, how the Spirit moved him to enter the order. Sylvester had been a secular priest in the city of Assisi,[164] from whom the man of God had at one time bought stones for the repairing of a church.[165] When this priest once saw Brother Bernard, who was the first little plant in the order of Friars Minor after the saint of God, making a perfect renunciation of his goods and giving them to the poor, he was moved to ravenous avarice and complained to the man of God over the stones he had sold him, that a fair price had not been given him for them. Francis smiled, seeing that the priest's soul was infected with the passion of avarice. But wishing to give some refreshment to that cursed burning, he filled the hands of the priest with money without counting it. The priest Sylvester rejoiced over what he had been given, but even more did he wonder at the liberality of the giver. He went home and often thought about what had happened. He complained with a blessed murmuring that though he was already growing old, he still loved the world, and he was astonished that that young man despised all things. Finally, after he had been filled with a fragrant odor, Christ opened to him the bosom of his mercy.

He showed him in a vision the works of Francis, what great worth they had, with what great luster they gleamed in his sight, and how they so magnificently filled the whole structure of the world. For he saw in his sleep a golden cross coming forth from the mouth of Francis; its top touched the heavens and its extended arms encircled both parts of the world in their embrace. Filled with compunction at the sight, the priest shook off harmful delay, left the world, and became a perfect imitator of the man of God. He began to live perfectly in the order and, by the grace of God, he brought his life to a perfect close.[166] But what is there to wonder at if Francis appeared crucified, since all his concern was with the cross? With the cross thus wonderfully rooted in him interiorly, why should it be such a surprising thing if, coming from good ground, it should bring forth such conspicuous flowers, leaves, and fruit? Nothing else could spring up in that soil, since from the first that wonderful cross claimed it for its own. But now I must return to the subject.

CHAPTER LXXVI

Of a certain brother freed from the assaults of the devil

110 It happened that a certain brother was assaulted for a long time by a temptation of the spirit, which is more subtle and much worse than the enticement of the flesh. Finally he came to St. Francis and humbly prostrated himself at his feet; shedding an abundance of bitter tears he could say nothing, prevented as he was by deep sobs. The kindness of the father went out to him and recognizing the fact that he was troubled by evil spirits, he said: "I command you, devils, by the power of God, not to assault my brother any more in the way you have presumed to do up until now." Soon the *blackness of darkness*[167] was dispelled and the brother arose freed; neither did he feel any more vexation, just as though he had never had any.

CHAPTER LXXVII

Of the wicked sow that ate a lamb

111 The fact that Francis' words had a wonderful effect on brutes too appears sufficiently clear elsewhere.[168] I will just touch on one instance that I have at hand. One night when the servant of the Most High was lodging at the monastery of St. Verecundus in the diocese of Gubbio,[169] a certain sheep brought forth a little lamb that night. There was also a very mean sow there that did not spare the life of the innocent lamb but killed it with its cruel jaws. Upon rising the next morning, the men found the lamb dead and they knew that the sow was guilty of the evil deed. When the kind father heard this, he was moved to wonderful compassion, and, remembering another Lamb,[170] he grieved over the dead lamb, saying before all: "Alas, brother lamb, innocent animal, you represent what is useful to all mankind! Cursed be that evil beast that killed you; let no man eat of it, or any beast either." Wonderful to say, that wicked sow immediately began to be ill, and after suffering torments of punishment for three days, it at last suffered avenging death. It was cast out into the monastery ditch, where it lay for a long time dried up like a board, and it did not furnish food for any hungry creature.

AGAINST FAMILIARITY WITH WOMEN

CHAPTER LXXVIII

Of avoiding familiarity with women, and how Francis talked with them

112 That honeyed poison, namely, familiarities with women, which lead astray even holy men, Francis commanded should be entirely avoided.[171] For he feared that from such things the weak spirit would be quickly broken and the strong spirit often weakened. Avoiding contagion from association with them, unless it were a question of a most proven man, Francis said, in accordance with Scripture, was as easy as walking in a fire without having the soles of one's feet burned.[172] And that he might speak from deeds, he always showed *himself an example of all virtue*.[173] Indeed, a woman was so unwelcome to him that you would think that his caution was not a warning or an example but rather a dread or a horror. When their importunate loquaciousness caused him difficulty in speaking with them, he would ask for silence with a humble and *speedy word*[174] and with his face cast down. Sometimes, though, *he looked up to heaven*[175] and seemed to draw from there the answers he gave to those who were muttering *out of the ground*.[176]

But those women in whose minds an urgency of holy devotion had set up the abode of wisdom, he taught by wonderful yet brief words. When he talked with a woman, he spoke what was to be said in a loud voice so that he could be heard by everybody. He said once to a companion: "I tell you the truth, dearest Brother, I would not recognize any woman if I looked into her face, except two. The face of the one and of the other is known to me, but I know no other." Rightly so, Father, for looking upon them makes no one holy. Rightly so, I say, for they provide no profit but only great loss, at least of time. They are an impediment to those who would walk the difficult way and who want to look up to the *face that is full of graces*.[177]

CHAPTER LXXIX

A parable against looking at women

113   Francis was accustomed to combat unclean

eyes with the following parable: "A very powerful king sent two messengers to the queen one after the other. The first came back and reported only her words in exact words. For *the eyes of a wise man are in his head*,[178] and he did not let them roam about. The other returned and after a few short words about her message, he recounted a long story of the lady's beauty. 'Truly, lord,' he said, 'I have seen a most beautiful woman. Happy he that enjoys her.' But the king said: 'Wicked servant, you have cast impure eyes upon my wife? It is evident that you wished to purchase what you looked upon so sharply.' He commanded that the first messenger be called back and said to him: 'What do you think of the queen?' And he said: 'I think very well of her, for she listened silently and replied wisely.' 'And there is no beauty in her?' the king said. 'It is for you, my lord,' he said, 'to look upon that; my business was only to deliver a message.' Then this sentence was pronounced by the king: 'You,' he said, 'are chaste of eye, and being even more chaste of body, you shall be my chamberlain. But let this other man depart from my house lest he defile my marriage bed.' "

But the blessed father would say: "Too much confidence makes one guard too little against the enemy. If the devil can get but one hair from a man, he will soon make it grow into a beam. Even if after many years he still has not made him fall whom he has tempted, he is not put out over the delay, as long as he catches him in the end. For this is his business, and he is busy about nothing else by day or by night."

CHAPTER LXXX

An example the saint gave against too great intimacy

114   Once it happened, when St. Francis was go-

ing to Bevagna,[179] that he was not able to reach the town because of his weakness from fasting. His companion, however, sending a messenger to a certain spiritual woman, humbly begged bread and wine for the saint. When she heard this, she ran to the saint along with her daughter, a virgin vowed to God, carrying what was necessary. But after the saint had been refreshed and somewhat strengthened, he in turn refreshed the mother and her daughter with the word of God. But while he preached to them, he did not look either of them in the face. When they departed his companion said to Francis: "Why, Brother, did you not look at the holy virgin who came with such great devotion?" The father answered: "Who must not fear to look upon the bride of Christ? But when a sermon is preached with the eyes and the face she looks at me, but not I at her."

Many times when Francis spoke of this matter he said that all talk with women is frivolous except only for confession, or, in so far as custom demands, a very short admonition. For he said: "What business should a Friar Minor have to transact with a woman, except when she piously asks for holy penance or for advice concerning a better life?"[180]

CONCERNING THE TEMPTATIONS FRANCIS SUFFERED

CHAPTER LXXXI

Of the saint's temptations and how he overcame temptation

115   As the merits of St. Francis increased, so too did his struggle with the ancient serpent. For the greater the gifts bestowed upon him, the more subtle were the temptations and the more serious the assaults hurled against him. Though the devil had often proved him to be a *man of war*[181] and a strenu-

ous battler and one who did not let up in the struggle
for even an hour, nevertheless he always tried to attack his always victorious foe. At one time there was
sent to the holy father a most serious temptation of
the spirit, of course for the increase of his crown. He
was in anguish as a result; and filled with sorrows,
he tormented and tortured his body, he prayed and
he wept bitterly. After being thus assailed for several years, he was praying one day at St. Mary of the
Portiuncula when he heard a voice within his spirit
saying: "Francis, *if you have faith like a mustard
seed, you will say to this mountain, 'Remove from
here and it will remove.'*"[182] The saint replied:
"Lord, what mountain do you want me to remove?"
And again he heard: "The mountain is your temptation." And weeping, Francis said: "Let it be unto me,
Lord, as you have said." Immediately all the temptation was driven out, and he was made free and put
completely at peace within himself.

CHAPTER LXXXII

*How the devil, calling to Francis, tempted him with
lust, and how the saint overcame the temptation*

116   At the hermitage of the brothers at Sar-
tiano,[183] he who is always envious of the children of
God, presumed to do the following against the saint.
For seeing the saint continuing to increase in holiness and not neglecting today's profit for yesterday's,
he called to Francis at prayer one night in his cell,
saying three times: "Francis, Francis, Francis." He
answered, saying: "What do you want?" And the
other: "There is no sinner in the world whom the
Lord will not forgive if he is converted; but whoever
destroys himself by harsh penance will not find
mercy forever." Immediately the saint recognized the
cleverness of his enemy by a revelation, how he was

trying to bring him back to lukewarmness. What then? The enemy did not stop short of inflicting upon him another struggle. For seeing that he could not thus conceal his snare, he prepared another snare, namely, the enticement of the flesh. But in vain, for he who had seen through the craftiness of the spirit could not be tricked by the flesh. The devil therefore tempted him with a most severe temptation of lust. But the blessed father, as soon as he noticed it, took off his clothing and beat himself very severely with his cord, saying: "See, brother ass, thus is it becoming for you to remain, thus is it becoming for you to bear the whip. The tunic belongs to the order; stealing is not allowed. If you want to go your way, go."

117   But when he saw that the temptation did not leave him in spite of the scourging, even though all his members were marked with welts, he opened his cell and went out into the garden and cast himself naked into a deep pile of snow. Then gathering handfuls of snow, he made from it seven lumps like balls. And setting them before him, he began to speak to his body: "Behold," he said, "this larger one is your wife; these four are your two sons and your two daughters; the other two are your servant and your maid whom you must have to serve you. Hurry," he said, "and clothe them all, for they are dying of cold. But if caring for them in so many ways troubles you, be solicitous for serving God alone." The devil then departed quickly in confusion, and the saint returned to his cell glorifying God. A certain spiritual brother, who was praying at the time, saw the whole thing by the light of the moon. But when the saint found out later that this brother had seen him that night, he was greatly distressed and commanded him to tell the thing to no one as long as he lived in this world.

CHAPTER LXXXIII

How Francis freed a certain brother from a temptation, and concerning the good that comes from temptation

118   On a certain occasion when one brother who was undergoing temptations was sitting alone with the saint, he said to Francis: "Pray for me, kind Father, for I am sure that I will be immediately freed from my temptations if you will be kind enough to pray for me. For I am afflicted above my strength and I know that this is no secret to you." St. Francis said to him: "Believe me, son, for I think you are for that reason more truly a servant of God; and know that the more you are tempted, the more will you be loved by me." And he added: "I tell you in all truth, no one must consider himself a servant of God until he has undergone temptations and tribulations. Temptation overcome," he said, "is in a way a ring with which the Lord espouses the soul of his servant to himself. There are many who flatter themselves over their long-standing merits and are happy because they have had to undergo no temptations. But because fright itself would crush them even before the struggle, they should know that their weakness has been taken into consideration by the Lord. For difficult struggles are hardly ever put in the way of anyone, except where virtue has been perfected."

CHAPTER LXXXIV

How devils beat Francis, and how courts are to be shunned

119   Not only was this man attacked by satan with

temptations, but he even carried on a hand to hand battle with satan. Once when he had been asked by the lord cardinal Leo of the Holy Cross[184] to stay with him for a little while in Rome, he chose a certain secluded tower that was divided by nine arched vaults into what looked like small cells for hermits. The first night, therefore, when he wanted to rest after he had poured out his prayers to God, the devils came and made preparations for a hostile struggle with the saint of God. They beat him for a long time very severely and in the end left him as though half dead. After they had gone and he had recovered his breath, the saint called his companion who was sleeping under one of the other arched vaults and said to him when he came: "Brother, I would like for you to stay near me, because I am afraid to be alone. For the devils beat me a little while ago." The saint was trembling and shaking in his members like a person suffering a severe fever.

120   The whole night, therefore, they remained awake, and St. Francis said to his companion: "The devils are the officers[185] of our Lord whom he sends to punish our excesses. But it is a sign of greater grace if nothing is left unpunished in his servant while he is living in this world. Indeed, I do not recall any offense that I have not washed away by satisfaction, through the mercy of God; for he has always so acted with me through his fatherly condescension, that he showed me when I prayed or meditated what was pleasing and displeasing to him. But it could be that he has permitted his officers to rise against me because my staying in the court of important persons does not give a good example to others. My brothers who live in poor places, hearing that I am staying with cardinals, will perhaps suspect that I am enjoying many comforts. Therefore, Brother, I think it better for him who is set as an example for others to

shun courts and to make strong those who, putting up with hardships, are bearing the same things." The next morning, therefore, they went to the cardinal and after telling him everything, they bade him farewell. Let the brothers who are court chaplains[186] take note of this and let them know that they have been drawn before their time from the womb of their mother. I do not condemn obedience, but I do condemn ambition, laziness, luxury. Lastly, I propose Francis as a model especially where it is a question of obedience. But let what is displeasing to God be tolerated, since such is pleasing to men.[187]

CHAPTER LXXXV

An example of what was said in the preceding paragraph

121   One thing happened that I think should not be passed over. A certain brother, seeing some brothers living at a certain court and attracted by what desire for glory I know not, wanted to become a court chaplain with them. And while he was curious about the court, he one night saw in his sleep such brothers placed outside of the place of the brothers and separated from their companionship. He also saw them eating from a very foul and unclean pigs' trough, from which they were eating peas mixed with human dung. Seeing this, the brother was greatly astonished and getting up long before daybreak he had no more desire for the court.

CHAPTER LXXXVI

Of the assaults Francis bore in a certain solitary place; a brother's vision

122   Once the saint came with a companion to a certain church situated a long way from any habita-

tion, and wanting to offer a prayer in solitude, he sent his companion away, saying: "Brother, I would like to remain here tonight alone. Go to the hospital and come back to me at dawn." Therefore, after he had remained alone and poured out long and very devout prayers to the Lord, he at length looked about for a place where he might lay his head to sleep. But suddenly, *troubled in spirit*,[188] he began *to feel dread and to be exceedingly troubled*,[189] while his body trembled in every part. He knew clearly that the devils were rising against him and that whole troops of them were rushing with much noise over the roof of the house. He therefore immediately arose and went outside and made the sign of the cross upon his forehead and said: "On the part of Almighty God, I say to you, devils, do with my body whatever is granted you to do with it. I will bear it willingly, for since I have no greater enemy than my body, you will take vengeance for me upon my adversary when you wreak vengeance upon it in my place." Therefore, when they who had come together to frighten his spirit saw that his spirit was ready even though his flesh was weak,[190] they quickly departed confused and in shame.

123   When morning had come, his companion returned to him, and finding the saint prostrate before the altar, he waited for him outside the choir and prayed fervently himself meanwhile before the cross. And behold, he went into ecstasy and saw among the many thrones in heaven one that was more honorable than the rest, ornamented with precious stones, and radiant with all glory. He wondered within himself at this noble throne and considered silently whose it might be. And while he was considering these things, he heard a voice saying to him: "This throne belonged to one of the fallen angels, but now it is reserved for the humble Francis." At length,

coming back to himself, the brother saw the blessed Francis coming from his prayers, and quickly prostrating himself at Francis' feet in the form of a cross, he said to him, not as to one living in this world, but as to one already reigning in heaven: "Pray for me to the Son of God, Father, that he will not impute to me my sins." The man of God *stretched forth his hand*[191] and *raised him up*,[192] realizing that something had been shown to him in his prayers. Finally, as they were leaving that place, the brother asked the blessed Francis, saying: "What, Father, is your opinion of yourself?" He replied: "It seems to me that I am the greatest of sinners, for if God had treated any criminal with such great mercy, he would have been ten times more spiritual than I." At these words the Holy Spirit immediately said in the heart of the brother: "Know that the vision you saw was indeed true, for humility will raise this most humble man to the throne that was lost through pride."[193]

CHAPTER LXXXVII

Of a certain brother who was freed from a temptation

124   A certain spiritual brother, long in religion, was afflicted with a great temptation of the flesh and he seemed almost to be sunk into the depths of despair. Every day his suffering was doubled, for his conscience, more tender than discreet, forced him to confess about nothing. Indeed, such great zeal should not be shown in confessing to have had a temptation but rather in confessing to have given in to a temptation. But he had such great shame that he was afraid to make known the whole thing to one priest, though it amounted to nothing, and so he divided up his thoughts and told different parts to different priests. One day, however, when he was walking with blessed Francis, the saint said to him:

"Brother, I tell you that you need confess your trouble to no one in the future. And do not be afraid, because what is going on in you beyond your responsibility will be unto your glory and not unto your guilt. But as often as you are tempted say with my permission seven *Pater Noster*." Astonished that the saint knew these things, and filled with very great joy, the brother very shortly escaped from all his trouble.

TRUE JOY OF SPIRIT

CHAPTER LXXXVIII

Praise of spiritual joy; the evil of dejection

125 St. Francis maintained that the safest remedy against the thousand snares and wiles of the enemy is spiritual joy. For he would say: "Then the devil rejoices most when he can snatch away spiritual joy from a servant of God. He carries dust so that he can throw it into even the tiniest chinks of conscience and soil the candor of mind and purity of life. But when spiritual joy fills hearts," he said, "the serpent throws off his deadly poison in vain. The devils cannot harm the servant of Christ when they see he is filled with holy joy. When, however, the soul is wretched, desolate, and filled with sorrow, it is easily everwhelmed by its sorrow or else it turns to vain enjoyments."

The saint, therefore, made it a point to keep himself in joy of heart and to preserve the unction of the Spirit and the *oil of gladness*.[194] He avoided with the greatest care the miserable illness of dejection, so that if he felt it creeping over his mind even a little, he would have recourse very quickly to prayer. For he would say: "If the servant of God, as may happen, is disturbed in any way, he should rise immediately to pray and he should remain in the presence of the heavenly Father until he *restores unto him the joy of salvation*.[195] For if he *remains stupified* in sadness,[196] the Babylonian stuff will increase, so that, unless it be at length driven out by tears, it will generate an abiding rust in the heart.[197]

CHAPTER LXXXIX

Of the angelic lute that Francis heard

126   During the days when Francis was staying at Rieti[198] to have his eyes cared for, he called one of his companions who had been a lute player in the world, saying: "Brother, the children of this world do not understand the hidden things of God. For musical instruments that were once destined for the praises of God[199] lust has changed into a means of pleasure for the ears. Therefore, Brother, I would like for you to borrow a lute secretly and bring it here so that with it you may give some wholesome comfort to brother body that is so full of pains." The brother replied: "I am not a little ashamed to do so, Father, because I am afraid men may suspect that I am being tempted to frivolity." The saint said: "Let us then forget about it, Brother. It is good to give up many things so that the opinion of others may not be harmed." The next night, when the saint was watching and meditating about God, suddenly there came the sound of a lute of wonderful harmony and very sweet melody. No one was seen, but the volume of the sound marked the going and coming of the lute player as he moved back and forth. Finally, with his spirit fixed on God, the holy father enjoyed so much the sweetness in that melodious song that he thought he had been transported to another world. When he got up in the morning he called the aforementioned brother and telling him everything just as it had

happened, he added: "The Lord who consoles the afflicted has never left me without consolation. For behold, I who could not hear the lutes of men have heard a far sweeter lute."

CHAPTER XC

How Francis would sing in French when he was cheerful in spirit

127   Sometimes Francis would act in the following way. When the sweetest melody of spirit would bubble up in him, he would give exterior expression to it in French, and the breath of the divine whisper which his ear perceived in secret would burst forth in French in a song of joy. At times, as we saw with our own eyes,[200] he would pick up a stick from the ground and putting it over his left arm, would draw across it, as across a violin, a little bow bent by means of a string; and going through the motions of playing, he would sing in French about his Lord. This whole ecstasy of joy would often end in tears and his song of gladness would be dissolved in compassion for the passion of Christ. Then this saint would bring forth continual sighs, and amid deep groanings, he would be raised up to heaven, forgetful of the lower things he held in his hand.

CHAPTER XCI

How Francis rebuked a brother who was sad and admonished him how to behave

128   Francis once saw a certain companion of his with a peevish and sad face, and not taking this lightly, he said to him: "It is not becoming for a servant of God to show himself sad or upset before men, but always he should show himself honorable. Examine your offenses in your room and weep and groan be-

fore your God. When you return to your brothers, put off your sorrow and conform yourself to the rest."[201] And after a few more things he said: "They who are jealous of the salvation of men envy me greatly; they are always trying to disturb in my companions what they cannot disturb in me." So much, however, did he love a man who was full of spiritual joy that he had these words written down as an admonition to all at a certain general chapter: "Let the brothers beware lest they show themselves outwardly gloomy and sad hypocrites; but let them show themselves joyful in the Lord, cheerful and suitably gracious."[202]

CHAPTER XCII

How the body should be treated so that it will not murmur

129 The saint also said once: "Brother body should be provided for with discretion, so that a tempest of bad temper be not raised by it. So that it will not be wearied with watching and that it may persevere with reverence in prayer, take away from it every occasion for murmuring. For it might say: 'I am weak with hunger, I cannot bear the burden of your exercise.' But if after it has eaten sufficient food it should mutter such things, know that a lazy beast needs the spur and a sluggish ass must expect the goad."

Only in this teaching did the most holy father's actions differ from his words.[203] For he subjected his own innocent body to scourgings and want, multiplying its *wounds without cause*.[204] For the warmth of his spirit had already so spiritualized his body, that with his soul thirsting after God, his most holy flesh also thirsted, *O how many ways*.[205]

CHAPTER XCIII

Against vainglory and hypocrisy

130   Welcoming true spiritual joy, Francis studiously avoided vainglory, because he knew that what contributes toward advancement should be loved fervently, while that which is harmful should be no less carefully shunned. He tried to crush vainglory in the seed, not permitting what might offend the eyes of God to endure even for a moment. For very often, when he was being offered much public commendation, weeping and sighing he would immediately change the feeling of his heart to sadness.

During winter, when his small, holy body was covered only with a single tunic, patched quite fully with poor pieces of cloth,[206] his guardian, who was also his companion, obtained a skin of a fox and giving it to him, said: "Father, you are suffering from an infirmity of the spleen and stomach;[207] I pray you, in your love for the Lord, let this skin be sewn beneath your tunic. If the whole skin does not please you, then at least let a part of it be put over your stomach." St. Francis replied to him: "If you want me to permit this under my tunic, then have a piece of the same size attached to the outside, which, sewn on the outside, will show men that there is a skin hidden inside too." The brother heard this, but did not approve; Francis insisted, but did not ask anything else. Finally, the guardian gave his consent and one piece was sewn over the other, so that Francis would not appear outwardly different from what he was inwardly. O you who were the same in word and in life, the same outwardly and inwardly, the same when you were a subject and when you were a superior! You, who gloried always in the Lord, loved nothing of outward glory, nothing of personal glory!

But I pray that I may not offend those who wear skins if I speak of one skin being added above the other; for we know that they who were despoiled of their innocence needed skins.[208]

CHAPTER XCIV

How Francis made a confession concerning hypocrisy

131   One time at the hermitage of Poggio[209] about Christmas time, when a large crowd of people had been called together for a sermon, Francis began with this prologue: "You believe me to be a holy man and for that reason you have devoutly come together. But I tell you," he said, "that during this whole period of fast[210] I have eaten food prepared with lard." In this way he often ascribed to pleasure what had been granted to him because of his infirmity.

CHAPTER XCV

How Francis made a confession of vainglory

132   With like fervor, when at times his spirit was moved to vainglory, he would immediately make it known by an open confession before all. Once when he was going through the city of Assisi, a certain old woman met him and asked an alms of him. Since, however, he had nothing but his mantle, he gave her that with speedy generosity. But feeling an impulse to vain complacency, he immediately confessed before all that he had had this feeling of vainglory.

CHAPTER XCVI

Francis' words against those who praised him

133   He tried to hide the good gifts of his Lord in the secret recesses of his heart, not wanting to let these become an object of praise, for they could then

be the cause of his ruin. For often when he was praised by many, he would answer with words like these: "I can still have sons and daughters; do not praise me as being secure. No one should be praised whose end is yet uncertain. If ever he who has lent these things to me would wish to take back what he has given me, only the body and soul would remain, and these even the unbeliever possesses." Such things he spoke to those who praised him. But to himself he said: "If the Most High had given such great things to a robber, he would have been more grateful than you, Francis."

CHAPTER XCVII

Francis' words against those who praised themselves

134   Francis would often say to his brothers: "No one should flatter himself with evil praise over what a sinner can do. A sinner," he said, "can fast, pray, weep, mortify his flesh. This, however, he cannot do, namely, be faithful to his Lord. Therefore in this should we glory, that we give glory to God, that we serve him faithfully, that we ascribe to him whatever he has given us. The greatest enemy of man is his flesh; it does not know how to recall anything to grieve over it; it does not know how to foresee things to fear them; its only aim is to misuse the present time. But what is worse," he said, "it claims as its own, it transfers to its own glory what was not given to it but to the soul. It seeks for praise for its virtues and the external favor of men for its watchings and prayers. It leaves nothing to the soul, but seeks a reward even for its tears."

CHAPTER XCVIII

How Francis replied to those who asked about his wounds and with what care he hid them

135 It would not be right to pass over in silence those marks of the Crucified that must be venerated even by the highest spirits, how Francis covered them over with a veil, with what great care he hid them.[211] From the very first when true love for Christ had transformed this lover into the very image of Christ, Francis began to conceal and hide his treasure with such great care that for a long time even his closest friends were unaware of it. But divine providence did not want it to be always hidden and not come to the eyes of his loved ones. Indeed, even the exposed location of his members did not permit it to remain concealed. Once when one of his companions saw the stigmata in his feet, he said to Francis: "What is this, good Brother?" But Francis replied: "Take care of your own business."

136 Another time the same brother asked for Francis' tunic to clean it. Seeing that there was blood on it, he said to the saint when he brought it back: "Whose blood is this on your tunic?" But the saint, putting his finger to his eye, said to him: "Ask what this is if you do not know that it is an eye." Rarely, therefore, did he wash his entire hands, but only his fingers, so that his secret should not be betrayed to those standing by. His feet he washed but very rarely, and not less secretly than rarely. When he was asked by anyone to let him kiss his hand, he would give him only half of it, extending only his fingers to be kissed; at times, in place of his hand, he extended his sleeve. He covered his feet with woolen socks, lest the wounds be seen, putting a skin above the wounds to ease the roughness of the wool. But though the holy father could not hide the stigmata in his hands and feet entirely from his companions, he nevertheless took it ill if anyone looked at them. Wherefore his companions, filled with prudence of spirit, averted their eyes when he uncovered either his hands or his feet out of necessity.

CHAPTER XCIX

How a certain brother saw the stigmata by a pious deception

137   While the man of God was living at Siena, it happened that a certain brother came there from Brescia;[212] he wanted very much to see the stigmata of the holy father and insistently demanded of Brothere Pacificus that he be allowed to do so. But the latter said: "When I am about to leave this place, I will ask to kiss his hands; when he gives them to me, I will wink with my eyes at you and you will see them." So, prepared to leave, they both came to the saint, and kneeling down, Brother Pacificus said to St. Francis: "Bless us, dearest Mother, and give me your hand to kiss."[213] He kissed the hand that was not willingly extended and made a sign to the other brother to look. And asking for the other hand, he kissed it and showed it to the other brother. As they were leaving, the father suspected there had been some pious deception there, as indeed there had been. And judging such pious curiosity to be impious, he immediately called Brother Pacificus back and said to him: "May the Lord forgive you, Brother, for sometimes you cause me a lot of distress." Pacificus immediately fell at his feet and humbly asked him, saying: "What distress did I cause you, dearest Mother?" But Francis said nothing, and the incident was closed with silence.

CHAPTER C

How a certain brother got to see the wound in his side

138   While the uncovered location of these members made the wounds in his hands and feet visible to some, no one was worthy to see the wound in his side while Francis was yet alive, with the exception of one person and then only once.[214] For whenever Francis had his tunic cleaned, he would cover the wound in his side with his right hand. At times, however, he covered the wound by putting his left hand over the pierced side. But when one of his companions was rubbing him, his other hand slipped down upon the wound and caused Francis great pain.[215] A certain other brother,[216] seeking out of prying curiosity to see what was hidden to others, said to the holy father one day: "Would it please you, Father, if we cleaned your tunic?" The saint replied: "May the Lord reward you, Brother, I do need it." Therefore, while Francis was taking off his tunic, that brother looked carefully and saw clearly the wound in his side. He was the only one who saw it while Francis was alive; none of the others saw it until he was dead.[217]

CHAPTER CI

How virtues are to be kept hidden

139   In this way this man renounced all glory that did not savor of Christ; in this way he placed an eternal anathema upon the favors of men. He knew that the price of fame diminishes the solitude of the conscience, and that it is by far more harmful to abuse virtues than not to have them at all. He knew that it was not less a virtue to protect what was acquired than to acquire it.[218] Alas, vanity moves us

to more things than does charity, and the favor of the world prevails over love for Christ. We do not fix our eyes on our afflictions, we do not *test the spirits*,[219] and when vainglory compels us to act, we think we have been moved by charity. Moreover, if we have done even a little good, we cannot bear its weight, but ridding ourselves of it while we live, we lose it at the shore of eternity. We bear patiently our not being good. We cannot bear at all not to seem good, not to be thought good. And thus we live completely amid the praise of men, because we are nothing else but men.

OF HUMILITY

CHAPTER CII

Of Francis' humility in dress, in opinion, in acts; against maintaining one's own opinion

140 Humility is the guardian and the ornament of all virtues. If the spiritual building does not rest upon it, it will fall to ruin, though it seems to be growing. This virtue filled Francis in a more copious abundance, so that nothing should be wanting to a man adorned with so many gifts. In his own opinion, he was nothing but a sinner, despite the fact that he was the ornament and splendor of all sanctity. He tried to build himself up upon this virtue, so that he would lay the foundation he had learned from Christ.[220] Forgetting the things he had gained, he set before his eyes only his failings in the conviction that he lacked more than he had gained. There was no covetousness in him except the desire to become better, and not content with what he had, he sought to add new virtues.

He was humble in dress, more humble in conviction, most humble in reputation. This prince of God was not known as anyone's superior except by this brightest jewel alone, namely, that among the lesser he was the least. This virtue, this title, this mark indicated that he was the minister general.[221] All lofty speaking was absent from his mouth, all pomp from his gestures, all ostentation from his actions.

In many things he had learned his opinion from a revelation; yet, conferring about it, he would set the opinions of others ahead of his own. He considered the advice of his companions safer, and the view of another seemed better than his own. He used to say that a brother had not given up all things for the Lord if he kept the purse of his own opinion. He preferred to hear blame spoken of himself rather than praise, for the former would lead one to amend his life, the latter to a fall.

CHAPTER CIII

Francis' humility toward the bishop of Terni and toward a certain peasant

141 Once when Francis preached to the people of Terni,[222] the bishop of that city praised him before all at the end of the sermon and said to them: "In this latest hour God has glorified his church in this poor and despised, simple and unlettered man; for this reason we are bound always to praise the Lord, knowing that *he has not done thus for any other nation.*"[223] When the saint heard these things, he accepted it with wonderful kindliness that the bishop had judged him to be contemptible in such express words. And when they were entering the church, he fell at the feet of the bishop, saying: "In truth, lord Bishop, you have done me a great favor, for you alone kept the things that are mine unharmed, whereas others take them away from me. Like a discerning man, you have separated, I say, the pre-

cious from the worthless, giving praise to God and ascribing to me my worthlessness."

142 Not only did the man of God show himself humble before his superiors; but also among his equals and those beneath him he was more ready to be admonished and corrected than to give admonitions. Wherefore when one day he was riding on an ass, because weak and infirm as he was he could not go by foot, he passed through the field of a peasant who happened to be working there just then; the peasant ran over to him and asked solicitously if he were Brother Francis. When the man of God humbly replied that he was the man he was asking about, the peasant said: "Try to be as good as you are said to be by all men, for many put their trust in you. Therefore I admonish you never to be other than you are expected to be." But when the man of God Francis heard this, he got down from the ass and threw himself before the peasant and humbly kissed his feet, thanking him for being kind enough to give him this admonition. Since, therefore, he was so famous as to be thought a saint by many, he considered himself lowly before God and men, neither did he feel any pride over his widespread fame or over his sanctity, not even over the many brothers and sons given him as a first reward for his merits.

CHAPTER CIV

How Francis resigned his office in a chapter, and about a certain prayer

143 A few years after his conversion, Francis, to preserve the virtue of holy humility, resigned the office of superior of the order in a certain chapter[224] before all the brothers, saying: "From now on I am dead to you. But see, here is Brother Peter of Catania, whom I and all of you shall obey." And bowing

down before him, he promised him obedience and reverence. The brothers, therefore, wept, and their sorrow brought forth deep sighs, when they saw themselves, in a certain way, to be orphaned from such a father. But Francis, rising and with his hands joined and his eyes raised to heaven, said: "Lord, I commend to you the family that you heretofore have entrusted to me. But now, because of my infirmities, as you know, most sweet Lord, I am unable to care for it and so I entrust it to the ministers. Let them be obliged to render an account before you, Lord, on judgment day, if any brother of them perishes because of their negligence, or example, or harsh correction." He remained thereafter until his death a subject, conducting himself more humbly than anyone else.

CHAPTER CV

How Francis gave up having any special companions

144 Another time Francis gave over all his companions to his vicar, saying: "I do not wish to appear singular because of a privilege, but let brothers go with me from place to place only as the Lord will inspire them." And he added: "I once saw a blind man with a little dog as his guide along the way." This therefore was his glory that, every vestige of singularity and ostentation having been put aside, *the strength of Christ* was dwelling in him.[225]

CHAPTER CVI

Francis' words against those who desired an office; his description of a Friar Minor

145 But Francis, seeing that some brothers were longing to hold offices, though, besides other things, their very ambition to be placed over others made them unworthy of office, said that such were not Friars Minor, but that, *forgetful of the calling with which* they *were called,*[226] *they had fallen away from that glory.*[227] Some, however, who took it ill when they were removed from office, in as much as it was not the burden they sought, but the honor, he would silence by many words.

Once he said to his companion: "I would not seem to myself to be a Friar Minor unless I were in the state I will describe to you." And he said: "Suppose I, being a prelate among the brothers, should go to the chapter and preach and admonish the brothers, and at the end this should be said against me: 'An unlettered and contemptible person is not suitable for us; therefore we do not want you to rule over us, because you have no eloquence, you are simple and unlettered.' At length I am thrown out with reproaches and despised by all. I say to you, unless I listen to these words with the same face, with the same joy, with the same purpose of sanctity, I am in no way a Friar Minor." And he added: "In an office is found an occasion for a fall; in praise, an occasion for complete destruction; in the humility of being a subject, an occasion for profit for the soul. Why then do we pay more attention to the dangers than to the profit, when we have time to gain profit?"

CHAPTER CVII

How and why Francis wanted the brothers to be subject to the clergy

146   But, though Francis wanted his sons to *be at peace with all men*[228] and to conduct themselves as little ones among all, he taught by his words and showed by his example that they were to be especially humble toward clerics. For he used to say: "We have been sent to help the clergy[229] toward the sal-

vation of souls so that what might be found insufficient in them might be supplied by us. Everyone will receive his reward, not according to the authority he exercises, but according to the labor he does. Know, brothers," he said, "the fruit of souls is most pleasing to God, and it can be better obtained by peace with clerics than by disagreements with them. If they hinder the salvation of people, the revenge pertains to God and he will *repay them in due time*.[230] Therefore, be subject to prelates, so that, in so far as you can help it, no jealousy will spring up. If you will be sons of peace, you will win the clergy and the people for the Lord, and the Lord judges this more acceptable than to win the people but scandalize the clergy. Hide their lapses, supply for their many defects; and when you have done this, be even more humble."

CHAPTER CVIII

Of the respect Francis showed the bishop of Imola

147   Once when St. Francis came to Imola,[231] a city of Romagna,[232] he presented himself to the bishop of the region,[233] asking his permission to preach. The bishop said to him: "It is enough, Brother, that I preach to my people." Bowing his head, St. Francis humbly went outside, and after a short time, he came back in. The bishop said to him: "What do you want, Brother? What are you seeking now?" And the blessed Francis said: "Lord, if a father drives his son out of one door, he must come back in by another." Subdued by this humility, the bishop embraced him with a happy countenance and said: "You and all your brothers may preach in my diocese in the future with my general permission, for your holy humility has merited this."

CHAPTER CIX

*Of the humility and charity of St. Francis and
St. Dominic toward one another*

148   Those two bright lights of the world, St.
Dominic and St. Francis, were together in Rome
once with the lord of Ostia,[234] who later became the
supreme pontiff. And after they had spoken affection-
ate words in turn about the Lord, the bishop finally
said to them: "In the primitive church the pastors
of the church were poor and were men of charity,
not men of greed. Why," he said, "do we not in the
future make bishops and prelates from among your
brothers who excel all others by their learning and
example? A dispute followed between the saints as
to which one should answer; they both strove not to
anticipate each other but to give way to each other;
what is more, each was urging the other to make the
reply. Each one gave preference to the other, for
each one was devoted to the other. But in the end,
humility conquered Francis, lest he put himself forward; and humility conquered Dominic, so that he
would humbly obey and answer first. Therefore,
replying, the blessed Dominic said to the bishop:
"Lord, my brothers have been raised to a high station, if they only knew it; and even if I wanted to,
I could not permit them to acquire any other dignity." After he had replied thus briefly, the blessed
Francis bowed before the bishop and said: "Lord,
my brothers are called *minors* so that they will not
presume to become greater. Their vocation teaches
them to remain in a lowly station and to follow the
footsteps of the humble Christ, so that in the end
they may be exalted above the rest in the sight of the
saints. If," he said, "you want them to bear fruit for
the church of God, hold them and preserve them in
the station to which they have been called, and bring

them back to a lowly station, even if they are unwilling. I pray you, therefore, Father, that you by no means permit them to rise to any prelacy, lest they become prouder rather than poorer and grow arrogant toward the rest." Such were the answers of these blessed men.

149 What then do you say, O sons of the saints? Jealousy and envy prove you are degenerate, and no less, ambition proves you are illegitimate sons. *You bite and devour one another,*[235] and your conflicts and strifes arise only from your concupiscences. Your wrestling is against the hosts of darkness;[236] your battle is against the armies of devils, and you turn the points of your swords against each other; your fathers, filled with wisdom and *their face being turned toward the propitiatory,*[237] looked familiarly upon one another, while their sons, filled with envy, are *grievous even to behold.*[238] What will the body accomplish, if it has a divided heart? Certainly, the teaching of piety would progress more fruitfully throughout the world, if the bond of charity joined the ministers of the word of God together more firmly. For what we speak or what we teach is rendered greatly suspect, because a certain leaven of hatred is made manifest in us today by evident signs. I know that the good on either side are not at fault, but the bad, who, I think, should be rooted out lest they infect the holy. What then shall I say of those who set their minds *on high things?*[239] The fathers came to the kingdom by the way of humility, not by the way of loftiness; the sons, walking about in the circle of their ambition, do not ask *the way of a city for their habitation.*[240] What is left, that we who do not follow their way should not attain glory? *Far be it from us, Lord!*[241] Make the disciples humble under the wings of their humble master; make kindred spirits kind; *and mayst thou see thy children's chil-*

dren, peace upon Israel.[242]

CHAPTER CX

How each commended himself to the other

150   When the answers of the servants of God had been given, as was narrated above,[243] the lord of Ostia was much edified by the words of both and gave great thanks to God. But as they left, the blessed Dominic asked St. Francis to kindly give him the cord he wore about his waist. St. Francis was reluctant to do this, moved by the same humility to refuse as the other was moved to ask. Finally, however, the blessed devotion of the petitioner won out and Dominic very devoutly put the cord that was given him about himself beneath his inner tunic. Then the two joined hands and commended themselves to one another with great kindliness. The one said to the other: "Blessed Francis, I wish that your order and mine might be made one and that we might live in the church according to the same rule." When at last they left one another, St. Dominic said to several who were there at the time: "In truth, I say to you, all other religious ought to follow this holy man Francis, so great is the perfection of his sanctity."

OF OBEDIENCE

CHAPTER CXI

How Francis always had a guardian for the sake of true obedience

151   In order that this most prudent merchant might profit in many ways and consume the entire present time in gaining merit, he wanted to be driven under the reins of obedience and to submit himself to the direction of another. For this reason he not only resigned the office of general,[244] but for the sake of the greater good of obedience, he requested a special guardian for himself whom he would cherish as his superior. For he said to Brother Peter of Catania, to whom he had earlier promised holy obedience:[245] "I ask you, for love of God, to give me one of my companions to take your place for me, so that I may devoutly obey him as I would obey you. I know," he said, "the fruit of obedience and that no time passes without profit for him *who submits* his *neck to the yoke* of another."[246] Therefore, after his earnest request had been granted, he remained everywhere subject until his death, always reverently obeying his personal guardian.

But once he said to his companion: "Among the other things the kindness of God has generously granted me, it has granted me this grace that I would obey a novice of one hour, if he were given me as my guardian, as carefully as I would obey the oldest and most discreet person. A subject," he said, "should not consider the man in his superior, but Him for whose sake he is a subject. But the more contemptible is he who rules, so much the more does the humility of him who obeys please."

CHAPTER CXII

How Francis described the truly obedient man, and of three kinds of obedience

152   Another time, sitting with his companions, the blessed Francis spoke something like this with a deep sigh: "There is hardly a religious in the whole world who obeys his superior perfectly." Greatly moved, his companions said to him: "Tell us, Father, what is the perfect and highest obedience." And he replied, describing the truly obedient man under the figure of a dead body: "Take a lifeless body and

place it where you will. You will see that it does not resist being moved, it does not murmur about its position, it does not cry out if it is allowed to lie there. If it is placed on a chair, it will not look up but down; if it is clothed in purple, it looks twice as pale. This," he said, "is a truly obedient man; he does not ask why he is moved, he cares not where he is placed, he does not insist on being changed elsewhere. Raised to an office, he retains his accustomed humility; the more he is honored, the more unworthy does he consider himself." Another time, speaking of these same things, he said that things that are granted after a request are more properly permissions; but if they are enjoined and not asked for, they are sacred obediences.[247] He said that both are good, but that the latter are safer. But that obedience he thought was the highest and was without anything of flesh and blood by which one goes by divine inspiration among the infidels,[248] either for the sake of profit for one's neighbors or out of a desire for martyrdom. To ask for this obedience he thought was highly acceptable to God.

CHAPTER CXIII

That a command under obedience is not to be lightly given

153 Francis therefore thought that a command should but rarely be given under obedience, that that weapon should not be hurled first which should be the last recourse. "The hand must not be quickly laid to the sword," he said. But he thought that he who does not hasten to obey a command of obedience does not fear God or respect men. Nothing is more true than this. For, in a rash superior what is the power to command but a sword in the hand of a madman? And what is more hopeless than a religious who spurns obedience?

CHAPTER CXIV

Of the brother whose capuche Francis threw into the fire because he came without an obedience, though he was drawn by devotion

154 On one occasion Francis took away the capuche from a brother who had come alone and without an obedience[249] and he ordered it to be thrown into a great fire. But when no one withdrew the capuche, for they were frightened whenever the face of their father was even somewhat disturbed, the saint commanded it to be withdrawn from the flames; and it had not been harmed. Although the merits of the saint could bring this about, perhaps merit was not entirely lacking on the part of that brother. For the desire to see the most holy father had spurred him on, though discretion, the charioteer of virtues, was not in him.

OF THOSE WHO GIVE A GOOD OR A BAD EXAMPLE

CHAPTER CXV

Of the example of a certain good brother and of the behavior of the older brothers

155 Francis used to say that the Friars Minor had been sent by the Lord in these latest times[250] to give examples of light[251] to those wrapped in the darkness of sins. He would say that he was filled *with the most sweet savour*[252] and anointed with the strength *of precious ointment*,[253] when he heard of the wonderful works of his holy brothers in distant parts of the world. It happened that a certain brother named Barbaro once hurled an abusive word against another brother in the presence of a certain nobleman from the island of Cyprus. When he saw that brother somewhat hurt by the conflict of words, he took some asses' dung and put it into his mouth to be eaten as vengeance upon himself; and he said: "Let the tongue that poured out the poison of anger upon my brother eat dung." Seeing this, the knight was struck with astonishment and departed greatly edified; and from that time on he generously placed himself and his goods at the will of the brothers.

All the brothers observed this unfailingly as a custom that if any of them at any time spoke a disturbing word to another, he would immediately cast himself upon the ground and impress kisses upon the other's foot even if the other were unwilling. The saint rejoiced in such things, whenever he heard his sons bring forth from themselves examples of holiness; and he heaped blessings most *worthy of entire acceptance*[254] upon those brothers who by word or deed led sinners to the love of Christ. He wanted his sons to have in themselves the same zeal for souls that filled himself.

CHAPTER CXVI

Of certain ones who gave bad example, and of the saint's curse upon them, and how seriously he took these things

156   Thus also those who brought dishonor upon religious life by their evil deeds or example incurred the heaviest sentence of his curse. For when one day it was told him that the bishop of Fondi[255] had said to two brothers who had come before him and who pretended great contempt for themselves by letting their beards grow rather long: "Beware, lest the beauty of religion be stained by novelties of this kind," the saint arose immediately and *stretching forth* his *hands to heaven*[256] and shedding many tears,

he burst out in words of prayer, or rather of imprecation, after this fashion: "Lord Jesus Christ, who chose your apostles to the number of twelve; though one of this number fell, the rest clung to thee and preached the holy Gospel, filled with one spirit; you, Lord, *in this last hour*,[257] mindful of your ancient mercy, planted the order of brothers as a support of your faith and that the mystery of your Gospel might be fulfilled through them. Who, therefore, will make satisfaction for them before you, if, though they are sent for this, they not only fail to display examples of light to all, but rather show forth the *works of darkness?*[258] By you, most holy Lord, and by the whole celestial court, and by me your little one, may they be cursed who by their bad example tear down and bring to ruin what you have built up in the past through holy brothers of this order and do not cease to build up." Where are they who say they are happy in his blessing and boast that they have gained familiarity with him as much as they have desired? If, which God forbid, they be found to have shown forth the *works of darkness*[259] to the peril of others without repentance, woe to them, woe because of eternal damnation!

157   "The best brothers are put to confusion by the works of the bad brothers," Francis used to say, "and where they themselves have not sinned, they must bear judgment because of the example of the wicked. They therefore transfix me with a sharp sword and plunge it through my bowels *all the day long*."[260] Mainly on this account did Francis withdraw himself from the company of the brothers, lest it happen that he hear anything evil of anyone unto the renewal of his grief.

And he would say: "The time is coming when the order beloved of God will be spoken ill of because of bad examples, so much so that it will be ashamed to

263

show itself in public. But those who will come to enter the order at that time will be led only by the operation of the Holy Spirit, and flesh and blood will put no stain upon them and they will indeed be blessed by the Lord. Although meritorious works may not be found in them, with that charity growing cold that makes saints work fervently, the greatest possible temptations will come upon them, and they who will be found just at that time will be better than those who have gone before them. But woe to those who applaud themselves for the mere appearance of the religious life; they will grow numb with sloth and they will not be able to resist steadfastly the temptations permitted as a trial for the elect; for only those who *have been tried will receive the crown of life,*[261] those whom meanwhile the malice of the wicked has put to the test."

CHAPTER CXVII

Of the revelation made by God to Francis concerning the state of the order and that the order would never fail

158 But Francis was greatly consoled by the visitations of God, by which he was made to feel sure that the foundations of his order would always remain unshaken. It was also promised to him that without a doubt the number of those who would fall away would be replaced by the substitution of elect. For once when he was disturbed over bad examples and, thus distressed, gave himself over to prayer, he brought back this rebuke from the Lord: "Why are you disturbed, little man?[262] Did I not place you over my order as its shepherd, and now you do not know that I am its chief protector? I chose you, a simple man, for this task, that what I would do in you to be imitated by the rest they might follow who wished to follow. I have called, I will preserve and feed, and I will choose others to repair the falling away of others, so that if a substitute is not born, I will make him to be born. Do not be disturbed, therefore, but *work out your salvation*,[263] for though the order were reduced to the number of three, it will by my grace remain unshaken." From then on Francis would say that the very great multitude of imperfect brothers would be overcome by the virtues of one saint, for the deepest darkness is dispersed by even a single ray of light.

AGAINST IDLENESS AND THE IDLE

CHAPTER CXVIII

A revelation made to Francis as to when one is a servant of God, when not

159 From the time that this man began to cling to the Lord, having put aside all transitory things, he allowed hardly a moment of time to pass unused. Indeed, though he had already laid up an abundance of merits in the *treasure house* of the Lord,[264] he was always ready, always zealous for spiritual exercises. Not to do something good he considered a grave offense; not to advance he judged to be a falling back. Once when he was staying in a cell at Siena, he called his sleeping companions one night, saying: "I have asked the Lord, brothers, to deign to show me when I am his servant. And the most kind Lord just now deigned to give me this reply: 'Know that you are then truly my servant when you think, speak, and do holy things.' Therefore have I called you, brothers, because I wish to be filled with shame before you if at any time I do nothing of these three things."

CHAPTER CXIX

The penance for idlc words at the Portiuncula

160   Another time, at St. Mary of the Portiuncula, the man of God, considering how much profit from prayer flows away because of idle words after prayer, ordained this remedy against the fault of idle words, saying: "If any of the brothers utters an idle or useless word, he shall be bound immediately to admit his guilt and to say a *Pater Noster* for each idle word. But thus I want it, that if he himself is first to admit the guilt of his fault, he shall say a *Pater Noster* for his own soul; if he is accused of his fault first by another, he shall offer the prayer for the soul of that other."

CHAPTER CXX

How Francis, working himself, despised the idle

161   Francis used to say that the lukewarm who did not make themselves acquainted familiarly with work would be quickly vomited forth from the mouth of the Lord.[265] No one could appear idle before him without being corrected by him with a sharp rebuke. Fcr he himself worked and labored with his hands as an example of all perfection, allowing nothing of that greatest gift of time to escape. But he said once: "I want all my brothers to work and to be employed, and those who do not know how should learn some crafts."[266] And he gave this reason: "That we may be less burdensome to men," he said, "and that the heart or tongue may not wander to unlawful things in idleness." But the profit or the reward of labor he did not commit to the free disposition of the laborer but to the disposition of the guardian or of the family.

CHAPTER CXXI

A lament over idle and gluttonous brothers addressed to St. Francis

162   Holy Father, permit us who are called your sons to raise on high today a lament. The exercise of virtue is odious to many who, wanting to rest before they have labored,[267] prove themselves to be sons of Lucifer rather than sons of Francis. We have a greater abundance of weaklings than of warriors, although they ought to consider this life a warfare, since they have been born to labor.[268] It does not please them to make progress through action; and they cannot do so through contemplation. When they have disturbed all by their singularity, working more with their jaws than with their hands, they hate *him that rebuketh them in the gate,*[269] and they do not permit themselves to be touched even by the tips of the fingers. But I wonder still more at the impudence of those who, according to the word of the blessed Francis, could not have lived at home except by their sweat, and now, without working, feed on the sweat of the poor. Wonderful prudence! Though they do nothing, they consider themselves always occupied. They know the hours of the meals, and if hunger takes hold of them, they complain that the sun has gone to sleep. Shall I believe, good Father, that these monsters of men are worthy of ·your glory? Not even of the habit! You always taught that we should seek in this wanton and fleeting time the riches of merits, lest it happen that we go begging in the future. These, though, have no part in their fatherland, and they will have to go into exile hereafter. This disease is rampant among subjects because superiors act as though it were not possible to merit a share in the punishment of those whose vices they are tolerating.

CHAPTER CXXII

What a preacher should be

163 Francis wanted such men to be ministers of *the word of God*[270] who give themselves to the study of spiritual things and are not hindered by other duties. For these, he used to say, have been chosen by a certain great king to deliver to the people the edicts that proceed from his mouth. But he said: "The preacher must first draw from secret prayers what he will later pour out in holy sermons; he must first grow hot within before he speaks words that are in themselves cold." He said that this is an office to be revered and that those who administer it should be reverenced by all. "These," he said, "are the life of the body; they are the attackers of the devils; they are the *light of the world*."[271]

But he considered doctors of sacred theology to be worthy of even greater honors. For he once had it written down for all: "All theologians and those who minister to us the words of God we must honor and venerate as those who minister to us spirit and life."[272] And when he wrote once to Blessed Anthony, he had this salutation placed at the beginning of the letter: "To Brother Anthony, my bishop."[273]

CHAPTER CXXIII

Against those who seek vain praise and an exposition of a word of prophecy

164 But Francis said that preachers who often sell what they do for the price of empty praise are to be pitied. The abnormal growth of such men he at times cured with such an antidote as this: "Why do you glory over men who have been converted when it was my simple brothers who converted them by

their prayers?" Finally these words, *So that the barren have borne many,*[274] he explained in the following way. "The *barren,*" he said, "is my poor little brother who does not have the duty of bringing forth children for the Church. This one will *bring forth many* at the judgment, because those he is now converting by his private prayers the Judge will give to him unto glory. *She that had many children is weakened*[275] suggests that the preacher who rejoices over many as though he had brought them forth by his own power will learn that he had nothing to do with them personally." But those who want to be praised rather as rhetoricians than as preachers, speaking as they do with elegance rather than with sincerity, Francis did not greatly love. These, he said, divide wickedly who spend all their time at preaching and none at devotion. But he praised the preacher, certainly, but only one who thinks of himself at the proper time and provides wisely for himself.

OF THE CONTEMPLATION OF THE CREATOR
IN HIS CREATURES

CHAPTER CXXIV

The love of the saint toward sensible and insensible creatures

165   Hurrying to leave this world in as much as it is the place of exile of our pilgrimage, this blessed traveler was yet helped not a little by the things that are in the world. With respect to the *world-rulers of this darkness,*[276] he used it as a field of battle; with respect to God, he used it as a very bright *image of his goodness.*[277] In every work of the artist he praised the Artist; whatever he found in the things made he referred to the Maker. He rejoiced in all the works of the hands of the Lord and saw behind things

pleasant to behold their life-giving reason and cause.[278] In beautiful things he saw Beauty itself; all things were to him good. "He who made us is the best," they cried out to him. Through his footprints impressed upon things he followed the Beloved everywhere; he made for himself from all things a ladder by which *to come even to his throne.*[279]

He embraced all things with a rapture of unheard of devotion, speaking to them of the Lord and admonishing them to praise him.[280] He spared lights, lamps, and candles,[281] not wishing to extinguish their brightness with his hand, for he regarded them as a symbol of Eternal Light. He walked reverently upon stones, because of him who was called the Rock.[282] When he used this versicle: *Thou hast exalted me on a rock,*[283] he would say for the sake of greater reverence: *Thou hast exalted me at the foot of a rock.*

He forbade the Brothers to cut down the whole tree when they cut wood, so that it might have hope of sprouting again. He commanded the gardener to leave the border around the garden undug, so that in their proper times the greenness of the grass and the beauty of flowers might announce the beauty of the Father of all things. He commanded that a little place be set aside in the garden for sweet-smelling and flowering plants, so that they would bring those who look upon them to the memory of the Eternal Sweetness.[284]

He removed from the road little worms, lest they be crushed under foot; and he ordered that honey and the best wines be set out for the bees, lest they perish from want in the cold of winter.[285] He called all animals by the name *brother,*[286] though among all the kinds of animals he preferred the gentle.[287] Who could possibly narrate everything? For that original goodness that will be one day *all things in all* already shown forth in this saint *all things in all.*[288]

CHAPTER CXXV

How the creatures themselves returned his love, and of the fire that did not give him pain

166 All creatures, therefore, tried to give their love in return to the saint and to reply by their own gratitude according as he deserved; they were glad when he caressed them, they agreed when he requested anything, they obeyed when he commanded anything. May the narration of a few instances please the reader. At the time when Francis suffered the infirmity of his eyes and was persuaded to permit treatment of them,[289] a doctor was called to the place. When he came, he brought an iron for cauterizing and ordered it to be put into the fire until it should be red-hot. But the blessed father, strengthening his body now struck with horror, spoke thus to the fire: "My brother fire, that surpasses all other things in beauty, the Most High created you strong, beautiful, and useful. Be kind to me in this hour, be courteous. For I have loved you in the past in the Lord. I beseech the great Lord who made you that he temper your heat now so that I may bear it when you burn me gently." When his prayer was ended, he made the sign of the cross over the fire and then remained fearless. The doctor took the glowing and hot iron in his hands; all the brothers, overcome by human weakness, fled; and the saint offered himself joyfully and eagerly to the iron. The iron was plunged into the tender flesh with a hiss, and it was gradually drawn from the ear to the eyebrow in its cauterizing. How much pain that fire caused, the words of the saint himself, who knows best, testify. For when the brothers who had fled returned, the father said, smiling: "O fainthearted and weak of heart, why did you flee? *In truth I say to you*,[290] I did not feel either the heat of the fire or any pain in my flesh." And

271

turning to the doctor, he said: "If my flesh is not sufficiently burned, burn it again." The doctor, knowing that in similar cases the experience was much different, proclaimed it a miracle from God, saying: "I say to you, brothers, I *have seen wonderful things today.*"[291] I believe that he had returned to primitive innocence, for whom, when he wished it, cruel things were made gentle.

CHAPTER CXXVI

Of the bird that rested in Francis' hands

167   When the blessed Francis was going across the lake of Rieti to the hermitage of Greccio, he was sitting in a certain little boat.[292] A certain fisherman offered him a waterfowl, that he might rejoice over it in the Lord. The blessed father accepted it joyfully, and opening his hands, he gently told it that it was free to fly away. But when it did not wish to leave, but wanted to rest there in his hands as in a nest, the saint raised his eyes and remained in prayer. And returning to himself as from another place after a long while, he gently commanded the bird to go back to its former freedom. So, upon receiving this permission along with a blessing, the bird flew away, showing its joy by a certain movement of the body.

CHAPTER CXXVII

Of the falcon

168   When the blessed Francis was staying in a certain hermitage, shunning in his usual way the sight and conversation of men, a falcon that was making its nest in the place attached itself to him in a great bond of friendship. For always during the night it announced with its song and noise the hour at which the saint was accustomed to rise for worship of God. This was very pleasing to the saint of God, in that, by reason of the great solicitude of the bird for him, any delay on his part because of laziness was driven away. But when the saint was afflicted more than usual by illness, the falcon would spare him and not give the signal for the time of the watches. Indeed, as if instructed by God, it would very gently sound the bell of its voice about dawn. Little wonder if all other creatures too venerated this eminent love of the Creator.

CHAPTER CXXVIII

Of the bees

169   On a certain mountain a cell was once constructed in which the servant of God performed penance most strictly for forty days. When this space of time was completed, he left the place and the cell remained without another inhabitant after him, placed as it was in a lonely spot. An earthen vessel, from which the saint used to drink, was also abandoned there. Once, however, when some men went to that place out of reverence for the saint, they found that vessel filled with bees. They had built little cells in the vessel with wonderful skill, signifying, surely, the sweetness of contemplation that the saint had experienced there.

CHAPTER CXXIX

Of the pheasant

170   A certain nobleman from the commune of Siena sent a pheasant to the blessed Francis while the latter was sick. He accepted it with alacrity, not with the desire of eating it, but, in the way he always rejoiced over such things, out of love for the Creator. And he said to the pheasant: "May our Creator be praised, brother pheasant!" And to the brothers he said: "Let us see now if brother pheasant will stay with us, or if it will go back to its usual and more suitable haunts." One of the brothers took it, at the command of the saint, and placed it at a distance in the vineyard. Immediately, however, it came directly back to the father's cell. Again Francis ordered it placed even farther away; but it came back with the greatest speed to the door of his cell and entered almost by force under the habits of the brothers who were standing at the door. The saint then ordered it to be fed diligently, embracing it and caressing it with soft words. When a certain physician who was quite devoted to the saint of God saw this, he begged the pheasant from the brothers, not wanting to eat it, but to raise it out of reverence for the saint. What more? He took it home with him; but the pheasant, as though it had suffered an injury in being separated from the saint, refused absolutely to eat as long as it was away from Francis' presence. The physician was astonished, and immediately taking the pheasant back to the saint, he told him everything just as it had happened. As soon as the pheasant was put upon the ground, it saw its father, and putting off all grief, it began to eat with joy.

CHAPTER CXXX

Of the tree cricket

171   Near the cell of the saint of God at the Portiuncula there was a tree cricket that used to perch on a fig tree and frequently sing sweetly. At times the blessed father would extend his hand to it and kindly call it to himself, saying: "My sister cricket, come to me." As though endowed with reason, it immediately got up on his hand. And Francis said to it: "Sing, my sister cricket, and praise your Creator

with a joyful song." Obeying without delay, it began to sing, and it did not cease to sing until the man of God, mingling his own praises with its songs, commanded it to go back to its usual haunt. It remained there for eight days in a row, as if bound there. But when the saint would come down from his cell, he would always touch it with his hands and command it to sing, and it was always ready to obey his commands. And the saint said to his companions: "Let us give our sister cricket leave to go now, for it has made us sufficiently happy now; we do not want our flesh to glory vainly over things of this kind." And immediately with permission from Francis, it left, and it did not ever show up there again. Seeing all these things, the brothers were greatly astonished.

OF CHARITY

CHAPTER CXXXI

Of Francis' charity and how he set himself as an example of perfection for the salvation of souls

172   Since the strength of Francis' love made him a brother to all other creatures, it is not surprising that the charity of Christ made him more than a brother to those who are stamped with the image of their Creator. For he used to say that nothing is more important than the salvation of souls, and he often offered as proof the fact that the Only-begotten of God deigned to hang on the cross for souls. This accounts for his struggles at prayer, his tirelessness at preaching, his excess in giving examples.[293] He did not consider himself a friend of Christ unless he loved the souls that Christ loved. And this was the main reason why he reverenced doctors so much,[294] namely, because, as Christ's helpers, they exercised one office with him. He loved his brothers beyond measure with an affection that rose from his inner-most being, because they were of the same *household of faith*[295] and united by participation in *an eternal inheritance according to the promise.*[296]

173   As often as the severity of his life was re-proved, he would reply that he had been given to the order as an example, that as an eagle he might en-courage his young ones to fly.[297] Wherefore, though his innocent flesh that always subjected itself of its own accord to the spirit did not need any scourging for its offenses, nevertheless, for the sake of example, he heaped punishments upon it, keeping *hard ways*[298] solely because of others. Indeed, rightly, for more respect is paid to the actions than to the words of superiors. By actions, Father, you spoke more sweet-ly, you persuaded more easily, and you showed the way more certainly. Though superiors *speak with the tongues of men and of angels,*[299] but do not show examples of charity, it profits me little, and them not at all. Indeed, where the one who reproves is in no way feared and will takes the place of reason,[300] will seals suffice for salvation?[301] However, we must do what they tell us, that the little streams may flow through narrow channels to the small garden beds.[302] Meanwhile, let a rose be gathered from thorns,[303] so that the *elder* may *serve the younger.*[304]

CHAPTER CXXXII

Of Francis' concern for his subjects

174   Who indeed is clothed with Francis' concern for his subjects? He was always raising his hands to heaven for the true Israelites,[305] and forgetful of himself at times, his first concern was for the salva-tion of his brothers. He prostrated himself at the feet of the Majesty, he offered a sacrifice of the spirit for his sons,[306] he compelled God to grant his graces to

them. With love and fear, he had compassion on the little flock he drew after himself, lest after they had lost the world they should lose also heaven. He believed that he would be without future glory unless he made those entrusted to him glorious with him, those whom his spirit brought forth with greater labor than a mother's labor in giving birth to her children.

CHAPTER CXXXIII

Francis' compassion for the sick

175   Francis had great compassion for the sick, great concern for their needs.[307] When the kindness of secular people sent him choice foods, even though he needed them more than others, he gave them to the rest of the sick. He transferred to himself the afflictions of all who were sick, offering them words of sympathy when he could not give them help. On days of fast he himself would eat, lest the sick should be ashamed to eat; and he was not ashamed to beg meat through the public places of the towns for a sick brother. But he admonished the ill to bear their troubles patiently and not to give scandal when all their wishes were not satisfied. Wherefore in one of his rules[308] he had these words set down: "I beg all my sick brothers that they do not become angry in their infirmities or disturbed either against God or against their brothers. Let them not be too solicitous in asking for medicines, nor too desirous that the flesh which is soon to die and which is the enemy of the soul be delivered. Let them *give thanks in all things*,[309] so that they may desire to be as God wants them to be. For whom God has *destined for eternal life*,[310] he instructs by the goads of scourgings and sicknesses, as he himself said: 'Those whom I love, I correct and chastise.' "[311]

176 Francis once took a certain sick brother, who he knew had a longing for grapes, into the vineyard and sitting down under the vine, he first ate to give the other courage to eat.[312]

CHAPTER CXXXIV

Of Francis' compassion toward those who were ill in spirit and of those who act contrary to what he said

177 But Francis cherished with greater kindness and supported with greater patience those sick who he knew were tossed about and bothered by temptations and were fainting in spirit. Therefore, avoiding sharp corrections where he saw there was no danger, he spared the rod to spare the soul. To forestall the occasion of failing and not to let him slip whom it would be difficut to raise up if he fell,[313] this Francis said is the duty of a superior who is a father and not a tyrant.[314] Alas for the pitiable madness of our time! Those who are liable to fall we not only do not raise up or support, but at times we even push them to make them fall. We think nothing of taking away from that Great Shepherd one little sheep for whom he offered on the cross a *loud cry and tears*.[315] You, holy Father, on the other hand, want the erring to amend rather than perish. But we know that the sickness of self-will is more deeply rooted in some and for these cauterizing is needed, not ointment. It is evident that for many it is more wholesome to be ruled *with a rod of iron*[316] than to be stroked with the hand. But *oil and wine*,[317] the *rod and the staff*,[318] harshness and pity, burning and anointing, the prison and kindness, all these *have their season*.[319] All of them the *God of revenge*[320] and the *Father of mercies*[321] needs, but he desires mercy rather than sacrifice.[322]

CHAPTER CXXXV

Of the Spanish brothers

178   Sometimes this most holy man was *out of his mind for God*[323] in a wonderful manner and he rejoiced in spirit as often as a *fragrance*[324] came to him about his brothers. It happened that a certain Spaniard, a cleric devoted to God, enjoyed the sight of and conversation with Francis. This man made Francis happy with this account, among other things, of the brothers who were in Spain. "Your brothers," he said, "live in our country in a certain poor hermitage and they have so established their way of living that half of them take care of domestic needs and the other half spend their time in contemplation. In this way each week those who lead the active life exchange with those who lead the contemplative life and the quiet of those giving themselves to contemplation is changed for the business of work.[325] One day when the table had been set and the absent summoned by the signal, all but one of the contemplatives came together. After a short wait they went to his cell to call him to the table; but he was being refreshed at the more abundant table of the Lord. For he was found prostrate upon his face on the ground, stretched out in the form of a cross; and there was no sign that he was alive either from breathing or from movement. Two candles were burning at his head and at his feet, and they lighted up the cell in a wonderful way with a bright light. He was left in peace, lest they disturb his rapture, lest they *make the beloved to awake,* before *she pleased.*[326] Then the brothers peeped through the chinks of the cell, *standing behind the wall and looking through the lattices.*[327] What more? While the friends were hearkening to her that dwelleth in the gardens,[328] suddenly the light was gone and the brother came to himself again. Immediately he arose and coming to the table, he confessed the fault of his tardiness. Thus," that Spaniard said, "does it happen in our land." St. Francis could not contain himself for joy, sprinkled as he was with such fragrance of his sons. Suddenly he arose to give praise, and, as if his only glory were to hear good things of his brothers, he cried out, moved to his innermost depths: "I give you thanks, Lord, sanctifier and director of the poor, who have given me such joy in hearing such things of my brothers. Bless those brothers, I pray, with your most generous blessing, and sanctify by a special gift all who through their good example cause their profession to give off a fragrant odor."

CHAPTER CXXXVI

Against those who live evilly in hermitages and how he wanted all things to be common to all

179   Though we therefore know the charity of the saint which led him to rejoice in the successses of his beloved brothers, still we believe that he rebuked with no small severity those who lived in a different manner in the hermitages. For many change the place of contemplation into a place of idleness and change the eremitical way of life, which was devised for the perfecting of souls, into a cesspool of pleasure. The norm for such hermits of the present time is to live as each one pleases. But this is not applicable to all, for we know some are living in a hermitage like saints in the flesh in accordance with the very best regulations. We know also that those fathers who were their predecessors bloomed as solitary flowers. Would that the hermits of our time would not fall away from that primitive beauty, the praise of the righteousness of which remains forever.

180   St. Francis, exhorting all moreover to charity,

admonished them to show to one another affability and the friendliness of family life. "I wish," he said, "that my brothers would show themselves to be children of the same mother and that if anyone asks for a tunic or a cord or anything else, the other should give it to him with generosity. Let them share their books and anything else that is agreeable, so much so that one would even force the other to take it." And lest in this matter he should speak anything of those things that Christ was not working through him, he was the first to do all these things.

CHAPTER CXXXVII

Of the two French brothers to whom he gave his tunic

181 It happened that two French brothers of great sanctity met St. Francis. Rejoicing with an unheard of joy over him, they felt a double joy in that they had wanted for a long time to see him. After kind greetings and heart to heart conversation, their ardent devotion led them to beg St. Francis for his tunic. Immediately he took his tunic off and standing there naked, he gave it to them with great devotion; then accepting the one brother's tunic that was poorer, he put it on. He was prepared not only to give away things like that, but he was ready to spend himself[329] and he gladly gave whatever was asked of him.[330]

OF DETRACTION

CHAPTER CXXXVIII

How Francis wanted detractors to be punished[331]

182 Finally, since the soul that is filled with charity hates what is hateful to God, this virtue flourish-

ed in St. Francis. Hating detractors deeply and more than any other kind of wicked men, he said that they carried poison on their tongues and infected others with their poison. Gossipers, therefore, those biting fleas, he avoided when they were speaking, and he averted his ears, as we ourselves have seen, lest they be defiled by hearing such things. For once, when Francis heard a certain brother blacken the reputation of another, he turned to Brother Peter of Catania, his vicar, and spoke this terrible sentence: "Disaster confronts the order, unless these slanderers are checked. Quickly the sweetest savor of the many begins to take on a horrible stench, unless the mouths of the stinking are closed. Arise, arise, examine diligently, and if you find any accused brother innocent, make the accuser known to all by a severe correction. Hand him over to the Florentine pugilist,"[332] he said, "if you yourself cannot punish him." (He used to call Brother John of Florence the pugilist; he was a man of great stature and great strength). "I want you to use the greatest care," he said, "you and all the ministers, lest this horrible disease spread further." But at times he decreed that he who had taken away the good name of a brother should have his tunic taken away and that he should not raise his eyes to God until he first restored what he had taken away. This is why the brothers of that time renounced this vice in a special way and firmly agreed among themselves that whatever would detract from the honor of others or smacked of evil talk should be strictly avoided. Rightly and excellently done! What then is a detractor but the gall of humanity, the leaven of wickedness, the disgrace of the world? What then is a double-tongued man but the scandal of religion, the poison of the cloister, the destroyer of harmony? Alas, the face of the earth is filled with poisonous animals, and no one can escape the teeth of envious rivals. Rewards are offered to those who inform, and when innocence has been destroyed, the palm is at times given to falsehood. Behold, where a person cannot live by his honesty, he may gain food and clothing by tearing down the good name of others.

183 St. Francis therefore often said: "This is what the detractor says: 'Perfection of life is not in me; I have no great knowledge or special grace; as a consequence I find no place either with God or with men. *I know what I will do:*[333] *On the elect I will lay a blot,*[334] and I will play up to those in authority. I know my superior is only a man and that he at times acts in the same way as I do; when therefore the cedars are cut down, only the bramble will be seen in the woods.'[335] Alas, wretched one, feed on human flesh; and since you cannot live otherwise, gnaw on the entrails of your brothers. Such men try to appear good, not to become good; and they accuse others of vices, but do not put off their own vices. They praise only those by whose authority they wish to be cherished; they withhold praise when they think their praise will not be reported to the one they praise. They sell the pallor of the face of fasting for ruinous praises, that they may appear to be spiritual men[336] who judge all things but do not themselves want to be judged by anyone. They rejoice in the reputation of sanctity, not in the fact of it; in the name of angel, but not in virtue."[337]

DESCRIPTION OF THE MINISTER GENERAL
AND OF OTHER MINISTERS

CHAPTER CXXXIX

How the ministers should conduct themselves toward their companions

184 Near the end of Francis' vocation in the

Lord,[338] a certain brother who was always solicitous for the things of God and filled with love for the order, made this request of Francis: "Father, you will pass away and the family that has followed you will be left abandoned in this valley of tears. Point out someone, if you know of anyone in the order, upon whom your spirit may rest and upon whom the burden of minister general may be safely placed." St. Francis answered, accompanying all his words with sighs: "I see no one, son, who would be capable of being the leader of an army of so many different men and the shepherd of so large a flock. But I would like to describe one for you and fashion one, as the saying goes, with my hand, one in whom it may be clearly seen what kind of man the father of this family must be.

185 "He must be a man of most serious life," he said, "of great discretion, of praiseworthy reputation. A man who has no private loves, lest while he shows favor to the one, he beget scandal in the whole group. A man to whom zeal for prayer is a close friend; a man who sets aside certain hours for his soul and certain hours for the flock committed to him. For the first thing in the morning he must begin with the holy sacrifice of the Mass and commend himself and his flock to the divine protection in a prolonged devotion. After his prayers," he said, "he should make himself available to be stormed by all, to give answers to all, to provide for all with kindness. He must be a man who will not commit the foul sin of showing favoritism, a man in whom the care of the lowly and the simple is no less pronounced than his care for the wise and the greater. A man who, though it be his gift to excel in learning, bears the image of pious simplicity in his actions and fosters virtue. A man who detests money as the chief cause of the corruption of our profession and perfection; one who,

as the head of a poor order, should show himself an example for imitation to the rest, does not make wrong use of the pocketbook. For himself a habit and a little book should suffice, and for his brothers it is enough if he has a box of pens and a seal. He should not be a collector of books, nor given to much reading, lest he be taking from his office what he gives to study. He should be a man who consoles the afflicted, since he is the last recourse for the troubled; and if they can find no healing remedies from him, there is danger that the illness of despair may prevail over the sick. He should bend stormy characters to meekness; he should debase himself and relax something of what is his right to gain a soul for Christ. Toward those who take flight from the order let him not shut up the bowels of his mercy, as if they were sheep who had perished, knowing that the temptations that bring a man to such a pass are overpowering temptations.

186   "I would want him to be honored by all as taking the place of Christ and to be provided with everything that is necessary in all charity. However, he must not take pleasure in honors, nor be pleased by favors more than by injuries. If some time he should need more abundant food because he has grown weak or is exhausted, he should take it not in private but in public, so that others may be spared shame in providing for the weaknesses of their bodies. Above all else it pertains to him to examine the secrets of consciences, to bring out the truth from hidden places, but not to listen to the talkative. He must be, finally, a man who in no way will bring down the strong fabric of justice by his eagerness for retaining honors, but who will consider so great an office a burden rather than a dignity. However, he should not let apathy grow out of excessive kindness, nor a letdown in discipline out of lax indulgence, so

that while he is loved by all, he will be none the less feared by those *that work evil*.[339] I would wish, however, that he have companions endowed with goodness of life who will show themselves, just as he does, *in all things an example of good works*:[340] men who are staunch against pleasures, strong against hardships, and so becomingly affable that all who come to them may be received with holy cheerfulness. Behold," he said, "this is what the minister general of the order must be."

CHAPTER CXL

Of the ministers provincial

187   The blessed father required all these same qualities in the ministers provincial too, though in the minister general the single ones had to stand out conspicuously. He wished them to be affable to those in lesser stations, and serene with such great kindness that those who had failed in some way might not be afraid to entrust themselves to their good will. He wanted them to be moderate in giving commands and generous in forgiving offenses; he wanted them to be more ready to bear injuries than to return them; he wanted them to be enemies of vices, but healers of the wicked. Finally, he wanted them to be such that their life would be a mirror of discipline to all the rest. Still he wanted them to be treated with all honor and to be loved, because they bear the burden of cares and labors. He said that they are deserving before God of the highest rewards who govern the souls entrusted to them according to such a norm and such a law.

CHAPTER CXLI

Francis' answer when he was asked about the ministers

188   Once when Francis was asked by a certain brother why he had renounced the care of all his brothers and given them over to strange hands, as though they did not in any way pertain to him, he answered: "Son, I love the brothers as much as I can; but if they would follow my footsteps, I would certainly love them even more and I would not make myself a stranger to them. For there are some among the number of superiors who draw them to other things, proposing to them the example of the ancients,[341] and putting little value upon my admonitions. But what they are doing will be seen in the end." And a little afterwards, when he was afflicted with grave infirmity, he raised himself upon his couch and said in vehemence of spirit: "Who are these who have snatched my order and that of my brothers out of my hands? If I go to the general chapter, I will show them what my will is." And that brother said: "Would you not also change those ministers provincial who have abused their freedom for so long a time?" And sighing deeply, the father spoke this terrible word: "Let them live as it suits them, for the damnation of a few is a lesser loss than the damnation of many!" He did not say this because of all the ministers, but because of some who seemed to claim their prelacy by a hereditary right since they had held office for so long a time. In every kind of regular prelates this he praised most of all, that they do not change their conduct except for the better, that they do not seek popularity, that they do not insist on their power, but fulfill their office.

CHAPTER CXLII

What true simplicity is

189   The saint was zealous with more than usual care to show forth in himself, and he loved in others, holy simplicity, the daughter of grace, the sister of wisdom, the mother of justice. Not all simplicity, however, was approved by him, but only that simplicity which, being content with its God, considers everything else as of little value. This is that simplicity that *glories in the fear of God*,[342] that knows not how to do or to speak evil. This is that simplicity that, examining itself, condemns no one by its judgment; that, surrendering due authority to a better, seeks no authority for itself. This is that simplicity that, not considering *Grecian glories for the best*,[343] chooses rather to act than to learn or to teach. This is that simplicity that, in all the divine laws, leaves wordy circumlocutions, ornaments, and embellishments, vain displays and curiosities, to those who are marked for a fall, and seeks not the bark but the pith, not the shell but the kernel, not the many things, but the much, the greatest and the lasting good. The most holy father demanded this virtue in both the learned and the lay brothers, not considering it contrary to wisdom, but true wisdom's sister, though he thought it easier to be gotten as a habit and more ready to be used by those who are poor as regards learning. Therefore in the *Praises of the Virtues*[344] he composed, he says this: "Hail, Queen Wisdom! The Lord save you, with your sister, pure, holy simplicity."

CHAPTER CXLIII

About John the Simple

190   When St. Francis was passing near a certain village[345] in the neighborhood of Assisi, a certain John, a very simple man, who was ploughing in a field, came to him and said: "I would like for you to make me a brother, for I have long wanted to serve God." The saint rejoiced, and when he had considered the simplicity of the man, he replied to his wish: "If, brother, you want to become our companion, give to the poor whatever you may have, and I will receive you after you have given everything away." Immediately he unhitched the oxen, and he offered one to St. Francis. "Let us give this ox to the poor," he said; "I deserve to receive that much at least of my father's goods." The saint smiled, but approved his disposition of simplicity not a little. When his parents and small brothers heard this, they came running in tears, unhappy, however, about losing the ox rather than about losing the man. The saint said to them: "Be of easy mind! Behold, I give you the ox and take your brother." He therefore took the man with him, and giving him the habit of religion, he made him his special companion because of his grace of simplicity.

When St. Francis would stand in any place to meditate, whatever gestures or movements he would make the simple John would himself repeat and copy. For if Francis spat, he spat; if Francis coughed, he coughed. He joined his sighs to Francis' sighs; and he accompanied Francis' weeping with his own weeping. When the saint raised his hands to heaven, John raised his too, diligently watching him as his model and copying everything he did. The saint noticed this, and once asked him why he did these things. He answered: "I have promised to do everything you do; it is dangerous for me to omit anything." The saint rejoiced because of the brother's simplicity, but gently forbade him to act like that in the future. Not long afterwards this simple brother went to the Lord in that purity of life. The saint often proposed his life for imitation, and with great joy he called him, not *Brother* John, but *Saint* John. Notice that it is a mark of pious simplicity to live according to the laws of one's superiors and to follow always the examples and the precepts of the saint. O that it were given to the *wisdom of men*[346] to follow him reigning in heaven with the great zeal with which simplicity conformed itself to him on earth! What then? Simplicity followed him in life, simplicity went before him to life.

CHAPTER CXLIV

How Francis fostered unity among his sons, and how he spoke of it figuratively

191   It was always Francis' anxious wish and careful watchfulness to preserve among his sons the bond of unity, so that those whom the same spirit drew together and the same father brought forth might be nurtured peacefully in the bosom of one mother. He wanted the greater to be joined to the lesser, the wise to be united with the simple by brotherly affection, the distant to be bound to the distant by the binding force of love. He once set before them this moral similitude that contains no little instruction. "Suppose that one general chapter should be held," he said, "of all the religious in the Church! Because, therefore, there are present the lettered and those without the knowledge of letters, the learned and those who know how to please God without learning, one of the learned and one of the simple are appointed to preach. The wise one, because he is wise, delib-

erates thus within himself: 'There is no place here for display of learning, where there are men perfect in learning; nor would it be becoming for me to make myself conspicuous for my strangeness by uttering subtleties among those most subtle men. To speak simply would probably be the most fruitful thing.' The appointed day dawns, the congregations of the saints are come together, and they are anxious to hear the sermon. The wise man goes forth clothed in sackcloth and his head sprinkled with ashes. And to the astonishment of all, preaching mostly by actions, he shortens his words. 'Great things,' he says, 'have we promised, still greater are promised to us; let us keep the former, let us strive after the latter. Pleasure is short, punishment eternal; suffering is small, glory without measure. Many are called, few are chosen, to all shall retribution be made.' The hearts of the listeners are touched and they break out into tears and indeed they venerate the wise man as a saint. But the simple man says in his heart: 'The wise man has stolen from me everything I was going to do and say. But I know what I will do. I know certain verses of the Psalms; I will play the part of a wise man, after that wise man has played the part of a simple one.' The next day's session comes, the simple man rises and proposes a psalm as his theme. Inspired by the Holy Spirit, he preaches so fervently, so subtly, so sweetly because of this inspired gift from God, that all are filled with amazement and say: 'God's *communication is with the simple.*'"[347]

192   This moral similitude, which he thus proposed, the man of God explained in this way. "Our order," he said, "is a very great company, a kind of general assembly, which has come together from every part of the world to live under one form of life. In it the wise turn to their own advantage what is characteristic of the simple, when they see the illiter-

ate seeking heavenly things with burning zeal and those who have not been taught by men learning to savor spiritual things through the Holy Spirit. In it also the simple turn to their own benefit the things that are proper to the wise, when they see renowned men who could live in glory everywhere in the world humbled in the same way as they themselves. This," he said, "is what makes the beauty of this family shine forth, whose many different ornaments please the father of the family not a little."

CHAPTER CXLV

How the saint wanted to be shaved

193 When St. Francis was shaved, he often said to the one who shaved him: "Be careful that you do not give me a large corona.[348] For I want my simple brothers to have a share in my head." He wished finally that the order should be for the poor and unlearned, not only for the rich and wise. "*With God*," he said, "there is *no respect of persons,*[349] and the minister general of the order, the Holy Spirit, rests equally upon the poor and the simple." He wanted this thought inserted into his rule, but since it was already approved by papal bull, this could not be done.[350]

CHAPTER CXLVI

How Francis wanted great clerics coming to the order to renounce all their possessions

194 Francis once said that a great cleric must in some way give up even his learning when he comes to the order, so that having renounced such a possession, he may offer himself naked to the arms of the Crucified. "Learning takes from many people their docility," he said, "and does not permit them to bend to humble practices. Wherefore I want the learned first to make this petition to me: 'Behold, Brother, I have lived in the world a long time and I did not truly know my God. I beg of you, give me a place that is removed from the noise of the world where I can think over my years in sorrow, where, recollecting my distracted heart, I can bring my soul to better things.' What kind of man," he said, "do you think he will become who starts out in this way? Surely he would go forth unto all things strong as an unchained lion, and the blessed moisture he has tasted at the beginning will increase constantly in him. He may be assigned confidently to the true ministry of the word, for he will pour out what is bubbling up within him." This is truly a pious teaching. For what is so necessary for a man coming back from such a different world as to eliminate and cleanse away through humble exercises his long standing and deeply imprinted worldly attachments? Quickly they reach perfection who enter the school of perfection.

CHAPTER CXLVII

How Francis wanted the brothers to learn, and how he appeared to a companion who was devoting himself to preaching

195   Francis was sad if learning was sought to the neglect of virtue, especially if each did not *remain in the calling in which he was called*[351] from the beginning. "My brothers," he said, "who are being led by curious craving after learning will find their hand empty on the day of retribution. I want them rather to be made strong in virtues, so that when the times of tribulation come, they will have the Lord with them in their distress. For tribulation will come," he said, "such that books, useful for nothing,

will be thrown out of windows and into cubby-holes."
He did not say this because Scripture studies displeased him, but in order that he might withdraw
all the brothers from a vain desire for learning and
because he wanted them to be good in charity rather
than superficially learned through curiosity.

He also sensed that times would not be long in
coming when he knew that knowledge would be an
occasion of ruin, but the striving after spiritual things
would be a bulwark of safety to the spirit. To a lay
brother who wanted to have a psalter and asked him
permission for it he offered ashes in place of the
psalter.[352] Appearing in a vision after death to one of
his companions who was once giving much time to
preaching, Francis forbade him to do this and commanded him to walk in the way of simplicity. *God is
my witness*,[353] that after this vision he felt sweetness
to the extent that for several days the dew-laden
words of his father seemed still to ring in his ears.

OF THE SPECIAL DEVOTIONS OF THE SAINT

CHAPTER CXLVIII

*How Francis was moved at the mention of the love
of God*

196 To touch briefly upon the special devotions
of St. Francis will perhaps be neither unprofitable
nor unfitting. For, though this man was devout in all
things, as one who enjoyed the anointing of the
Spirit, nevertheless he was moved toward certain
special things with a special love. Among other words
used in ordinary conversation, he could never hear
the love of God without a kind of transformation
within himself. For immediately upon hearing *the
love of God,* he would become excited, stirred, and
inflamed, as though an inner chord of his heart had

been plucked by the plectrum[354] of the outward voice of the speaker. He said that to offer the love of God to get an alms was a noble prodigality, and those who valued it less than money were most foolish men.[355] He himself kept unfailingly to his death the resolution he had made while he was still enmeshed in worldly things, namely, that he would never turn away a poor man who asked an alms for the love of God.[356] For on one occasion when a poor man asked an alms for the love of God and he had nothing, he took a scissors and was going to quickly cut up his tunic. He would have done this too, but he was detected by his brothers, and instead he saw to it that the poor man was provided for by some other means.[357] "The love of him," he said, "who loved us much is much to be loved."

CHAPTER CXLIX

Of Francis' devotion to the angels, and what he did out of love for St. Michael

197   Francis venerated with a very great affection the angels who are with us in our struggle and who walk *in the midst of the shadow of death* with us.[358] Such companions who were everywhere with us, he used to say, are to be venerated, such are to be invoked as our guardians. He used to teach that their presence must not be offended, and that we must not presume to do before them what we would not do before men. Because in choir we sing *in the sight of the angels,*[359] he wanted all who could do so to come together in the oratory and there *sing wisely.*[360] He often said that the blessed Michael should be honored more especially than the rest in as much as he has the office of presenting souls to God.[361] He also kept most devoutly a fast of forty days in honor of St. Michael between the feast of the Assumption and

his feast.[362] For he said: "Everyone should offer to God, to honor so great a prince, some praise or some special gift."

CHAPTER CL

Of Francis' devotion to our Lady, to whom in particular he entrusted his order

198 Toward the Mother of Jesus he was filled with an inexpressible love, because it was she who made the Lord of Majesty our brother. He sang special *Praises* to her, poured out prayers to her, offered her his affections, so many and so great that the tongue of man cannot recount them.[363] But what delights us most, he made her the advocate of the order and placed under her wings the sons he was about to leave that she might cherish them and protect them to the end. — Hail, advocate of the poor! Fulfill toward us your office of protectress *until the time set by the Father.*[364]

CHAPTER CLI

Of Francis' devotion at Christmas and how he wanted all things to be treated on that feast

199 The birthday of the Child Jesus Francis observed with inexpressible eagerness over all other feasts, saying that it was the feast of feasts, on which God, having become a tiny infant, clung to human breasts. Pictures of those infant members he kissed with thoughts filled with yearning, and his compassion for the Child flooded his heart and made him stammer words of sweetness after the manner of infants. His name was like honey and the honeycomb in Francis' mouth. When the question arose about eating meat that day, since that Christmas day was a Friday,[365] he replied, saying to Brother Morico: "You sin, Brother, calling the day on which the Child was born to us[366] a day of fast. It is my wish," he said, "that even the walls should eat meat on such a day, and if they cannot, they should be smeared with meat on the outside."

200   On this day Francis wanted the poor and the hungry to be filled by the rich, and more than the usual amount of grain and hay given to the oxen and asses. "If I could speak to the emperor," he said, "I would ask that a general law be made that all who can should scatter corn and grain along the roads so that the birds might have an abundance of food on the day of such great solemnity, especially our sisters the larks." He would recall, not without tears, what great want surrounded the poor Virgin on that day.[367] Once when he was sitting at dinner, a certain brother talked about the poverty of the Blessed Virgin and recalled the want of Christ, her Son. Francis immediately arose from the table and, with great sighs and many tears, ate the rest of the meal on the bare ground. For this reason he used to say that this virtue that shone forth so eminently in the King and Queen was a royal virtue. And when the brothers were discussing at a gathering which virtue does more to make one a close friend of Christ, Francis, as though making known to them a secret of his heart, answered: "Know, my sons, that poverty is the special way to salvation; its fruit is manifold, but it is really well known only to a few."

CHAPTER CLII

Of Francis' devotion to the Body of the Lord

201   Francis burned with a love that came from his whole being for the sacrament of the Lord's body, and he was carried away with wonder at the loving condescension and the most condescending love

297

shown there. Not to hear at least one Mass each day, if he could be there, he considered no small contempt. He frequently received Holy Communion, and he did so with such devotion that he made others also devout. Showing toward that sacrament deserving of all reverence all the reverence he could, he offered a sacrifice of all his members; and receiving the Lamb that was offered,[368] he immolated his own spirit with the fire that burned always upon the altar of his heart. He loved France as a friend of the Body of the Lord,[369] and he longed to die there because of its reverence for sacred things. He wished at one time to send his brothers through the world with precious pyxes, so that wherever they should see the price of our redemption kept in an unbecoming manner, they should place it in the very best place.[370] He wanted great reverence shown to the hands of priests, for to these has been given authority from God over the consecrated bread and wine. Often he would say: "If it should happen that I would meet at the same time some saint from heaven and any poor priest, I would first show honor to the priest and quickly go to kiss his hands. And I would say to the other: 'Wait, St. Lawrence,[371] for the hands of this one touch the *Word of Life*,[372] and have something about them that is more than human.'"

CHAPTER CLIII

Of Francis' devotion to the relics of saints

202   This man, beloved of God, showed himself most devoted to divine worship and he left nothing pertaining to God dishonored because of neglect. When he was at Monte Casale, in the province of Massa,[373] he commanded his brothers to bring the holy relics from a church that had been abandoned by all to the place of the brothers in a most reverent

manner. He was deeply grieved that they had been deprived of the devotion due them already for a long time. But when for some reason his sons had to go to some other place, they forgot the command of their father and neglected the merit of obedience. But one day, when the brothers wanted to celebrate Mass, they removed the cloth from the altar, as is customary, and there they found some very beautiful and fragrant bones. Quite astonished, they were looking at what they had never seen before. When the saint of God returned a little later, he diligently inquired if what he had commanded about the relics had been carried out. Humbly confessing the guilt of their neglected obedience, the brothers merited pardon along with punishment. And the saint said: "Blessed be the Lord my God, who himself carried out what you were to do." Consider diligently the devotion of Francis, notice the *good pleasure of God*[374] concerning our dust, and *magnify with praise* holy obedience.[375] For God obeyed the prayers of him whose voice man did not obey.

CHAPTER CLIV

Of Francis' devotion to the cross and of a certain hidden mystery

203   Finally, who can express, who can understand how far Francis was from glorying in anything *save in the cross of our Lord?*[376] To him alone is it given to know to whom alone it is given to experience it. For, though in some sense we should perceive these things in ourselves, words would in no way suffice to express such wonderful things, defiled as words are by everyday and common things. And perhaps it had therefore to appear in the flesh, because it could not be explained in words. Therefore let silence speak where words are wanting, for the thing itself

cries out where the word fails.[377] Let this alone be made known to human ears that it is not yet fully clear why that mystery appeared in the saint; for, as far as it has been revealed by him, it must get its explanation and reason in the future. He will be found true and trustworthy unto whom nature, the law, and grace will be witnesses.[378]

OF THE POOR LADIES

CHAPTER CLV

How Francis wanted his brothers to deal with the Poor Ladies[379]

204   It would not be proper to pass over the memory of the spiritual edifice, a much nobler edifice than that earthly building, which the blessed Francis founded in that place, under the guidance of the Holy Spirit, after he had repaired that material building.[380] It is not to be thought that it was to repair a church that would perish and was falling down that Christ spoke to him from the wood of the cross in a manner so stupendous that it filled those who heard of it with fear and sorrow. But, as the Holy Spirit had once foretold,[381] the Order of Holy Virgins was to be established there, which, like a polished mass of *living stones*,[382] was one day to be brought there unto the restoration of the heavenly house. Indeed, after the virgins of Christ began to come together in that place, gathered together there from various parts of the world, they professed the greatest perfection in observing the highest poverty and in adorning themselves with all virtues. Though their father gradually withdrew his bodily presence from them, he nevertheless gave them his affection in the Holy Spirit by caring for them. For when the saint recognized by many signs of highest perfection that they had been proved and were ready to make every

sacrifice for Christ and endure every difficulty without ever wanting to depart from Christ's holy commandments, he firmly promised them and others
who would profess poverty in a similar way of life
that he would always give them his help and counsel
and the help and counsel of his brothers. This he
always diligently carried out as long as he lived, and
when he was close to death, he emphatically commanded that it should be always so, saying that *one
and the same spirit*[383] had led the brothers and the
poor ladies out of the world.

205   At times the brothers wondered that Francis
did not visit the holy servants of Christ with his
corporal presence more often, and he would say: "Do
not believe, dearest brothers, that I do not love them
perfectly. For if it were a fault to cherish them in
Christ, would it not have been a greater fault to have
united them to Christ? Indeed, not to have called
them would not have been a wrong; not to care for
them once they have been called would be the greatest unkindness. But I give *you an example, that as I
have done to you, so you also should do.*[384] I do not
want anyone to offer himself of his own accord to
visit them, but I command that unwilling and most
reluctant brothers be appointed to take care of them,
provided they be spiritual men, proved by a worthy
and long religious life."

CHAPTER CLVI

*How Francis reprimanded certain ones who went of
their own accord to the monasteries*[385]

206   Once when a certain brother who had two
daughters of perfect life in a certain monastery said
he would willingly take some poor little gift to that
place for the saint, Francis rebuked him very severe-

ly, saying things that should not now be repeated. So he sent the little gift by another brother who had refused to go, but had not persisted obstinately in his refusal. Another brother went in the winter to a certain monastery on an errand of sympathy, not knowing the saint's strong will about not going on such visits. After the fact had become known to the saint, he made the brother walk several miles naked in the cold and deep snow.[386]

CHAPTER CLVII

Of the sermon Francis preached more by example than by words

207   Repeatedly asked by his vicar to preach the word of God to his daughters when he stopped off for a short time at St. Damian's, Francis was finally overcome by his insistence and consented. But when the nuns had come together, according to their custom, to hear the word of God, though no less also to see their father, Francis raised his eyes to heaven, where his heart always was, and began to pray to Christ. He then commanded ashes to be brought to him and he made a circle with them around himself on the pavement and sprinkled the rest of them on his head. But when they waited for him to begin and the blessed father remained standing in the circle in silence, no small astonishment arose in their hearts. The saint then suddenly rose and to the amazement of the nuns recited the *Miserere mei Deus*[387] in place of a sermon. When he had finished, he quickly left. The servants of God were so filled with contrition because of the power of this symbolic sermon that their tears flowed in abundance and they could scarcely restrain their hands from inflicting punishment on themselves. By his actions he taught them that they should regard themselves as ashes and that there was noth-

ing in his heart concerning them but what was fitting this consideration. This was the way he acted toward these holy women; his visits to them were very useful, but they were forced upon him and rare. And this was his will for all his brothers: he wanted them to serve these women in such a way for Christ, whom they serve, that like *them that have wings* they would always guard against the snare laid out for them.[388]

CHAPTER CLVIII
How the blessed Francis commended the rule, and of a brother who carried it about with him

208 Francis glowed most ardently for the common profession and the rule, and he blessed with a very special blessing those who would be zealous about it. For he called the rule the *book of life,*[389] the *hope of salvation,*[390] the marrow of the Gospel,[391] the way of perfection, the key to paradise, the agreement of a *perpetual covenant.*[392] He wanted it to be had by all, to be known by all,[393] and he wanted it to speak everywhere to the interior man unto his comfort in weariness and unto a remembrance of the vows he had made.[394] He taught them to keep it ever before their eyes as a reminder of the life they were to live, and, what is more, that they should die with it.

A certain brother, not unmindful of this direction, who, we believe, is to be venerated among the number of martyrs, gained the palm of a glorious victory. For when he was brought to martyrdom by the Saracens, holding the rule in his hands and kneeling humbly, he said to his companion: "I confess my guilt before the eyes of God's majesty and before you, most dear Brother, concerning everything I have done against this holy rule." The sword followed this brief confession and brought his life to its end by martyrdom; afterwards he became famous for *miracles and wonders.*[395] This brother had entered the order so young that he could hardly bear the fast of the rule, and yet, though a young man, he wore an iron corslet next to his skin. Happy young man, who began happily so that he might finish even more happily.[396]

CHAPTER CLIX

A vision that commended the rule

209 The most holy father once saw a vision, wrought by a heavenly wonder, concerning the rule. At the time when there was a discussion among the brothers about the confirmation of the rule,[397] the following things were shown to Francis, who was greatly anxious about the matter, in his sleep. It seemed to him that he had to gather the finest crumbs of bread from the ground and to distribute them to the many hungry brothers who were standing around him. But while he was afraid to distribute such small crumbs lest such minute particles of dust should fall from his hands, a voice spoke to him from above: "Francis, make one host out of all these crumbs and give it to those who want to eat of it." When he did this, those who did not receive devoutly, or who despised the gift they had received, were soon seen to be greatly infected with leprosy. The saint told all these things to his companions in the morning, regretting that he did not understand the mystery of the vision. But after a little while, while he continued to keep watch in prayer, this *voice came down to him*[398] from heaven: "Francis," it said, "the crumbs of last night are the words of the Gospel, the host is the rule, the leprosy is wickedness." This fidelity to the rule that they had sworn, the brothers of those times, who were eager to go beyond what was required, did not consider difficult or harsh. Neither was there any place for laziness or idleness where the stimulus of love urged them on to ever greater things.

CHAPTER CLX

How Francis discussed with a certain brother about the care of his body

210 Francis, the herald of God, walked in the footsteps of Christ through innumerable labors and severe illnesses, and he did not draw back his foot until he had brought what he had perfectly begun to an even more perfect end. For though he was enfeebled and completely broken in body, he never halted his pursuit of perfection, he never suffered· himself to relax the rigor of discipline. For even when his body was exhausted he could not give it even a little relief without his conscience murmuring. Therefore, when it became necessary, even though he was unwilling, to ease with some soothing remedies the inconveniences of his body, which were beyond his strength, he one day spoke kindly to a certain brother who he knew would give him suitable counsel. "What do you think, my dearest son, of the fact that my conscience murmurs so frequently about the care of my body? It is afraid that I will indulge it too much in its illness and be anxious to come to its aid by means of delicacies carefully sought after. Not that it can take delight any more in anything after it has been worn down so long by illness and after all urge to satisfy taste has left it."

211 The son, acknowledging that the words of his answer were given to him by the Lord, replied faithfully to the father: "Tell me, if you will, Father, with how much diligence did your body obey your commands when it could?" He answered: *"I bear*

305

witness concerning[399] it, son, that it was obedient in all things; it spared itself in nothing, but rushed almost headlong to obey all my commands. It shirked no labor, it refused no discomfort, so long as it could do what was commanded. In this I and it agreed perfectly that we would *serve the Lord Christ*[400] without any reluctance." And the brother said: "Where then, Father, is your generosity, where are your kindness and discretion? Is this a worthy way to repay faithful friends, to accept a kindness willingly, but when the giver is in need not to repay him as he deserves? What could you have done up till now in the service of Christ your Lord without the help of your body? Has it not, as you said, exposed itself to every danger on this account?" "I confess, son," said the father, "this is very true." And that son said: "Is this reasonable then that you abandon so faithful a friend in such great need, a friend who has exposed himself and all that is his for you even unto death? *Far be it from you,*[401] Father, help and staff of the afflicted; *far be from* you *this sin against the Lord.*"[402] "May you be blessed, son," he said, "who propose wisely such salutary remedies for my uncertainties." And he began to speak joyfully to his body: "Rejoice, brother body, and forgive me, for, behold, I now gladly fulfill your desires, I hasten to give heed to your complaints." But how could his exhausted body rejoice now? What could support what had collapsed in every part? Francis was now dead to the world, but Christ was living in him.[403] All the pleasures of the world were a cross to him, because he carried the cross of Christ rooted in his heart. And therefore the stigmata shone forth exteriorly in his flesh, because interiorly that deeply set root was sprouting forth from his mind.

CHAPTER CLXI

What was promised Francis by the Lord for his infirmities

212   Since Francis was thus worn out in every part by sufferings, it is surprising that his strength was sufficient to bear them. But he looked upon these trials not under the name of sufferings but of *sisters*. That they proceeded from many causes is beyond doubt. Indeed, that Francis might be more renowned because of his triumphs, the Most High not only entrusted difficult things to him when he was as yet inexperienced, but now too when he was a veteran in the battle there was given to him the opportunity of triumphing. His followers had in this also an example, for he did not act more slowly because of age nor more indulgently because of illness. Nor was it for no reason that his purgation was completed in this valley of tears, for thus he might give an account even to the last penny, if anything that could be burned clung to him; and thus cleansed most perfectly he might at length take his flight to heaven without delay. I think the best way to understand his suffering is this, that, as he said of others, in bearing them *there is a great reward.*[404]

213   For one night, when he was exhausted more than usual because of the many severe pains of his infirmities, Francis began to pity himself in the depths of his heart. But lest that ready spirit yield carnally to the flesh in anything even for an hour, he kept the shield of patience unshaken by praying to Christ. At length, as he prayed thus in agony, he was given a promise of eternal life by the Lord under this simile: "If the whole *bulk of the earth*[405] and the whole universe were precious gold without price, and if there were given to you as a reward for these severe sufferings you are enduring, after all the pain

had been removed, a treasure of such great glory, in comparison with which that aforementioned gold would be nothing or not even worthy of mention, would you not be happy and would you not willingly bear what you are bearing at the moment?" "I would indeed be happy," the saint said, "and I would rejoice *beyond all measure.*"[406] "Rejoice, therefore," the Lord said to him, "for your sickness is an earnest of my kingdom; and await the inheritance of that kingdom, steadfast and assured, because of the merit of your patience." But with what great exultation do you think that man rejoiced, blessed as he was by such a happy promise? And not only with what great patience, but also with what great love do you believe he embraced the sufferings of his body? He now knows perfectly, but he was not then able to give expression to what he felt. But he did tell his companions some few things, as much as he could. It was at this time that he composed the *Praises of Creatures*[407] and inflamed them as much as he could to praise their Creator.

OF THE DEATH OF THE HOLY FATHER

CHAPTER CLXII

How Francis exhorted his brothers and blessed them at the end

214   The Wise Man says: *In the end of man is the disclosing of his works.*[408] We see this gloriously fulfilled in this saint. Running *the way of God's commandments*[409] with alacrity of mind, he reached the summit by means of the steps of all the virtues; and like a *beaten work*,[410] he was brought to perfection by the hammer of many kinds of tribulation, and he saw *an end of all perfection.*[411] For it was then that his wonderful works shone forth; and that the way he

lived was from God was shown by a judgment of truth, for after he had trampled upon all the allurements of mortal life, he went free to heaven. For to live for the world he considered a disgrace; he *loved his own to the end*,[412] and he accepted death singing. When he was approaching his last days, and the eternal light was taking the place of the temporal light that was being withdrawn, he showed by an example of virtue that he had nothing in common with the world. For, worn down by his serious illness that was being brought to an end with every suffering, he had himself placed naked upon the naked ground, so that in that final hour when the enemy could still rage against him, he might wrestle naked with a naked enemy.[413] He waited without fear for his triumph, and with his hands clasped he was grasping a *crown of justice*.[414] Placed thus upon the ground, with his garment of sackcloth laid aside, he raised his face to heaven as was his custom, and giving his whole attention to that glory, he covered the wound in his right side with his left hand lest it be seen. And he said to his brothers: "I have done what was mine to do; may Christ teach you what you are to do."

215   Seeing these things his sons shed streams of tears and sighing deeply from their innermost being, they were overwhelmed by grief in their compassion. Meanwhile, when their sighs were somewhat quieted, Francis' guardian, who knew the saint's wish more exactly by reason of divine inspiration, hurriedly arose and taking a tunic and trousers and a little cap of sackcloth, he said to their father: "Know that this tunic and trousers and cap have been lent to you by me, by command of holy obedience. But, that you may know that you have no ownership with regard to them, I take away from you all authority to give them to anyone." The saint rejoiced and was glad out of the gladness of his heart, for he saw that he

had kept faith with Lady Poverty to the end.[415] For he had done all these things out of zeal for poverty, so that he would not have at the end even a habit that was his own, but, as it were, lent to him by another. The little cap of sackcloth, however, he wore on his head to cover the wounds he had received when he sought health for his eyes, for which purpose a soft cap of finer wool was rather necessary.

216   After these things, the saint raised his hands to heaven and praised his Christ, because, freed now of all things, he was going to him free. Indeed, that he might show himself to be a true imitator of Christ his God in all things, he *loved to the end*[416] his brothers and sons whom he had loved from the beginning. He had all the brothers present there called to him and soothing them with comforting words in view of his death, he exhorted them with paternal affection to love God. He spoke a long time about practicing patience and poverty, setting the counsels of the holy Gospel ahead of all other prescriptions. Then, with all the brothers sitting about, he extended his right hand over them and beginning with his vicar, he placed it upon the head of each one. "Farewell," he said, "all you my sons, *in the fear of the Lord*,[417] and may you remain in him always! And because a future temptation and tribulation is approaching, happy will they be who will persevere in the things they have begun. I am hastening to the Lord, to whose grace I commend you all."[418] And he blessed in those who were present also all his brothers in the world and all who would come after them unto the end of the world. Let no one claim this blessing for himself which Francis spoke for the absent upon those who were present. As it is set forth elsewhere,[419] the blessing had a special significance, but mainly with regard to the exercise of an office.[420]

CHAPTER CLXIII

Of Francis' death and what he did before he died

217   While therefore the brothers were weeping very bitterly and grieving inconsolably, the holy father commanded that bread be brought to him. He *blessed and broke it*[421] and gave a small piece of it to each one to eat. Commanding also that a book of the Gospels be brought, he asked that the Gospel according to St. John be read to him from the place that begins: *Before the feast of the Passover.*[422] He was recalling that most holy supper which the Lord celebrated as his last supper with his disciples.[423] He did all of this in reverent memory of that supper, showing thereby the deep love he had for his brothers.

Then he spent the few days that remained before his death in praise, teaching his companions whom he loved so much to praise Christ with him. He himself, in as far as he was able, broke forth in this psalm: *I cried to the Lord with my voice: with my voice I made supplication to the Lord.*[424] He also invited all creatures to praise God, and by means of the words he had composed earlier,[425] he exhorted them to love God. He exhorted death itself, terrible and hateful to all, to give praise, and going joyfully to meet it, he invited it to make its lodging with him. "Welcome," he said, "my sister death."[426] To the doctor he said: "Tell me bravely, brother doctor, that death, which is the gateway of life, is at hand." Then to the brothers: "When you see that I am brought to my last moments, place me naked upon the ground just as you saw me the day before yesterday;[427] and let me lie there after I am dead for the length of time it takes one to walk a mile unhurriedly." The hour therefore came, and all the mysteries of Christ being fulfilled in him, he winged his way happily to God.

*How a certain brother saw the soul of the holy
father at his death*[428]

217a   One of Francis's brothers, a man of some
renown, saw the soul of the most holy father, like a
star, but with the immensity of the moon and the
brightness of the sun, ascending over many waters
and borne aloft on a little white cloud, going directly to heaven.[429] There was therefore a great concourse
of people there, praising and glorifying the name of
the Lord. The whole city of Assisi rushed in a body
and the whole region hastened to see the wonderful
things of God that the Lord had made manifest in
his servant. Francis' sons were filled with sorrow at
being deprived of so great a father and they showed
the pious affection of their hearts by their tears and
sighs. However, a new miracle turned their laments
to joy and their weeping to jubilation.[430] They saw
the body of their blessed father adorned with the
stigmata of Christ, in the middle, namely, of his
hands and feet; not indeed the holes made by nails,
but the nails themselves formed out of his flesh, indeed imbedded in that same flesh, and retaining the
blackness of iron; and his right side was red with
blood.[431] His flesh, naturally dark before, but now
gleaming with a dazzling whiteness, gave promise of
the rewards of the future life. His members, finally,
had become pliable and soft, not rigid as they generally are in the dead; and they were changed into the
likeness of the members of a little child.[432]

CHAPTER CLXIV

*Of the vision Brother Augustine saw when he was
dying*

218   The minister of the brothers in the Terra di
Lavoro[433] was Brother Augustine. When he was

312

brought to his last hour, he suddenly cried out in the hearing of those who were standing about, even though he had lost his faculty of speech long before this: "Wait for me, Father, wait for me! Behold, I am coming with you." When the brothers asked in astonishment to whom he was speaking thus, he boldly replied: "Do you not see our father Francis going to heaven?" And immediately that brother's soul, released from his flesh, followed the most holy father.

CHAPTER CLXV

How the holy father appeared after his death to a certain brother

219 The glorious father, clad in a purple dalmatic,[434] appeared on the night and at the hour of his death to another brother of praiseworthy life who was absorbed in prayer at the time; he was accompanied by a great multitude of men. From this multitude of men several separated themselves and said to the brother: "Is not this Christ, Brother?" And he said: "It is he." But the others asked again: "Is not this St. Francis?" The brother answered again in the same way that it was he. Indeed, it seemed to the brother and all that great multitude that Christ and Blessed Francis were one and the same person. This does not seem to understanding people to be in any way a rash judgment, for he who cleaves to God is made one spirit with him,[435] and God will work *all things in all*.[436] The blessed father came at length with that astonishing multitude to a very pleasant place, which, watered with crystal clear waters, gave growth to the fairest plants and was covered with beautiful flowers and filled with every delightful kind of trees. There was a palace there of wonderful size and outstanding beauty, and the new inhabitant of heaven entered it eagerly, for he found in it very many brothers; and he began to eat happily with them at a table prepared most splendidly and filled with many delicious foods.

CHAPTER CLXVI

The vision the bishop of Assisi had about the death of the holy father

220   The bishop of Assisi[437] had gone at that time to the church of St. Michael[438] on a pilgrimage. The blessed father Francis appeared to him in a vision on the night of his death when the bishop was coming back to Benevento where he was staying. Francis said to him: "Behold, Father, I am leaving the world and I go to Christ." Rising in the morning, the bishop told his companions what he had seen, and sending for a notary, he recorded the day and the hour of Francis' death. He was made very sad because of these things, and shedding many tears, he grieved over the loss of his distinguished father. So, when he had gone back to his see, he made known everything in order and gave boundless thanks to the Lord because of his gifts.

Of the Canonization and Translation of St. Francis[439]

220a   *In the name of* the Lord *Jesus.*[440] Amen. In the year of our Lord's incarnation 1226, on October 4, the day he had foretold, twenty years after he had given himself perfectly to Christ and followed the life and footsteps of the Apostles,[441] the apostolic man Francis was freed from the shackles of this mortal life and went happily to Christ;[442] and after he had been buried in the city of Assisi, he began to shine forth with so many and such great and varied miracles, that in a short time he had brought a great part of the world to the admiration of a new age.[443] Because now he was becoming renowned around the various parts of the world by reason of the light of his miracles and everywhere those were coming together who rejoiced over being freed through him from their ailments, the lord pope Gregory, when he was at Perugia with all the cardinals and other prelates of churches, began to have discussions concerning his canonization.[444] All agreed and all said the same thing. They read and approved the miracles that the Lord had worked through his servant and they commended the life and conduct of the blessed father with the highest praises. The princes of the land were first called together for the great solemnity, and the whole assembly of prelates, with an infinite multitude of people, entered the city of Assisi on the appointed day with the blessed pope,[445] to celebrate his canonization there, because of the greater reverence for the saint in that place. When they had all come to the place that had been prepared for so solemn a gathering, Pope Gregory first preached[446] to the whole gathering and with sweet affection announced *the glorious works of God*.[447] He also praised our father Francis in that most noble sermon and when he spoke of the purity of his life, he was bathed in tears. Therefore, when the sermon was finished, Pope Gregory, extending his hands to heaven, proclaimed in a loud voice:[448] "To the praise and glory of Almighty God, the Father, Son, and Holy Spirit, and of the glorious Virgin Mary and of the blessed apostles Peter and Paul, and to the honor of the glorious Roman Church, at the advice of our brothers and of the other prelates, we decree that the most blessed father Francis, whom the Lord has glorified in heaven and whom we venerate on earth, shall be enrolled in the catalogue of saints and that his feast shall be celebrated on the day of his death."[449]

THE PRAYER OF FRANCIS' COMPANIONS
TO HIM[450]

221   Behold, you our blessed Father, the efforts of
our simplicity have sought to praise in some measure
your magnificent deeds and to recount in part for
your glory some few of the many virtues of your
sanctity. We know that our words have detracted
much from the splendor of your outstanding virtues,
for they are unequal to the task of recording the very
great deeds of such great perfection. We beg of you
and of our readers to consider our love as against our
effort, and to rejoice that human pens are really over-
powered by the greatness of your wonderful life. For
who, great one among the saints, could either frame
within himself or impress upon others the ardor of
your spirit? Who would be able to conceive of those
ineffable affections that flowed uninterruptedly from
you to God? But we have written these things out of
happiness over your sweet memory, about which,
while we live, we will try to tell others, if only in a
stammering way. You who were once famishing, are
now fed *with the fat of wheat;*[451] you, who up till
now were thirsting, drink *of the torrent of pleasure.*[452] But we do not believe that you are so *in-
ebriated with the plenty*[453] of the house of God that
you have forgotten your sons, for even he whom you
drink is *mindful of us.*[454] Draw us therefore to yourself, worthy Father, that we may run *after thee to the
odor of thy ointments,*[455] we who you see are lukewarm because of our sloth, languid because of our

idleness, half-living because of our negligence. The little flock is following you with hesitant steps; our weakened eyes cannot bear the dazzling rays of your perfection. *Renew our days as from the beginning,*[456] O mirror and model of the perfect, and do not suffer us who are like you in our profession to be unlike you in our life.

222   Behold, we now lay before the clemency of the Eternal Majesty our humble prayers for the servant of Christ, our minister, the successor of your holy humility and the imitator of your true poverty, who is exercising solicitous care for your sheep with tender affection *from love of* your *Christ.*[457] We beg of you, O holy one, so to stand by him and encompass him that, always following your footsteps, he may obtain forever the praise and glory you have attained.

223   We beseech you also, with all the affection of our hearts, most kind Father, for this your son who now and earlier has devotedly written your praises.[458] He, together with us, offers and dedicates this little work; though it is not done in a way that is worthy of what you deserve, it is done lovingly to the best of our ability.[459] Deign to preserve and deliver him from every evil; increase in him his holy merits; and by your prayers join him forever with the fellowship of the saints.

224   Remember all your sons, Father, who, surrounded by inextricable dangers, follow your footsteps, though from how great a distance, you, most holy Father, know perfectly. Give them strength that they may resist; purify them that they may gleam forth; rejoice them that they may be happy. Pray that *the spirit of grace and of prayers*[460] be poured upon them; that they may have the true humility you had;

that they may observe the poverty you observed; that they may be filled with the charity with which you always loved Christ crucified. Who with the Father and the Holy Spirit lives and reigns world without end. Amen.

PART III

Treatise on the Miracles of Blessed Francis
by Thomas of Celano

Treatise on the Miracles of Blessed Francis
by Thomas of Celano

SELECTIONS

TREATISE ON THE MIRACLES
OF THE BLESSED FRANCIS[1]

CHAPTER III

*Of Francis' controls over insensible creatures
and especially over fire*[2]

18   In the province of Rieti a very serious pestilence broke out that so cruelly took the lives of the
oxen that there was hardly an ox left there. It was
made known at night in a vision to a certain God-
fearing man that he should hurry to the hermitage
of the brothers and get the water in which the blessed Francis, who was living there at the time, had
washed his hands and feet, and sprinkle it upon all
the oxen. Rising early in the morning, that man,
anxious about his own needs, went to that place and,
not knowing the saint, he took the water secretly but
with the help of other brothers and he sprinkled it
upon all the oxen in accordance with the command
that had been given him. From that hour, by the
grace of God, the pestilence ceased and did not rage
again in that region.

CHAPTER IV

Of Francis' control over sensible creatures[3]

31   Once, when the man of God was traveling
from Siena to the Spoleto valley, he came to a certain
field on which a rather large flock of sheep was graz-
ing.[4] When he greeted them kindly, as was his custom,
they all ran to him, raising their heads and returning
his greeting with loud bleating. Francis' vicar noted

with very careful attention of his eyes what the sheep did and said to the other companions who were following along behind more slowly: "Did you see what the sheep did to the holy father? Truly he is a great man whom the brutes venerate as their father and, though they lack reason, recognize as the friend of their Creator."

32   The larks[5] are birds that love the noonday light and shun the darkness of twilight. But on the night that St. Francis went to Christ, they came to the roof of the house, though already the twilight of the night to follow had fallen, and they flew about the house for a long time amid a great clamor, whether to show their joy or their sadness in their own way by their singing, we do not know. Tearful rejoicing and joyful sorrow made up their song, either to bemoan the fact that they were orphaned children, or to announce that their father was going to his eternal glory. The city watchmen who guarded the place with great care, were filled with astonishment and called the others to witness the wonder.

CHAPTER V

How the divine clemency responded immediately to Francis' desires[6]

34   When St. Francis was returning from Spain, because he could not go to Morocco as he had wished, he fell into a very grave illness.[7] For, after suffering privation and weakness and having been driven from a lodging place by the incivility of the host, he lost his speech for three days. But after he had somewhat recovered his strength, he said to Brother Bernard[8] while they were going along the way that he would eat a bird if he had one. And behold, a certain horseman came riding across the field, carrying a very

fine bird; he said to the blessed Francis: "Servant of God, kindly accept what the goodness of God sends you." He took the gift with joy, and seeing how Christ was taking care of him, he blessed him for all his gifts.

CHAPTER VI

Of the Lady Jacoba of Settesoli[9]

37   Jacoba of Settesoli,[10] equally renowned for her nobility and her sanctity in the city of Rome, had merited the privilege of a special love from St. Francis. It is not necessary for me to repeat unto her praise her illustrious origin, the dignity of her family, her great wealth, nor finally the wonderful perfection of her virtues, or her long continence as a widow. When therefore the saint lay in that illness that was to end all his suffering and bring to a most happy conclusion the happy course of his life, a few days before his death he wanted to send word to Rome for the Lady Jacoba, that if she wanted to see him whom she loved so ardently in this land of exile before he would go home to his fatherland, she should come with the greatest speed. A letter was written, a swift messenger was sought, and when one was found, he was gotten ready for the journey. Suddenly there was heard at the door the sound of horses, the noise of soldiers, and the crowd of a company of men. One of the companions, the one who had instructed the messenger, went to the door and found her there whom they had wanted to summon from afar. He was completely astonished, ran very quickly to the saint, and not being able to contain himself for joy, said: "I have something good to tell you, Father." And the saint immediately said in quick reply: "Blessed be God, who has guided the Lady Jacoba, our brother, to us. Open the door and bring her in, for

our Brother Jacoba does not have to observe the decree against women."[11]

38   There was a great rejoicing among the noble guests, and amid the rejoicing of spirit there was also a flowing of tears. And that nothing should be lacking to the miracle, the woman was found to have brought what the letter that had been previously written had contained about what should be brought for the father's burial. For God had seen to it that she brought the ashen-colored cloth with which to cover his dying body, also many candles, the cloth for his face, the little pillow for his head, a certain sweetmeat the saint had wanted to eat,[12] and everything the spirit of this man had wanted. I want to tell the outcome of this true pilgrimage, lest I dismiss that noble pilgrim without consolation. A great multitude of nobles, especially the many devout people of the city, awaited the approaching birthday in death of the saint. But the saint was made stronger by the coming of these devout people from Rome, and it seemed for a little while that he would live a little longer. Wherefore that Lady ordered the rest of the company to leave, and only she herself with her children and a few attendants would remain. The saint said to her: "No, for I will depart on Saturday; on Sunday you may leave with all who have come with you." And so it happened. At the time he had foretold, he who had fought so hard in the church militant entered the church triumphant. I will pass over[13] the concourse of people, the cries of rejoicing, the solemn ringing of the bells, the streams of tears; I will pass over the weeping of his sons, the sighs of those dear to him, the lamenting of his companions. I want only to speak of those things that that pilgrim, deprived of the consolation of her father, did to be consoled.

39   She was led quietly, streaming with tears, to Francis, and his body was placed in her arms. "See," said the vicar, "he whom you loved in life you shall hold in your arms in death." She wept hot tears over his body, wept aloud, and sighed deeply; and holding him in her arms and kissing him, she loosened the veil so that she could see him unhindered. Why should we add more? She looked upon that precious body in which also a precious treasure lay hidden, ornamented as it was with five pearls.[14] She saw that work that only the hand of the Almighty had wrought to the astonishment of the whole world, and filled with unaccustomed joy, she drew new life from her deceased friend. On the spot, she gave the advice that the unheard of miracle should not be hidden or covered over in any way, but that with prudent foresight it should be unveiled before the eyes of all. They then all eagerly ran to see the miracle and they found in truth what God had *not done in like manner to every nation,*[15] and they wondered in astonishment. I break off my description, for I do not want to stammer over what I cannot explain. John Frigia Pennates,[16] who at that time was a young man and afterwards a proconsul of the Romans and a count of the papal palace, admitted to the doubts he had had about it, but swore willingly to what at that time he and his mother had seen with their eyes and touched with their hands. Let the pilgrim now return to her fatherland,[17] consoled with such unusual graces, and let us pass on to other things that happened after the death of Francis.

CHAPTER VII

Of the dead who were brought to life through the merits of Blessed Francis[18]

41   To show that all men should love with all

their hearts the wonderful gift of God of confession and to worthily make known that this saint was always close to Christ, it must certainly be told what he did in so wonderful a way while he was living in this world and what his Christ did for him even more wonderfully after his death. For when the blessed father Francis was approaching Celano to preach there, a certain knight invited him with humble devotion, but with great insistence, to dine with him. Francis excused himself and begged off, but in the end he was overcome by the importunate persuasion of the knight. The mealtime came and the table was splendidly prepared. The devoted host was happy and the whole family rejoiced at the coming of the poor guests. Blessed Francis stood, his eyes raised to heaven, and he spoke to the host who had invited him. "Behold," he said, "brother host, I have come to your house to eat, conquered by your prayers. Listen quickly to my admonitions, for you are not going to eat here but elsewhere. Confess your sins with devout contrition, and let nothing remain in you that you do not make known by a true confession. The Lord will repay you today, because you have received his poor ones with such great devotion." The man immediately consented to the holy words, and when the companion of Francis who was a priest was called, he revealed all his sins to him in a good confession. He put his house in order and expected the word of the saint to be surely fulfilled. At length they went in to the table, and when all had begun to eat, that man, after making the sign of the cross upon his breast, extended his hand fearfully toward the bread. But before he drew his extended hand back, he bowed his head and breathed forth his spirit. O how much is not the confession of sins to be loved! Behold, a dead man is brought back to life so that he can make his confession;[19] and that a living person might not perish forever, he is freed from his sins by the gift of an opportunity to confess them.

CHAPTER XIV

Of the blind, deaf, and dumb[20]

124 Bevagna, a noble city, is located in the Spoleto valley. In that city there lived a certain holy woman with an even more holy daughter and a granddaughter who was very devoted to Christ. St. Francis had honored their hospitality by visiting them a number of times. For that woman had a son in the order, a man of accomplished perfection. But one of these people, the granddaughter, was deprived of the light of her external eyes, though her interior eyes, through which God was seen, were endowed with wonderful sight. Asked once to show mercy to her, St. Francis took into consideration their work; he marked the eyes of the blind girl with his spittle three times in the name of the Trinity and restored to her the sight she desired.

CHAPTER XVII

Of the lame and the invalids[21]

174 Many miracles of this kind Francis worked while he was still living in the flesh. Once when he was passing through the diocese of Rieti, he came to a certain village where a woman, bathed in tears, brought an eight year old son in her arms and placed him before Francis. Already for four years the boy had lived enormously swollen, so that he could not even see his legs. The saint picked him up kindly and placed his most holy hands upon the boy's abdomen. At his touch, the swelling went down. He was immediately made whole again, and he gave abundant thanks to God and to his saint along with his mother who was happy again.

178   Once Francis came to the city of Orte to take up lodging there. A boy, James by name, who had lain for a long time twisted up, came with his parents and begged for health from the saint. As a result of his long illness the boy's head was bent down to his knees and some of his bones were broken. After he had received the sign of a blessing from St. Francis, he began in that moment to stand straight again, and he became perfectly straight and was completely cured.

179   Another citizen of that city had a tumor between his shoulders the size of a large loaf of bread. After he was blessed by St. Francis, he was suddenly so completely healed that no trace of the tumor remained.

	Events	Church History	Francis and the Franciscan Family
Birth of Francis			1182 (1181)
Pontificate of Innocent III		1198-1216	
Battle near the bridge of San Giovanni			1202
Francis' imprisonment at Perugia			1202-1203
Francis' release from prison, illness			1203
Journey to Apulia, dreams, returns to Assisi			1205
Francis' pilgrimage to Rome, the voice of the crucifix at St. Damian's			1206
Renunciation before bishop of Assisi			1206 (1207)
Francis restores St. Damian's, St. Peter's, the Portiuncula			1207-1208
First followers: Bernard, Peter, Giles			1208 (1209)
Oral approbation of the primitive rule			1209 (1210)
Founding of the III Order			perhaps as early as 1209 or 1210
Investment of St. Clare, founding of the II Order			1212
Uncompleted missionary trip to Syria			1212
Uncompleted missionary trip to Morocco, illness in Spain			1213-1214
Return to Portiuncula			1214 or 1215
IV Lateran Council		1215	
Ponaificate of Honorius III		1216-1227	
Pentecost chapter at Portiuncula, division of order into provinces			1217 (5/5)
Meeting of Cardinal Hugolino and Francis at Florence			1217
Pentecost chapter at Portiuncula			1218 (6/3)
Pentecost chapter at Portiuncula			1219 (5/26)
Francis' trip to Orient, at Damietta, before sultan, Palestine			1219 (last half)
Protomartyrs (Morrocco)			1220 (1/16)
Pentecost chapter at Portiuncula, Peter of Catania becomes vicar			1220 (5/17)
Introduction of novitiate year			1220 (9/22)
Meeting between St. Dominic and St. Francis			1220 (probably)
Death of Peter of Catania, Elias vicar			1221
Pentecost chapter at Portiuncula, First Rule			1221 (5/30)
Rule of the III Order redacted by Cardinal Hugolino and orally approved by Honorius III			1221
Pentecost chapter at Portiuncula			1222 (5/22)
Pentecost chapter at Portiuncula, discussions of Second Rule			1223 (6/11)
Approbation of Second Rule by Bull			1223 (11/29)
First crib at Greccio			1223 (12/25)
Pentecost chapter at Portiuncula			1224 (6/2)
Francis receives the stigmata on Alverna			1224 (9/c14)
Francis' death			1226 (10/3, 4)
Francis' burial in St. George's Church			1226 (10/4)
Pontificate of Gregory IX		1227-1241	
Francis' canonization			1228 (7/16)
Translation of Francis' remains to the new basilica			1230 (5/25)

INTRODUCTION FOOTNOTES

1. Celano lies about eighty miles southeast of Assisi in the region of Abruzzi and the province of Aquila, near the bed of what was once Lake Fucino. In the past there was some discussion about Thomas' place of origin, but it is now generally accepted that it was Celano. Writing in the *Archivum Franciscanum Historicum* (II, 517) in 1909, Fr. Atanasio Masci O.F.M. said: It is absoulutely certain that Brother Thomas, the first biographer of St. Francis, was from Celano in the diocese of Marsica in Abruzzi.

2. The *First Life of St. Francis,* no. 56.

3. *Ibid.,* no. 57.

4. Thomas says it took place *sexto namque conversionis suae anno,* the sixth year of his conversion. *Ibid.,* no. 55.

5. *Tempore non multo post. Ibid.,* no. 57.

6. English translation in *XIIIth Century Chronicles,* Placid Hermann O.F.M., Franciscan Herald Press, 1961.

7. Brother Jordan tells us that ninety brothers volunteered and that "twelve clerics and thirteen lay brothers" were chosen to go. See his *Chronicle,* no. 19.

8. An earlier attempt to establish the order in Germany had met with failure, mainly because the brothers did not know the German language. *Ibid.,* no. 5.

9. *Ibid.,* no. 30.

10. *Ibid.,* no. 31.

11. *Ibid.,* no. 33.

12. Brother Mark was appointed custos of Franconia; Brother Angelus of Worms, custos of Bavaria and Swabia; Brother James, custos of Alsace; and Brother John of Pian di Carpine, custos of Saxony. The places over which Brother Thomas had been custos, Mainz, Worms, Cologne, and Speyer, were absorbed into the new custodies of Franconia and Alsace.

13. With the one exception mentioned just below when he gave the relics to Brother Jordan to take back to Germany.

14. In the *First Life,* no. 88, Brother Thomas says: We will now add to this work briefly the rest of the things he [Francis] did from the second last year of his life on, in so far as we have been able to get proper knowledge of them.

15. Brother John Parenti (1227-1232).

16. Brother Otto.

17. See Brother Jordan's *Chronicle,* no. 58-59. Glassberger (*Chronica fratris Nicolai Glassberger, Ordinis Minorum*

observantium, Analecta Franciscana, II, 54) says the relics were of his hair and clothing.

18. May 25, 1230. The new basilica was being built under the direction of Brother Elias and by authorization of Pope Gregory IX. Only the lower church was finished by this date.

19. Minister general from 1244-1247.

20. See the discussions below concerning the various works of Brother Thomas.

21. Minister general from 1247-1257.

22. Pope from 1254-1261.

23. The letters S.F.D. are interpreted to mean *Sancti Francisci Discipulus.* The final *R* in *Cronicar* and in *Mortuor* has a stroke through it, signifying the genitive plural. The inscription therefore commemorates Celano's writing of the two lives of St. Francis and of the sequence of the Requiem Mass, the *Dies Irae.*

24. The Bull *Recolentes, Bullarii Franciscani Epitome,* Sbaralea-Eubel, I, 43.

25. Prologue of the *First Life.* Because this life was so commissioned by Pope Gregory IX, it is often known as the *Legenda Gregoriana.*

26. At Perugia the blessed lord pope Gregory IX, on February 25, in the second year of his glorious pontificate, received, confirmed, and judged this legend worthy to be accepted. The text is quoted here from the *Analecta Franciscana,* X, p. 115.

27. See the section below concerning the literary character of the works of Celano.

28. To my knowledge, no one has actually proposed, with any real conviction, that Brother Thomas was the author of that allegory, though the possibility was suggested by the Quaracchi editors of that little work. The work is ascribed to one of several authors by various writers, but Thomas is not among them. However, the thought and in some parts the expression of the *Sacrum Commercium* bear a striking similarity to the thoughts and expression especially in Brother Thomas' *First Life.*

29. Prologue, no. 1.

30. In the Prologue Brother Thomas says: I have tried ... to set forth ... at least those things that I have heard from his own mouth or that I have gathered from faithful and trustworthy witnesses.

31. The theory that the *Legenda Trium Sociorum,* or at least part of it, was in existence already before Brother Thomas wrote his *First Life* can in no way be substantiated. Nor is it likely that Celano used some written sources embodying an older tradition that is more faithfully represented in the *Legenda Trium Sociorum.* Michael Bihl O.F.M. refuted this latter theory of J. R. H. Moorman *(The*

Sources for the Life of St. Francis, Manchester University Press, 1940, p. 68-75) in the *Archivum Franciscanum Historicum* XXXIX, 1946.

32. *Chronica XXIV Generalium,* in the *Analecta Franciscana,* III, 262: *In quo capitulo [anno 1244] idem Generalis [Crescentius] praecepit universis fratribus quod sibi in scriptis dirigerent, quidquid de vita, signis et prodigiis beati Francisci scire veraciter possent.*

33. This compliment is paid, no doubt, to Brother Thomas' *First Life* and also to that of Julian of Speyer, based upon Celano's *First Life* and written between 1232-1235.

34. In the Latin: *Graecii, 3 idus augusti an. Dom. MCCXLVI.*

35. In the Parma edition, p. 60; in the Holder-Egger edition, p. 176.

36. It seems obvious that Brother Thomas is not merely referring to the order to send in whatever material could be gathered about St. Francis but also to the order he received personally to write the life. He is of course speaking, as it were, in the name of the several companions who had supplied the material, but even Celano by this time could be considered one of those to whom these things were better known, not only because he had already written a legend, but also because, to the new generation of friars, he would seem to have been a rather close companion of St. Francis.

37. The first part of the prayer contains a kind of apology for the work and a word of praise of St. Francis. The second part is a prayer for the minister general. The third part is a prayer for the author himself "who now and earlier has devotedly written your praises." The fourth part is for all the sons of St. Francis.

38. No. 2.

39. No. 94, 98, 198. In these places it seems that the author is using the phrasing of the original material.

40. For instance, no. 26, 34, 68, 82, 100, 101, 111, 121.

41. Prologue, no. 2.

42. *Loc. cit.*

43. See no. 220 of the *Second Life.*

44. *Chronica XXIV Generalium, Analecta Franciscana,* III, p. 269.

45. It is possible, as the Quaracchi editors think, that Crescentius gave his approbation of the *Second Life* in advance of the general chapter and then sent it on to the chapter. *Analecta Franciscana,* X, xxvi.

46. The date given in the manuscript was 1557. Melchiorri's work was entitled: *Leggenda di San Francesco d'Assisi scritta dalli suoi compagni che tut'hora conversavano con lui,* Recanati, 1856.

47. Latin text published by the Bollandists in the *Acta Sanctorum,* and Rinaldi's edition of 1806.

48. *Vie de S. Francois d'Assise,* Paris, 1894.
49. St. Bonaventure's *Legenda Major* was completed about 1262. Bernard of Bessa's work about 1285 or shortly thereafter.
50. Little or no attention is paid anymore to the theory that the *Legenda Trium Sociorum* is the lost *Legenda* written, on the testimony of Bernard of Bessa, by John Ceperano, beginning *Quasi Stella Matutina.*
51. Manuscript found by S. Minocchi in the convent of All Saints at Florence. The error in the date was one that could easily occur. The copyist wrote MCCXXVIII for MCCCXVIII.
52. *Documenta Antiqua,* Quaracchi, I, p. 10, no. 3, and II.
53. The treatment of these much discussed points is necessarily brief here. We hope, however, that it will suffice as an introduction to so complicated yet important a subject, and that it may serve as an incentive for the reader to pursue the subject further.
54. There are four paragraphs toward the end of the *Second Life* (217a-220) that narrate the appearances of St. Francis to certain persons after his death.
55. Arnald of Sarrant O.F.M., the author of the *Chronica XXIV Generalium* (written 1369-1379), speaks of the *Second Life* of Brother Thomas as the *legenda antiqua* in relation to the *Legenda Major* of St. Bonaventure, which was more recent.
56. The *First Life* of Brother Thomas was unknown to Arnald of Sarrant; therefore he speaks of the *Second Life* as the first treatise.
57. *Hic Generalis praecepit, multiplicatis litteris Fr. Thomae de Celano, ut* Vitam B. Francisci, *quae* Antiqua Legenda *dicitur, perficeret, quia solum de ejus conversatione et verbis in primo* Tractatu, *de mandato Fr. Crescentii Generalis compilato, omissis miraculis, fecerat mentionem. Analecta Franciscana,* III, 276.
58. Judging from the fact that John of Parma had to write to Brother Thomas repeatedly to get him to carry out the command to write a new treatise, we may conclude that it was not finished before 1250. In addition, in relating the story of the visit of Lady Jacoba of Settesoli to Francis shortly before Francis' death, Celano makes mention of her son, John, as a witness of the things that had occurred on that visit and that he had obtained his information from John. John was therefore living at the time of the writing. It is known however, that John died before 1254, and probably already the first part of 1253, since his two children died after his death and they too were dead by 1254. Hence it is safe to say that the *Treatise on the Miracles* was written between 1250-1253. See *Analecta Franciscana,* X, xxxvii-xxxviii.

59. *Et sic secundum* Tractatum *qui de ejusdem ... agit miraculis, compilavit, quem cum* Epistola *quae incipit*: Religiosa vestra sollicitudo, *misit eidem Generali. Analecta Franciscana*, III, p. 276.

60. Of the 198 paragraphs, 54 are taken from the *First Life*, 10 from the *Second Life*, and one from the *Legenda ad usum chori* — 65 in all.

61. She left home on Palm Sunday, March 18 or 19.

62. 1243-1254.

63. From December 1254 to May 1261.

64. See the English translation, *Legend and Writings of Saint Clare of Assisi*, The Franciscan Institute, St. Bonaventure, N. Y., 1953, p. 17.

65. *Ibid.*, p. 18.

66. *Analecta Franciscana*, X, p. 119.

67. *Ibid.*, p. xx.

68. This *Legenda* can be conveniently found in the *Analecta Franciscana*, p. 119 to 126.

69. According to the reckoning of that time the day extended from nightfall to nightfall. October 4 therefore began at nightfall of Saturday, the 3.

70. Paragraph 13 of the legend. *Analecta Franciscana*, X, p. 124.

71. *Dictionary of Hymnology*, John Julian, D.D., Dover Publications, Inc., New York, new edition 1957, p. 295-301.

72. *Analecta Franciscana*, X, p. L. Fr. Luke Wadding, however, ascribed both of them to Thomas of Celano.

73. *First Life*, no. 64.

74. Just as examples, see: the *First Life*: 63, 116, 120, 121. There are many others, for instance, the *Second Life*, 76.

75. See, for instance, the *Second Life*: 5, 6.

76. In quoting Holy Scripture in this English volume we have used the Challoner-Douay version for the Old Testament because this version gives more exactly the idea the author of the lives had in mind in using the quotation. For the New Testament we have generally used the new version of the Confraternity of Christian Doctrine.

77. Seneca, Cicero, Sallust, Quintillian, Virgil, Ovid, Juvenal.

78. Sulpicius Severus, St. Gregory the Great, St. Augustine, St. Bernard.

79. The *cursus* or end-pattern is based of course on the last two accents together with the unaccented syllables that accompany them.

80. Among these were E. Lempp, S. Minocchi, L. de Kerval, and others of lesser importance.

81. General chapters were held of course while Brother Elias was vicar. While he was minister general, 1232-1239, apparently no general chapters were held, and this was one point that led up to his deposition. But this was later than the *First Life*.

82. Related opinions hold that Elias told Brother Thomas what to write and Thomas naively accepted for true whatever he was told and consequently that he was completely ignorant of the true state of affairs (e.g. E. Lempp).
83. E. Lempp again, among others.
84. Paragraphs 69, 95, 98, 105, 108, 109.
85. No. 105.
86. *Loc. cit.*
87. In no. 28 he is called "the vicar of the saint." In no. 216 he is referred to as "his vicar."
88. In no. 156 where Francis utters a threat of damnation.
89. In no. 138. We know that the reference is to Elias since the story is told briefly in the *First Life* and Elias is mentioned by name.
90. No. 95.
91. See also the letter Brother Elias wrote to announce to the friars the death of their father.
92. See the *Chronicle of Brother Jordan,* no. 61: But Brother Elias, having been elected minister general, wishing to complete the building he had begun at Assisi in honor of St. Francis, ordered levies upon the whole Order to complete the work.
93. Minister general 1232-1239.
94. At Assisi and at Le Celle near Cortona.
95. He died, however, repentant and absolved in 1253.
96. This is a Scriptural passage, Eph. 4, 6.
97. *First Life,* no. 108.
98. Ecclus. 9, 22.
99. Rom. 1, 9. The passage is from the *First Life* again, no. 108.
100. *Ibid.,* no. 109.
101. Ecclus. 9, 22.
102. The *Second Life,* no. 216.
103. The added details of the placing of the hand upon each one's head and of the blessing of the bread are in no way essential changes. They may simply be details that escaped him in the *First Life* or that came to his attention later.
104. Bonaventure became minister general in 1257 and remained in office until his death in 1274.
105. *Analecta Franciscana,* X, no. 3, p. 558.
106. *Loc. cit.*
107. It soon came to be called the *Legenda Major S. Francisci* to distinguish it from the *Minor Vita B. Francisci* that Bonaventure prepared almost immediately for use in choir.
108. *Analecta Franciscana,* X, lxxii.
109. Brothers Leo and Illuminato were still living at that time.
110. *Archivum Franciscanum Historicum,* VII, 678.
111. Much has been made of this decree, especially by those

who see in it the shadow of the growing dispute between the Spirituals and the Community over poverty in particular. Perhaps something of these troubles did enter in. Bonaventure was a moderate, in his good sense, and perhaps he did try to restore unity among his brethren by his *legenda*.

112. The Assisi and Marseille manuscripts.
113. In the Marseille manuscript.

FIRST LIFE

PROLOGUE FOOTNOTES

1. Acts 1, 1: In the former book, O Theophilus, I spoke of all that Jesus did and taught, ...
2. Gregory IX became pope March 19, 1227. Before this he was known as Hugolino. In 1198 he was created cardinal and in 1206 he was made cardinal-bishop of Ostia. He became a close friend of St. Francis and the first cardinal protector of the Franciscan Order in 1220 or 1221. He died at Rome August 22, 1241.
3. Purity here implies the renunciation of self and of all earthly goods for the sake of living entirely for God.
4. Philip. 1, 22 and 1 Pet. 4, 2. The first book has 30 chapters arranged into 87 paragraphs so numbered by early editors. The historical or chronological order is not, however, followed strictly.
5. The second book has 10 chapters, with the paragraphs numbered from 88 through 118.
6. St. Francis was canonized July 16, 1228. The third book has two parts, in the reverse order of how they are mentioned here. The first part treats of the canonization of St. Francis (paragraphs 119-126); the second part narrates some of the miracles attributed to St. Francis (paragraphs 127-150). The whole is brought to a close with a short epilogue.

BOOK ONE FOOTNOTES

1. The Spoleto valley lies in central Italy, northeast of Rome.
2. Job. 1, 1. The early biographers do not give the year in which Francis was born. Most modern writers are agreed that he was born either late in 1181 or early in 1182. See the *Second Life*, number 3, for the naming of Francis.
3. The poet is Seneca and the quotation alluded to seems to be from his *Epistulae Morales*, LX: *"Jam non admiror, si omnia nos a prima puerita mala secuntur; inter execrationes parentum crevimus."* (It is no surprise to me, that

nothing but evil attends us from our early youth; for we
have grown up amid the curses invoked by our parents).
The Loeb Classical Library, *Seneca Epistulae Morales* I,
p. 422-423.

4. Rom. 11, 16 and Mt. 7, 17.
5. Rom. 6, 19, Jn. 8, 34, and Rom. 6, 13.
6. "Up to the twenty-fifth year" could mean the beginning
   of his twenty-fifth year or "until he was nearly twenty-
   five." The date of his birth would be either late in 1181 or
   early in 1182, since his perfect conversion took place in
   1206 (or 1207).
7. 2 Mach. 4, 1-2.
8. Gal. 1, 14.
9. St. Augustine, *Confessions*: "Behold with what companions I walked the streets of Babylon, and I wallowed myself in the mire of it,..." The Loeb Classical Library,
   English translation by William Watts, Vol. I, p. 75.
10. Ps. 32, 13.
11. Is. 48, 9.
12. Ezech. 1, 3.
13. Celano speaks of Francis' youth with severe words. He
    does so, speaking in hyperbole, after the fashion of bio-
    graphers of his day, to set up a strong contrast between
    what Francis was before his conversion and what he be-
    came afterwards. Francis did take an active part in the
    amusements and frivolities of his day, but undoubtedly the
    Legenda Trium Sociorum is correct in its estimate of
    Francis as a cheerful and generous person by nature, a
    kind and courteous person who spoke no injurious words
    and would listen to nothing impure; people who knew him
    thought surely he was marked for great things (Cap. I).
    See also no. 83 below.
14. Osee 2, 6.
15. Is. 5, 18.
16. An allusion to Gen. 27, 40: the time shall come, when
    thou shalt shake off and loose his yoke from thy neck.
17. Cicero, in his *De finibus bonorum,* says: *Quin etiam ipsi
    voluptarii deverticula quaerunt et virtutes habent in ore
    totos dies voluptatemque dumtaxat primo expeti dicunt,
    deinde consuetudine quasi alteram quandam naturam
    effici, qua impulsi multa faciant nullam quaerentes volup-
    tatem.* English: Even the votaries of pleasure take refuge
    in evasions: the name of virtue is on their lips all the
    time, and they declare that pleasure is only at first the
    object of desire, and that later habit produces a sort of
    second nature, which supplies a motive for many actions
    not aiming at pleasure at all. The Loeb Classical Library,
    translation by H. Rackham, M.A., Book V, xxv, 74.
18. 1 Cor. 7, 34.
19. Wis. 9, 13: For who among men is he that can know the

counsel of God?

20. The nobleman, according to the *Legenda Trium Sociorum,*
    was a certain count, Gentile by name (Chapter 2). In
    Apulia Walter of Brienne, famed in the songs of the
    troubadours, had been fighting since 1202. After Henry
    VI of Germany had died in 1197, his widow entrusted
    their son, Frederick II, to the tutelage of Pope Innocent
    III. This angered the German princes and they joined
    Markwald, lieutenant under Henry VI, against the Holy
    Father. In 1202 Walter joined the forces of Innocent III
    and won victory after victory. Francis, like so many
    others of his day, dreamed of knighthood and wanted to
    join Walter of Brienne. He had fought earlier in the war
    between Assisi and Perugia but had been taken prisoner
    in 1202 at the bridge of San Giovanni. He had been re-
    leased the following year (cf. *II Cel.* 4 and *Legenda
    Trium Sociorum,* chapter 2). The journey to Apulia took
    place in 1205 and early in the year for Walter was killed
    in June of that year. Apulia lay some 200 miles southeast
    of Assisi.
21. Mk. 9, 5.
22. 1 Kg. 17, 26: What shall be given to the man that shall
    kill this Philistine, and shall take away the reproach from
    Israel?
23. 1 Kg. 17, 45.
24. An allusion to Eph. 3, 16: and to have Christ dwelling
    through faith in your hearts.
25. An allusion to Mt. 13, 44: The kingdom of heaven is like
    a treasure hidden in a field; he who finds it hides it,
    and in his joy goes and sells all that he has and buys that
    field.
26. Who this person was is not known.
27. Is. 3, 8.
28. 1 Cor. 13, 12.
29. A city southeast of Assisi, some ten miles or so distant.
30. St. Damian's was about a half mile outside of Assisi.
31. Lk. 2, 44.
32. An allusion to Prov. 16, 16: Get wisdom because it is
    better than gold: and purchase prudence, for it is more
    precious than silver.
33. Francis' father was Pietro Bernardone, a rich cloth mer-
    chant of Assisi, but not of noble origin. His mother was
    Lady Pica. Though some authors have attempted to give
    her a French origin, this cannot be confirmed. There were
    at least two other children in the family besides Francis,
    according to the *Legenda Trium Sociorum,* (IX). One of
    these, Angelo, had two sons of his own, Piccardo and
    Giovanni. Angelo's descendants, according to Wadding,
    were reduced to begging in the streets of Assisi. Francis
    was first called John, when his mother had him baptised

while his father was away. But the father seems to have given him the name Francis upon his return. (See *II Cel.*, 3 and the *Legenda Trium Sociorum,* I).

34. Gen. 6, 6.
35. Ps. 6, 4.
36. Rom. 12, 19: Do not avenge yourselves, beloved, but give place to wrath, for it is written, "Vengeance is mine. I will repay, says the Lord."
37. An allusion to Ps. 108, 31: Because he hath stood at the right hand of the poor, to save my soul from persecutors.
38. Joel 2, 12.
39. Ps. 54, 23.
40. Dan. 2, 22.
41. The reference is not clear, but perhaps the author is referring to Seneca: *Habet enim hoc optimum in se generosus animus, quod concitatur ad honesta.* English: for this is the most excellent quality that the noble soul has within itself, that it can be roused to honorable things. *Epistulae Morales,* translated by Richard M. Gummere, Ph.D., The Loeb Classical Library, **XXXIX**, p. 260-261.
42. Mt. 4, 10-12: Blessed are you when men reproach you and persecute you, and, speaking falsely, say all manner of evil against you, for my sake. Rejoice and exult,...
43. Ps. 31, 6.
44. Prov. 14, 26.
45. The Latin *pater carnalis* might signify *father according to the flesh* or, most probably, the idea used here of a contrast between the father's concern over earthly things of the flesh and Francis' sole concern over the things of the spirit.
46. Guido II, bishop of Assisi from about 1204 until his death July 30, 1228.
47. See St. Gregory, *Hom. in Evan.,* 32, as contained in the Roman breviary, IX lesson for the feast of the Stigmatization of St. Francis: *Nihil autem maligni spiritus in hoc mundo proprium possident: nudi cum nudo luctari debemus.*
48. 1 Cor. 7, 34.
49. Seneca, *Epistulae Morales,* XIV, 9, The Loeb Classical Library, p. 88.
50. Probably the Benedictine abbey of St. Verecundus, about six miles south of Gubbio.
51. About twenty miles north of Assisi.
52. Count Spadalunga of Gubbio. See *Archivum Franciscanum Historicum,* Vol. I, p. 144-147.
53. II Paral. 26, 8.
54. In *The Words of Saint Francis,* James Meyer O.F.M., Franciscan Herald Press, 1952, p. 243.
55. Mt. 5, 42.
56. 1 Cor. 3, 11.

57. St. Clare was born in Assisi most probably in 1194 of the noble family of the Offreducci di Coccorano. Her father's name was Faverone; her mother's Ortolana. In 1212 she ran away from home and was received by Francis at the Portiuncula and given a habit similar to his own. Several others followed her, including her sister, Agnes. Francis soon wrote a short rule for them, consisting mainly of Scripture passages. Clare and her sisters lived at St. Damian's. Innocent III granted her the privilege of the highest poverty 1215-1216. In 1218-1219 Cardinal Hugolino (later Gregory IX) prepared a rule for them that did not include strict poverty as she desired it. In 1245 Innocent IV confirmed this rule for all the monasteries of the Poor Clares, but in 1247 he gave them a new rule permitting common property. Clare did not accept it, however, and in 1250 Innocent IV declared that no sister could be forced to accept it, thus nullifying it. Clare wrote a new rule in 1253 which Innocent IV approved orally for her while visiting her on her deathbed. He later approved it by bull. This rule was in accord with Clare's original plan of complete poverty. She died August 11 (12), 1253 and was canonized August 15, 1255. (See: *Legend and Writings of St. Clare of Assisi,* Franciscan Institute, 1953.)
58. The name *Clare* is from the Latin *clara,* meaning bright or clear.
59. Rom. 2, 29.
60. An allusion to Sallust: *nam idem velle atque idem nolle, ea demum firma amicitia est* (for agreement in likes and dislikes—this, and this only, is what constitutes true friendship). The Loeb Classical Library, *Bellum Catilinarium,* XX, 4, p. 34-35.
61. An allusion to James 1, 17: Every good gift and every perfect gift is from above.
62. 1 Cor. 5, 13.
63. See footnote 57 above.
64. Thomas of Celano later wrote a life of St. Clare at the order of Pope Alexander IV, in 1256.
65. St. Bonaventure tells us the church was that of St. Peter, "rather distant from Assisi." *Legenda Major,* II, 7. Most probably it was the church of St. Pietro della Spina, about two miles southeast of Assisi. It no longer exists.
66. The Portiuncula lay deep in the woods about a mile southwest of Assisi. Today this little church is enclosed within the basilica of St. Mary of the Angels. The little church had belonged to the Benedictines of Mount Subasio, but was at that time no longer in use. St. Francis always regarded it as the cradle of his Order.
67. It was the feast of St. Matthias, February 24, probably 1208.

68. Mt. 10, 9. Lk. 10, 4. Mk. 6, 8. Lk. 9, 3.
69. Lk. 9, 2. Mk. 6, 12. Penance is a central point of Franciscan spirituality, meaning a complete turning of the heart to God *(metanoia),* a complete resignation to the will of God and to his commandments, renunciation of self, complete abandonment to God. This is the sense in which St. Francis used the term (see his *Testament*) and in which Celano uses it. See *The Changing Heart,* Chrysostom Dukker O.F.M., Franciscan Herald Press, 1959.
70. Francis' perfect conversion (the renunciation at the court of the bishop of Assisi) took place in 1206. The "third year of his conversion" would therefore start early in 1208.
71. 2 Cor. 7, 4.
72. An allusion to Gal. 5, 24: And they who belong to Christ have crucified their flesh with its passions and desires.
73. Ecclus. 23, 22.
74. The church of St. George. He was at first buried there, but his remains were translated to the basilica in 1230.
75. See the *Testament* of St. Francis: "The Lord revealed to me this salutation that we should say: The Lord give you peace."
76. Not even the name of this one is known. He is not generally counted among the first followers of Francis, since he is otherwise unknown. Evidently he soon left again.
77. Bernard of Quintavalle. He belonged to a noble and wealthy family of Assisi. He died between 1241 and 1246. The story of his conversion is told at greater length in the *Legenda Trium Sociorum* (VIII). A life of Bernard is given in the *Analecta Franciscana,* III, p. 35-45.
78. Lk. 14, 32: Or else, whilst the other is yet at a distance, he sends a delegation and asks the terms of peace.
79. Mt. 13, 44.
80. The phrases *conceived* and *bring forth* are used several times in Scripture in a similar way: Job 15, 35; Is. 59, 4; Ps. 7, 15.
81. Mt. 19, 21.
82. See no. 30 below.
83. This last sentence occurs at the beginning of the next paragraph in various manuscripts, but it is placed here where it obviously belongs.
84. This seems to have been Peter of Catania. His epitaph attached to the wall of the church of St. Mary of the Angels reads: *Anno Domini MCCXXI, VI° id. martii . . . migravit ad Dominum.* Peter went to the Orient with Francis in 1219 (see the Chronicle of Brother Jordan of Giano, 11) and returned with Francis to be present at the general chapter at Pentecost of 1220, where it seems he was made vicar for Francis. He died March 10, 1221.

85. Job 1, 8.
86. Tit. 2, 12.
87. He was received on the feast of St. George (April 23), two years after the conversion of St. Francis. Therefore in 1208. He died April 22, 1262.
88. Philip the Long was especially zealous for the Poor Clares. According to the *Legenda Trium Sociorum,* Sabbatino and Morico were received before Philip. See footnote 110 below.
89. Is. 6, 6.
90. Jn. 7, 15: How does this man come by learning, since he has not studied?
91. That is, the apostles. Acts 4, 13: Now seeing the boldness of Peter and John, and finding that they were uneducated and ordinary men, they began to marvel, and to recognize them as having been with Jesus.
92. Tob. 13, 6.
93. Zach. 4, 14.
94. Is. 38, 15.
95. Lk. 18, 13.
96. Eph. 6, 10. Phil. 3, 1.
97. Gen. 12, 2.
98. Lk. 5, 6.
99. Mt. 13, 47-48: Again the kingdom of heaven is like a net cast into the sea that gathered in fish of every kind. When it was filled, they hauled it out, and sitting down on the beach, they gathered the good fish into vessels, but threw away the bad.

100. In number 25 above it was said that with the coming of Fhilip the number of brothers was brought to seven. Apparently Francis was included in that number, for from what is said here in number 29, it is apparent that the number is eight in all with the admission of this last brother. His name is uncertain since we do not know for sure from any of the sources the precise order in which the brothers were admitted. See footnote 110 below.
101. Mk. 1, 4.
102. Rom. 12, 12.
103. See Mt., Chapter 5. The *Legenda Trium Sociorum* (IX) tells of what seems to have been an earlier trip. Immediately after Giles had joined the group Francis went with him to the Marches of Ancona; the other two (Bernard and Peter) went "to another region." They then returned to the Portiuncula, where Sabbatino, Morico, and John of Capella were admitted. Chapter XI tells of four more being admitted but without giving

names. That brought the number to eleven besides St. Francis. See footnote 110.

104. 1 Mach. 5, 54.

105. This is cited from the Roman psalter. The Vulgate reads: "Cast thy care upon the Lord, and he shall sustain thee."

106. St. James Compostella in the province of Galicia in northwest Spain. Next to Jerusalem it was the most popular place of pilgrimage in the Middle Ages.

107. Ps. 146, 2.

108. An allusion to Lk. 17, 10: Even so you also, when you have done everything that was commanded you, say, "We are unprofitable servants; we have done what it was our duty to do."

109. This last sentence is generally found at the head of the next paragraph, but it belongs more logically at the end of this paragraph.

110. This brought the number to twelve, including St. Francis. The names of the first twelve are generally given as: Francis, Bernard of Quintavalle, Peter of Catania, Giles, Sabbatino, Morico, John of Capella, Philip the Long, John of St. Constantia, Barbaro, Bernard Viridante, Angelo Tancredi. The *Legenda Trium Sociorum* (IX) tells the story of Sylvester's conversion just after it tells how Bernard disposed of his money, with Sylvester receiving generous hands full. But it indicates that Sylvester was received a little later. In the same way *The Little Flowers of St. Francis (Actus B. Francisci)* puts the reception of Sylvester a little later. The *Chronica XXIV Generalium* lists them as above. See footnotes 100 and 103 above.

111. Acts 2, 47: And day by day the Lord added to their company such as were to be saved.

112. In his *Testament* Francis said: And after the Lord gave me some brothers, there was nobody to show me what to do; but the Most High himself revealed to me that I was to live according to the form of the Holy Gospel. And I caused it to be written down simply and in a few words, and the Lord Pope approved it for me. *(The Words of St. Francis,* Meyer, p. 245.) This was the very first or primitive rule, which is no longer extant. A reconstruction of it can be found in *Via Seraphica,* Placid Hermann O.F.M. Franciscan Herald Press, 1959, p. 11.

113. John Lothar, count of Segni, elected pope January 8, 1198, died at Perugia July 16, 1216. He was the greatest pope of the middle ages. During his pontificate the two great mendicant Orders were founded, the Dominicans and the Franciscans.

114. The same into whose hands Francis made his complete renunciation in 1206.

115. Cardinal John of St. Paul died in 1215.
116. That is, he persuaded him to join one of the already existing orders.
117. The date was April 16, 1209. There has been considerable discussion in the past as to whether the year was 1209 or 1210. For a discussion of the year 1209 see Fr. Paschal Robinson O.F.M., Vol. II of the *Archivum Franciscanum Historicum*, p. 181-196. For a discussion of the year 1210 see Fr. Dominic Mandic O.F.M., *De Legislatione Antiqua O.F.M. 1210-1221*, Mostar, 1924. More recently the year 1209 was accepted by the Order of Friars Minor in their celebration of the 750th anniversary, 1959. In that year the minister general, the Most Reverend Augustinus Sepinski O.F.M., wrote in his encyclical letter, dated February 11, 1959: *"Vobis sane compertum est in hunc eundem MCMLIX annum, anniversarium DCCL memoriam incidere primae religiosae Professionis, cum nempe seraphicus Conditor a Summo Pontifice Innocentio PP. III, una cum primis Sociis, sanctae Regulae approbationem vivae vocis oraculo obtinuit."* Englsih: "You are indeed aware that in this same year 1959 falls the 750th anniversary of the first religious profession, for the seraphic Founder, with his first companions, obtained from the Supreme Pontiff Pope Innocent III oral approbation of his holy Rule."
118. Job 5, 11.
119. An allusion to Mt. 14, 15: Now when it was evening, his disciples came to him, saying: "This is a desert place and the hour is already late; send the crowds away, so that they may go into the villages and buy themselves food."
120. About forty miles north of Rome.
121. Acts 24, 3.
122. Is. 30, 29.
123. This last sentence is generally found with the next paragraph but it belongs logically here.
124. 2 Cor. 5, 15.
125. Mt. 9, 35.
126. 1 Cor. 2, 4.
127. Acts 9, 28.
128. Prov. 7, 9.
129. Joel 2, 2.
130. Ecclus. 24, 23.
131. Is. 51, 3.
132. This whole section has a strong resemblance to the Bull of Canonization, dated July 19, 1228.
133. An allusion to the three orders St. Francis founded; the first order of Friars Minor; the second of Poor Clares; the third for those living in the world.

134. The Latin equivalent of "lesser brothers" is *minores;* hence, the Order of Friars Minor. The reference here is to the so-called First Rule of 1221, where we read: "And let them be lesser brothers and subject to all who are in the same house." *Opuscula Sancti Patris Francisci Assisiensis,* Quaracchi, 1904, p. 33.

135. Mt. 6, 22: If thy eye be single, thy whole body shall be lightsome (Douay version).

136. Prov. 15, 4: A peacable tongue is a tree of life; but that which is immoderate, shall crush the spirit.

137. Prov. 15, 1: A mild answer breaketh wrath.

138. *Testament* of St. Francis: And they were content with one tunic patched within and without.

139. Seneca, *Epistulae Morales,* XII, 9: *Ille beatissimus est et securus sui possessor, qui crastinum sine solicitudine expectat* (That man is happiest, and is secure in his own possession of himself, who can await the morrow without apprehension). The Loeb Classical Library, p. 71.

140. First Rule, Chapter 7: And the brothers who know how to work, should work,... Second Rule, Chapter 5: Those brothers to whom the Lord has given the grace of working, should work,...

141. First Rule, Chapter 7: nor are they to accept any position that may cause scandal.

142. Heb. 12, 14.

143. 1 Jn. 3, 18.

144. The twisted river. The place was called thus from the twisting river that flowed down from the heights of Mount Subasio on which Assisi was located. Rivo Torto was a mile or so south of the Portiuncula.

145. This saying was attributed by Peter Cantor (died 1197) to "a certain hermit." *Analecta Franciscana,* Vol. X, p. 33, footnote 5.

146. These words are based on the hymn *Sanctorum meritis* of the Vespers from the common of several martyrs: *Non murmur resonat, non querimonia,* / *Sed corde impavido, mens bene conscia* / *Conservat patientiam.*

147. There is some doubt about Celano's statement here that the emperor passed close to Rivo Torto enroute to Rome for his coronation. Most authors think that this was not the case, but that he passed close by on his return from Rome. Those who have made a careful study of the question say that Otto proceeded along the old Via Aemilia from Faenza to Rimini. From Rimini he went along the Via Flaminia through Fano, Cagli, Nocera, Spoleto (at the end of September), and on to Rome, where he was crowned by Innocent III on October 4, 1209. Between October and December 1209, Otto visited in Tuscany. On December 3 he was in Florence. From Decem-

ber 12-14 he was in Foligno. On December 20, in Terni. From January 5-8, 1210, he was again in Foligno. On November 4, 1210, he was in Assisi. Apparently he was in Assisi also much earlier than this, namely between early December 1209 and early January 1210. The Via Flaminia passed through Nocera and Spoleto on its way to Rome. Hence, the emperor would have passed within 20 to 25 miles of Assisi on his way to Rome and within a little less than this of Rivo Torto. This is not a great distance, yet it is questionable if it fits Celano's description of a "road close to the hovel" at Rivo Torto. Still, there is no particular reason why St. Francis could not have sent one of the brothers that comparatively short distance to cry out to the emperor as he passed by, while he himself and his other brothers did "not go out to watch." Such an unusual occurrence as the emperor passing so close to Rivo Torto might very easily have made the brothers look upon it as really close by. However, most authors think Celano is in error in saying that the emperor passed by on his way to Rome and regard it as more probable that he passed close by on his return from Rome when he was most probably in Assisi itself.

148. Otto was excommunicated October 18, 1210, because he did not carry out his promise to safeguard the rights of the Church. He thereafter lost the support of the Hohenstaufen party and eventually suffered a crushing defeat in 1214. He made some further effort to secure his throne in 1217 and 1218, but had little success. He died May 19, 1218, reconciled to the Church.

149. See numbers 33 and 36 above.

150. A biblical phrase. Gen. 32, 9 and 12: Return to thy land and to the place of thy birth, and I will do well for thee.

151. Is. 5, 8: Woe to you that join house to house and lay field to field.

152. Number 21 above.

153. Prov. 20, 7.

154. The Divine Office.

155. Lk. 11, 2.

156. This prayer Francis inserted also in his *Testament*.

157. Similar thoughts were expressed by Francis in his *Admonitions*, III, *De perfecta et imperfecta obedientia*. See *Opuscula*, p. 6-7.

158. Literally the Latin should be rendered "with both men," but the meaning evidently is, with the spiritual and bodily man, or body and soul.

159. In his *Testament*, Francis said later: I do not wish to consider sin in them [that is, priests] because I see in in them the Son of God, and they are my masters.

160. In the Rule of 1221 we read: "And though they be called

hypocrites, let them not quit their good life, nor let them look for expensive clothes in this world, so that they can have their robe in the kingdom of Heaven." *The Words of St. Francis*, p. 252.

161. St. Bonaventure places the apparition narrated here among the things that happened at Rivo Torto. *Legenda Major*, IV, 4.

162. John Bonelli of Florence. St. Bonaventure, *Legenda Major*, IV, 10, and the *Chronica XXIV Generalium, Analecta Franciscana*, III, p. 230, also record this incident.

163. The province of Provence was established as early as 1219 by John Bonelli, sent there by St. Francis.

164. The chapter was held at Arles in 1224. See St. Bonaventure, *loc. cit.*

165. Col. 4, 3: Praying withal for us also, that God may open unto us a door of speech to speak the mystery of Christ (Douay version).

166. Monaldo died at Arles, it is thought.

167. St. Anthony of Padua (Fernando de Bulhoes) was born in Lisbon, Portugal, though his name is inseparably connected with the Italian city of Padua. The year of his birth is not certain, but it may have been as early as 1190. He joined the Order of Canons Regular of St. Augustine in Spain some time not long after 1206. But after the five Franciscan missionaries had been martyred in Morocco in 1220 and their bodies brought to Spain, Anthony felt a great desire to enter the Franciscan Order. This he did shortly after. There is some doubt as to whether he had been ordained before his entry or whether he was ordained as a Franciscan. He was a great theologian and was appointed by St. Francis to be the first lector of theology in the Order (at Bologna). He died June 13, 1231 and was canonized within a year thereafter by Pope Gregory IX. In 1946 he was declared a Doctor of the Church by Pope Pius XII.

168. An allusion to Lk. 24, 45: Then he opened their minds that they might understand the Scriptures.

169. Ps. 18, 11.

170. Jn. 19, 19.

171. Acts 9, 31.

172. Riccerio of Muccia in Piceno. He died in 1236 and was later venerated as a saint. He is mentioned in the Franciscan martyrology on February 7.

173. 2 Cor. 6, 13: Now as having a recompense in kind — I speak as to my children — be you also open wide to us.

174. See Celano's *Second Life*, number 60.

175. Rom. 1, 1; 1 Thess. 2, 9.

176. Lk. 10, 8: Eat what is set before you. II Rule: And ac-

cording to the holy Gospel it is lawful to eat of whatever food is placed before you (chapter III).

177. Acts. 2, 37.
178. Ps. 30, 13.
179. Lk. 4, 15.
180. In the Latin the form is *filium Petri de Bernardone*. The implication seems to be this: Francis is the son, Peter the father, Bernardone the grandfather. Apparently the grandfather was poor, while the father was wealthy. Hence, Francis, thinking of his grandfather, recalls his humble origin.
181. In the second half of the year 1212.
182. Slavonia, on the coast of Dalmatia, on the Adriatic Sea.
183. Ancona, a seaport on the Adriatic, in east-central Italy.
184. Jn. 15, 2: Every branch in me that bears no fruit he will take away; and every branch that bears fruit he will cleanse, that it may bear more fruit.
185. The name is Latinized from Emir-el-mumenin, meaning "head of the believers." He was the sultan of Morocco. The year of this trip was 1213.
186. Gal. 2, 11.
187. Francis returned from Spain in 1214 and was back at the Portiuncula at the end of 1214 or early in 1215. It is possible that Thomas of Celano entered the order at this time; perhaps he was one of the educated and noble men who entered at this time. Some, however, think he entered as early as 1213.
188. Several years are passed over here. This next trip to Syria, "in the thirteenth year of his conversion," took place in 1219. Francis had been present at the Pentecost chapter of that year at the Portiuncula (May 26). He left not long thereafter for the Orient and arrived at Damietta in Egypt on August 29.
189. His companion was Brother Illuminato, as St. Bonaventure tells us in his *Legenda Major*, IX, 8. See the *Second Life* where several companions seem to have been with him. No. 30.
190. The sultan was Melek-el-Khamil, 1217-1238. The crusaders had been fighting from May 9, 1218 at Damietta. After the battle of August 29, 1219, the Christians and Saracens tried to arrange a peace. But war broke out anew on September 26. During this interval of peace Francis spent several days with the sultan.
191. Celano is referring to the stigmata which Francis was to receive in 1224. While Francis was away in Syria, the two vicars Francis had left behind to conduct the affairs of the order (Matthew of Narni and Gregory of Naples) held a chapter and enacted certain constitutions at variance with the Rule. A certain Brother Stephen brought

347

word of this to Francis and Peter of Catania in Syria. They, together with Elias, provincial of Syria, and Caesar of Speyer, immediately returned to Italy, and Francis went directly to Pope Honorius (who was staying at Orvieto, at the time) and requested a cardinal protector for his Order (Hugolino). This was probably in 1220. See the English translation of Brother Jordan of Giano's *Chronicle* in *XIIIth Century Chronicles,* Placid Hermann O.F.M., Franciscan Herald Press, 1961, numbers 10-14.

192. In ancient times it was known as Mevania. The incident took place at a place called Pian d'Arca, midway between Bevagna and Cannara, about three miles or so south of Assisi.

193. The Latin form is *monadae,* though some codices have *monedula.* The modern Italian form is *mulacchia,* a crow-like bird or daw.

194. Mt. 6, 12 and Lk. 12, 24.

195. Lk. 4, 30.

196. About thirty miles southwest of Assisi.

197. Jud. 13, 16.

198. Lk. 24, 53.

199. About forty-five miles south of Assisi.

200. Literally, a hare. But rabbit sounds better in the complete setting, and much better than the technical lagomorph. A little farther on, the literal meaning is rabbit.

201. Lake Trasimene, about twenty-five miles west of Assisi.

202. This sentence is generally in the preceding paragraph 60, but it seems to belong more logically here.

203. The city of Rieti is about thirty-seven miles northeast of Rome. The lake is about three and a half miles northwest of the city.

204. *Tinca* is the popular Italian name for it. It was probably a tench, belonging to the carp family.

205. About six miles northeast of Narni in Umbria.

206. Mt. 8, 27: What manner of man is this, that even the winds and the sea obey him?

207. See number 58 above.

208. In the Marches of Ancona. Today it is called Ascoli-Piceno.

209. An old Etruscan city, Arezzo lies about thirty-five miles southeast of Florence.

210. About seventeen miles northwest of Orvieto, or some thirty-seven miles west southwest of Assisi.

211. Acts 10, 21.

212. About eleven miles west of Viterbo.

213. Lk. 8, 11 ssq. The parable of the sower and the seed.

214. On the river Nera, some six miles southwest of Terni, not too far from Rieti.

215. Narni.

216. About thirty miles south of Assisi.
217. Mt. 15, 2.
218. Esther 13, 13.
219. Osee 13, 14.
220. About twenty-five miles north of Perugia.
221. 1 Cor. 13, 5: Charity ... seeketh not her own.
222. Phil. 1, 23.
223. Cant. 2, 14.
224. The Latin is *caelibes mansiones,* perhaps an allusion to Quintillian's: *ingenioseque visus est Gavius* caelibes *dicere veluti* caelites, ... That is: And Gavius thought himself a perfect genius when he identified *caelibes,* "bachelors," with *caelites,* "gods," ... The meaning may be: places where there were no women. Cf. Acts 14, 4. See *Institutio Oratoria* of Quintillian in *The Loeb Classical Library,* I, 6, 36.
225. Honorius III became pope July 18, 1216. He died March 18, 1227. It was Honorius who gave the final approbation to St. Francis' rule of life in 1223, the so-called *Regula Bullata.*
226. Hugo is the form used here, though generally Hugolino is used.
227. Acts 2, 37.
228. Hugolino became the first cardinal protector of the Order in 1220 or 1221. See footnote 1 above and footnote 232 below.
229. Jer. 2, 21.
230. Is. 22, 2.
231. Acts 5, 36.
232. Cardinal Hugolino was legate for the first time in Lombardy and Tuscany from January 23, 1217 until September 14, 1219. His second term began with March 14, 1221. Francis met him in the summer of 1217 at Florence, according to various authors. See *Archivum Franciscanum Historicum,* Vol. 19, 1926, p. 530-558.
233. An allusion to Lk. 12, 14: I have come to cast fire upon the earth, and what will I but that it be kindled?
234. Acts 10, 25.
235. See the *Second Life,* number 25.
236. See the *Second Life,* numbers 5 and 90.
237. See also the *Second Life,* numbers 86 and 87.
238. For example, Is. 16, 1; 53, 7; Acts 8, 32, and many others.
239. The Marches of Ancona are northeast of Assisi, on the coast that faces the Adriatic Sea. The city of Ancona is on the coast itself, a good sixty-five miles from Assisi.
240. Osimo is about eight miles or so south of Ancona.
241. The Marches of Ancona formed a province in the Order some years before the death of St. Francis.
242. Gen. 6, 6.
243. This was the monastery of Poor Clares, S. Salvatore in

Colpersito, close to San Severino. San Severino lay about thirty-one miles southwest of Ancona. This monastery was founded in 1223, but it is today a Capuchin friary.

244. Literally the Latin means "of both men," but the meaning is given better as "of the inner and outer man," or "of his soul and body." See also footnote 158.

245. Ps. 21, 7.

246. See Dan., chapter 3.

247. Celano, no doubt, has in mind St. Francis' *The Canticle of Brother Sun,* which Francis composed during a long illness in 1225, while he was staying at San Damiano. For an Italian version of this canticle see *Via Seraphica,* Placid Hermann O.F.M., Franciscan Herald Press, 1959, p. 32.

248. See the *Second Life,* number 165.

249. Is. 11, 1.

250. Ecclus. 50, 8.

251. Rom. 8, 21.

252. The Latin reads: *scriptum aliquid, sive divinum sive humanum.* It could be rendered "whether the word of God or of man," or as here, "whether about God or about man." The idea is the same, the name of God can be made from all letters.

253. Jud. 13, 6.

254. Mt. 6, 22: If thy eye be sound, thy whole body will be full of light (Confraternity of Christian Doctrine version).

255. Prov. 15, 4: A peaceable tongue is a tree of life.

256. Tit. 3, 2.

257. These words are from the so-called First Rule (1221) of St. Francis. In the Second Rule *(Regula Bullata,* 1223), it is stated: The rule and life of the Friars Minor is this, namely, to observe the holy Gospel of our Lord Jesus Christ, by living in obedience, without property, and in chastity.

258. Some forty-five miles south of Assisi.

259. Therefore on December 25, 1223.

260. Jn. 8, 56.

261. This is a close imitation of the words used above in number 83.

262. See Ps. 35, 8.

263. 3 Kings 8, 63.

264. 1 Pet. 1, 19.

265. 1 Cor. 1, 10.

BOOK TWO FOOTNOTES

1. The title of this chapter is missing in certain manuscripts.
2. In number 55 of this first life of St. Francis Celano spoke of the sixth year of Francis' conversion *(sexto namque conversionis suae anno)*, which was 1212; and in number 57 he spoke of the thirteenth year of his conversion *(tertio decimo anno conversionis)*, which was 1219. So here the eighteenth year is 1224. According to Celano's reckoning, the "second last year of his life" *(paenultimo vitae suae anno)* would run from September 14, 1224, to September of 1225, and the last year from that time to Francis' death, October 4, 1226.
3. The indiction was a recurring cycle of 15 years, called in full *the cycle of indiction*. The number attached to the indiction indicated the specific year within the cycle, as here, the fourteenth year within the indiction is meant. Celano is using the Roman or Papal indiction. According to this system the indiction is found by adding 3 to the year in question; thus, 1226 plus 3. The sum is then divided by 15. Hence, the number of the indiction was 82. And within the 82nd cycle, it was the fourteenth year.
4. According to the reckoning of the time (and still used at the present time in some regions of Italy, e.g., Umbria, Tuscany), the day ran from evening to evening (not from midnight to midnight, as we know it). St. Francis died, according to our reckoning, on a Saturday evening, about an hour after dark, October 3. But, according to the reckoning of that time, Sunday, October 4, had already begun with sunset. Hence, as Brother Elias put it in his letter announcing the death of Francis: *Quarto nonas Octobris, die dominica, prima hora noctis praecedentis, pater et frater noster Franciscus migravit ad Christum.* For the entire letter see *Analecta Franciscana*, Vol. X, p. 525-528. Celano too in his *Legenda ad Usum Chori* gives the date very precisely in these words: *Anno Dominicae Incarnationis 1226, quarto nonas Octobris sanctus Franciscus, expletis viginti annis, ex quo perfectissime Christo adhaesit, vitae mortalis compedibus absolutus, die sabbati in sero feliciter migravit ad Deum, sepultus in die dominico. Analecta Franciscana*, X, p. 125-126.
5. Rom. 6, 7.
6. Ps. 76, 11.
7. Lk. 1, 35.
8. Jn. 5, 33.
9. 1 Cor. 1, 20.
10. 1 Cor. 1, 21.
11. 1 Pet. 1, 5.
12. James 5, 17.

13. Ps. 118, 96.
14. 1 Cor. 12, 31.
15. Eph. 5, 32.
16. An adaptation of Lk. 10, 11: Even the dust from your town that cleaves to us we shake off against you.
17. Ps. 30, 21.
18. Ps. 33, 9: O taste and see that the Lord is sweet.
19. Ps. 72, 1.
20. Wis. 1, 1.
21. 1 Cor. 7, 40.
22. 2 Cor. 1, 3.
23. St. Augustine says he did the same thing *(Confessions* VIII, 12); so too St. Gregory of Tours and others.
24. Dan. 3, 39: That we may find thy mercy: nevertheless in a contrite heart and humble spirit let us be accepted.
25. The exact part is not clear but all the evangelists speak of the passion to come and all narrate the passion.
26. Acts 14, 21.
27. Lk. 19, 17.
28. Mt. 25, 21.
29. Alverna is a mountain in Tuscany, in the province and diocese of Arezzo near the middle of the Apennines. This mountain was given to Francis by Count Orlando of Chiusi in Casentino. The count's sons later gave the friars a document confirming the gift. This document stated that the original gift had been made on September 8, 1213. See Johannes Joergensen, *St. Francis of Assisi,* 1913, Longmans, Green, and Co., p. 162.
31. Is. 6, 2: Upon it stood the seraphims: the one had six wings, and the other had six wings: with two they covered his face, and with two they covered his feet, and with two they flew.
32. Brother Elias of Assisi or of Cortona. Not much is known of his early life. He must have been a man of rather exceptional qualities since he merited to be esteemed so highly by St. Francis. Francis appointed him his vicar, that is, after the death of Peter of Catania. He served in this capacity until after the death of St. Francis. In 1227 he was not elected minister general, but was engaged by Pope Gregory IX to superintend the building of a basilica to honor St. Francis. However, he was elected minister general in 1232, an office he held until he was deposed in 1239 because he was abusing the office entrusted to him. He was later excommunicated, but he died penitent and absolved on April 22, 1253.
33. Rufino was a cousin of St. Clare of Assisi. He died in 1270. A life of Rufino is found in the *Chronica XXIV Generalium, Analecta Franciscana,* III, 46-54.
34. Ecclus. 3, 19: My son, do thy works in meekness, and thou shalt be beloved above the glory of men.

35. Ps. 118, 11.
36. 1 Cor. 9, 27: But I chastise my body and bring it into subjection.
37. See number 88 above.
38. Mt. 26, 41: the spirit indeed is willing.
39. Lk. 8, 11: the seed is the word of God.
40. Mk. 6, 6.
41. Lk. 8, 1.
42. Ps. 62, 2.
43. See footnote 17 in Book One.
44. 2 Cor. 4, 16: Wherefore we do not lose heart. On the contrary, even though our outer man is decaying, yet our inner man is being renewed day by day.
45. Ecclus. 18, 6.
46. Mt. 26, 41: The spirit indeed is willing, but the flesh is weak.
47. Phil. 1, 23.
48. Col. 1, 24.
49. Gal. 6, 17.
50. Ps. 35, 8: O how hast thou multiplied thy mercy, O God!
51. The reference is to the appointment of Elias as Francis' vicar, after the death of Peter of Catania. See footnote 32 of Book Two.
52. 1 Jn. 5, 13.
53. Ecclus. 38, 4.
54. The curia was in Rieti from June 23, 1225 to January 31, 1226, as quoted in the *Analecta Franciscana*, X, 76, from Potthast, *Regesta Pontificium Romanorum*, Berolini, 1874, I, n. 7434-7526.
55. Honorius III.
56. See the *Chronicle of Brother Jordan of Giano*, English version in *XIIIth Century Chronicles*, numbers 16-18.
57. Is. 50, 4.
58. Phil. 3, 18.
59. Jn. 5, 35.
60. Is. 49, 2.
61. Ps. 31, 6.
62. Lk. 14, 32.
63. Jerem. 7, 5.
64. Ezech. 31, 8.
65. Jerem. 2, 21.
66. Ps. 79, 12: It stretched forth its branches to the sea and its boughs unto the river.
67. This of course took place earlier, not during the last two years of Francis' life. Francis asked Hugo (or Hugolino) as early as 1216 probably to act in some such capacity and this was later confirmed by Honorius III, probably in 1220 or 1221.
68. Mt. 24, 45.

69. He was bishop of both places. Ostia is at the mouth of the Tiber river, Velletri inland, some thirty miles east.
70. Gen. 49, 26.
71. Tob. 2, 14.
72. Ephes. 1, 3.
73. 2 Mach. 14, 35.
74. Prov. 22, 15.
75. Not enough information is given in any of these instances to determine definitely just who is meant. But most authors think that Brother Angelo Tancredi is meant here. He died in 1258.
76. Brother Rufino is probably meant here. See number 95 above.
77. This is probably Brother Leo, the father confessor of St. Francis, his secretary, and his trusted friend. Leo died in 1271. For a sketch of his life see *Analecta Franciscana*, III, 65-74.
78. This is probably Brother John de Laudibus (of Lodi). Brother Bernard of Bessa wrote of him in his *Liber de Laudibus S. Franciscis*. While Francis was still in the flesh, he merited to touch the wound of the stigmata in his side. *Analecta Franciscana*, III, 668. He died about 1250. Some think, however, that Brother Masseo may be meant. He died in 1280.
79. Gen. 32, 2.
80. Dan. 9, 25.
81. Rom. 12, 12.
82. Phil. 3, 13: Brethren, I do not consider that I have laid hold of it already.
83. Rom. 6, 4.
84. Apoc. 2, 5.
85. Rom. 12, 3.
86. April, 1226.
87. Siena is some seventy miles northwest of Assisi.
88. Le Celle was one of the first places of the friars. It was about two miles north of Cortona. Cortona itself lies about thirty-seven miles northwest of Assisi.
89. Esther 8, 15.
90. Lk. 1, 10.
91. Mk. 1, 24.
92. Phil. 1, 24.
93. See numbers 21 and 22 above.
94. Ezech. 34, 13.
95. Rom. 8, 33.
96. See the *Second Life,* number 19.
97. Ps. 41, 5.
98. This revelation is given more fully in number 109 below.
99. Gen. 49, 1-27.
100. Gen. 33, 1 ssq.

101. Ephes. 4, 6.
102. Ecclus. 9, 22.
103. Rom. 1, 9.
104. See the *Second Life,* number 216.
105. See number 88 above.
106. These two were Brother Angelo Tancredi and Brother Leo, according to the *Speculum Perfectionis,* chapter 10 of the first redaction (Fr. Leonard Lemmens O.F.M., in *Documenta Antiqua Franciscana,* Vol. II), chapter 123 in the Sabatier redaction.
107. That is, Francis' *The Canticle of Brother Sun.*
108. Ps. 141, 28.
109. This is Brother Elias, as is evident from what follows.
110. See the Letter of Brother Elias to all the friars announcing the death of St. Francis, *Analacta Franciscana,* Vol. X.
111. The text, Jn. 13, 1, actually begins: Before the feast of the Passover. The opening words as given here, Six days before the Passover, are the opening words of the preceding chapter, 12, 1.
112. The Latin text has simply *minister,* which could also mean the minister provincial of that province, or even just one who waited on Francis. Minister general, however, seems to be meant, since Brother Elias, the vicar of Francis, was present. The early writers use the terms *minister general* and *vicar* of Francis synonomously for those early years.
113. See number 92 above.
114. Acts 7, 60.
115. Bernard of Besse *(Liber de Laudibus S. Francisci)* says it was Brother James of Assisi. See *Analecta Franciscana,* III, 668.
116. Acts 2, 34.
117. Cant. 6, 9.
118. Rom. 9, 5.
119. Lk. 2, 13.
120. .The whole description that follows here and in the next paragraph is evidently based upon the encyclical letter of Brother Elias announcing the death of Francis.
121. 1 Pet. 1, 19.
122. Jn. 19, 34.
123. 1 Pet. 1, 19.
124. Rom. 16, 27.
125. Ecclus. 36, 6: Renew thy signs, and work new miracles.
126. Jn. 3, 13.
127. 2 Cor. 1, 3.
128. That is, the order of seraphim.
129. Celano here explains in allegorical fashion the vision in Is. 6, 1-3 and Ezech. 1, 5-14, 22-25.
130. Mt. 6, 22-23.

131. Mt. 12, 34.
132. St. Bernard of Clairvaux wrote this of him. (See Migne, P. L., 185, 238).
133. An allusion to Francis' *The Canticle of Brother Sun.*
134. 1 Cor. 2, 2.
135. The Portiuncula.
136. See number 18 above.
137. Is. 46, 4: Even to your old age I am the same, and to your gray hairs I will carry you: I have made you, and I will bear you: I will carry and will save.
138. A play on words: *Clara*, by name; and *clara erat.*
139. Josue 3, 3.
140. Ps. 45, 2.
141. Ephes. 2, 19.
142. Is. 33, 7: Behold they that see shall cry without, and the angels of peace shall weep bitterly.
143. Francis was first buried in the church of St. George. In 1230 his remains were translated to the new basilica erected in his honor.
144. Ps. 39, 3.

BOOK THREE FOOTNOTES

1. Ps. 8, 6.
2. Ezech. 28, 14.
3. Heb. 1, 3. The phrases are arranged a little differently here.
4. Phil. 3, 10.
5. Ps. 65, 20.
6. Mt. 8, 11.
7. In the Holy Saturday canticle *Exultet* the deacon sings: *Qui licet divisus in partes, mutuati tamen luminis detrimenta non novit.* English: And though the fire was spread to kindle other flames, such sharing does not lessen the force of its light.
8. The king was Louis IX who was later canonized. He was born in 1214 and while he was a minor his kingdom was ruled by his mother Blanche. Louis married Margaret, the daughter of Raymond Berengarius, in 1234.
9. The Latin is *adorandum,* but obviously the word is used in its improper sense.
10. Here is meant the university of Paris.
11. There is a bit of a play on words here in the Latin: *Franciscus,* qui super omnes cor *francum* et nobile gessit.
12. Jn. 3, 29.
13. Celano speaks here of the cardinals as *collaterales papae,* using the same phrase St. Bernard used for them *(De*

Considerationis ad Eugenium III, IV, 4, 9). There is also a play on words here in the *cardines mundi* for the *cardinales*.

14. An allusion to 1 Cor. 1, 27-28: But the foolish things of the world has God chosen to put shame the "wise," and the weak things of the world has God chosen to put to shame the strong, and the base things of the world and the depised has God chosen, and the things that are not, to bring to naught the things that are.

15. An allusion to Jn. 12, 32: And I, if I be lifted up from the earth, will draw all things to myself.

16. 1 Mach. 14, 31. On March 27, 1228, the party of Frederick II rebelled against the pope.

17. Ps. 128, 4.

18. Gregory IX left Rome on April 20 or 21, 1228.

19. The Roman curia was at Rieti from April 25 to May 10, 1228.

20. This was the Poor Clare monastery of St. Paul near Spoleto.

21. He was in Assisi from May 26 to June 12, 1228.

22. The pope was in Perugia from June 13 to July 13, 1228.

23. 1 Jn. 1, 1.

24. This was John of Brienne. Born in 1148, he was crowned king of Jerusalem on October 3, 1210. On March 9, 1225 his daughter married the emperor Frederick II who usurped all the rights of the king of Jerusalem. John was crowned emperor of Constantinople in 1228. He later entered the Franciscan Order, but died shortly thereafter, March 23, 1237. His remains were later translated to the church of St. Francis.

25. The church of St. George, then just outside the walls of Assisi; now Santa Chiara, enclosed by a mid-thirteenth century outer wall.

26. Job. 3, 19.

27. Ecclus. 45, 14.

28. Ecclus. 45, 13.

29. Is. 4, 2.

30. Ps. 44, 10.

31. Jer. 25, 10.

32. Ecclus. 1, 6-7.

33. 1 Tim. 1, 15.

34. Octavian Ubaldini de Mugello. He was made a cardinal by Pope Innocent IV (1243-1254) on May 28, 1244.

35. Raynerius Capocci de Viterbo, O. Cist. He had been made a cardinal by Pope Innocent III (1198-1216) in 1216. He was the author of the hymn *Plaude turba paupercula* of the Lauds for the feast of St. Francis and of the antiphon *Coelorum candor splenduit*. He was present at the chapter of 1221, according to the chronicle of Brother Jordan of

Giano (no. 16). He died in 1250.

36. The complete Bull of canonization can be conveniently found in *Via Seraphica,* Placid Hermann O.F.M., Franciscan Herald Press, 1959.
37. It may be that already then one or the other of the hymns in honor of St. Francis had been composed. Pope Gregory IX himself wrote several, like the hymn *Proles de caelo,* and the responsory of the office of St. Francis, *De paupertatis horreo.* The *Sancte Francisce propera* and the *Plange turba paupercula* are also attributed to him.
38. Num. 29, 39.
39. The holy sacrifice of the Mass.
40. Ecclus. 50, 13.
41. Ecclus. 50, 24.
42. In the reckoning of the time this would be the year from March 21, 1228 to March 20, 1229.
43. July 16, 1228, the ninth Sunday after Pentecost. It is apparent from the whole narrative that Brother Thomas of Celano was an eyewitness to the whole ceremony of canonization.
44. This miracle is repeated in Celano's *Tractatus de Miraculis,* no. 160.
45. This is told in shortened form in the *Tractatus de Miraculis,* no. 161.
46. *Ibid.,* no. 162.
47. *Ibid.,* no. 163.
48. Fano lies on the Adriatic Sea, about thirty miles northeast of Ancona.
49. This is told again in the *Tractatus de Miraculis,* no. 164.
50. *Ibid.,* no. 165.
51. There were two cities in Umbria by this name: one was near Perugia, the other near Todi. There was another city by the same name in the region of Sabina, near Rieti.
52. Francis' body lay in the church of St. George at this time.
53. This is told also in the *Tractatus de Miraculis,* no. 166.
54. Coccorano lies about seven miles north of Assisi.
55. This is told also in the *Tractatus de Miraculis,* no. 167.
56. This is told in a greatly condensed version in the *Tractatus de Miraculis,* no. 173.
57. *Ibid.,* no. 130.
58. About five miles southeast of Assisi.
59. This is also told in the *Tractatus de Miraculis,* no. 143.
60. About twenty-three miles east of Assisi.
61. This is told again in the *Tractatus de Miraculis,* no. 136.
62. *Ibid.,* no. 137.
63. *Ibid.,* no. 138.
64. *Ibid.,* no. 139.
65. The shrine at Monte Gargano in Apulia was famous.
66. This is told also in the *Tractatus de Miraculis,* no. 150.

67. *Ibid.*, no. 151.
68. In Umbria, about twenty-three miles south of Perugia.
69. Even today this is a popular nickname for Francis, under the form *Cecco*.
70. This is repeated more briefly in the *Tractatus de Miraculis*, no. 67.
71. *Ibid.*, no. 68.
72. *Ibid.*, no. 69.
73. *Ibid.*, no. 78.
74. *Ibid.*, no. 80.
75. *Ibid.*, no. 79.
76. *Ibid.*, no. 70.
77. *Ibid.*, no. 76.
78. *Ibid.*, no. 71.
79. *Ibid.*, no. 77.
80. *Ibid.*, no. 197.
81. *Ibid.*, no. 113.
82. *Ibid.*, no. 196, in a condensed version.
83. *Ibid.*, 146, in a condensed version.
84. *Ibid.*, 147.
85. *Ibid.*, no. 125, in a condensed version.
86. *Ibid.*, no. 140.
87. *Ibid.*, 141.
88. *Ibid.*, 142.
89. Apoc. 5, 13.
90. Rom. 16, 27.
91. 1 Cor. 12, 6.
92. Mss. 3817, National Library, Paris, adds this note: *Apud Perusium felix dominus Papa Gregorius nonus, secundo gloriosi Pontificatus sui anno, quinto kalendas Marcii, Legendam hanc recepit, confirmavit et censuit fore tenendam. Gratias omnipotenti Deo et Salvatori nostro super omnia dona sua nunc et per omne saeculum. Amen.* English: At Perugia the happy lord pope Gregory the ninth, in the second year of his glorious pontificate, on the fifth day of the calends of March, received and confirmed this legend and decreed it was to be held fast. Thanks be to Almighty God and our Savior for all his gifts now and forever. Amen. — The date was February 25, 1229. Gregory IX was indeed at Perugia at this time with the Roman curia.

SECOND LIFE

PROLOGUE FOOTNOTES

1. This was the general chapter held at Genoa in 1244.
2. The minister general was Fr. Crescentius of Jesi.
3. From the way this is put here it would seem that Thomas of Celano is writing not in his own name alone but in the name of Francis' closest companions. See the introduction to the *Lives* in this volume.
4. 2 Mach. 14, 20.
5. Rom. 12, 2.
6. The first part or *opus* of this *Second Life* contains 25 numbered paragraphs distributed among 17 chapters. It is a chronological account of the early life of St. Francis and of the early days of his order up to the naming of Cardinal Hugolino to be the protector of the order. In general, however, it is supplementary only to what was said in the *First Life*. The second part or *opus* consists of paragraphs numbered from 26 to 224, distributed over 167 chapters. It covers a wide range of subjects and ends with the canonization and translation of Francis and a prayer to him.
7. It is evident from this that Celano is writing not only from what he knows personally but also from what he has been able to gather from others; and the latter part of the prologue seems to be written in his own name, unlike the first part of the prologue.

BOOK ONE FOOTNOTES

1. Is. 26, 8: *nomen tuum et memoriale tuum in desiderio animae.* English: thy name and thy remembrance are the desire of the soul.
2. Though the name was not used too often at that time, it became common after St. Francis' day.
3. Jn. 3, 5.
4. Eph. 2, 3: and were by nature children of wrath even as the rest.
5. Lk. 1, 60: And his mother answered and said, "Not so, but he shall be called John."
6. Lk. 1, 45: Elizabeth's words to Mary when Mary visited her cousin after the annunciation.
7. See the *First Life,* no. 16. When Francis was asked by the robbers who he was, he answered: "I am the herald of the great King."
8. In his *First Rule* (1221), chapter 23, he placed John the Baptist immediately after the archangels and angels in his

final prayer.

9. Mt. 11, 11.
10. Lk. 1, 44: The babe in my womb leapt for joy (at the coming of Mary and the unborn child Jesus).
11. Francis was taken prisoner at the bridge of San Giovanni during the battle between the Perugians and the citizens of Assisi in 1202. He was released about a year later, 1203.
12. Tob. 4, 7: And turn not away thy face from any poor man.
13. See the *First Life* where these things are given more at length, no. 4.
14. St. Martin, bishop and confessor, whose feast is celebrated on November 11. The incident referred to here is recounted in the lessons of the second nocturn.
15. Is. 16, 14: *parvus et modicus,* small and feeble.
16. Sulpicius Severus, Epistola III, no. 21: *Martinus hic pauper et modicus caelum dives ingreditur.*
17. Mt. 5, 42: To him who asks of thee give; and from him who would borrow of thee, do not turn away.
18. See the *First Life,* no. 5.
19. About two hundred miles southeast of Assisi.
20. See the *First Life,* no. 7 and 4.
21. Ezech. 23, 17.
22. See the *First Life,* no. 2.
23. Gen. 38, 18.
24. Ps. 31, 6.
25. An allusion to the stories of the multiplication of the loaves and fishes in the Gospel.
26. Mt. 14, 23.
27. See the *First Life,* no. 33, 36, 43.
28. *Ibid.,* no. 46, 62.
29. *Ibid.,* no. 6
30. Eph. 6, 10.
31. Prov. 27, 7.
32. In the opening words of his *Testament* Francis said: And when I came away from them [i.e., lepers], what seemed bitter to me was changed to sweetness of spirit and body for me.
33. Painted in Byzantine style, it is still preserved in the church of St. Clare where it was placed in 1260.
34. The church of St. Damian was about a half mile outside of Assisi.
35. Cant. 5, 6.
36. Actually, it was about eighteen years later.
37. Acts 20, 28.
38. See no. 13 of the *First Life* (and footnote 45 under it). We choose here also to render *pater carnalis* as *carnally minded* rather than as *according to the flesh* because it seems that Celano wishes to emphasize the contrast between the spiritually minded Francis and his father.

39. Ps. 108, 28.
40. The bishop was Bishop Guido. See the *First Life*, no. 14-15.
41. Mt. 6, 9. See the *First Life*, no. 53.
42. Here *according to the flesh* is to be preferred, since that is the emphasis Celano seems to intend.
43. See the *First Life*, no. 120.
44. Probably an allusion to Virgil: "*Omnia vincit amor.*" Eclogue X, 69.
45. Bernard of Quintavalle. See the *First Life*, no. 24.
46. *Ibid.*, no. 92.
47. Mt. 19, 21. See also the *First Life*, no. 24.
48. Lk. 9, 3. See also the *First Life*, no. 22.
49. Lk. 9, 23.
50. Gen. 30, 25: And when Joseph was born, Jacob said to his father in law: Send me away that I may return into my country, and to my lord.
51. Phil. 3, 14: I press on towards the goal, to the prize of God's heavenly call in Christ Jesus.
52. In 1209. See the *First Life*, 32-33.
53. See the *First Life*, no. 36-37.
54. *Ibid.*, no. 33.
55. *Ibid.*, no. 36.
56. Mt. 9, 35.
57. Fortini quotes a document from the year 1160 that calls this place "S. Maria de Porzuncula"; *Nova Vita di S. Francesco d'Assisi,* p. 385, (Milan, 1926).
58. See the *First Life*, no. 22, 106.
59. *Ibid.*, 24-30, 44, 57, 106.
60. *Ibid.*, 106.
61. *Ibid.*, 44. See also the *Speculum Perfectionis* (Lemmens, chapter 27; Sabatier, chapter 55). Also below, no. 57 and 59.
62. See the *First Life*, no. 39-41, 41, 51. Also below, no. 160.
63. 2 Tim. 4, 3.
64. Heb. 11, 35-38.
65. See the *First Life*, no. 40.
66. Dan. 13, 52.
67. See the *First Life*, no. 74.
68. Col. 2, 18.
69. Mt. 1, 24.
70. See the *First Life*, no. 33.
71. Ps. 30, 21.
72. Deut. 13, 13.
73. See the *First Life*, no. 73.
74. That is, the cardinals.
75. Hugolino, cardinal bishop of Ostia, later Gregory IX. Hugolino became cardinal protector of the order in 1220 or 1221.

76. Chapter 12 of the *Regula Bullata* (1223) says: I enjoin on the ministers by obedience that they ask of the Lord Pope one of the cardinals of the holy Roman Church to be governor, protector, and corrector of this brotherhood: so that submissive and subject always at the feet of the same holy Church, grounded in the Catholic faith, we may, as we have firmly promised, observe the poverty and the humility and the Holy Gospel of our Lord Jesus Christ. (apud *The Words of St. Francis,* James Meyer O.F.M., Franciscan Herald Press, 1952, p. 294).

77. He died August 22, 1241. The same story of Francis' asking for a cardinal to act as his pope is told in Brother Jordan of Giano's *Chronicle,* no. 14. See the English version: *XIIIth Century Chronicles,* Placid Hermann O.F.M., Franciscan Herald Press, 1961.

78. See the *First Life,* no. 90.

BOOK TWO FOOTNOTES

1. In Wis. 7, 26, wisdom is called: "the unspotted mirror of God's majesty, and the image of his goodness."

2. See the *First Life,* no. 91.

3. *Ibid.,* prologue, no. 1.

4. *Ibid.,* prologue, no. 2.

5. Apoc. 19; 10. See also the *First Life,* no. 26-27.

6. See also the *First Life,* no. 30, 47-50.

7. Most likely Brother Elias is meant here. By the time the second life was written by Brother Thomas, Elias had been deposed from the office of general (1239) and excommunicated. Celano does not mention him any more by name.

8. Prov. 26, 11: As a dog that returneth to his vomit, so is the fool that repeateth his folly.

9. Ps. 106, 26.

10. Damietta had been besieged for a year by the crusaders. This battle mentioned here took place on August 29, 1219. Though the crusaders suffered a great setback in the battle, they (under John of Brienne) ultimately took Damietta, Nov. 5, 1219, after they had been reinforced by Cardinal Pelagio. But of the original 70,000 inhabitants, only about 3,000 survived.

11. Among his companions were Brothers Illuminato, Peter of Catania, Elias, Caesar of Speyer. See also the *Chronicle* of Brother Jordan of Giano, no. 11, 12, 14.

12. See the *First Life,* no. 11.

13. The fact that there were many Spaniards along on this crusade is confirmed by a document of Pope Honorius III

(March 15, 1219) quoted by Fr. Ferdinand M. Delorme O.F.M. See the *Archivum Franciscanum Historicum,* Vol. XVI (1923), p. 245-246.

14. Ecclus. 46, 8.
15. Eccles. 4, 10: If one fall he shall be supported by the other: woe to him that is alone, for when he falleth, he hath none to lift him up.
16. Ps. 68, 2.
17. Prov. 7, 23: as if a bird should make haste to the snare, and knoweth not that his life is in danger.
18. Ecclus. 11, 13: Yet the eye of God hath looked upon him for good.
19. Ps. 110, 1-2.
20. Prov. 27, 17.
21. *Ibid.* 18, 19.
22. Jam. 1, 12.
23. Mt. 18, 6: it were better for him [he who gives scandal] to have a great millstone hung around his neck, and to be drowned in the depths of the sea.
24. Zach. 5, 7: And behold a talent of lead was carried, and behold a woman sitting in the midst of the vessel.
25. See the *First Life,* no. 84-87.
26. Lk. 3, 8.
27. Prov. 26, 11.
28. Ps. 106, 38.
29. *Ibid.* 105, 21.
30. In 1242 Emperor Frederick II besieged Rieti. Greccio is only a short distance from that city and it may be that it was burned at this time. See *Analecta Franciscana,* Vol. X, p. 152, footnote 20.
31. No. 35 just above.
32. See the *Second Life,* no. 4.
33. The Quaracchi editors of Celano *(Analecta Franciscana,* X, p. 153-154) say that this civil war between the nobles of Perugia and the people began in 1214 and was settled by Pope Innocent III that same year, but that it was renewed in 1217 and again in 1223. They conjecture that Francis' sermon was in 1213 (or 1217).
34. 1 Tim. 1, 5: Now the purpose of this charge is charity, from a pure heart and a good conscience and faith unfeigned.
35. See the *First Life,* no. 105.
36. This city canot be identified. The Quaracchi editors suggest several possibilities: Lisciano Niccone, Reschio, Lusignano, Lucignano. *(Analecta Franciscana,* X, p. 154, footnote 3.)
37. Gen. 28, 56.
38. 4 Kings, 16, 15.
39. 1 Cor. 7, 14.

40. A region just below central Italy, on the western coast. This was one of the early Franciscan provinces.

41. Lucca is about ten miles northeast of Pisa.

42. See the *First Life,* no. 99.

43. According to the Quaracchi editors this man was bursar of the cathedral at Rieti from 1213-1216. He died some time between 1236 and 1246, but the precise date is unknown.

44. In the extreme south of the region of Abruzzi, in the diocese of Marsica.

45. See no. 144 below.

46. Who the doctor was is not known for certain. A certain "magister Nicolaus medicus" is mentioned in documents at Rieti between 1203 and 1233. This may have been Francis' doctor. See *Analecta Franciscana,* X, p. 158, footnote 1.

47. The following paragraph, marked 44a, is omitted in several of the manuscripts. It repeats, to some extent even in the wording, the story told in the *First Life,* no. 49-50.

48. St. Francis is considered the first. See the *First Life,* no. 24, for Bernard's reception into the order.

49. This companion was Brother Leo, a priest and confessor of St. Francis.

50. The original is preserved yet today in the basilica of St. Francis of Assisi. The words of both the Praises of God and of the blessing can be found in the *Opuscula,* p. 124-125, 198-200. Brother Leo added a note to the original in which he said that the paper was given him in the month of September 1224, just after Francis had received the stigmata.

51. That is, the palace of the bishop of Assisi. See the *First Life,* no. 108.

52. See the *First Life,* no. 120. Also no. 181 below. In the latter number is told of another habit taken to England by Brother Lawrence of Beauvais.

53. 1 Cor. 13, 5.

54. Amos 8, 11.

55. Mt. 23, 27: Woe to you, Scribes and Pharisees, hypocrites! because you are like whited sepulchres.

56. 2 Cor. 11, 13: For they are false apostles, deceitful workers, disguising themselves as apostles of Christ.

57. Lk. 21, 9.

58. Celano, no doubt, is exaggerating somewhat, but the rebellion of the Romans against the pope occurred in 1228 (see the *First Life,* no. 122). Frederick II had been excommunicated by Gregory IX in 1227 because he had delayed too long the crusade to Palestine. He went, however, in June 1228. While he was gone, some of his soldiers in Italy attacked the Marches of Ancona and the duchy of Spoleto and later Naples. Thus the war was rather widespread.

59. Several contemporary sources speak of a famine in 1227. Brother Salimbene mentions it in his *Chronicle.* So too the *Chronicum Parmense, 1138-1338* and others. See the *Analecta Franciscana,* X, p. 163-164, footnote 16.

60. The veiled implication here seems to be that the dead child was eaten.

61. Lam. 3, 41.

62. Gen. 2, 24.

63. This whole passage, as well as other similar passages in the *Lives,* is so reminiscent of the *Sacrum Commercium S. Francisci cum Domina Paupertate* that it suggests the thought that perhaps Celano was the author of that work too

64. See St. Francis' *Testament*: And those who came to take up this life, gave all they would possess to the poor, and they were content with one tunic patched inside and out if they wished, besides a cincture and drawers. And we wished to have nothing else. Apud *The Words of St. Francis,* English by James Meyer O.F.M., Franciscan Herald Press, 1952, p. 245.

65. Mt. 19, 29: And everyone who has left house, or brothers, or sisters, or father, or mother, or wife, or children, or lands, for my name's sake, shall receive a hundredfold, and shall possess life everlasting.

66. Mt. 8, 20. In quoting the Gospel passage Celano uses *Son of God* and the past tense *had,* in the latter half of the sentence.

67. See number 25 above.

68. See the *First Life,* no. 74. Apparently, from the context, the legate was not in Bologna itself, but must have been somewhere close by. This incident may have happened in 1219, but more probably it took place in 1221, after Francis' return from the Orient.

69. This, however, is probably not Celano, but the brother who supplied the story at the request of the minister general. This story apparently was amplified by later writers who wanted to use it to show that Francis was opposed to studies in the order. Angelo of Clareno, one of the *Spirituals,* added the detail that the house was a house of studies founded by Peter of Stacia and that Francis drove out the brothers because it was devoted to studies. He also added that Francis cursed Peter and would not retract his curse even after Peter became ill and was dying. At the end of the 14th century an additional chapter was inserted into the *Actus B. Francisci (Little Flowers of St. Francis)* in which the story was repeated from Angelo and this detail added that when Peter was dying, a blob of burning sulphur fell upon him and he burned to death and "the devil came and carried away his soul." It should be emphasized that Celano (and the *Speculum*

Perfectionis) gives the reason for Francis' action precisely as that the people considered the house as being owned by the friars. The whole thing is a good example of how an anecdote grows to suit the purposes of the narrators.

70. In the province of Siena, northwest of Assisi.

71. The Latin word is *carcer,* which here means desert.

72. That is, in the Rule (Second Rule, 1223): The brothers are to take nothing as their own, neither a house, nor place, nor anything, and as pilgrims and strangers in this world, . . . let them go confidently in quest of alms (Chapter 6).

73. Lk. 24, 18: Art thou the only stranger in Jerusalem who does not know the things that have happened there in these days?

74. *Ibid.,* 32: Was not our heart burning within us while he was speaking on the road and explaining the Scriptures?

75. Hugolino. See no. 58 above.

76. There is a strong play on words in this sentence: *Ostiensis* (of Ostia), *ostium* (door), *hostibus* (foes), *hostiam* (victim).

77. See the *First Life,* no. 99-101 where Celano praises Hugolino at some length.

78. A wild grass often found growing amid grain.

79. Chapter 8 of the *First Rule* (1221) speaks of money like this: ". . . because we ought to have no greater use and regard for money and coin than for stones . . . And should we find coins anywhere, let us not bother about them any more than the dust we tread under foot." The *Second Rule* (1223) says (chapter 4): "I firmly command all the brothers that they must not in any way accept coins or money, either themselves or through an intermediary person."

80. The Latin is *leprosis pecuniae famulis offerendum.* Lepers were supported by alms, but they always needed money. It is not surprising that some of them became *servants of money* or *greedy for money.* This seems to be a good way to translate the phrase.

81. See footnote 79 just above.

82. This is very similar to Prov. 28, 23: He that rebuketh a man, shall afterward find favor with him.

83. He became vicar probably in 1220, though some have argued that he functioned as vicar, especially in the absence of Francis, even earlier than this. However, the only mention of vicars before this occurs in Brother Jordan of Giano's *Chronicle,* no. 11, at the time of Francis' going to the Orient when he appointed two vicars to act in his place. See also the *First Life,* no. 25, footnote 84.

84. Both the First and the Second Rule bid those entering the order to give their things to the poor, by which is understood, not to the order. And the brothers are forbidden to

meddle in their affairs.

85. The Latin is *funda* (Italian *fonda*), literally a sling; perhaps it is best translated as a money belt.
86. Mt. 18, 16.
87. Lk. 22, 41.
88. Phil. 2, 21.
89. Num. 14, 2-4: And all the children of Israel murmured against Moses and Aaron, saying: Would God that we had died in Egypt:... and they said one to another: Let us appoint a captain, and let us return into Egypt.
90. Thereafter let them give them the clothes of probation, to wit, two tunics without a capuche, a cincture, drawers, and a caperon reaching to the cincture,... And those who have promised obedience, shall have one tunic with a capuche and, such as wish, another without a capuche. *Rule* (1223), chapter 2.
91. And all the brothers shall dress in garments of low value and they may patch them with sacking and other patches with the blessing of God. *Ibid.*
92. See the *First Life,* no. 110. Also below, 225-226.
93. Ps. 17, 46.
94. Ps. 26, 12.
95. Ps. 9, 19.
96. Ps. 68, 33.
97. Both the *First* and the *Second Rule* speak of the obligation of seeking alms. The *Testament* says: And should the wages of our work not be given to us, let us take recourse to the table of the Lord by seeking alms from door to door.
98. Mt. 25, 40.
99. That is, Christ.
100. That is, the *least* brothers.
101. Francis wanted not more than three or four to live in hermitages. Two were to live like Martha, the other one or two like Mary. See his little work *De Religiosa Habitatione in Eremo, Opuscula,* p. 83.
102. That is, Lady Poverty.
103. A fief, Latin *feudum,* in the terminology of the Middle Ages, meant some immovable goods given over by a prince to his trusted servants for a time, during which they might enjoy the usufruct of it.
104. Mt. 5, 3: Blessed are the poor in spirit, for theirs is the Kingdom of heaven.
105. 2 Cor., 8, 9.
106. The present Nocera Umbra, about fourteen miles east of Assisi.
107. The Satriano that lies between Nocera Umbra and Assisi. The incident mentioned here took place probably in September 1226.
108. Lk. 10, 8: And whatever town you enter, and they receive

you, eat what is set before you, ... See the *Second Rule,* chapter 3: Into whatever house they enter, let them first say, Peace to this house. And according to the holy Gospel, they shall be free to eat of whatever foods are put before them.

109. 1 Kings 25, 17. He was probably a member of a heretical sect, like the Cathari.

110. Mt. 5, 31.

111. *Ibid.,* 19, 21: If thou wilt be perfect, go, sell what thou hast, and give it to the poor, ...

112. Ps. 72, 17.

113. Gen. 20, 3.

114. See no. 106 below.

115. Ps. 11, 7.

116. The reference is to Dan. 2, 36-45; that is, Daniel's interpretation of Nabuchodonosor's dream of the great statue; the succession of the four kingdoms (golden, silver, brass, iron).

117. That is, the Blessed Virign Mary.

118. 1 Cor. 12, 6.

119. Cant. 1, 12.

120. Ps. 83, 10.

121. Is. 53, 3. Celano touched frequently on this subject in the *First Life,* e.g., no. 84, 91, 92, 102, 103.

122. The author's birthplace.

123. About fifteen miles east of Rome. Apparently, therefore, Francis came to Celano on the old Via Valeria.

124. The diocese of Marsica is not named after a city but rather after a stretch of land that was the home of the ancient Marsi. The cathedral church was in the little city called S. Benedetto dei Marsi. After 1580 the episcopal see was located at Pescina, just about seven miles southeast of Celano. Today it is at Avezzano. See *Franziskanische Studien,* 22 (1935), p. 133 ssq.

125. Collestrada was an ancient village about three miles southeast of Perugia, near the bridge of San Giovanni. It marked the boundary between Perguia and Assisi.

126. The Latin text used the popular word *gaida,* meaning the edge or border or part of a garment.

127. See the *First Life,* no. 25. Also no. 67 of the *Second Life.*

128. For example, Lk. 12, 33: See what you have and give alms.

129. See above, no. 41.

130. It was probably a town near Rieti, but it no longer exists.

131. This was in April 1226. See the *First Life,* no. 105, and below, no. 137.

132. There were several towns named Campiglia in that general neighborhood. Going from Rieti to Siena, Francis could have gone along a route that would have taken

him through Campiglia d'Orcia, not too far away from Siena. Or he could have taken another route that would have taken him past Campiglia di Val d'Ombrone. There is no way of knowing which town is meant here.

133. See no. 82 above. Celano is speaking with philosophical terms here in the single form perfecting a threefold matter.

134. 2 Cor. 5, 6: Always full of courage, then, and knowing that while we are in the body we are exiled from the Lord ....

135. Eph. 2, 19: Therefore, you are now no longer strangers and foreigners, but you are citizens with the saints and members of God's household.

136. Eph. 2, 14: For he himself is our peace, he it is who has made both one, and has broken down the intervening wall of the enclosure, the enmity, in his flesh.

137. Celano may be speaking here in the name of those who supplied the information.

138. See the *First Life,* no. 96.

139. Apoc. 2, 17: To him who overcomes, I will give the hidden manna.

140. It is not clear whether or not Celano is referring to a particular trip by boat by Francis.

141. 2 Cor. 6, 1: Yes, working together with him we entreat you not to receive the grace of God in vain.

142. See the *First Life,* no. 105, 130.

143. That is, without putting the capuche over his head.

144. Ps. 94, 3: For the Lord is a great God, and a great King above all gods.

145. A town about twenty-two miles northeast of Arezzo.

146. The bishop was Guido. He was bishop of Assisi from about 1204 until his death on July 30, 1228.

147. This was the Benedictine abbey of St. Giustino, about twelve miles northeast of Perugia. See *L'Umbria Francesana,* Nicholas Cavanna O.F.M., Perugia, Unione Tip. Cooperativa, 1910, p. 183.

148. Phil. 4, 15.

149. 2 Cor. 5, 10.

150. See the *First Life,* no. 23.

151. The degree of master, the equivalent of doctor, was the highest academic degree conferred by the universities of the Middle Ages.

152. This is a free quotation of Ezech. 3, 18: If, when I say to the wicked, Thou shalt surely die: thou declarest not to him, nor speak to him, that he may be converted from his wicked way, and live: the same wicked man shall die in his iniquity, but I will require his blood at thy hand.

153. From the following account, however, it does not appear that the swords proceeded from his mouth but were across the body. See the vision of Brother Sylvester,

below in no. 109.

154. Frederick II.

155. Is. 5, 18.

156. 2 Kings, 14, 14.

157. The reference is probably to the same convent of nuns mentioned in the *First Life,* no. 78, and it was probably at this time yet a monastery of Benedictine nuns. Only in 1223 did it become a Poor Clare monastery, and Brother Pacificus entered the order perhaps in 1212, as some say, or in 1215 or 1216, according to others.

158. The *Tau* is a letter of the Greek alphabet. Ezech. 9, 4: And the Lord said to him: Go through the midst of Jersualem: and mark Thau upon the forehead of the men that sigh.

159. See the *First Life,* no. 73, and above no. 25.

160. Ps. 67, 34.

161. The Latin *physicus* meant in the Middle Ages a medical doctor.

162. Is. 55, 11: So shall my word be, which shall go forth from my mouth: it shall not return to me void.

163. See the next paragraph for Sylvester's conversion.

164. It appears from a document quoted by Arnaldo Fortini that Sylvester had been a canon of the church of St. Rufino, but little else is known about him. See Fortini's *Nova Vita di San Francesco d'Assisi,* Milan 1926, p. 178, note 17, and p. 406-408.

165. Most probably St. Damian's. See the *First Life,* no. 18. It could, however, also be the church of St. Mary of the Angels at the Portiuncula. *Ibid.,* no. 21.

166. It is clear that he was already dead at the writing, 1246.

167. 2 Peter 2, 17.

168. See below, no. 167-171 and also the *First Life,* no. 56-61.

169. A Benedictine abbey. See the *First Life,* no. 16.

170. That is, Christ. Jn. 2, 29: Behold, the Lamb of God, who takes away the sin of the world.

171. The Rule of 1223 says in chapter 11: I strictly command all the brothers not to have suspicious associations or conversations with women.

172. ·Prov. 6, 28: Or can he walk upon hot coals and his feet not be burnt?

173. Ruth 4, 11.

174. Rom. 9, 28.

175. Acts 7, 55.

176. Is. 29, 14: and out of the ground thy speech shall mutter.

177. Esther 15, 17: For thou, my lord, art very admirable, and thy face is full of graces.

178. Eccles. 2, 14.

179. See the *First Life,* no. 58.

180. In the First Rule (1221), chapter 12: The brothers all,

wherever they are or go, shall be on their guard against evil looks and associations with women, and none shall confer alone with them. Let the priests speak respectfully with them in administering Penance or any spiritual advice.

181. Is. 3, 2.
182. Mt. 17, 19.
183. See no. 59 above.
184. Leo Brancaleo was made a cardinal deacon in 1200 and a cardinal priest in 1202. His titular church was that of the Holy Cross in Jerusalem. He died about 1230.
185. The Latin is *castaldus* or *gastaldus*. It has the meaning, in the dialect of the Lombards, of a kind of prefect with the power to punish and coerce people. See *Analecta Franciscana*, X, p. 201, note 3.
186. The Latin is *palatinus*. Brothers were sometimes requested by nobles to serve as a kind of court chaplain. Some were assigned to the task by obedience.
187. Celano evidently does not approve of the friars being at the courts and thinks such a practice was displeasing to God.
188. Jn. 13, 21.
189. Mk. 14, 33.
190. Mt. 26, 41: The spirit indeed is willing, but the flesh is weak.
191. Mt. 14, 31.
192. Acts 3, 7.
193. In his *Sermo de S. Francisco (Opera Omnia,* IX, 577) St. Bonaventure attributes this vision to Brother Pacificus (see above, no. 82, 106) and explains that it was the throne of Lucifer that was reserved for Francis. The *Speculum Perfectionis* too (first redaction, chapter 33; the second redaction, chapters 59-60) attributes the vision to Brother Pacificus. A later tradition attributes it to Brother Amasseo of Marignano (e.g., Ubertino da Casale in the *Arbor vitae crucifixae jesu*).
194. Ps. 44, 8.
195. Ps. 50, 14.
196. Hab. 2, 3.
197. Celano used a similar expression in the *First Life,* where he said that Francis walked about the streets of Babylon with evil companions. Here he is using it for dejection. See no. 2 of the *First Life.*
198. See above, no. 92.
199. See, for instance, Ps. 70, 22; 91, 4; 97, 5. The latter passage reads: Sing praise to the Lord with the harp, with the harp and melodious song.
200. It could be that Celano is using here the words of those who supplied the material, but it seems more likely that he is speaking for himself.

201. See no. 99 above.
202. We read in the First Rule: And let the brothers take heed not to appear sad exteriorly and be gloomy hypocrites, but let them prove to be joyful in the Lord, and merry and becomingly courteous (chapter 7).
203. See below, no. 210-211.
204. Ps. 23, 29.
205. An allusion to Ps. 62, 2: For thee my soul hath thirsted; for thee my flesh, O how many ways.
206. See above, no. 69.
207. See above, no. 69.
208. The reference seems to be to our first parents after their fall in paradise. Gen. 3, 21.
209. Most probably this is Poggio Bustone, about seven miles north of Rieti.
210. The fast from the feast of All Saints until Christmas which was prescribed by the third chapter of the Rule.
211. See the *First Life,* no. 95-96.
212. A city in northern Italy.
213. Since it is Brother Pacificus speaking here, the King of Verses, it is not surprising to see him use the term *mother.*
214. Celano then goes on to explain this, but see the next few notes.
215. This was Brother Rufino. See the *First Life,* no. 95.
216. This is understood to be Brother Elias. *First Life,* no. 95.
217. In the *First Life,* no. 95, Celano expresses his wonder that so few were permitted to see the wound in Francis' side while the saint was yet alive. He then goes on to tell that Brother Elias merited to see it and that Brother Rufino touched it. In no. 102 he then tells how Francis entrusted the care of his person to certain brothers, four in number, but the names are withheld. Their identity can be surmised from the description of each: Angelo Tancredi, Rufino, Leo, John of Lodi. Of the latter Bernard of Bessa *(Liber de Laudibus S. Francisci)* says that he too touched the wound *(Analecta Franciscana,* III, 668). In the *Second Life* here the incident of Brother Rufino is repeated briefly, and also the trickery of Brother Elias is explained. But the statement in the paragraph that only one brother and only once saw the wound is hard to understand. In other sources Rufino is said to have placed his hand into the wound (his life in *Analecta Franciscana,* III, and in the Fourth Consideration on the Stigmata in the *Little Flowers of St. Francis*), and this seems to be implied here. Are we to picture it that Rufino, in his rubbing of St. Francis (presumably his back; the Latin *scalpere* is difficult to render), stood behind him and only touched the wound without seeing it? Incidentally, the *Tractatus de Miraculis* says that many saw the wounds while Francis lived (no. 5), but here

Celano is speaking of the stigmata in general.

218. There is an allusion here to Ovid, *The Art of Love*, II, 13: *Nec minor est virtus, quam quaerere, parta tueri. The Loeb Classical Library.*

219. 1 Jn. 4, 1.

220. Mt. 11, 29: learn of me, for I am meek and humble of heart.

221. That is, the servant of all. In the second Rule, chapter 8, we read: All the brothers shall be bound always to have one of the brothers of this order as the minister general and servant of the whole brotherhood and shall be strictly bound to obey him.

222. A city about fifteen miles northwest of Rieti.

223. Ps. 147, 20.

224. It seems that this was the general chapter of 1220. The expression "a few years after his conversion" cannot be taken too strictly. Some, however, argue that Peter acted as the vicar of Francis prior to this time.

225. 2 Cor. 12, 9. Francis said in his *Testament* that he had always wanted "to have a cleric to do the Office" with him.

226. Eph. 4, 1.

227. Gal. 5, 4.

228. Ps. 12, 18.

229. Francis seems to have been mindful of the decree of the Lateran Council (1215) that there be in cathedral and other churches suitable men to assist the bishop and the clergy in caring for souls. See the *Analecta Franciscana,* X, p. 214, note 8.

230. Deut. 32, 35.

231. A city along the ancient Via Aemilia about twenty miles southeast of Bologna.

232. A region between the Adriatic Sea, the Po River, and the Apennines Mountains.

233. A certain Meinardinus Aldigerii (1207-1249). See note 2, p. 215 of the *Analecta Franciscana,* X.

234. Hugolino was the bishop of Ostia and later Pope Gregory IX. The meeting of these three probably took place after the summer of 1217 and before August 6, 1221, the date of St. Dominic's death. The papal court was at Rome from October 2, 1217 to June 1, 1219; again from December 30, 1219 to January 3, 1220; again from October 21, 1220 to February 21, 1222. In between it was at various other places, especially Rieti and Viterbo. Francis was in the Orient during the summer and early fall of 1219. And Dominic apparently was in Rome early in 1218, late in 1219, early in 1220 and again late in 1220 and the first part of 1221. Most probably the meeting of the three took place in 1220. That seems to be the conclusion of some more recent authors. Others put it back a bit.

Incidentally, Pope Gregory IX canonized both St. Francis (July 16, 1228) and St. Dominic (July 3, 1234). See *Analecta Franciscana*, X, p. 215.

235. Gal. 5, 15.

236. Eph. 6, 12: For our wrestling is not against flesh and blood, but against the Principalities and the Powers, against the world-rulers of this darkness, . . .

237. Exod. 25, 20.

238. Wis. 2, 15.

239. Rom. 12, 16: Do not set your minds on high things.

240. Ps. 106, 4.

241. Acts 10, 14.

242. Ps. 127, 6.

243. See no. 148, above.

244. See above, no. 143.

245. *Loc. cit.*

246. Ecclus. 51, 34.

247. See the *First Life,* no. 45.

248. The Rule (1223), chapter 12: Whoever of the brothers may wish on divine inspiration to go among the Saracens and other non-believers should ask leave for it from their provincial ministers.

249. An obedience is the command of the superior of the province (or of the order), especially of transfer from one place to another, usually a written or printed document.

250. See the *First Life,* no. 36, 37, 89.

251. The expression *exempla lucis* is probably taken from St. Gregory the Great, as found in the homily of the III Nocturn of Matins of the *Commune Confessoris non Pontificis*: *cum, per bona opera, proximis nostris lucis exempla monstramus.*

252. Exod. 29, 18.

253. Mt. 26, 7.

254. Tim. 1, 15.

255. In the province of Gaeti. Robert, a Cistercian, was at the head of the diocese from 1210 to 1227.

256. 2 Mach. 14, 34.

257. 1 John 2, 18.

258. Rom. 13, 12.

259. *Loc. cit.* There seems to be a rather veiled reference in these lines to Brother Elias who received a special blessing from Francis. See the *First Life,* no. 108.

260. Ps. 43, 9.

261. Jam. 1, 12.

262. The Latin is the diminutive *homuncio,* a word that was used already by such ancient writers as Cicero and Juvenal.

263. Phil. 2, 12.

264. Dan. 1, 2.
265. Apoc. 3, 16: But because thou art lukewarm, and neither cold nor hot, I am about to vomit thee out of my mouth.
266. Francis' *Testament*: And I worked with my hands, and I wish to work; and I wish earnestly to have all the rest of the brothers work at employment such as conforms with propriety. Those who know none, should learn, ...
267. An allusion to what is said in Gen. 2, 2 about God resting on the seventh day after the work he had done.
268. Job 5, 7: Man is born to labor and the bird to fly.
269. Amos 5, 10.
270. Acts 6, 4. Chapter 17 of the First Rule speaks at length of preachers and Chapter 9 of the Second Rule. But Celano is not quoting here from either place.
271. Mt. 5, 14.
272. The *Testament* of St. Francis.
273. St. Anthony of Padua. See no. 48 of the *First Life*. The letter seems to have been written when St. Anthony was appointed to teach the young students of the Order at Bologna. It is now generally accepted as authentic. See the *Chronica XXIV Generalium (Analecta Franciscana,* III, 132) and *Franziskanische Studien,* 31, 1949, p. 135 ssq.; 36, 1954, p. 244-249. Also, *AFH,* 45, 1952, p. 474-492.
274. 1 Kings 2, 5.
275. *Loc. cit.*
276. Eph. 6, 12.
277. Wis. 7, 26.
278. See the *First Life,* no. 80-81.
279. Job. 23, 3.
280. *First Life,* no. 58-61, 77-79.
281. *Ibid.,* no. 80.
282. 1 Cor. 10, 4: And all ate the same spiritual food, and all drank the same spiritual drink (for they drank from the spiritual rock which followed them, and the rock was Christ).
283. Ps. 60, 3.
284. See the *First Life,* no. 81.
285. *Ibid.,* no. 80.
286. *Ibid.,* no. 81. See also above, no. 47, 75, and the following paragraphs here.
287. See the *First Life,* no. 77-79.
288. 1 Cor. 12, 6.
289. See the *First Life,* no. 98-101.
290. Lk. 4, 25.
291. *Ibid.,* 5, 26.
292. See the *First Life,* no. 61.
293. See the *First Life,* no. 90, 97.
294. See no. 163 above.
295. Gal. 6, 10.
296. Heb. 9, 15.

297. Deut. 32, 11: As the eagle enticing her young to fly.
298. Ps. 16, 4: for the sake of the words of thy lips, I have kept hard ways.
299. 1 Cor. 13, 1-3.
300. An allusion to Juvenal, *Satires,* VI, 223: *Sic volo, sic jubeo, sit pro ratione voluntas* (this I wish, this I command, let my will stand in the place of reason). *The Loeb Classical Library.*
301. The use of the seal pertains to superiors. The idea is that mere authority will not do any good under such circumstances.
302. The expression seems to have been prompted by Cant. 6, 1: My beloved is gone down into his garden, to the bed of aromatical spices, . . .
303. Perhaps with Mt. 7, 16 in mind (Do men gather grapes of thorns) Celano switches to "rose be gathered from thorns."
304. Gen. 304. The general idea seems to be that no matter how difficult obedience may be it is still profitable for eternity at least.
305. That is, the good brothers. Jesus said of Nathanael that he was "a true Israelite," Jn. 1, 47.
306. Ps. 50, 19: A sacrifice to God is an afflicted spirit.
307. The *Second Rule,* chapter 6: And if anyone of them fall into illness, the rest of the brothers must wait on him as they themselves would want to be waited on.
308. The *First Rule,* chapter 10, but the wording is slightly changed.
309. 1 Thess. 5, 18: In all things give thanks.
310. Acts 13, 48.
311. Apoc. 3, 19: As for me, those whom I love I rebuke and chastise.
312. See no. 22 above.
313. An allusion to Ps. 144, 14: The Lord lifteth up all that fall.
314. Francis set down in his rule how superiors were to act toward their subjects and he asked mainly for kindness.
315. Heb. 5, 7.
316. Ps. 2, 9.
317. Lk. 10, 34.
318. Ps. 22, 4.
319. Eccles. 3, 1.
320. Ps. 93, 1.
321. 2 Cor. 1, 3.
322. Osee 6, 6: For I desired mercy and not sacrifice.
323. 2 Cor. 5, 13: For if we were out of our mind, it was for God.
324. *Ibid.,* 2, 15: For we are the fragrance of Christ for God.
325. This is what Francis wanted, though he did not suggest the weekly changeover. See his *De religiosa habitatione*

in eremo, Opuscula, 83-84.

326. Cant. 2, 7.

327. *Ibid.,* 2, 9.

328. *Ibid.,* 8, 13: Thou that dwellest in the garden, the friends hearken.

329. 2 Cor. 12, 15: But I will most gladly spend and be spent myself for your souls.

330. We read in Thomas of Eccleston's *De Adventu Fratrum Minorum in Angliam (XIIIth Century Chronicles,* Placid Hermann O.F.M., p. 96) that Brother Lawrence of Beauvais was given a tunic by St. Francis and took it back to England. He had been among the first brothers to go to England in 1224. Most likely he went back to see Francis not too long thereafter and probably received the habit from him in 1226. At the time Brother Thomas of Eccleston was writing, Brother Lawrence was desperately ill; this would be about 1258 or 1259. The "one brother" whose tunic here was poorer would very likely be this Brother Lawrence of Beauvais. See also above in no. 50 for the story of the habit taken to France.

331. Detraction, in its more technical meaning, means revealing a hidden fault of someone, while calumny or slander means the false report of some evil in another. Celano, however, seems to be using the Latin term *detractio* in a broader sense of slander, or perhaps both detraction and slander.

332. The Florentine pugilist or Brother John of Florence is probably the same as John de Laudibus or of Lauds or of Lodi. He is praised in the *Speculum Perfectionis* (second redaction) as a man of "bodily and spiritual courage," "who in his time had been physically stronger than all men." See the English translation, *St. Francis of Assisi,* translated by Leo Sherley-Price, Harper & Brothers, 1959, p. 106.

333. Lk. 16, 4.

334. Ecclus. 11, 33.

335. The idea is somewhat lost behind the metaphorical language here. There is an obvious allusion to Joatham's parable in Judg. 9, 7, ssq, especially verse 15: And it [the bramble to the trees] answered them: If indeed you mean to make me king, come ye and rest under my shadow; but if you mean it not, let fire come out from the bramble, and devour the cedars of Libanus. The meaning of the words here that Francis is putting into the mouth of the slanderer may possibly be this: the slanderer, wanting to slander the good, cuts down the cedars, so that he himself will then stand out, the bramble.

336. Mt. 6, 16: And when you fast, do not look gloomy like the hypocrites, who disfigure their faces in order to appear to men as fasting. Amen I say to you, they have

received their reward.

337. It may be that the last four sentences of this paragraph are Celano's own words rather than a continuation of the words of St. Francis.

338. That is, not long before Francis' death.

339. Prov. 10, 29.

340. Tit. 2, 7.

341. That is, the founders of the older monastic orders.

342. Ecclus. 9, 22.

343. 2 Mach. 4, 15.

344. Also called *Salute to the Virtues*. See *The Words of St. Francis,* James Meyer O.F.M., Franciscan Herald Press, 1952, p. 73.

345. Probably Nottiano, about five miles east of Assisi.

346. 1 Cor. 2, 4.

347. Prov. 3, 32.

348. Or tonsure. Among Franciscans it is frequently called the corona. The meaning of the next sentence is not too clear, but the idea seems to be that Francis did not want the distinction between clerics and lay brothers to be emphasized by too great a difference in the size of the tonsure.

349. Rom. 2, 11.

350. The final rule was approved by Honorius III, November 29, 1223.

351. 1 Cor. 7, 20.

352. Even though it was said in the *First Rule,* chapter 3, that lay brothers might have a psalter if they knew how to read it. The *Speculum Perfectionis* (second redaction, chapter 4) says that this lay brother was a novice.

353. Rom. 1, 9.

354. A plectrum is a tiny piece of ivory, or metal, used in playing a lyre or other such stringed instrument.

355. See above, no. 77.

356. See the *First Life,* no. 17, 115; also above, no. 5.

357. See above, no. 90.

358. Ps. 22, 4.

359. Ps. 137, 1.

360. Ps. 46, 8.

361. The same thought is expressed, for instance, in the Offertory of the Requiem Mass: *Signifer S. Michael repraesentet eas in lucem sanctam.*

362. September 29.

363. See the *Salute to the Blessed Virgin,* composed by Francis, in *The Words of St. Francis,* James Meyer O.F.M., Franciscan Herald Press, 1952, p. 197.

364. Gal. 4, 2.

365. According to the rule Friday is a day of fast, as well as abstinence. Chapter 3.

366. An allusion to the Introit of the III Mass on Christmas: *Puer natus est nobis.*

367. Lk. 2, 7: And she brought forth her firstborn son, and wrapped him in swaddling clothes, and laid him in a manger because there was no room for them in the inn.

368. 1 Pet. 1, 18-19: You know that you were redeemed from the vain manner of life handed down from your fathers, not with perishable things, with silver or gold, but with the precious blood of Christ, as of a lamb without blemish and without spot.

369. The Blessed Eucharist was especially venerated in the region which is now modern Belgium. See *Analecta Franciscana,* X, p. 245, note 6.

370. Francis frequently spoke on this subject; for instance, in his letter to all clerics, *Opuscula,* p. 22-23, and in his *Testament.* In the latter he said: And I want these most holy mysteries above all else to be honored and venerated and kept in choice places.

371. He chose St. Lawrence as an example because, like himself, he was a deacon.

372. 1 Jn. 1, 1.

373. Massa is a mountainous region between Perugia and Arezzo. Monte Casale is only a mile or so from Borgo San Sepolcro.

374. Ps. 68, 14.

375. *Ibid.,* 31.

376. Gal. 6, 14.

377. Celano uses technical terms here from philosophy: *signaculum* or the thing signed or the thing itself, and *signum* or the sign or the word.

378. Celano is speaking of the stigmata in a rather enigmatic way. Writing about 1258, Thomas of Eccleston wrote: But Brother Leo, the companion of St. Francis, told Brother Peter, the minister of England, that the apparition of the Seraph came to St. Francis while he was rapt up in contemplation and more clearly even than was written in his life [i.e. Celano's *legenda*]; and that many things were revealed to him at that time that he did not communicate to any living person. But he did tell Brother Rufino, his companion, that when he saw the angel from afar, he was greatly afraid, and that the angel treated him harshly; and he told him that his Order would continue to the end of the world, that no one of evil will would remain long in the Order, that no one who hated the Order would live long, and that no one who truly loved the Order would come to a bad end. But St. Francis commanded Brother Rufino to wash and anoint with oil the stone on which the angel had stood; this he did. These things Brother Warin of Sedenefeld wrote down from the lips of Brother Leo.

See *XIIIth Century Chronicles,* Placid Hermann O.F.M., Franciscan Herald Press, 1961, p. 161-162.

379. That is, the Poor Clares.
380. St. Damian's church.
381. See above no. 13, where the prophecy is given.
382. 1 Pet. 2, 5.
383. 1 Cor. 12, 11.
384. Jn. 13, 15.
385. The term monastery at that time meant simply a dwelling place of nuns.
386. See above, no. 85.
387. That is, Ps. 50.
388. Prov. 1, 17: But a net is spread in vain before the eyes of them that have wings.
389. Apoc. 3, 5.
390. 1 Thess. 5, 8.
391. No. 32 of the *First Life* explains this.
392. Gen. 17, 13.
393. In this *First Rule,* chapter 23, we read: In the name of the Lord I beseech all the brothers to learn the text and sense of what is written down in this rule of life for the salvation of our soul, and often to call it to mind. *The Words of St. Francis,* p. 283.
394. That is, religious profession.
395. 2 Cor. 12, 12.
396. This was Brother Electus, killed certainly before 1246 and perhaps while Francis was still alive.
397. This was between 1221 and 1223 before the final rule was approved.
398. 2 Pet. 1, 17-18.
399. Jn. 5, 31.
400. Col. 3, 24.
401. Gen. 18, 25.
402. 1 Kings 12, 23.
403. Gal. 2, 20: It is now no longer I that live, but Christ lives in me.
404. Ps. 18, 12.
405. Is. 40, 12.
406. 2 Cor. 4, 17.
407. Otherwise called *The Canticle of Brother Sun.* It was probably composed while Francis was staying at the Poor Clares place at St. Damian's. The verse concerning pardon and peace was added later at the time of a quarrel between the religious and civil authorities of Assisi. The verse about Sister Death was added after the doctor had told him he would surely die. The poem is one of the first in the common language of the people. See one version of it in *Via Seraphica,* Placid Hermann O.F.M.

408. Ecclus. 11, 29.
409. Ps. 118, 32.
410. Exod. 25, 31.
411. Ps. 118, 96. See the *First Life,* no. 90.
412. Jn. 13, 1.
413. The same quotation from St. Gregory, used in the *First Life,* no. 15.
414. 2 Tim. 4, 8.
415. See above, no. 70.
416. Jn. 13, 1.
417. Acts 9, 12.
418. The wording here is very similar to the wording of the blessing in the *First Life,* no. 108.
419. *Ibid.,* no. 108.
420. The idea here is that the blessing should not be considered a personal thing, in so far as Elias is concerned, but as pertaining to his office of vicar. In the *First Life* the very special blessing given to Elias is given in detail. When Celano was writing this *Second Life* Elias had been deposed as general (1239) and was excommunicated by Gregory IX and again by Innocent IV. In referring to the blessing of the *First Life* Celano is implying that Elias had made himself unworthy of it.
421. Mt. 14, 19.
422. Jn. 13, 1. In the *First Life,* no. 110, Celano had misquoted these opening words; here he corrects himself.
423. Mt. 26, 20-29; Mk. 14, 17-25, Lk. 22, 14-38.
424. Ps. 141. See the *First Life,* no. 109.
425. See above, 213 and the *First Life,* no. 109. The reference is to *The Canticle of Brother Sun.*
426. From the *Canticle of Brother Sun.*
427. See above, no. 214.
428. The paragraph that follows here, numbered 217a, is missing in codex A; it is supplied for the most part from the *First Life,* no. 110.
429. These first lines are from the *First Life,* no. 110.
430. The preceding section is found for the most part in the same life, no. 112.
431. *Ibid.,* no. 113.
432. *Ibid.,* no. 112.
433. A region just below central Italy on the western coast.
434. The vestment proper to the deacon.
435. 1 Cor. 6, 17: But he who cleaves to the Lord is one spirit with him.
436. *Ibid.,* 12, 6.
437. Bishop Guido, the same before whom Francis renounced the world.
438. At Monte Gargano, north of Foggia, in Apulia.
439. The following paragraph, numbered 220a, is also missing in codex A. It is made up of passages from various

places of the *First Life*.

440. 1 Cor. 6, 11.
441. See the *First Life,* no. 23.
442. *Ibid.,* no. 88. The *Legenda ad usum chori* adds that it was *late Saturday night* when Francis died. *Analecta Franciscana,* Vol. X, p. 126.
443. *First Life,* no. 119-120.
444. *Ibid.,* 120-124.
445. Most of the preceding is from the *First Life,* no. 123.
446. *Ibid.,* 125.
447. Ecclus. 18, 5.
448. Here the manuscripts break off and the latter part of the proclamation and the translation are missing. We complete the proclamation here from the *First Life,* 126.
449. These words are really from the Bull of Canonization, the text of which can be found in the *Via Seraphica,* Placid Hermann O.F.M. The *Legenda ad usum chori* of Celano adds (no. 13) this little notation: Francis' body remained in the church of St. George "until the wonderful church had been built in his honor and named after him, in which afterwards his sacred body was translated by the brothers of the general chapter." This was May 25, 1230. See *Analecta Franciscana,* Vol. X, p. 124.
450. This final prayer has really four parts to it: a) a part specially directed to St. Francis; b) a prayer for the minister general; c) a prayer for "this your son who now and earlier has devotedly written your praises"; d) a prayer for all the sons of Francis. At first Celano speaks in the name of the several companions who supplied the material; then in his own name.
451. Ps. 80, 17.
452. Ps. 35, 8-9.
453. *Loc. cit.*
454. Ps. 113, 12.
455. Cant. 1, 3.
456. Lam. 5, 21.
457. Rom. 8, 35. The minister general was Crescentius of Jesi.
458. Celano of course is speaking of himself in this elaborate literary apostrophe and prayer.
459. In a sense, the *Life* is considered by Celano the work of himself and of the companions of Francis who supplied the material. But there is no question but what Celano himself wrote the entire work.
460. Zach. 12, 10.

TREATISE ON THE MIRACLES

1. The *Treatise on the Miracles* contains in all 198 paragraphs distributed over 19 chapters. Of these 198 paragraphs 41 pertain to things that happened while Francis
   was yet alive and therefore have some reference to his
   biography. However, of these 41, all but 13 are already
   contained in the two *Lives*. We include in this Appendix
   only these last 13.
2. Of the six paragraphs in this chapter, four have reference
   to things that happened while Francis was still alive.
   However, only paragraph 18 contains material not already
   contained in the *Lives*.
3. Twelve of the thirteen paragraphs of this chapter pertain to things that happened while Francis was yet alive,
   but only the two paragraphs given here contain material
   not already included in the *Lives*.
4. For other stories of sheep see the *First Life*, no. 77-79.
5. See the *Second Life*, no. 200.
6. All of the paragraphs of this chapter (4) refer to things
   that happened while Francis was alive, but only paragraph 34 contains material not already included in the
   Lives.
7. See the *First Life*, no. 56. But what follows is new.
8. *Ibid.*, no. 24.
9. This whole chapter is new and is given here.
10. Jacoba Giacoma of Settesoli, the widow of Graziano
    Frangipani. After St. Francis' death she moved to Assisi
    where she died in 1239. She was buried in the lower
    church of the basilica of St. Francis.
11. See the *Second Life*, no. 19.
12. The *Speculum Perfectionis* (2nd redaction), no. 112, says:
    "This is the sweatmeat the people of Rome call *mostaciolli,*
    and is made of almonds, sugar, and other ingredients."
13. Since they were given in the *First Life*, no. 112-113, 116-
    118.
14. That is, the five wounds.
15. Ps. 147, 20.
16. The oldest son of Lady Jacoba. The name as it is given
    here is another form of Frangipani.
17. That is, back to her home in Rome.
18. Of the nine paragraphs of this chapter only paragraph
    41 pertains to what happened during Francis' life and is
    new.
19. An example of this was given in the preceding paragraph
    40.
20. Of the thirty paragraphs of this chapter only three per-
    tain to things that happened during Francis' life, and of
    these three only paragraph 124 is new material not con-

tained in the *Lives*.

21. Of the twenty-five paragraphs of this chapter only four pertain to things that happened during Francis' life, and of these four only paragraphs 174, 178, and 179 contain new material.

BIBLIOGRAPHY

This list contains only the books and articles that were especially helpful in making this translation. It would be impossible to list the works from which incidental help was derived.

Analecta Franciscana, ex Typographia Collegii S. Bonaventurae, Quaracchi, Italy. Volume X (1941) of this set contains the best edition of Thomas of Celano's works. This edition was used in making this translation.

The Legend and Writings of Saint Clare of Assisi, an English translation and studies. The Franciscan Institute, St. Bonaventure, New York. 1953.

The Lives of S. Francis of Assisi by Brother Thomas of Celano, translated by A. G. Ferrers Howell, LL.M., Methuen & Co., London, 1908.

Thomas von Celano, Leben und Wunder Des Heiligen Franziskus von Assisi, translation by P. Engelbert Grau O.F.M., Dietrich-Coelde-Verlag, Werl, Westphalia, 1955.

Le due Leggende di San Francesco d'Assisi, translation by Prof. Fausta Casolini, Quaracchi, 1923.

Documenta Antiqua Franciscana, Leonard Lemmens O.F.M.; Quaracchi, 1901. Pars I: *Scripta Fratris Leonis;* Pars II: *Speculum Perfectionis,* redactio prima.

Legenda Trium Sociorum, typis Fratrum Monaldi, Rome, 1880.

Chronica XXIV Generalium, in *Analecta Franciscana, III,* Quaracchi, (1897).

Early Franciscan Government, Elias to Bonaventure, Rosalind B. Brooke, Cambridge at the University Press, 1959.

XIIIth Century Chronicles, chronicles of Brother Jordan of Giano and of Thomas of Eccleston; selections from the chronicle of Brother Salimbene. Translation by Placid Hermann O.F.M., Franciscan Herald Press, 1961.

Via Seraphica, selected readings from the early documents and writings pertaining to St. Francis and the Franciscan Order. Placid Hermann O.F.M., Franciscan Herald Press, 1959.

Archivum Franciscanum Historicum, Quaracchi. An indispensable magazine on Franciscan subjects. Of the many articles used from this collection, these two were the most important: *Disquisitiones Celanenses,* by Michael Bihl O.F.M., Vol. 20 and 21; *De Codicibus Vitae I S. Francisci Assisiensis Auctore Fr. Thoma Celanensi,* by Michael Bihl O.F.M., Vol. 29 and 30.

INDEX

In this Index of the *First* and *Second Life* and the selections from the *Treatise on the Miracles* the Roman I stands for the *First Life;* the Roman II for the *Second* Life; the capital M for the *Miracles*. The Arabic numerals without parentheses stand for the numbers of the various paragraphs of these works, not the pages. The Arabic numerals within parentheses stand for the numbers of the footnote related to the paragraph number that immediately precedes. The occasional small p indicates the Prologue of the *First Life*.

to bishop of Assisi, 220

Apulia, I: 4, 5-7, 21, 24, 25, 138 (65); II: 6, 68

Arbor vitae crucifixae Jesu, II: 123 (193)

Arezzo, I: 63, 63 (209), 140; II: 108

Arles, chapter of, I: 48 (164)

Ascoli, I: 62

Assisi, I: 1, 4, 4 (20), 6, 8, 11, 18, 42, 52, 88, 105, 112, 116, 123, 124, 126, 136; II: 4, 7, 40, 50, 57, 76, 77, 109, 132, 190, 213 (407); M: 37 (10)

Augustine, Br., minister of Terra di Lavoro, II: 218, 218 (433)

Augustine, St., I: 22 (9), 92 (23)

Augustine Sepinski O.F.M., 33 (117)

Avezzano, II: 86 (124)

Babylon, I: 2; II: 7, 125 (197)

Barbaro, Br., I: 31 (110); II: 155

Bari, II: 68

Bartholomew, of Narni, I: 135

bashfulness, II: 13, 74

beds, II: 63

bees, I: 80, 165; II: 169

begging, II: 10, 14, 78-79

Benedictine, abbot, I: 16; II: 101, 101 (147)
        monastery, I: 16, 21 (66); II: 101, 101 (147)

Bernard, of Bessa, Br., I: 102 (78), 111 (115)

Bernard, of Clairvaux, I: 115 (132), 121 (13)

Bernard, of Quintavalle, Br., I: 24, 24 (77), 25, 29 (103), 30, 31 (110); II: 15, 48, 109; M: 34

Bernard, Viridante, Br., I: 31 (110)

Bernardone, Peter, father of Francis, I: 10, 10 (33); II: 12
        grandfather of Francis, I: 53 (180)

Bethlehem, I: 84-87

Bevagna, I: 58, 58 (192); II: 114

birds, I: 58, 59; II: 47, 167, 168

Blanche, mother of Louis IX, I: 120 (8)

blind, M: 124

body, treatment of, II: 22, 129, 210-211

Bologna, II: 58, 58 (69), 147 (231), 163 (273)

Bonaventure, St., Br., I: 21 (65), 47 (161), 48 (162), 57 (183), 57 (189); II: 123, 123 (193)

Bontadosus, I: 142

Bonushomo, I: 146

books, II: 62, 102, 195

Borgo San Sepolcro, II: 98, 98 (145)

Brancaleo, Leo, cardinal, II: 119, 119 (184)

Elias, of Cortona, Br., I: 57 (191), 69, 95, 95 (32), 98, 105, 108,
    109, 109 (109), 110 (111); II: 28 (7), 30 (11), 138, 138
    (216), 157 (259), 216 (420), M: 39
Elizabeth, mother of John Bap., II: 3
Eucharist, devotion to, II: 201
Example, good, II: 155
    bad, II: 155-157
expropriation, I: 24; II: 80-81
Exultet, I: 119 (7)
Ezechiel, passage explained, II: 103

Faenza, I: 43 (147)
falcon, II: 168
familiarity, with women, II: 112-114
famine, foretold, II: 52, 53 (59)
fast, of Rule, II: 53 (59), 131, 208
    in honor of St. Michael, II: 197
fasting, II: 21
Faverone, father of St. Clare, I: 18 (57)
fire, and Francis, II: 166
fish, and Francis, I: 61
Florence, I: 43 (147)
Foligna, I: 8, 43 (147), 129, 137
Fondi, bishop of, II: 156 (255)
France, II: 201, 201 (369)
Francis, of Assisi, St.,
    birth, I: 1 (1)
    naming, II: 3
    early training, 1: 1-2, 89
    captive at Perugia, II: 4, 4 (11)
    early illness, I: 3
    leader of revels, II: 7
    his grotto, I: 6
    dream of arms, II: 6
    changes garments with knight, II: 5
    vision of spouse, I: 7
    sells father's cloth, I: 8
    hides in church, I: 10
    persecution by father, I: 10-15; II: 12
              by brother, II: 12
              by citizens, I: 11
    before bishop, I: 13-15
    seized by robbers, I: 16
    with Benedictines, I: 16
    with lepers, I: 17; II, 9

Giles, of Assisi, Br., I: 25, 30, 30 (103), 31 (110)
Giovanni, nephew of Francis, I: 10 (33)
gluttony, II: 22, 75, 162
Gospel way of life, I: 7, 22, 24, 32, 51, 84, 89, 93; II: 15, 24, 28, 80, 208, 216
Greccio, I: 60, 84-87, 150; II: 35, 36, 36 (30), 45, 61, 64, 167
    burning of, II: 36, 36 (30)
greed, II: 47
Gregory IX, I: p1, 1 (2), p2, 122-126, 126 (37), 127; II: 25
    (75), 53 (58), 73, 148 (234), 216 (420), 220a, *see
    Hugolino, Ostia*
Gregory, the Great, I: 15, 15 (47); II: 155 (251), 214 (413)
Gregory, of Naples, Br., I: 57 (191)
grotto, of Francis, I: 6
guardian, of Francis, II: 92, 130, 151, 215
Gubbio, I: 67, 132, 134, 136, 142; II: 111
Guido, bishop of Assisi, I: 14, 14 (46), 15, 32, 108; II: 12, 12
    (40), 100, 100 (146), 220, 220 (437)
hail storms, at Greccio, II: 35-36
hands of a priest, II: 201
healing of sick, *see miracles*
Henry VI, of Germany, I: 4 (20)
hermitages, II: 71, 71 (101), 178, 178 (325), 179-180
Honorius III, I: 57 (191), 73, 73 (225), 99-100; II: 30 (13)
houses, II: 56-58
Hugolino (Hugo), I: 18 (57), 73-75, 73 (228), 74 (232), 99-
    101, 100 (67); II: 2 (6), 25, 25 (77), 58, 63, 73, 148,
    148 (234), *see Gregory IX*
humility, I: 17, 34, 51-54, 71, 91-92, 102-103; II: 18, 123, 135-
    139, 140-150
hypocrisy, II: 130-131
idle, words, at Portiuncula, II: 160
idleness, II: 159-162
illnesses, of Francis: I: 3, 97-98, 99-101, 105-107; II: 96, 105,
    210-213; M: 34
Illuminato, Br., I: 57 (189); II: 30 (11)
Imola, bishop of, II: 147, 147 (231)
Imperator, man of Spello, I: 144
Indiction, I: 88 (3)
Innocent III, I: 4 (20), 18 (57), 32, 32 (113), 125 (35); II: 16
Innocent IV, I: 18 (57), 125 (34); II: 216 (420)
invalids, M: 174, 178, 179

Jacoba, lady, of Settesoli, M: 37-39
James, of Assisi, Br., I: 110, 110 (115)
James, boy cured, M: 178
James, St. Compostella, shrine, I: 30, 30 (106)
Jerusalem, II: 61

Sermo de S. Francisco, St. Bonaventure, II: 123 (193)
sheep, I: 77-79; M: 31
Sibyl, I: 136
sick brothers, II: 175-176
    in spirit, II: 177
Siena, I: 105; II: 33, 87, 93, 103, 170; M: 31
simplicity, I: 44, 46, 47, 50, 75 102, 104; II: 189-195
singularity, II: 14, 29
Slavonia, I: 55, 55 (182)
snake, money turned to, II: 68
solitude, I: 71; II: 9, 94
sow, that ate lamb, II: 111
Spain, I: 55; M: 34
Spaniards II: 30, 30 (13)
Spanish brothers, II: 178
Speculum Perfectionis, I: 109 (106); II: 18 (61), 58 (69), 123
    (193), 182 (332); M: 38 (12)
Spello, I: 136, 144
Spoleto, I: 43 (147), 122; II: 53 (58)
    valley, I: 1 (1), 34, 35, 58; M: 31
spouse of Francis, I: 7
Stephen, Br., I: 57 (191)
stigmata I: 57, 57 (191), 90, 94-95, 112-114, 118, 119; II: 11,
    135-139, 203, 203 (378), 211, 217a; M: 39
striving after virtue, I:p2, *see various virtues*
Sulpicius Severus, II: 5 (16)
sultan, I: 57, 57 (190)
superiors, I: 45, 104, II: 141, 142, 151-153, 173, 177 183, 184-
    188
swallows, I: 59
swords, vision of, II: 105
Sylvester, Bro., I: 31 (110); II: 108-109, 109 (164)
Syria, I: 55, 55 (188), 57
Tau, sign of, II: 106, 106 (158)
teachings of Francis, I: p2, 38-41
temptations, I: 42, 43; II: 115-124
    value of, II: 118
Terni, I: 43 (147); II: 141
    bishop of, II: 141
Terra di Lavoro, II: 39, 39 (40), 218, 218 (433)
Testament, of Francis, I: 17 (54), 23 (75), 32 (112), 39 (138)
    46 (159); II: 9 (32), 55 (64), 71 (97), 144 (225), 161
    (266), 163, 201 (370)
theologians, II: 163